Guide to Equine Assisted Therapy

Yuval Neria • Prudence W. Fisher
Allan J. Hamilton
Editors

Guide to Equine Assisted Therapy

Springer

Editors
Yuval Neria
Department of Psychiatry and the New York State Psychiatric Institute
Columbia University Irving Medical Center
New York, NY, USA

Prudence W. Fisher
Department of Psychiatry and the New York State Psychiatric Institute
Columbia University Irving Medical Center
New York, NY, USA

Allan J. Hamilton
Department of Neurosurgery, Artificial Intelligence Division of Health Sciences
University of Arizona
Tucson, AZ, USA

ISBN 978-3-031-74425-9 ISBN 978-3-031-74426-6 (eBook)
https://doi.org/10.1007/978-3-031-74426-6

This Springer imprint is published by the registered company Springer Nature Switzerland AG
The registered company address is: Gewerbestrasse 11, 6330 Cham, Switzerland

Acknowledgments

This book would not have been possible without the support of many individuals who believe in the power of horses. The editors are grateful to Neal Prasad, Chana Fisch, Adeen Izzathullah, and Bradley Tao for supporting the creation of this book along all editorial stages and to our dear friends and colleagues Drs. John C Markowitz, Amit Lazarov, Xi Zhu, Jane Hamilton, and Ari Lowell, who were central to the Equine Assisted Therapy (EAT) research at Columbia University, and to the EAT treatment team at Bergen County Equestrian center for all they taught us along the way: Jody Jacob-McVey, Bonnie E. Malajian, Debra G. Farber, and April Neumann. We will always be grateful for the generous support of Earle I. Mack, who believed in us and founded the Man O' War Project at Columbia University Irving Medical Center out of his desire to support both retired race horses and veterans' mental health—without him we wouldn't have entered the EAT world, and to Anne Poulson, J.D., for her consistent commitment, advice, and expertise which has been instrumental in the success of the Man O' War Project. We are indebted to Matt Ryba for playing such a central role in making EAT work sustainable and available to war veterans, and to Takeisha Hall-Ruff and John Darlington for sharing our vision of providing EAT to heal traumatized populations and helping us to disseminate this work. And above all, we are grateful to the equine world at large: horses, horse owners, veterinarians, farriers, jockeys, and horse lovers who believe in the magical power of horses as healers, and who make the EAT work so exciting and promising.

Introduction: Horses as Emotional Healers

Strong bonds between humans and horses have existed for thousands of years, with some evidence that horses were domesticated since at least 3500 BCE (Zeder, 2012). Throughout history, horses have served a variety of purposes, including transportation, agriculture, and warfare. Over time, as the roles of horses in society have evolved, our understanding of their potential to contribute to human well-being has grown beyond their physical capabilities.

Horses have long been recognized for their therapeutic qualities, with early records dating back to ancient Greece (Zeder, 2015), where horse riding was considered an effective treatment for various physical ailments. In more recent times, horses have been employed in therapeutic settings for individuals with physical disabilities, as well as in programs aimed at promoting personal growth and development.

The emergence of equine-assisted treatment (EAT; also known as equine-assisted psychotherapy, EAP) can be traced back to the twentieth century, when therapists began to recognize the unique and powerful benefits that horses could offer in the context of mental health treatment. Until recently, little research accompanied the development of EAT. In fact, numerous modalities of EAT were developed over the years, representing a fusion of traditional psychotherapy techniques with equine-facilitated activities, capitalizing on the unique attributes of horses to promote self-awareness, emotional regulation, and interpersonal skills in clients.

In this book, we will explore the foundations of equine-assisted psychotherapy, delving into the history of human-equine relationships, as well as examining the current state of the field and the potential for future growth. Specifically, the book includes a comprehensive description of various approaches to EAT, presenting recent research in psychiatric and psychological fields, in both adults and children with various psychiatric disorders, highlighting the perspective of the horses. The book aims to provide a thorough understanding of equine-assisted treatment and its potential to transform mental health programs.

The book includes four parts. The first part focuses on various perspectives on EAT. It starts with the mindful approaches, discussing the integration of Zen Buddhist principles into EAT and equine-assisted learning. The chapter draws on material from Buddhist folklore and historical anecdotes, but also contrasts that with modern neuroscientific research highlighting the unique role right hemispheric brain activity plays in spiritual experiences (Hamilton, 2024). Next, this part includes a comprehensive review of the history, rationale, and applications of the use of equine-assisted services (EAS) among veterans with psychiatric disorders (Marchand, 2024). The chapter highlights both progress in EAS in veterans, as well as what is still needed to bolster high-quality research that will test the efficacy of new EAS protocols as well as their mechanisms of action. Next, the part includes a thorough comparison between equine-assisted therapy programs on the ground versus riding programs. Specifically, differences in methodologies, rationale, and outcomes between M-EAT and G-EAT are examined, as well as the clinical implications of these distinctions. The chapter highlights cost considerations, estimates potential therapeutic value in both approaches, and discusses how communication styles between horses and clients differ in the two approaches (Ward et al., 2024). Next, a discussion of EAT evolution and methodological challenges is presented. Particular attention is given to the nature of relationships between humans and equines typically formed in EAT, the emotional connections between the horse and the patients, and the potential development of human-animal bonding and its hormonal underpinnings (Moshe-Grodofsky, 2024). The next chapter focuses on a recent approach to group-based groundwork EAT, focusing on facilitating self-awareness, emotion regulation, and interpersonal skills (Strong et al., 2024). The last chapter in this part discusses a manualized EAT based on a modification of cognitive processing therapy (CPT), a well-established treatment for Posttraumatic stress disorder (PTSD) (Wharton et al., 2024).

The second part of the book focuses on equine therapies for adults. A range of studies is presented involving applying EAT among adult patients with psychiatric disorders including PTSD, schizophrenia, and substance abuse. Regarding PTSD, two chapters describe EAT-induced treatment changes on both clinical measures, such as PTSD and depression (Fisher et al., 2024), and functional and structural brain measures (Neria et al., 2024) among American veterans with PTSD. Next, the idea that EAT might be beneficial for schizophrenia is presented, reviewing previous and recent research in this area (Cerino, 2024). Next, EAT might be beneficial for neurorehabilitation of comorbid PTSD and neurological deficits stemming from traumatic brain injury, spinal cord injury, and stroke. Viruega et al. (2024) describe how riding EAT (also known as hippotherapy) can utilize the movement of the horses at a walk to promote functional recovery and well-being in individuals with neural disabilities. Hippotherapy may effectively stimulate neural pathways and improve emotional regulation and mental processes, thus relieving PTSD, anxiety, and depressive symptoms. Lastly, this part reviews progress in applying EAT in patients with substance abuse disorders. Targeting deficits in the ability to experience trust, self-efficacy, and positive emotional affect, the Gaustad model of EAT discussed in Espen Ajo Arnevik's chapter (Arnevik, 2024) focuses on strengthening attachment and relationships.

In the next part, recent EAT approaches for children and youth are described. Applications of EAT among children and youth with anxiety and ADHD, as well as utilizing cross-diagnostic targets such as social competence and stress regulation, are presented. First, the Acri et al. (2024) chapter discusses Reining in Anxiety (RiA), a 10-session, manualized adaptive horseback riding program that incorporates evidence-based cognitive-behavioral elements for children and adolescents with anxiety. Utilizing EAT as a mental health service for youth in naturalistic settings with alternative, highly trained providers also address key barriers to help-seeking as well as expands the workforce to meet the need for services. Next, two chapters focus on applying EAT for ADHD. In the first chapter, Aviv outlines key deficits in ADHD and how EAT can address them (Aviv, 2024). Then, Helmer and Bart (Helmer et al., 2024) present a pilot study of the ADHD Skills Therapy Ride (ASTride), an Equine-Assisted Occupational Therapy (EAOT) intervention protocol designed for children aged 6–12 with ADHD. Applying both mounted and unmounted activities in the stables surrounding, the protocol's success and limitations are described in this chapter. Lastly for this part, Pendry lays out theoretical models and empirical evidence supporting Equine-Assisted Interventions (EAIs) aiming to boost adolescents' social competence and ability to regulate stress (Pendry, 2024). Special attention is given to the Human Animal Interaction (HAI)–Hypothalamic Pituitary Adrenal (HPA) transactional model, a framework for understanding the mechanisms that underlie the effects of EAI on cortisol—a marker of HPA axis activity and its correlates. A pilot study examining the efficacy of the Equine-Assisted Learning (EAL) program on adolescent social competence is described.

In the last part, several perspectives on the horse's side are described. First, Ryba describes the major role horses have played throughout military history (Ryba, 2024). They were highly instrumental for fighting men and women in a variety of uses, from convoys for hauling gear to cavalry engagement, reconnaissance, and navigating difficult terrain. Importantly, horses on the battlefield also provided a psychological impact. The horse's companionship to the troops was found to boost morale and give troops a tangible purpose to continue fighting. The chapter presents several historic examples of horses that were known for their contribution to soldiers and senior officers and reflects on how the partnership between fighting men and women and their service equines may inform some aspects of the relationship between horses and veterans who seek equine therapy for PTSD and other service-related mental health issues. Lastly, the book concludes with how to facilitate horse welfare throughout the EAT range of applications. Welfare assessment and steps to increase horse well-being are discussed. The chapter outlines and discusses the Five Freedoms and the Five Domains, which are broad models for welfare assessment, and then addresses the potential consequences of horse well-being for human outcomes.

Taken together, this book is the first effort to focus on the current state of research in EAT, its accomplishments and gaps, informing future studies to help establish a stronger evidence base for its efficacy in treating various mental health problems. By addressing both progress and limitations, the book provides valuable insights and guidance to both mental health professionals and horse experts, fostering a deeper understanding of equine-assisted psychotherapies and their potential to improve mental health treatment outcomes.

Yuval Neria, yuval.neria@nyspi.columbia.edu
Prudence W. Fisher, prudence.fisher@nyspi.columbia.edu
Allan J. Hamilton, allan@surgery.arizona.edu

References

Acri, M., et al. (2024). Reining in Anxiety (RiA): A 10-session, manualized adaptive horseback riding program. In Y. Neria, P. Fischer, & A. J. Hamilton (Eds.), *Equine-assisted therapy*. Springer.

Arnevik, E. A. (2024). Espen Ajo Arnevik chapter. In Y. Neria, P. Fischer, & A. J. Hamilton (Eds.), *Equine-assisted therapy*. Springer.

Aviv, R. (2024). Key deficits in ADHD and how EAT can address them. In Y. Neria, P. Fischer, & A. J. Hamilton (Eds.), *Equine-assisted therapy*. Springer.

Cerino, S. (2024). EAT and schizophrenia. In Y. Neria, P. Fischer, & A. J. Hamilton (Eds.), *Equine-assisted therapy*. Springer.

Fisher, P. R., Neria, Y., & Hamilton, A. J. (2024). Clinical measures of PTSD and depression among veterans. In Y. Neria, P. Fischer, & A. J. Hamilton (Eds.), *Equine-assisted therapy*. Springer.

Hamilton, A. J. (2024). Mindful approaches: The integration of Zen Buddhist principles into EAT. In Y. Neria, P. Fischer, & A. J. Hamilton (Eds.), *Equine-assisted therapy*. Springer.

Helmer, O., & Bart, D. (2024). ADHD Skills Therapy Ride (ASTride): An Equine-Assisted Occupational Therapy intervention. In Y. Neria, P. Fischer, & A. J. Hamilton (Eds.), *Equine-assisted therapy*. Springer.

Marchand, W. R. (2024). Equine-assisted services among veterans with psychiatric disorders. In Y. Neria, P. Fischer, & A. J. Hamilton (Eds.), *Equine-assisted therapy*. Springer.

Moshe-Grodofsky, M. (2024). Human-animal bonding and its hormonal underpinnings in EAT. In Y. Neria, P. Fischer, & A. J. Hamilton (Eds.), *Equine-assisted therapy*. Springer.

Neria, Y., et al. (2024). Functional and structural brain measures in veterans with PTSD. In Y. Neria, P. Fischer, & A. J. Hamilton (Eds.), *Equine-assisted therapy*. Springer.

Pendry, P. (2024). The Human Animal Interaction (HAI) – Hypothalamic Pituitary Adrenal (HPA) Transactional model in EAIs. In Y. Neria, P. Fischer, & A. J. Hamilton (Eds.), *Equine-assisted therapy*. Springer.

Ryba, M. (2024). The major role of horses throughout military history. In Y. Neria, P. Fischer, & A. J. Hamilton (Eds.), *Equine-assisted therapy*. Springer.

Strong, A., et al. (2024). Group-based groundwork EAT for self-awareness and emotion regulation. In Y. Neria, P. Fischer, & A. J. Hamilton (Eds.), *Equine-assisted therapy*. Springer.

Viruega, S., et al. (2024). Riding EAT (hippotherapy) for neurorehabilitation. In Y. Neria, P. Fischer, & A. J. Hamilton (Eds.), *Equine-assisted therapy*. Springer.

Ward, T., et al. (2024). Comparison between equine-assisted therapy programs on the ground versus riding programs. In Y. Neria, P. Fischer, & A. J. Hamilton (Eds.), *Equine-assisted therapy*. Springer.

Wharton, R., et al. (2024). Manualized EAT based on cognitive processing therapy (CPT) for PTSD. In Y. Neria, P. Fischer, & A. J. Hamilton (Eds.), *Equine-assisted therapy*. Springer.

Zeder, M. A. (2012). The domestication of animals. *Journal of Anthropological Research, 68*, 161–190. https://doi.org/10.3998/jar.0521004.0068.201

Zeder, M. A. (2015). Core questions in domestication research. *Proceedings of the National Academy of Sciences*, 112, 3191–3198. https://doi.org/10.1073/pnas.1501711112

Contents

Part I Perspectives on Equine Assisted Therapy

Mindful Approaches: Zen Principles in the Theory and Practice of Groundwork in Equine-Assisted Therapy and Learning 3
Allan J. Hamilton

An Overview of the History, Rationale, and Clinical Application of the Use of EAS in Veterans with Psychiatric Disorders 25
William R. Marchand

Equine-Assisted Therapy Programs on the Ground Versus Programs in the Saddle: How Do You Choose? 53
Jessica Ward, Angela Hovey, and Keith Brownlee

Equine-Assisted Therapy Development: Methodology and Rationale ... 75
Merav Moshe-Grodofsky

The Equus Effect: Somatic Experiencing with Horses 97
Jane Strong, David Sonatore LCSW, and Elizabeth E. Lloyd-Richardson

Equine-Facilitated Cognitive Processing Therapy (EF-CPT) for Psychotherapy with Adults 119
Tracy Wharton, James Whitworth, and Marguerite Malone

Part II Equine Assisted Therapies for Adults

Equine-Assisted Therapy for PTSD (EAT-PTSD): The Man O' War Protocol 139
Prudence W. Fisher, Allan J. Hamilton, and Yuval Neria

Discovering Brain-Based Mechanisms and Predictors of Clinical Outcomes of EAT for Patients with PTSD 161
Yuval Neria, Xi Zhu, Prudence W. Fisher, Neal Prasad, and Allan J. Hamilton

Therapeutic Riding for Patients With Schizophrenia 169
Stefania Cerino

How Hippotherapy Can Tackle Posttraumatic Stress Disorders in Traumatic or Vascular Conditions of the Central Nervous System 187
Hélène Viruega and Manuel Gaviria

Equine-Assisted Therapy for Substance Use and Mental Health Disorders 213
Espen Ajo Arnevik and Christina Thorpe

Part III Equine Assisted Therapy for Children and Youth

Equine-Assisted Interventions for Youth with Anxiety 231
Mary C. Acri, Aviva Vincent, Meghan A. Morrissey, Lauren Seibel, and Kimberly Eaton Hoagwood

From Disability to Advantage: Equine-Assisted Therapy (EAT) in Children with Attention-Deficit/Hyperactivity Disorder 245
Tal-li Matild Aviv

Introducing ASTride: An Equine-Assisted Occupational Therapy Intervention for Children with ADHD 265
Anne Helmer and Orit Bart

Efficacy of EAIs on Relieving Adolescent Stress and Improving Social Competence: Theoretical Models and Empirical Evidence 285
Patricia Pendry

Part IV Cherishing Equines: A Journey of Remembrance and Care

Horses in Service: A Historical Military Context 303
Matthew Ryba

Horse Well-Being in Therapies Integrating Horses 317
Ellen M. Rankins and Karyn Malinowski

Index 331

Part I
Perspectives on Equine Assisted Therapy

Mindful Approaches: Zen Principles in the Theory and Practice of Groundwork in Equine-Assisted Therapy and Learning

Allan J. Hamilton

> *A society is great when old men plant trees in the shade of which they know they will never sit. –A Greek Proverb*

Introduction

This chapter on the application of Zen Buddhist principles to horsemanship in general, and equine-assisted therapy (EAT) in particular, came about for two reasons: the first is that I had written a popular book on training horses entitled *Zen Mind, Zen Horse: The Science and Art of Training Horses* (Hamilton, 2011). In that book, I described a peaceful and patient approach to establishing the horse–human partnership that lies at the heart of all natural horsemanship techniques. The second is that my approach to training and partnering with horses created a series of therapeutic maneuvers and exercises that my wife (a clinical psychologist) and I incorporated into an equine-assisted therapy (EAT) training manual (Hamilton & Hamilton, 2022). The manual was originally commissioned by the Man O' War Project to create a systematic and reproducible approach to providing EAT programming for veterans with post-traumatic stress disorder (PTSD). Throughout the manual, we employed the model originally promulgated by the Equine-Assisted Growth and Learning Association (EAGALA) that an EAT session is delivered by a team consisting of a horse, the equine professional (EP), and the mental health professional (MHP) to deliver a coordinated, customized equine experience with therapeutic objectives tied to the clients' individual needs (EAGALA). This manual would later serve as a foundation for the principal investigators, the equine professionals, and the mental health professionals who would ultimately conduct the Columbia University and New York Psychiatric Institute Study on the effects of EAT on

A. J. Hamilton (✉)
Department of Neurosurgery, Artificial Intelligence Division of Health Sciences, University of Arizona, Tucson, AZ, USA
e-mail: allan@surgery.arizona.edu

Y. Neria et al. (eds.), *Guide to Equine Assisted Therapy*,
https://doi.org/10.1007/978-3-031-74426-6_1

veterans suffering with PTSD (Zhu et al., 2021; Arnon et al., 2020; Fisher et al., 2021). The manual as specifically used in the PTSD study is outlined in Arnon et al. (2020).

Since much of this volume is devoted to how horses can be useful in providing therapeutic support for individuals suffering from the effects of trauma and other mental health disorders, the editors believed that discussing the principles of Zen Buddhism, as they relate to mindful training of horses, would be useful. Not only would such a discussion help to provide a better understanding of what makes horses so unique when they lend their power and grace to a therapeutic initiative but would also be useful in understanding my approach to training horses for EAT. For organizational purposes, this chapter is divided into two major parts. The first part focuses on how the tenets of Zen Buddhism are reflected in the horse–human partnership at the heart of natural horsemanship. This part of the chapter focuses on the general principles and teachings of Zen scholars and practitioners and then drills down on specific aspects of Zen Buddhism as they relate specifically to horsemanship (Suzuki, 1994). As such, the first part of this chapter may be of interest to those who live and work with horses but just as valuable an exposure to a lay person, an equine professional (EP), a mental health professional (MHP), or an educator who may be using equine-assisted learning (EAL) as an immersive adjunct to classroom learning. The second part of this chapter reviews the selection and training of horses in general for EAT or EAL. As such, this part of the chapter tends to contain practical and specific advice for the EP who is charged with the selection of horses for EAT or EAL. The EP must concentrate his or her efforts on ensuring that the horses employed in these activities are of the right age, and mental and physical disposition to make a reliable partner to engage in groundwork with students, clients, and patients.

Zen Principles and Natural Horsemanship

At the heart of Zen Buddhism lies the notion of enlightenment, or "satori." Individuals who are unfamiliar with the study of Zen may find themselves occasionally frustrated that a seemingly vague and transcendental concept is the engine that drives Zen Buddhism from within. D.T. Suzuki, who was one of the great twentieth-century scholars of modern Buddhism, wrote:

> Satori is the raison d'être of Zen without which Zen is no Zen. Therefore, every contrivance, disciplinary or doctrinal, is directed toward satori. Zen masters could not remain patient for satori to come by itself; that is, to come sporadically or at its own pleasure. In their earnestness to aid their disciples in the search after the truth of Zen their manifestly enigmatical presentations were designed to create in their disciples a state of mind which would more systematically open the way to enlightenment. (Suzuki, 1964, 1959)

There are two approaches to attaining satori: one through zazen meditation and the second is actional. The latter is distinct to highlight that enlightenment is an experiential awakening and not an intellectual concept. One of the many wonderful

Zen Buddhist stories about enlightenment involves Rinzai Gigen, the father of the great school of Rinzai Zen in the ninth century, which flourished in the age of the samurai and was grounded in actional discipline. The story goes that a Zen student enquired of Rinzai what was the essence of Zen. Rinzai bolted down from the dais, grabbed the student firmly by the collar of his robe, slapped him powerfully across the face, and then released him. Naturally, the student was aghast. One of the monks seated nearby said to the student: "Why don't you bow?", implying that the student should recognize the great service Master Rinzai had just done him. The student shook off his surprise and, as the story goes, when he began to bow, he attained enlightenment.

Similarly, there is a story told about Tennō Dōgo, a great Zen swordsman in the eighth century. A disciple named Sōshin was studying swordsmanship with Dōgo. The practice sessions consisted of the master attacking him at the most inopportune moments: while he was returning with his arms full of kindling, or carrying cups of tea, or kneeling in the garden tending to the vegetables. These random attacks with the wooden training sword always ended in some painful calamity for Sōshin, as not only were these random attacks meant to be disruptive but the rebuking blow with the wooden sword was quite painful. This routine continued for years with Dōgo attacking his disciple from every conceivable angle, during any activity, and at all hours of the day or night. Gradually, it became the second nature to Sōshin to expect an attack from any quarter and at any time, and he began to use his own wooden sword to fend off the master's blows but always doing it quite naturally as he attended to whatever activity he was doing. Soon, the master noticed that no matter how or when he attacked his student, Sōshin would swipe with his sword and very matter-of-factly parry the blow. The master explained to the student that his enlightenment had been reached without any conceptualization or intellectualization about the nature of satori. He explained: "In the study of Zen, conceptualization must go. As long as we tarry at this level, we can never reach the area where Zen has its life" (Suzuki, 1964, 1959). I will return to these notions of awareness in action when we focus on the principles of Zen as they apply to horsemanship.

In trying to explain the essence of Zen, D.T. Suzuki enumerated, first, that the discipline at the heart of Zen consists of attaining enlightenment. Second, the key to finding enlightenment was to look for it in everyday experiences, not an esoteric set of exercises or asceticism. Third, enlightenment is not something that is found outside of us; rather, it is discovered in the act of being itself. Suzuki refers to satori as grasping the "isness" of reality, grounded in the present of the senses and "purged of all intellectual sediments" (Suzuki, 1994).

Zen teachings reinforce that satori arises from direct personal experience. Again, stories passed down with various Zen masters embodying these concepts. One of the most famous is the story of the so-called Finger Pointing at the Moon. In this account, the Zen master sits beneath a tree surrounded by his students. He raises his hand and points to the moon. One student gazes at the moon and another student at the master's finger. He rebukes the one who is looking at his finger, stating: "The finger is not the moon, and you will never understand the moon by looking only at the finger." The implication is that one cannot grasp satori by relying on teaching and texts (the finger). The student who is looking at the moon has taken the suggestion offered by the master's finger and looked where it points to experience the moon for himself.

Another elegant story is that of "The Empty Mirror." Mirrors are recurrent symbols throughout Zen teachings and stories. In this story, the master is polishing a mirror when one of his students interrupts him: "Master," he says, "why are you polishing the mirror? The mirror is already empty. What is there for you to polish?" This notion of a mirror being empty stems from the metaphor that is widely used in Zen to point that the mirror holds nothing. While we see ourselves in the mirror, we are the ones who stood in front of the mirror to create the reflection and the image of ourselves is not our real physical selves. So, the master answers back: "Of course, you are correct. I am polishing the mind that waits to see something appear." The story reinforces that the individual who seeks enlightenment must be keenly prepared to be aware of and focused on the present moment, unencumbered by preconceptions or biases.

A final story illustrates these tenets of Zen Buddhism that we must free ourselves of our preconceived notions to gain access to satori. A Zen master sits down for tea with one of his students. He begins to pour tea into the student's cup. The cup fills up and the master continues to pour tea as the cup overflows. "Your mind," the master says, "is like this cup of tea. It is full of your own opinions, judgments, and preconceptions. There is no room for you to become enlightened. To reach satori, you must empty the mind, The empty mind is the proper state of mind that is prepared for enlightenment. Empty your mind! Empty your cup!"

Connectivity and Right Hemisphere Function in Humans

We have already seen in Zen Buddhism that words—verbalism and intellectualization—impede our access to the experience of enlightenment. There is a correlate between this tenet and neuroscience, which relates to what Antonio Damasio called "the autobiographical self" (Damasio, 1999). He identified it as the singular and separate identity that is lent to us by language and gives us out internal dialogue. However, because that identity makes us consider how we experience an encounter internally and will react to it externally, it separates the cognitive processing of the event from the simple awareness of the sensation of the experience. This is why myriad spiritual practices, ranging from drumming to chanting and singing to dancing, are all specifically "right-brain" activities that favor and are associated with functions housed in the right hemisphere and encourage spirituality through communion with Nature, or God, or with community, or with family. These activities tend to inhibit the dominant left hemisphere from imposing the supremacy of language and separating us from connecting with an entity or power greater than ourselves. This prevents our internal voice from inserting itself between us and our direct unprocessed and unabridged experience of the world around us.

The emerging consensus is that brain mechanisms supporting spiritual connectivity and religious experience appear to reside primarily in the nonverbal right hemisphere. It has been said that the left hemisphere concerns itself with theory, while the right specializes on the nature of experience. Iain McGilchrist, an Oxford scholar, psychiatrist, and the author of *The Master and His Emissary*, asserts that:

> Every attempt to reflect on life, understand the world or convey its true nature in language—in other words, every project of philosophy or theology—is an attempt to reconcile fundamentally incompatible models of the world, each of which can claim to reveal aspects of underlying reality. These attempts can, I suggest, be illuminated by an awareness of the conflicting models of the world yielded by the two hemispheres of our brains. (McGilchrist, 2019)

To the extent that we can see the right and left hemispheres creating two different experiential models, the left hemisphere would impose a more narrowly constrained, focused, and analytic vantage point, while the right would provide a more holistic and integrative perspective. This distinction becomes important when we discuss the implications of undertaking activities that promote a working partnership between horses and human that relies on nonverbal communication.

Horses and Nonverbal Communication

Over 50 million years of evolution as a prey animal and, later, a herd animal have taught the horse to excel at using nonverbal language as its preferred mode of communication. This stems from the fact that loud or repetitive vocalization runs the risk of tipping off a predator as to the location of individuals in a herd. Instead, the horse has evolved an elegant body language (sometimes referred to as Equus) that is made up of bodily postures, head tilt and carriage, ear position, and stance to communicate not just rank in the herd but also to lead or drive other horses in the herd. Unlike primates, horses do not rely on varied facial expression as a means of displaying emotion for two reasons. The first is a lack of effective musculature to permit a wide range of facial expression. Second, herds communicate over great distances, sometimes over hundreds of meters, so the use of subtle changes in facial musculature would serve little purpose. Contrast that with chimps in a tightly knit troupe where facial expression is vital to understanding differences between individuals. And, as such, the evolution of verbalization in primates has proceeded in a stepwise fashion, linking vocalization and facial expression into a game-changing, winning combination for impactful, varied communication.

The tight coordination of herd movement is the primary reason that unequivocal nonverbal language is essential to the well-being of herd members. Interestingly, studies have looked at whether domesticated horses could match vocalizations to human photographs displaying concordant or dissonant emotion. Horses appeared to show most interest in the photograph when the vocalization (say, anger) did not match the photograph (e.g., smiling). Using bradycardia and tachycardia as relative indices of whether a horse was reacting negatively or positively to a stimulus, these same researchers found that vocalization had the strongest effect on the horse's reaction and that facial expression was quite minor by comparison (Trösch et al., 2019). This correlates with the experience of most horse trainers, where they find there is relatively little response on the part of the horse to actual words used to formulate commands and more attention paid by the animal to the tone of voice the trainer uses to give the command. So, for example, a horse may make little distinction between the words "go and "whoa" if they are spoken with same intonation—even though these two commands have diametrically different meanings.

This is not to say that horses never vocalize; they do. Often the loudest vocalizations are reserved for stallion-on-stallion aggression (where the well-being of the herd takes a distant second to the demands of sire competition) and circumstances where one herd member has become separated from its herd mates. This can represent a particularly dire situation in the wild as a solitary horse, without the benefit of the herd, can be easily defeated by a large predator (e.g., a grizzly bear) or a coordinated pack of predators (e.g., wolves). Mares will often vocalize to their foals, but it is almost always in low-volume, low-frequency vocalization, which does not carry far and carries little risk of tipping off a predator as to the location of the foal.

This reliance on nonverbal communication has important implications not only for the Zen qualities of horsemanship but on the nature of the human–horse partnership itself. With respect to the human–horse dyad, the horse relies mostly on the horseman's or horsewoman's body language, their soothing tone of voice, and gestures such as petting or lightly slapping the horse on the shoulders or neck to tell the horse whether it has succeeded. I remember one particular Kentucky Derby where the owners were gathering in the winner's circle to pose with their horse. A woman (one of the owners) was so excited that she suddenly started screaming and jumping up and down. The result was that she spooked the horse, and it reared up and almost dumped its jockey on the ground.

The horse's lack of sophisticated and nuanced facial expression and its reliance on nonverbal behavior makes it uniquely suited as a species for working with individuals with autism spectrum disorder (ASD), and indeed, there are numerous equine programs with focus on serving youth with ASD. Individuals with ASD exhibit impaired social communication and interaction with diminished ability to respond to or exhibit the emotional content of facial expression. Horses are a wonderful method to therapeutically engage youngsters and others with ASD because neither of these deficits significantly impairs the affected individuals from having meaningful engagement with a horse.

Implications of a Prey Reward System

As prey animals, horses also function with a different reward system than that of humans. As predators, humans are uniquely tuned to stimulus-response learning. For example, the ease of rewarding a dog for learning a trick can often be an excited praise from the trainer, along with a food treat. We understand that pairing of stimulus and response. Because that is a hallmark of predatory, food rewards, they work well while training dogs. Horses, on the other hand, are prey animals and their biggest reward comes from being left alone, unmolested, and free from the pressures of any predators or threats in sight. While humans, as predators, hardly give a moment's thought to being stalked, herd animals like horses never forget "the flight imperative" that is the birthright of every prey animal. Thus, horse trainers must therefore keep in mind that a horse will be far less motivated by being given a piece of apple (as much as horses love them!) as a reward than being permitted to stand still and relax. It also means that we motivate a horse by applying energy to the animal either directly (e.g., through a halter and lead) or indirectly (e.g., swinging a lariat or training wand in the animal's vicinity). To reward the horse, that energy must cease. And the more instantaneously we can make that release from a high-energy state to a low or relaxed energy state, the more rapidly our horse will learn a new skill. One of my fellow horse trainers described it as "the horse seeks peace and is motivated by finding it." Unfortunately, in decades of horse training, I have only seen the timing of the release improve with concerted and sustained practice. Major differences in this reward system have profound consequences for clients and trainers interacting with horses.

By way of contrast, with a predator—let's use a dog as an example—it often helps to get the animal "amped up" (as they say) as they are tackling a training task. So, if I am asking a dog to make a jump, getting him excited with encouragement can make him more willing to attempt the jump. So, I can motivate him positively to make the jump by increasing my level of energy. By contrast, if I increase my own energy levels in front of the horse, I may negatively affect the horse. I may discourage him from making the jump. With the horse, I want to get him to understand that when the jump is made, release, relaxation, and peace await him. I will use a soothing, soft voice to praise him. This is one of the horse's greatest gifts to humans: because of its prey nature, the horse teaches us to control our impulses, to sublimate them, and to replace them with calm, peaceful energy. As we will see below, this becomes a powerful tool to teach individuals to control their aggressive, high energy and even violent impulsive tendencies.

I summarize these principles below because they are so important in training horses:

1. The horse is rewarded by release from a high-energy state to a lower one.
2. The more pronounced the energetic transition from high to low and the quicker the release follows the desired response, the easier it is for the horse to learn the task at hand.
3. Quick release with impeccable timing only comes with concerted and sustained practice.

Zen Principles in Horsemanship

Let Go We have already observed one of the central tenets of Zen Buddhism at work; namely, that attachment leads to sorrow and that in those moments when we relinquish notions of performing poorly, we gain transformative insight. Pema Chödrön is an ordained Catholic nun who went onto a lifelong study of Buddhism as a disciple of the venerable Chögyam Trungpa Rinpoche and was elevated to the status of acharya within the sect of Shambhala Buddhism. She wrote about this notion of no longer struggling for control:

> …feelings like disappointment, embarrassment, irritation, resentment, anger, jealousy, and fear, instead of being bad news, are actually very clear moments that teach us where it is that we're holding back. They teach us to perk up and lean in when we feel we'd rather collapse and back away. They're like messengers that show us, with terrifying clarity, exactly where we're stuck. This very moment is the perfect teacher, and, lucky for us, it's with us wherever we are. (Chödrön, 2005)

Horses drive home the same lesson: when we hold on tightly to the horse, there will be a struggle. And we will always lose that struggle. Pit yourself against the horse, and you will always be defeated. But it is not horse that vanquished you; it was you, deciding to assert control.

The horse's primary line defense is to flee. If you try to thwart that drive, the horse will only struggle harder. If the trainer then responds by fighting harder for control—by pulling harder on the reins or the lead rope or kicking deeper with the spurs—then both the horse and the trainer have plunged down the rabbit hole. The horse will only struggle that much more violently. It can turn into an unimaginably forceful and even deadly contest.

It is only when we let the horse go that it will cease to struggle and be prepared to listen to us. One of my adages in training: "If you want the horse to move away from you, walk towards him briskly. Conversely, if you want him to follow you, turn your back on him and walk away." Horses want to move away from high or tension-filled energy, and they like to move toward tranquil, low energy. By turning yourself off, by lowering your eyes, and swinging the front of your body away from the horse, you have given up control. Right? You've let go of your own agenda enough to walk away from the horse. So, think of horses as Zen-like sages on four hooves, waiting patiently out there in the pastures: when the student is ready, the teacher will appear.

In this regard, horses are uniquely suited to helping individuals assert control over their physically aggressive impulses. If a client is aggressive, prone to using excessive amounts of energy to get his way, then this characteristic of horses is useful for teaching the individual to dial down their physical response and lower the energy signature of their body and gestures. Only by learning to assume a calm, peaceful demeanor will the horse let the client approach (Nurenberg et al., 2015).

Interactions with horses help teach us to lose our preconceived notions of control. Truth be told, a human being on the ground weighing between 100 and 200 pounds cannot "out-muscle" a horse weighing in at 1000 pounds. In fact, as one of my fellow trainers likes to point out: "The only really powerful tool we can use to control a horse is the strength of the bond between the trainer's mind and that of his horse." So, we have to relinquish our sense of physical control: we can only compel the horse to do what he wants to do to please himself and his trainer. Again, this is a powerful lesson for an individual who has learned to rely on physical dominance, bullying, or simply reactive violence to get their way. Nine times out of ten, such individuals behave the way they do because they are fearful and insecure about their own situation.

Breath Control Meditation and meditative breathing are central to the study and practice of Zen Buddhism (Cysarz & Büssing, 2005). One of the favorite adages is that practicing Zen is easy: You start by sitting. Then, be quiet. After that, just breathe. Sitting meditation, known as zazen, is also carefully attended to by the head monks to ensure that the breathing is deep and purposefully taps into the hara (the lower abdomen) to encourage diaphragmatic breathing. The general thought is that as one gets into one's head (i.e., becomes more absorbed in one's own thoughts), the less likely the breathing is to be diaphragmatic and the higher the likelihood it is to be shallow and powered in the rib cage and chest. The more practiced a practitioner could become at reacquiring the deeper, diaphragmatic type of breathing, the more quickly one would be able to reacquire a more composed, contemplative demeanor. Peter Matthiessen, an acclaimed writer and a practicing Buddhist priest, wrote in his book, *The Snow Leopard*: "In this very breath that we now take lies the secret that all great teachers try to tell us" (Matthiessen, 2016).

In natural horsemanship, we use our breathing a great deal. In part, this is because horses are finely attuned to the nuances of our respirations, i.e., short and shallow panting might be seen as a cause of alarm or threat, while deep abdominal breathing relaxes muscle tension and puts the horse at ease. We can often use breath control to signal to a horse on the ground that he should pick up his speed or shift gait by increasing the rate of respirations and to slow down by taking slower, deeper cleansing breaths. With clients suffering from either anxiety or panic disorders or poor impulse control, learning to apply relaxation techniques that use meditative breathing with horses can be useful as they can see the change that it induces in their equine partner. Finally, grooming activities can often constitute an important part of a client's initial interaction with his or her horse at the beginning of each therapeutic session. Grooming can often calm a horse and can be enhanced by the client adding meditative breathing to the rhythmic stoking; it can be doubly so.

Be Mindful Zen Buddhism emphasizes the centrality of practicing mindfulness in our lives. This means that the individual horseman or horsewoman is aware of his or her surroundings and stays grounded in the present, paying little heed to what has happened in the past or might happen in the future. One of the important tenets of working with horses is that when the trainer is not fully present to the horse's needs, he or she is risking compromising the integrity of the partnership with the horse. For example, if I remain angry or upset with a horse because he failed to make a jump, then I am compromising the ability of the horse to clear the jump right in front of us, in the present. By the same token, if I am worrying about how high a jump my horse will make in an upcoming steeplechase event, then again, I have handicapped his performance in the present because I am focusing on future expectations.

In a similar vein, students are inclined to use a dressage whip on the ground and intervene when they feel the horse is preparing to slow down. I warn the student not to anticipate the horse making an error but, instead, to simply observe and if—and only if—the horse commits the error, then to simply correct this in a straightforward, matter-of-fact manner—without aggression, without shouting. Again, we don't need to imagine a future when the horse makes a mistake. We will remain in the present and simply respond to what occurs. As someone once said: "You can't arrest someone for thinking about robbing a bank. And you can't correct a horse because you think he might make an error."

Have Present Attention The other aspect of mindfulness that relates to both horsemanship and EAT is the concept of impeccable attention. In Zen Buddhism, especially in the martial arts (such as swordsmanship, horsemanship, and archer), the student is taught that "…the arrow is just a tool to bring you into the present moment, and the real target is yourself. If you think of the target as outside of yourself, then you have already missed the point." The archer is instructed that his or her awareness in the present moment is the key to hitting the target. Dan Millman, a world champion athlete and coach, wrote in *The Inner Athlete*: "When the archer shoots, he can think of nothing else. If he does, he is certain to miss the bullseye. This is the secret of the art of archery" (Millman, 1994). Archers schooled in these Zen-based methods were reported to be incredibly skillful with the bow and arrow. Yuzuru was a master archer who lived in Japan during the Edo period (1603–1868), when the martial arts flourished under the Tokugawa shogunate. He practiced a unique shot where his arrow would pass through a hole in a leaf hanging from a tree without touching the leaf or the branch. In Zen archery, this unique shot was iconic and came to be named the mokomokai, which means "peeping through the leaves."

In groundwork and EAT, the trainer (or EP) must be cognizant that the horse is sensitive to even small lapses in attention that can arise from sharing brief instructions with a client during an exercise on the ground and such lapses can cause a horse to "lose his eye" (meaning he is no longer trained on the individual at the center of the round pen) or to alter his gait (e.g., change his speed or length of his stride). Similarly, a horse may be willing to "hook on" to a client as part of a "joining-up" exercise but quickly wanders off if the client's attention flags.

EAT gives the individual a unique opportunity to visualize what happens when one's attention remains focused versus when it becomes diffuse or distracted. In limited clinical studies in children between the ages of 6 and 13 years old, EAT significantly diminished the severity of attention deficit hyperactivity disorder (ADHD) symptoms along with improvement in measures of social and psychomotor functions (Jang et al., 2015). A separate pilot study in ten children (mean age 8.3 ± 1.3 years) with ADHD measured baseline activity on functional MRI (fMRI) scans using a 3 Tesla magnet 2 weeks before and 2 weeks after a 12-week-long program of EAT. The functional neuroimaging revealed improved connectivity in two specific areas of the brain known as the precuneus and pars orbitalis. Aberrant activity along with micro-bursts of deactivation in the precuneus has been implicated in the momentary lapses seen in children with mild to moderate ADHD. Likewise, impaired function in the pars orbitalis has been hypothesized to interfere with behavioral inhibition and executive motor control in individuals suffering with ADHD. These signal changes observed on MRI have been hypothesized to underlie the symptomatic improvement seen in the children with ADHD treated with EAT (Yoo et al., 2016).

Accepting the No-Self Zen Buddhism teaches that the individual should seek to end the cult of the self; the cultivation of the non-self called for in Buddhist teachings is based on seeing the idea of personal identity as an illusion, and the first step on that journey is to turn off desire (Shiah, 2016). This concept of non-self is a powerful idea in trying to understand natural horsemanship. By contrast, the notions of the self and the ego lie at the very heart of Western psychology. Our culture has supported the reinforcement of the ego, along with fostering hedonic principles that heighten the self's obsession with fulfilling its desires.

Instead of "breaking" the horse, in the old parlance of the cowboy tradition, natural horsemanship is built around the premise that we develop the partnership between human and animal to the point that the horse becomes perfectly comfortable undertaking an activity of its own volition. The earlier traditions of horse training were based on what would be termed "flooding" in psychological parlance. If a horse would not accept a saddle, then one broke the horse's resistance by, first, tightly binding it to a snubbing post, cinching the saddle down tightly, and then allowing the horse to buck until he does not have the strength to show further resistance to the presence of the saddle. Contrast that with a natural horsemanship approach where we are lightly "sacking the horse out," gently rubbing the horse's back, shoulders, legs, and underbelly with blankets. We then proceed on to a light belt or cinch, then to a light saddle, and finally to a heavier Western rig (if that is the chosen endpoint). By using systematic desensitization, we have the luxury of proceeding at the horse's pace of acceptance and ensuring all steps are assimilated willingly and thoroughly. Of course, the great hidden benefit is that at every step of the way, the trainer is building trust with the horse. In this fashion, one gets to see the direct benefits of sublimating the needs of the trainer's ego to those of the horse.

Many of these same principles can also be applied with psychotherapy clients. It can often be hard to provide clients with practical instruction or exercises to help them learn to sublimate their own anxieties, fears, and emotions in order to foster a more constructive basis for social and familial relationships. However, interactions with the horse in ground exercises provide a ready opportunity to see how much better the relationship begins to work when we learn to proceed at the pace of the horse's needs rather than that of our own agendas. This is perfectly in keeping with the Zen saying: "A true horseman is not one who can make a horse do what he wants, but one who can understand what the horse wants."

Simplicity Zen encourages pursuing a simple, uncluttered life, stripped of unnecessary possessions and materialistic attachments. In a way, the quintessential interaction between the horse and the horse trainer is embodied in the round pen: just one individual exerting the influence of his or her energy at the same level as the horse, eye to eye. Many of the foundational exercises we employ in EAT and EAL either originate in the round pen or the latter is simply replaced with a long line. But this is the bond of the horse simplified to its essence, free from the complications of saddles, bridles, bits, and spurs. There is a clean, streamlined quality to the horse–human partnership: in pure groundwork, there is no other goal than to further the relationship with the horse. Yes, there are exercises of escalating difficulty (as we will see in the next section devoted to training horses for EAT and EAL), but the notions of success or failure fall away, because all that matters is did the horse and trainer engage with each other? There is no other objective than to endeavor together as a team to see what can be achieved.

Moderation or the Middle Way When Buddha grasped for the first time that death and disease were part of the nature of human suffering, he left his royal palace in the middle of the night, renouncing all of his worldly possession as a prince. He sought to wander the countryside as ascetic beggar and starvation soon brought his emaciated body close to death. But he had failed to attain enlightenment. He realized that zealous asceticism and denial were not the path to satori. He had not attained enlightenment living the most privileged of lifestyles as a prince nor had been able to reach it depriving himself of the most basic human needs. He reasoned that neither of these extreme paths led one to reach enlightenment, so, the path must be the "Middle Way", where both extremes were avoided. In this way, one of the fundamental tenets of Zen Buddhism is that opposites must be integrated into a unique balance of one harmonious entity in order to create the path to follow to enlightenment. Horses learn groundwork exercises or maneuvers by avoiding extremes and holding to the middle way in four distinct stages of learning.

The first is the learning phase of progressive exposure where the animal learns the task as a succession of easily accomplished "baby steps." The horse has to be able to search for the correct solution without any sense of pressure from punishment.

The second is the "lumping" stage, where we help the horse to take the small, discrete steps and begin to bring them together into a more holistic, integrated exercise. In this stage, again, praise serves to reinforce the horse's efforts at lumping.

The third step is consolidation when the integrated practices are assembled into a unified, orchestrated maneuver or movement. This means that horse's conception of assembly becomes the organizing principle but always with reward for integration.

The fourth and final stage is rehearsal, where the maneuver is practiced and repeated until the horse has comfortably assimilated it into his repertoire of behaviors. A cautionary note: horses are easily bored, and it is a mistake to endlessly repeat an exercise. Instead, it should be rotated in and out of the horse's repertoire almost at random. Here, the middle way is delight and playfulness to ensure that rehearsals do not become tedious. The middle way at each stage avoids the extreme of tedium on the one hand or punishment on the other.

We must balance the horse's experience so that, yes, he is practicing the repertoire he has already consolidated, but I also need to keep his mind engaged and playful by undertaking new challenges that are neither too aggressively ambitious nor too tediously boring. The Middle Way keeps the horse emotionally engaged and self-disciplined.

Withhold Judgment One of the things I have noticed working with horses is that they will engage whatever you are—expert, novice, clumsy, or graceful, the horse just accepts you the way you are. I want you to fold that back into the notion of Zen we just outlined. In other words, horses don't judge us. Or, more specifically, they don't pre-judge us. The idea that horses accept individuals regardless of their level of expertise or ability can be related to the Zen concept of nonjudgmental awareness. In Zen, the practice of nonjudgmental awareness involves cultivating a state of mind that is free from preconceived notions, biases, and judgments. This state of mind allows individuals to experience the world as it is, without imposing their own subjective interpretations on their experiences.

Similarly, horses do not have preconceived notions or biases toward humans, and they do not judge individuals based on their level of expertise or ability. Instead, they respond to individuals in the present moment based on their own unique personalities and behaviors. This can create a space of nonjudgmental awareness in which individuals can experience a sense of acceptance and connection with the horse, without the pressure of judgment or evaluation.

The experience of working with horses in this way can be a powerful reminder of the importance of nonjudgmental awareness in our daily lives. By cultivating a state of mind that is free from notions and judgments, individuals can experience greater acceptance and connection with themselves and others. This can lead to a greater sense of well-being, compassion, and equanimity.

Selection and Training of Horses for EAT

There are several variables that impact the selection of horses for an EAT/EAL program.

Breed The single most important quality when it comes to selecting horses for EAT programming is temperament. No one breed of domestic horse can lay claim to having the most suitable personality for EAT. Horses with a calm, gentle, and patient temperament are ideal for EAT. Some breeds that are known for their docile temperament include Quarter Horses, Haflingers, Norwegian Fjords, and draft horses such as Clydesdales, Percherons, and Belgians. So-called hot-blooded horses, such as thoroughbreds or Arabians, may require more assessment for EAT. However, I will say that some of the greatest horses for EAT were hot-blooded breeds like thoroughbreds or Arabians.

Size The size of the horse should be considered in relation to the clients who will be participating in the therapy. For adult clients, larger breeds such as Quarter Horses, Thoroughbreds, and Warmbloods may be appropriate, while for children or smaller clients, ponies or miniature horses may be better suited.

Gender I have never been impressed that one gender is better suited for EAT. Generally, most male horses are geldings, but even this rule is not inviolate. One of the best horses I ever used for my own EAT programming was an intact stallion that was also active in our breeding program. Under most circumstances, no one was even aware that there was a stud horse in the line-up.

Movement I am limiting my discussion to EAT and EAL that is confined to groundwork exercises. Separate from hippotherapy, however, horses selected for EAT should be sound. I believe people make a mistake using horses with advanced age that have been retired from work under saddle because of joint or back issues.

Age The age of horses used in equine-assisted therapy (EAT) can vary depending on the program's goals and the individual needs of the clients. But one can establish some general guidelines to consider when selecting horses based on age for EAT:

Older Horses While older horses may often exhibit the calm and reliable temperaments suitable for EAT programs, advanced age can also be a relative contraindication to including them into equine programming if their movement is limited and painful. Older horses tend to have more experience working with people and may be less reactive to sudden movements or noises. They may also be more patient and forgiving with less-experienced handlers.

Younger Horses Younger horses (e.g., 3–5-year-olds) are typically more reactive but can also be suitable for EAT programs. These horses tend to have more energy and enthusiasm, which can be useful for clients who need more physical support or stimulation. However, they may require more training and supervision by HPs to ensure their behavior is appropriate for therapy sessions.

Middle-Aged Horses Horses in their prime, typically between 6 and 12 years old, can often be the best choice for EAT programs. These horses are often at the peak of their physical fitness and may have a good balance of energy and maturity, making them well suited for a variety of clients. I prefer the horses I use for EAT be in their prime and in excellent athletic condition. Many of my EAT horses may also be engaged in active competition (such as hunter jumper, dressage, Western pleasure, and cutting), and I often use them for chores and livestock operations around the ranch. This gives them lots of novel opportunities to keep their minds and work ethic engaged.

Retirement-Aged Horses Horses that have retired from other disciplines or are no longer able to perform at a high level may also be included in EAT programs. I am excluding horses that have been "retired" from the racetrack as these are often quite young horses (typically 3-year-olds) although many of these horses can become suitable EAT and EAL horses with patience and training. Horses that have been retired because of advanced age tend to have a lot of experience working with people and may be more relaxed and easygoing in their interactions.

Ultimately, the age of the horse should not be the sole factor in determining its suitability for EAT. The horse's temperament, health, and training should be the primary considerations. The horses used in EAT programs should be well trained, calm, and reliable, regardless of age. Programs should also have a plan in place for monitoring the horses' health and well-being and providing them with appropriate care and retirement when necessary.

Training It is a mistake to believe that horses used in EAT programs do not require specific training to ensure their fitness and preparation before participating in an EAT or EAL program. Rather, EAT horses should have specific training that focuses on preparing them for the unique challenges of working with clients in a therapeutic setting and to ensure that only the safest horses are employed.

Desensitization Table 1 summarizes the qualities one looks for in EAT horses with respect to personality and demeanor. Horses used in EAT should be desensitized to a wide variety of stimuli, such as unusual equipment on the grounds (e.g., wheelchair; see Fig. 1) as well as sudden and/or loud noises (backfires, air horns, feedback from Av equipment, etc.), unexpected movements (plastic bags, jackets, tarps, etc.), unfamiliar equipment (e.g., cones, helium balloons, large inflatable beach balls, etc.), and uneven terrain (teeter-totter boards, walking across a large pile of recycled

Table 1 "The seven Ss:" What to look for when selecting horses for equine-assisted therapy and learning programs

Characteristics	Qualities
Socialization	Horse is comfortable around a variety of clients and well integrated into herd with other horses (sign of well-adjusted horse)
Submission	Horse will readily cede leadership role to human handler or client and will not seek to dominate hesitant or younger clients
Suspicion versus susceptibility	Horse has not lost his sense of fear or self-preservation, but once he is clear that there is no danger involved, he will give himself over to curiosity, playfulness, and susceptible to investigating a novel stimulus
Sensitivity versus desensitization	Horse is light and responsive, willing to respond to light touch but can desensitize itself quickly to a stimulus that is nonthreatening
Security	Horse is outgoing and has moderate self-confidence and self-possession and is not too fearful or shy
Safe	Horse that has good "ground manners" and is respectful of human beings (i.e., no biting, nipping, pushing)
Sustainability	Horse is in good physical condition and has many years of use left for an EAT program

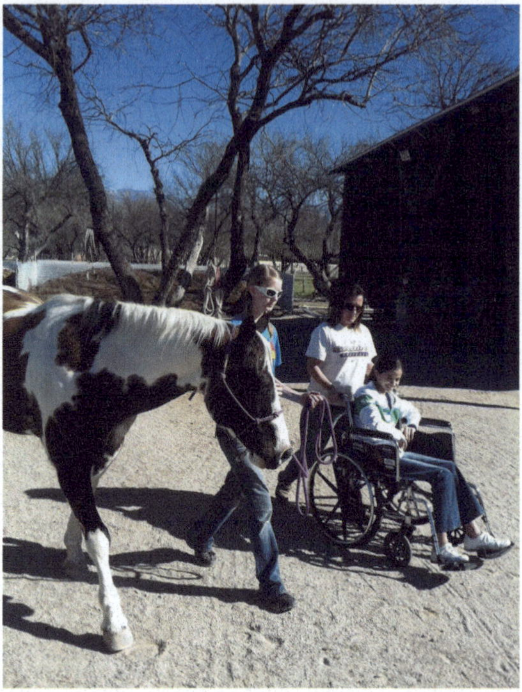

Fig. 1 Horses used for equine-assisted therapy (EAT) must be able to accommodate a wide range of clients, including those with disabilities. Wheelchairs can represent a novel challenge for a horse that has never seen one. It is wise to expose horses used for EAT to a wide range of novel experiences. (Photo courtesy of the author and Rancho Bosque LLC)

plastic bottles, and even balloons; see below). This helps to ensure that the horse remains calm and focused during therapy sessions and will be less likely to shy or rear when confronted by unfamiliar stimuli. That said, there is no such thing as a horse that will not spook under the right (or wrong) set of circumstances. No matter how well trained one's horse may be, something unexpected can happen for which the trainer and the horse were never prepared. As cowboys are fond of saying about desensitizing horses to loud noises: "Any fool can shoot a gun off the back of a horse—once. It's the second time that matters." The point of all this training is to ensure that the horse is confident, seasoned, and sufficiently mature to handle the most common of life's surprise on a ranch or farm.

Groundwork: Horses used in EAT should be trained in ground handling skills, such as leading, standing quietly, and responding to basic cues (backing up, side-stepping, etc.) from their handlers. This training helps to ensure that the horse is safe and reliable during therapy sessions.

Range of Behaviors The horses used in an EAT program may often need to be switched out of rotation, so their behaviors are best matched to the needs of the clients. For example, some clients may need a quieter, more calming presence, while others may require a more responsive horse. Once EAT horses have been trained and thoroughly evaluated for temperament, matching horses to clients is a relatively easy task to leave in the hands of a EP.

Therapeutic Techniques Horses used in EAT should be schooled to any specific therapeutic techniques used in a particular program. For example, horses may need additional training to stand quietly during guided meditation (see Fig. 2) or to walk slowly at liberty, off lead, during sensory integration exercises. It is important to note that the specific training required for EAT horses may vary depending on the program's goals and the individual needs of the clients. Experienced HPs with knowledge and expertise in EAT and equine training should develop a training plan that is tailored to the program's specific needs. There is an almost infinite variety of groundwork exercises, and one should consult training guides for additional inspiration.

Training Regimen Preparatory for EAT The exercises recommended here are the minimum that a horse must be able to carry out safely around clients. In the learning phase through the consolidation phases of training for each maneuver, the environment should remain quiet. Once the horse has mastered the task, then the environment can be allowed to become noisier and distracting. In this regard, many of the same methods used to train horses for police work are employed to create the most reliable and "bombproof" equine partners (see Fig. 3) for working with clients, who can occasionally behave in unpredictable ways.

Fig. 2 It is important to use horses with a calm demeanor for EAT. Horses are trained to feel comfortable leading next to clients without requiring lead ropes and exhibit a willingness to partner with individuals who may never have had any prior experience moving around the horse. (Photo courtesy of the author and Rancho Bosque LLC)

Fig. 3 The author is preparing one of his cutting horses for EAT work and is working on desensitizing the mare to the presence of a noisy, flapping plastic bag that is tied to the end of a training wand. It is important to never accelerate the desensitization process faster than what the horse can comfortably and willingly accept. (Photo courtesy of the author and Rancho Bosque LLC)

Grooming Horses must be able to stand quietly while being groomed by one or more individuals. The horse also needs to be able stand and allow clients to clean his hooves with a hoof pick. In some instances, grooming may be deeply therapeutic. For example, in cancer patients with treatment-related alopecia, clients often wish to lavish attention on grooming, especially of the mane and tail. Appropriate detanglers should always be applied to the mane and tail to prevent the horse's hair being inadvertently damaged or pulled out.

Leading The horse must be trained to lead with minimal to no pull on the lead ropes or halters. Horses need to be able to readily sidestep as well as move forward and backward, both in a straight line and on a curve. They need to be able to move backward at the walk and be able to easily back up the length of the round pen and, later, along one entire revolution of the riding arena. Horses need to be able to carry out both inside and outside circles (with respect to the client's position relative to the circle the horse is making) at will and to readily yield on the hindquarters and forehand. Later, as horses are comfortable leading, they are then usually asked to perform the same maneuvers at liberty (i.e., without a lead rope). Horses must be able to lunge comfortably at the walk, trot, and slow lope near a client.

Training Wands The horse needs to be fully desensitized to the presence of training wands and lead ropes. This also means the horse is comfortable with lengths of

Fig. 4 Training a horse to cross over a tarp to increase a horse's confidence when confronting uneven, noisy footing. (Photo courtesy of the author and Rancho Bosque LLC)

ropes being draped over the back and cross the rear and front legs. Horses must be permitted to become completely at ease with training wands and lead ropes (14-foot length, 25-foot length, and 50-foot lariat) and trust completely that no training aid will ever be used to punish them. Horses need to be able to lunge in the round pen at all gaits except the gallop (not advised because of stress on legs inside round pen). The horse also needs to be able to stop, change direction, and "upshift" or "downshift" gaits through various speeds.

Other Training Aids The horse needs to be able to lunge over jumps or jump at liberty. Jumps need not be more than 3 or 4 feet high, and routine jump standards should be used for stability. Care should always be taken in jumps to adequately protect the coronet band of the hooves. Horses should be completely desensitized to plastic bags, helium-filled balloons, walking across tarps (see Fig. 4), noisy and uneven footing (such as recycled plastic bottles), and across puddles or other shallow bodies of water (such as ponds or running streams). It can be expected that horses may occasionally get tangled up in their lead rope in difficult or tight maneuvers in an obstacle course (see Fig. 5), and it is useful to get the horse accustomed to finding itself with the lead rope occasionally tangled around the front or hind legs. In such situations, the horse should be trained to stop and stand quietly until a handler or EP comes by to undo the lead rope.

Fig. 5 Horses being used for EAT should be exposed to a wide variety of challenges. Here, the horse is being taken through an obstacle course that includes ground poles and jumps. There is also a large group of participants as well as the sound of loudspeakers that are required for working in a large arena. (Photo courtesy of the author and Rancho Bosque LLC)

Conclusion

Like any disciplined course of study, horsemanship lends itself to lifelong learning, and there is no end point at which complete mastery will ever be achieved. Nor does one set of guidelines, principles, philosophy, or approach have all the answers. There is an old Japanese story about an old man who has lived more than 100 years and spent his life as a horse master, training students in ways and tradition of horsemanship. He is on his deathbed and his son is by his side. He confesses to his son: "I wish I had more time I could spend with my horses."

"Why?" asked his son. "You are the most revered horseman in all of Japan. Why would you need more time with your horses?"

"I was just beginning to understand the creatures," he chuckled. And that is the point. I studied horsemanship with some of the luminaries of school of natural horsemanship, including the legendary Ray Hunt. I once asked him how long he thought a person needed to train with horses before one would no longer have to label oneself a novice. He said: "Oh, I don't know. Maybe ten thousand hours."

"My god," I exclaimed, "Ten thousand hours!"

He looked at the shock on my face and said: "You think that's too little?". Again, Ray Hunt's point was that it took a lifetime to learn about horses. And you never finish.

Learning about horses is an opportunity to see the world through the eye of a prey animal. You can learn to see it with what Zen Buddhists call "the beginner's mind," which is free from biases and ore-conceived notions. And you get the opportunity to partner closely with an animal that accepts you just the way you are, without the confusion of the verbal lies you tell others or yourself. There are few activities more humbling or uplifting. As the Zen horse master suggested: one lifetime—no matter how long—is not enough to absorb all the lessons that horses can teach us.

Conflicts of Interest The author has no conflicts of interest to declare.

References

A cautionary note is warranted here: it is relatively contraindicated to place individuals with a history physical aggression or violent—but especially those with a history of sadism or cruelty towards animals—into an environment with horses except under the most supervised situations and, always, the welfare of the horse must be paramount in the horse professional's mind.

Arnon, S., Fisher, P., Pickover, A., Lowell, A., Turner, B., Hamilton, J. H., Hamilton, A. J., Markowitz, J. C., & Neria, Y. (2020, June 8). Equine assisted therapy for PTSD: Treatment development and pilot findings among military personnel. *Military Medicine, 185*(5–6), e557–e564. https://doi.org/10.1093/milmed/usz444

Birke, L. (2007). "Learning to speak horse": The culture of "natural horsemanship". *Society & Animals, 15*(3), 217–239.

Chödrön, P. (2005). *When things fall apart: Heart advice for difficult times* (p. 14). Shambhala Publications.

Cysarz, D., & Büssing, A. (2005). Cardiorespiratory synchronization during Zen meditation. *European Journal of Applied Physiology, 95*, 88–95.

Damasio, A. R. (1999). *The feeling of what happens: Body and emotion in the making of consciousness*. Houghton Mifflin Harcourt.

Equine-Assisted Growth and Learning Association (EAGALA). P. O. Box 6568, Elgin, IL 60121. https://www.eagala.org/index

Fisher, P. W., Lazarov, A., Lowell, A., Arnon, S., Turner, J. B., Bergman, M., Ryba, M., Such, S., Marohasy, C., Zhu, X., & Suarez-Jimenez, B. (2021). Equine-assisted therapy for post-traumatic stress disorder among military veterans: An open trial. *The Journal of Clinical Psychiatry, 82*(5), 36449.

Hamilton, A. J. (2011). *Zen mind, Zen horse: The science and spirituality of working with horses*. Storey Publishing.

Hamilton, A. J., & Hamilton, J. F. (2022). T*he neuro-equine model: A manual on the scientific approach to the application and practice of equine-assisted therapy and learning* (Expanded 2nd ed.). Ranch in the Woods Publishers. ISBN: 979-9-9858554-0-1.

Herrigel, E. (1999). *Zen in the art of archery* (p. 29). Vintage Books. ISBN: 978-0375705090.

Jang, B., Song, J., Kim, J., Kim, S., Lee, J., Shin, H. Y., Kwon, J. Y., Kim, Y. H., & Joung, Y. S. (2015). Equine-assisted activities and therapy for treating children with attention-deficit/hyperativity disorder. *Journal of Alternative and Complementary Medicine (New York, N.Y.), 21*(9), 546–553. https://doi.org/10.1089/acm.2015.0067

Matthiessen, P. (2016). *The snow leopard* (p. 245). Viking Press. ISBN: 9780143129523.

McGilchrist, I. (2019). Cerebral lateralization and religion: A phenomenological approach. *Religion, Brain & Behavior, 9*(4), 319–339. https://doi.org/10.1080/2153599x.2019.1604411

Millman, D. (1994). *The inner athlete* (2nd ed., p. 50). Stillpoint Publishing. ISBN: 978-0913299975.

Nurenberg, J. R., Schleifer, S. J., Shaffer, T. M., Yellin, M., Desai, P. J., Amin, R., Bouchard, A., & Montalvo, C. (2015). Animal-assisted therapy with chronic psychiatric inpatients: Equine-assisted psychotherapy and aggressive behavior. *Psychiatric Services (Washington, D.C.), 66*(1), 80–86. https://doi.org/10.1176/appi.ps.201300524

Shiah, Y. J. (2016). From self to nonself: The nonself theory. *Frontiers in Psychology, 7*. https://doi.org/10.3389/fpsyg.2016.00124

Suzuki, D. T. (1964). *An Intriduction to Zen Buddhism* (p. 65). New York: Grove Press.

Suzuki, D. T. (1959). *Zen and the Japanese culture* (p. 15). N. J: Princeton University Press.

Suzuki, D. T. (1994, January 13). *An introduction to Zen Buddhism* (p. 95). Grove Press.

The author realizes that the term "horsemanship" represents one of those maddening words which needlessly cling to masculine context for the noun and offer no good or useful alternative to a more gender-free synonym. This is all the more frustrating today as the vast majority of individual working in the area of horsemanship are, in fact, women. The term is therefore employed with the author's apologies and regrets.

The issue of gender and pronoun use is an understandably touchy one. And having bred horses, I am well aware that there are stallions, geldings, and mares. I find the "he or she" awkward when referring to a horse and I have found that in my own line of horsework and training, I am working with male horses more than ninety percent of the time. So, my convention is to always label a horse he/him unless I am discussing a specific horse that is a mare or I am talking about, say, reproductive behavior unique to mares. On a working ranch, almost all the stock are geldings, so it is just commonplace to refer ot horses as "he/him" unless biology corrects you.

The term "equine professional" is synonymous with the designation of "equine specialist" that appears elsewhere in the book.

Trösch, M., Cuzol, F., Parias, C., Calandreau, L., Nowak, R., & Lansade, L. (2019). Horses categorize human emotions cross-modally based on facial expression and non-verbal vocalizations. *Animals: An Open Access Journal from MDPI, 9*(11), 862. https://doi.org/10.3390/ani9110862

Yoo, J. H., Oh, Y., Jang, B., Song, J., Kim, J., Kim, S., Lee, J., Shin, H. Y., Kwon, J. Y., Kim, Y. H., Jeong, B., & Joung, Y. S. (2016). The effects of equine-assisted activities and therapy on resting-state brain function in attention-deficit/hyperactivity disorder: A pilot study. *Clinical Psychopharmacology and Neuroscience: The Official Scientific Journal of the Korean College of Neuropsychopharmacology, 14*(4), 357–364. https://doi.org/10.9758/cpn.2016.14.4.357

Zhu, X., Suarez-Jimenez, B., Zilcha-Mano, S., Lazarov, A., Arnon, S., Lowell, A., Bergman, M., Matthew, R., Hamilton, A., Hamilton, J., Turner, J. B., Markowitz, M., Fisher, P. W., & Neria, Y. (2021, February 5). Neural changes following equine-assisted therapy for PTSD: A longitudinal multimodal brain imaging study. *Human Brain Mapping*, 1930. https://doi.org/10.1002/hbm.25360

An Overview of the History, Rationale, and Clinical Application of the Use of EAS in Veterans with Psychiatric Disorders

William R. Marchand

Introduction

The goal of this chapter is to provide an overview of the use of equine-assisted services (EAS) for veterans with psychiatric illness. The scope of this chapter includes definitions, findings and limitations from the extant literature, potential mechanisms of action, treatment needs of the veteran population, challenges associated with conventional interventions, potential benefits, and strategies to move the field forward. The overarching focus is to provide an outline of potential benefits, and underlying mechanisms, of EAS for veterans as well as to delineate the limitations of our understanding given the field is in the early stages of scientific development.

Animal-Assisted Interventions and Equine-Assisted Services

Animal-assisted interventions (AAIs) are therapeutic processes that utilize animals with a goal of helping humans in various ways. EAS refer to a group of AAIs that utilize horses to fulfill the mission of benefiting humans (Wood et al., 2020). EAS include psychotherapy incorporating horses (PIH), therapeutic or adaptive riding, hippotherapy, and equine-assisted learning (Wood et al., 2020). PIH is focused on self-awareness, behavior change, and symptom reduction, and it requires that a licensed mental health professional (MHP) be a member of the team providing the intervention (Wood et al., 2020). PIH is typically facilitated by at least one MHP and one equine professional and may include groundwork, mounted activities, or both. Generally, the MHP focuses on the therapeutic aspects of the intervention and

W. R. Marchand (✉)
Whole Health Service, VA Salt Lake City Health Care System, Salt Lake City, UT, USA
e-mail: william.marchand@va.gov

Y. Neria et al. (eds.), *Guide to Equine Assisted Therapy*,
https://doi.org/10.1007/978-3-031-74426-6_2

the equine professional manages the equestrian portion, but this may vary somewhat based upon the training and skill sets of the providers. Therapeutic and adaptive riding utilize primarily mounted activities to provide a therapeutic intervention and/or facilitate recreational riding for individuals with psychiatric and/or medical conditions. For example, if provided as a component of a PIH intervention, mounted activities would be termed therapeutic. In contrast, if aimed at helping an individual with a medical or psychiatric condition participate in recreational riding, the activity would be labeled as adaptive. While these interventions focus primarily on mounted activities, they typically include some groundwork, such as leading, tacking, and grooming. Hippotherapy refers to interventions provided by occupational therapy, physical therapy, and speech–language pathology professionals using the horse movement to increase functioning in conditions such as stroke, cerebral palsy, multiple sclerosis, spinal cord injury, and traumatic brain injury (American Hippotherapy Association; House Armed Services Committee, 2015). Finally, equine-assisted learning facilitates acquisition of new knowledge and/or skills and may include mounted activities, groundwork, or both (Wood et al., 2020).

Equine-Assisted Services for Veterans

AAIs in general are often used as complementary interventions for trauma survivors (Chandler, 2012; Beetz et al., 2019; McCardle et al., 2011), and since the 1990s, the use of EAS has increased significantly in both the United States and Europe (Bachi et al., 2012) for both civilian (Alfonso et al., 2015; Anderson & Meints, 2016; Borgi et al., 2016; Cerino et al., 2011; Corring et al., 2013; Cuypers et al., 2011; Earles et al., 2015; Frederick et al., 2015; Gabriels et al., 2015; Harris & Williams, 2017; Hession et al., 2014; Hoagwood et al., 2017; Holm et al., 2014; Hyun et al., 2016; Jang et al., 2015; Jormfeldt & Carlsson, 2018; Kang et al., 2018; Kern et al., 2011; Malcolm et al., 2018; Nurenberg et al., 2015; Srinivasan et al., 2018; Trzmiel et al., 2019) and military/veteran populations (Arnon et al., 2020; Lanning et al., 2018; Burton et al., 2019; Duncan et al., 2014; Ferruolo, 2016; Fisher et al., 2021; Gehrke et al., 2018a, b; Hoopes et al., 2022; Johnson et al., 2018; Lanning & Krenek, 2013; Lanning et al., 2017; Malinowski et al., 2018; Marchand et al., 2022a, b, 2023; Meyer & Sartori, 2019; Monroe et al., 2019; Romaniuk et al., 2018; Rosing et al., 2022; Shelef et al., 2019; Steele et al., 2018; Sylvia et al., 2020; Wharton et al., 2019; Zhu et al., 2021). In addition to the number of studies published in recent years, other types of evidence include the fact that the Professional Association of Therapeutic Horsemanship International (PATH Intl) centers providing services to veterans increased from 89 to 335 from 2009 to 2016 (PATH Intl). Also, the Equine-Assisted Growth and Learning Association (EAGALA) has added a "Military Services Designation" for practitioners of that model of EAS. While EAS interventions are being frequently used for the military/veteran population, the field remains in the initial stages of scientific development and rigorous research is absent (Marchand et al., 2021a).

Research Supporting the Use of EAS for Veterans

Despite the increasing use of EAS interventions for veterans, the evidence of effectiveness is limited. However, a scientific literature of studies assessing benefits exists. Studies of nonveteran populations report benefits for depression (Frederick et al., 2015), autism-spectrum disorder (Anderson & Meints, 2016; Borgi et al., 2016; Gabriels et al., 2015; Harris & Williams, 2017; Hoagwood et al., 2017; Holm et al., 2014; Kern et al., 2011; Malcolm et al., 2018; Srinivasan et al., 2018; Trzmiel et al., 2019), social anxiety (Alfonso et al., 2015), schizophrenia-spectrum illness (Cerino et al., 2011; Corring et al., 2013; Jormfeldt & Carlsson, 2018; Nurenberg et al., 2015), and attention-deficit/hyperactivity disorder (Cuypers et al., 2011; Hyun et al., 2016; Jang et al., 2015). Studies have also reported trans-diagnostic benefits, such as improvements in cognition, quality of life, and well-being (Bachi et al., 2012; Bunketorp-Kall et al., 2017; Cerulli et al., 2014; Fields et al., 2018).

Given the fact that many veterans have trauma histories, community studies of EAS for this population are particularly relevant. Studies of EAS for children and youth have revealed reduction of depression (Signal et al., 2013), anxiety, externalizing behaviors (Kemp et al., 2014), and post-traumatic stress disorder (PTSD) symptoms (McCullough et al., 2015). These investigations suggest promise; however, rigorous research is lacking (Marchand et al., 2021a). Specifically, large multisite randomized controlled trials have not been done. Finally, these results may not generalize to veteran populations.

A developing literature reports investigations of EAS specifically for veterans (Arnon et al., 2020; Lanning et al., 2018; Burton et al., 2019; Duncan et al., 2014; Ferruolo, 2016; Fisher et al., 2021; Gehrke et al., 2018a, b; Hoopes et al., 2022; Johnson et al., 2018; Lanning & Krenek, 2013; Lanning et al., 2017; Malinowski et al., 2018; Marchand et al., 2022a, b, 2023; Meyer & Sartori, 2019; Monroe et al., 2019; Romaniuk et al., 2018; Rosing et al., 2022; Shelef et al., 2019; Steele et al., 2018; Sylvia et al., 2020; Wharton et al., 2019; Zhu et al., 2021). Please see Table 1 for an overview of published studies. However, of the published studies, only three studies (Lanning et al., 2018; Burton et al., 2019; Johnson et al., 2018) have a control group and only one (Johnson et al., 2018) is a randomized trial. Finally, a case study (Nevins et al., 2013) of a single veteran reported improved psychological functioning. A 2019 systematic review by Kinney et al. (2019) concluded that EAS interventions for veterans were found to be promising but continued research is necessary to establish their efficacy. Further, an older study by Hayes, Inc. in 2016 (House Armed Services Committee, 2015) assessed the effectiveness of using EAS for military service members and concluded that existing evidence was insufficient to determine the effectiveness for psychological disorders. Thus, the field is currently in the early stage of scientific development, and rigorous randomized controlled trials are needed to fully establish the benefits of EAS for veterans.

Despite the lack of rigorous research, the existing veteran-specific literature is promising. For example, investigators have reported decreased depression (Arnon et al., 2020; Lanning et al., 2018; Fisher et al., 2021; Marchand et al., 2022b, 2023;

Table 1 Investigations of EAS interventions for veterans

Authors	Intervention	Study design	Sample size	Participant diagnoses	Outcomes
Arnon et al.	*EAT-PTSD*, a manualized, eight 90-minute weekly sessions, group psychoeducation and horsemanship skills training (groundwork only)	Pre- to post-intervention NR/NC	8	PTSD and psychiatric comorbidities	↓ PTSD SX ↓ Depressive SX No Adverse Outcomes
Burton et al.	6-week, metaphor-based group (groundwork only)	Two-arm parallel group NR, PTSD TAU = control group	20 (10 per group)	PTSD	↓ PTSD SX ↑ Resilience No change in salivatory cortisol
Duncan et al.	*Can Praxis*, a 7-day, group EAL for couples	Post NR/NC	31 Canadian veterans and 27 partners	PTSD (for veteran participants)	↓ PTSD SX
Ferruolo	1- or 2-day group intervention consisting of psychoeducation, experiential equine activities, and group processing	Pre- to post NR/NC Qualitative	8	Not given	Locally developed survey revealed themes of learning about self, spiritual connection, trust, and respect
Fisher et al.	*EAT-PTSD*, a manualized, eight 90-minute weekly sessions, group psychoeducation and horsemanship skills training (groundwork only)	Pre- to post NR/NC	63	PTSD	↓ PTSD SX ↓ Depressive SX

(continued)

Table 1 (continued)

Authors	Intervention	Study design	Sample size	Participant diagnoses	Outcomes
Gehrke et al.	Eight weekly sessions of 3 hours each (mounted and groundwork)	Pre- to post NR/NC	17	PTSD	↑ Affect ↑ HRV
Gehrke et al.	Eight weekly sessions of 3 hours each (mounted and groundwork)	Pre- to post NR/NC Mixed methods	9	PTSD	↑ Affect Theme clusters were positive impact, connection with the horse, being present, horse mirroring, translating, and power dynamic
Hoopes et al.	One-time recreational trail ride, approximately 2 hours duration	Pre- to post NR/NC	18	Addictive disorders and PTSD	↑ Positive affect ↓ Negative affect ↓ Anxiety ↓ Craving No adverse outcomes
Johnson et al.	6-week, therapeutic horseback riding, conducted once per week (ground and mounted work)	C/R, WL = control group	29	PTSD	↓ PTSD SX No adverse outcomes
Lanning et al.	*Rainier Therapeutic Riding's Riding Through Recovery*, 8-week, 90-minute sessions (ground and mounted work)	Repeated measures, comparison group = TAU NR	89	PTSD	↓ PTSD SX ↓ Depressive SX ↓ Functional disability
Lanning et al.	8-week, 90-minute sessions (ground and mounted work)	Multi-method, repeated measures NR/NC	51	PTSD	↓ PTSD SX ↑ Functioning

(continued)

Table 1 (continued)

Authors	Intervention	Study design	Sample size	Participant diagnoses	Outcomes
Malinowski et al.	Five 1-hour sessions over 5 days (ground and mounted work)	Pre- to post NR/NC	7 veterans and 9 equines	PTSD	*Humans*: ↓ PTSD SX ↓ PD ↓ Blood pressure on 1 day *Equines*: No change in cortisol ↓ Heart rate No change in HRV No change in oxytocin
Marchand et al.	One 4-hour session of EAL/PIH for veterans enrolled in VA residential substance abuse treatment (groundwork only)	Pre- to post NR/NC	33	Addictive disorders and PTSD	↑ Positive affect ↓ Negative affect ↓ Anxiety ↓ Craving No adverse effects
Marchand et al.	Two sessions of horsemanship skills training and two trail rides (ground and mounted work)	Pre- to post NR/NC	18	PTSD and many had psychiatric comorbidity	↑ Positive affect ↓ Negative affect ↓ Depressive SX ↑ Psych flexibility ↓ PTSD SX Enjoyed activity No adverse effects
Marchand et al.	*Whispers with Horses*, a six-session manualized intervention providing mindfulness and self-compassion training in the context of developing horse–human relationship offer as individual and group therapy (groundwork only)	Pre- to post NR/NC	33	All had trauma histories, 73% had PTSD, many had additional psychiatric comorbidity	↑ Positive affect ↓ Negative affect ↓ Depressive SX ↑ Psych flexibility No adverse effects

(continued)

Table 1 (continued)

Authors	Intervention	Study design	Sample size	Participant diagnoses	Outcomes
Meyer and Sartori	Very limited description	Qualitative study	5	PTSD	Themes were positive changes in thoughts and behaviors, beliefs about horses' cognition and emotions, EAS-induced emotions and emotional regulation, and interpersonal and interspecies relationships
Monroe et al.	Eight-week group intervention with 3-hour sessions (ground and mounted work) utilizing components of CBT	Pre- to post NR/NC	48	Self-identified as having PTSD, 76% met diagnostic criteria	↓ PTSD SX ↓ Anxiety ↓ Depressive SX ↑ Quality of life
Romaniuk et al.	Separate individual and couples group therapy. Based on Relational Gestalt Therapy, mindfulness, grounding techniques, and natural horsemanship. Couple group for veterans and partners	Within-subject longitudinal study NR/NC	25 veterans 22 couples	Not given but many experienced PTSD symptoms	↓ PTSD SX ↓ Anxiety ↓ Stress ↓ Depressive SX ↑ Quality of life ↑ Happiness
Rosing et al.	Group, 3 hours/ week for 6 months (ground and mounted work), included the EAGALA model	Pre- to post NR/NC Qualitative	13	PTSD	Themes were the ability to relax, forming relationships and transformation and hope

(continued)

Table 1 (continued)

Authors	Intervention	Study design	Sample size	Participant diagnoses	Outcomes
Shelef et al.	Group, 3 hours/ week for 6 months (ground and mounted work), included the EAGALA model	Open case series NR/NC	23	PTSD	
Steele et al.	Trauma and Resiliency Resources, Inc.'s *Warrior Camp* is a program of 7-day intensive intervention including EMDR, PIH, yoga, and narrative writing (groundwork only)	Pre- to post NR/NC	85	Not given but all participants were military veterans, and most had been deployed to a combat zone	
Sylvia et al.	Two-day retreat, veterans and family members participated in three 2-hour sessions of EAS (ground and mounted work)	Post NR/NC	62 veterans 44 family	PTSD was primary diagnosis for 53 participants, other diagnoses were TBI, AUD, and depression	
Wharton et al.	Equine-facilitated cognitive processing therapy, 12 sessions	Pre- to post NR/NC	27	PTSD	
Zhu et al.	*EAT-PTSD*, a manualized, eight 90-minute weekly sessions, group psychoeducation and horsemanship skills training (groundwork only)	Pre- to post NR/NC	19	PTSD	

This table was adapted from Table 1 in Marchand (2023)

C/R controlled/randomized, *WL* wait list, *R* randomized, *PTSD* post-traumatic stress disorder, *SX* symptoms, *PD* psychological distress, *NR* non-randomized, *NR/NC* non-randomized/non-controlled, *MOA* mechanism of action, *EAL* equine-assisted learning, *HRV* heart rate variability, *PIH* psychotherapy incorporating horses, *psych* psychological, *EMDR* eye movement desensitization and reprocessing therapy, *TBI* traumatic brain injury, *AUD* alcohol use disorder, *fMRI* functional magnetic resonance imaging, *DTI* diffusion tensor imaging, *FC* functional connectivity, *CBT* cognitive behavioral therapy, *HRV* heart rate variability

Monroe et al., 2019; Romaniuk et al., 2018; Steele et al., 2018; Zhu et al., 2021), anxiety (Hoopes et al., 2022; Marchand et al., 2022a; Monroe et al., 2019; Romaniuk et al., 2018), craving for substances (Hoopes et al., 2022; Marchand et al., 2022a), and PTSD symptoms (Arnon et al., 2020; Lanning et al., 2018; Burton et al., 2019; Duncan et al., 2014; Fisher et al., 2021; Johnson et al., 2018; Lanning et al., 2017; Malinowski et al., 2018; Monroe et al., 2019; Romaniuk et al., 2018; Shelef et al., 2019; Steele et al., 2018; Wharton et al., 2019; Zhu et al., 2021). Additionally, improvements in psychological flexibility (Marchand et al., 2022b, 2023) and affect (Gehrke et al., 2018a, b; Hoopes et al., 2022; Marchand et al., 2022a, b, 2023) have been reported. Several investigations revealed that participants enjoyed the EAS experience (Marchand et al., 2022b; Sylvia et al., 2020), and that there were no adverse effects (Arnon et al., 2020; Hoopes et al., 2022; Johnson et al., 2018; Marchand et al., 2022a, b, 2023; Shelef et al., 2019). Taken together, these studies suggest that EAS participation is associated with both trans-diagnostic benefits and symptom reduction. Further, there appears to be a low risk of adverse outcomes.

Although studies are promising, there are challenges to the field beyond the lack of rigorous studies. One of the major problems in the field is a lack of standardized terminology, which has created challenges for both practice and research (Hallberg, 2018). This has occurred in part because numerous organizations offer trainings and certifications for EAS professionals and may use different terminology and definitions (Hallberg, 2018). Such organizations include the Equine Assisted Growth and Learning Association (https://www.eagala.org/index), the Professional Association of Therapeutic Horsemanship International (https://pathintl.org/), Pet Partners (https://petpartners.org/), Eponaquest (https://eponaquest.com/), Horse Boy Foundation (https://www.horseboyfoundation.org/), Natural Lifemanship (https://naturallifemanship.com/), and others. The lack of standardization has made it difficult to understand mechanisms of action and compare outcomes across studies. To move the field forward with rigorous studies that can be replicated, the field will need to adopt a standardized nomenclature (Hallberg, 2018). To address this issue, a consensus terminology paper (Wood et al., 2020) was written and published by experts in the field. However, it is still unknown whether the recommendations will be adopted in full or in part by the EAS field. Further, the authors acknowledge that there was disagreement during the consensus building process and that the publication is intended to be a living document subject to revision.

Finally, in addition to a lack of standardized terminology, there is a lack of standardization of EAS interventions used for veterans, which severely limits both between-study comparisons and the ability to draw conclusions from the existing literature. However, several interventions for veterans (Arnon et al., 2020; Lanning et al., 2018; Marchand et al., 2022b, 2023; Wharton et al., 2019; Zhu et al., 2021) were designed to be manualized to facilitate both fidelity and replication studies. Rigorous investigations of these interventions can potentially move the field forward, and if some are shown to be effective then disseminated to the field.

Mechanisms of Action

In addition to the challenges to the field stated above, little is currently known about the mechanisms of action underlying the benefits of EAS. Further, it is likely that various EAS interventions may have different mechanisms of change and outcomes. Thus, it is unclear which of the various components of interventions contribute to benefit for participants. This section reviews potential psychological and physiological mechanisms of action.

One psychological component likely underlying the benefits is the horse–human relationship, which may, in some cases, include bonding. Human–horse interactions are thought to contribute to benefits of EAS in general (Hallberg, 2018), and several investigators (Lanning & Krenek, 2013; Lanning et al., 2017; Nevins et al., 2013) of veteran-specific studies have hypothesized that human–horse bonding has contributed to outcomes. Further, it has been conjectured that the horse could serve as an attachment figure in some EAS encounters (Bachi, 2013; Yorke et al., 2008). The general AAI literature, as well as EAS-specific studies, suggests that horse–human relationships might contribute to positive outcomes in several ways. For those who have a trauma history, the experience of trauma can significantly impair the ability to bond with other humans (Pearlman & Courtois, 2005) and horse–human relationships might be a safer form of attachment (O'Haire et al., 2019). Also, trauma survivors may trust an animal more easily than another person (Chandler, 2005; Pichot & Coulter, 2007). Finally, animals may provide unconditional affection and non-judgmental support (O'Haire et al., 2019). However, while many EAS interventions provide an opportunity for participants to form a relationship with an equine, not all do (Fry, 2019). Furthermore, interventions that do not focus on the horse–human bond, such as the Equine Assisted Growth and Learning Association (EAGALA) model (Fournier et al., 2018; Notgrass & Pettinelli, 2014), have evidence of benefit for both community (Buck et al., 2017; Coetzee et al., 2022; Harvey et al., 2020) and veteran populations (Burton et al., 2019; Steele et al., 2018). Thus, additional mechanisms must underlie the benefits in some EAS interventions.

The EAGALA model, mentioned above, is an experiential and solution-focused intervention based on the use of metaphor (Fournier et al., 2018; Notgrass & Pettinelli, 2014). Horses, arena props, and the equine facility setting serve as potential metaphors for situations in the participant's life. The metaphors serve as physical and visual representations of the participant's emotions and cognitions (Fry, 2019) and facilitate self-distancing. Self-distancing through metaphor facilitates the participant working safely with distressing emotions and cognitions and can result in psychological insight as well as the opportunity to practice new behaviors in a low-risk setting (Fry, 2019). Thus, metaphor and self-distancing are apparent mechanisms of action for EAGALA, and perhaps other interventions.

Another postulated mechanism of action is improvement of assertiveness, sense of control, and autonomy (Lanning & Krenek, 2013; Nevins et al., 2013). EAS interventions that include horse handling or mounted work require the participant to be a leader (Bachi et al., 2012). This can give participants a sense of control and autonomy, as well as provide an opportunity to practice appropriate assertiveness.

Psychological flexibility is defined as pursuing objectives despite feeling distress (Kashdan et al., 2020). Greater psychological flexibility is associated with decreased depression, anxiety, substance abuse, self-harm, chronic pain, prejudice, and stress (Biglan, 2009), as well as contributing to overall psychological health (Kashdan & Rottenberg, 2010) and resilience (Kashdan et al., 2006; Kashdan & Rottenberg, 2010; Meyer et al., 2019). There is limited evidence (Marchand et al., 2022b, 2023) that some EAS interventions may enhance psychological flexibility, and if so, this effect this could contribute to some of the trans-diagnostic benefits of EAS. Mindfulness is paying attention to the present moment without judgment and is closely related to psychological flexibility (Silberstein et al., 2012). It has been theorized that AAIs in general can serve as a method of mindfulness training (Beetz & Schöfmann-Crawford, 2019). Interacting with horses affords a compelling reason to focus on the present for safety and communication purposes (Fry, 2019). At least one EAS intervention designed for veterans (Marchand et al., 2023) provides mindfulness training and gives participants a real-world opportunity to practice while in the arena with an equine.

Biophilia (Wilson, 1984) is the human affinity for nature. The biophilia effect (Beetz & Schöfmann-Crawford, 2019; Julius et al., 2013) is the psychological and physiological relaxation around calm, resting animals that some humans experience (Beetz & Schöfmann-Crawford, 2019) and is thought to have developed as a mechanism to enhance survival (Julius et al., 2013; Wilson, 1984). Biophilia may play a role in EAS outcomes, but studies are lacking. Indirect evidence is that many of the trans-diagnostic benefits of EAS, including enhanced resilience (Wilson, 1984), are similar to those associated with nature exposure. Also, there is some evidence that both nature exposure not involving equines (Marchand et al., 2018, 2021b) and EAS (Marchand et al., 2022b, 2023) are associated with enhanced psychological flexibility, which could be a common underlying mechanism.

Finally, emotional mirroring and heart rate synchronization are related potential mechanisms underlying the benefits of EAS that have both psychological and physiological components. Horses are prey animals and must evade predators to survival (Jones, 2020). Therefore, horses are extremely sensitive to, and aware of, their immediate environment, including awareness of humans (Jones, 2020). This awareness includes behaviors that could indicate a potential attack, such as agitation, inconsistencies, and autonomic arousal among nearby animals, including humans (Wharton et al., 2019). Thus, equines often sense and may mirror human emotional states. This may benefit participants by providing nonjudgmental feedback about one's emotion state, behaviors, and body language. This may facilitate insight, and self-awareness, as well as offer a way to safely examine one's emotional state. Finally, there is some evidence (Baldwin et al., 2023; Drinkhouse et al., 2012; Hockenhull et al., 2015; Lanata et al., 2016) indicating that equine sensitivity to the environment may result in horse–human heart rate synchronization during some, but not all (Hockenhull et al., 2015), horse–human interactions.

There is some evidence regarding physiological mechanisms that may underlie the benefits of EAS; however, most of the evidence is indirect and comes from studies of non-equine AAIs.

Heart rate variability (HRV) is a physiological marker that may be associated with EAS. HRV is a measure of autonomic nervous system function and can be used to evaluate stress in both horses and humans (Gehrke et al., 2011; McCraty et al., 2009). HRV is a beat-to-beat variation resulting from the interaction between parasympathetic and sympathetic branches of the autonomic nervous system (Gehrke et al., 2011). Stress activates the sympathetic branch, and variation between heartbeats is decreased. In contrast, the parasympathetic branch engages to counter the stress, and the variation between heartbeats is higher (Gehrke et al., 2016); therefore, reduced stress is associated with increased HRV. Increased HRV is associated with enhancement of cognition and decreased anxiety (McCraty et al., 2006). Studies of nonveteran populations have revealed that HRV can be measured in EAS (Baldwin et al., 2018; Nqwena & Naidoo, 2016). A review by Garcia-Gomez and colleagues (Garcia-Gomez et al., 2020) found studies that reported increased HRV and enhanced parasympathetic activity to be associated with EAS participation. Additionally, one nonveteran study (Gehrke et al., 2016) demonstrated that it is feasible to measure HRV during EAS for this population, and a study (Gehrke et al., 2018a) of a veteran population demonstrated that increased HRV was associated with EAS participation. Thus, future studies evaluating HRV may make meaningful contributions to the understanding of physiological mechanisms of EAS.

Related to HRV, one physiological benefit of AAIs in general is decreased arousal. The AAI literature indicates that human–animal interactions result in decreases in physiological signs of arousal, including blood pressure, skin conductance, and heart rate (Friedmann et al., 1983; Nagengast et al., 1997; Odendaal & Meintjes, 2003; Vormbrock & Grossberg, 1988). A systematic review (Rathish et al., 2021) of canine–human interactions reported reduction of heart rate, blood pressure, and/or cholesterol levels. Studies have reported decreased human heart (Clark et al., 2020; Coakley et al., 2021; Krause-Parello et al., 2018; Wolynczyk-Gmaj et al., 2021) and respiratory rates (Coakley et al., 2021) and blood pressure (Krause-Parello et al., 2018), as well as increased heart rate variability (Clark et al., 2020). Further research is needed to determine whether EAS participation is associated with decreased arousal among veterans.

Studies using functional neuroimaging have the potential to enhance our understanding of the neural mechanisms underlying the benefits of EAS. A study (Yoo et al., 2016) of the effects of EAS on participants with attention-deficit/hyperactivity suggests that EAS participation may be associated with connectivity changes in the default mode network and the behavioral inhibition system. Another study (Zhu et al., 2021) used function and structural imaging to assess changes among veterans with PTSD who participated in an EAS intervention. Results indicated a significant increase in caudate functional connectivity as well as a reduction in the gray matter density of the thalamus and basal ganglia. These investigations suggest that functional neuroimaging may be a useful tool to investigate neural mechanisms underlying the benefits associated with EAS.

Cortisol is a glucocorticoid hormone produced by the adrenal cortex and is stimulated by activation of the stress response of the sympathetic nervous system. While intended to support the acute stress response, long-term elevation of cortisol levels is harmful (Lanning et al., 2018). The AAI literature indicates evidence of attenuated cortisol response in some (Beetz et al., 2012a; Jennings et al., 2021; Krause-Parello et al., 2019; Machova et al., 2019; Meints et al., 2022; Wijker et al., 2021) but not all studies (Branson et al., 2017; Coakley et al., 2021). In contrast, a study (Rodriguez et al., 2018) of military veterans with PTSD indicated that those individuals with service dogs had higher cortisol response. Regarding EAS, one study (Hoagwood et al., 2022) of a youth population found some evidence of decreased cortisol but no overall pre- to post-intervention changes. Finally, a study (Burton et al., 2019) of an EAS intervention for veterans found no evidence of changes in cortisol response associated with the intervention. Studies of cortisol have revealed mixed findings, but further research into possible cortisol changes associated with EAS investigations for veterans is warranted.

Oxytocin is a hypothalamic neuropeptide (Carter, 2022), which has both hormonal and neurotransmitter functions (Carter, 2022; Beetz & Schöfmann-Crawford, 2019). It has essential functions in birth and lactation; however, it is also a stress-modulating hormone (Carter, 2022; Beetz & Schöfmann-Crawford, 2019) and could underlie many of the positive benefits of AAI (Beetz & Schöfmann-Crawford, 2019). Oxytocin is released because of touch, including breastfeeding (Beetz & Schöfmann-Crawford, 2019). Activation of the oxytocin system likely occurs during AAI interactions that involve touch and may result in enhanced trust, communication, social interaction, and calmness, as well as a reduction of stress, anxiety, and pain (Beetz et al., 2012b; Carter, 2022; Beetz & Schöfmann-Crawford, 2019). Studies of the possible role of oxytocin in the benefits of EAS for veterans are warranted.

Needs of the Veteran Population

The literature (Arnon et al., 2020; Lanning et al., 2018; Burton et al., 2019; Duncan et al., 2014; Ferruolo, 2016; Fisher et al., 2021; Gehrke et al., 2018a, b; Hoopes et al., 2022; Johnson et al., 2018; Lanning & Krenek, 2013; Lanning et al., 2017; Malinowski et al., 2018; Marchand et al., 2022a, b, 2023; Meyer & Sartori, 2019; Monroe et al., 2019; Romaniuk et al., 2018; Rosing et al., 2022; Shelef et al., 2019; Steele et al., 2018; Sylvia et al., 2020; Wharton et al., 2019; Zhu et al., 2021) regarding the use of EAS for veterans is exclusively focused on potential mental health benefits for trauma survivors; thus, the primary focus of this chapter is on the utilization of EAS to enhance mental health outcomes. Future studies should explore whether EAS might be beneficial for commonly occurring medical conditions, such as traumatic amputations, traumatic brain injury and other neurological injuries, hearing impairment, and musculoskeletal injuries.

Among active duty military personnel and veterans, rates of PTSD approach 30% (Hoge et al., 2004; Suris & Lind, 2008), and this condition is associated with impairment in social, occupational, and physical functioning as well as reduced quality of life and physical health problems (American Psychiatric Association, 2022). Functional impairment is exhibited across social, interpersonal, and occupational areas and often negatively impacts relationships, and work, as well as educational and occupational success. Those with PTSD often suffer from mental disorders and have a higher risk of suicide (American Psychiatric Association, 2022). Up to 80% of veterans with PTSD may have complex PTSD (Letica-Crepulja et al., 2020), which increases the risk of suicide and psychiatric comorbidities (Wisco et al., 2014, 2016).

The core feature of PTSD in an amplified fear response (Neria, 2021), and research indicates that this is due to anomalies of fear learning and extinction (Neria, 2021). A meta-analysis (Suarez-Jimenez et al., 2020) of functional magnetic resonance imaging studies suggests neural underpinning of increased fear circuit activation during all stages of fear learning and extinction. Other neuroimaging studies indicate that PTSD is also linked to aberrations of the default mode, salience, and executive control networks (Koch et al., 2016; Sripada et al., 2012).

In addition to PTSD, there are several other trauma sequelae that may result in unique needs for veterans. The first is that rates of military sexual trauma (MST) can be as high as 15% among female veterans (Kimerling et al., 2010) and can result in complicated aftereffects, which can include, but are not limited to, PTSD (Steenkamp et al., 2015). Additionally, veterans may experience psychological effects of experiencing the transgressive acts of combat. Trauma-related guilt and associated beliefs about the trauma (Wharton et al., 2019) are one such impact, and there is evidence of a link between beliefs about traumatic and the ability to recover (Kubany, 1994; Kubany et al., 1995). Guilt can be associated with cognitive distortions and disengagement, which may be associated with depression, and aggressive behaviors (Marx et al., 2010). Moral injury is a related concept, which is defined as feeling anguish related to experiences that have violated one's moral beliefs or causes one to doubt the morality of the world (Litz et al., 2009). Moral injury is associated with increased risk of both substance use (Currier et al., 2014) and suicide (Frankfurt & Frazier, 2016; Litz et al., 2009). Finally, disruptions of attachment may be associated with trauma (Meyer & Sartori, 2019).

In summary, veterans who have experienced trauma have needs not only for effective treatments for PTSD but also for interventions that address MST, guilt, moral injury, and disruptions of attachment.

Challenges Associated with Conventional Interventions

Both psychotherapeutic and pharmacological interventions are available for PTSD. Evidence-based psychotherapies for PTSD fall into two broad categories: past- and present-focused evidence-based treatments (Najavits, 2007). Past-focused models, such as cognitive processing therapy (CPT), prolonged exposure (PE), eye movement desensitization and reprocessing (EMDR), and narrative exposure therapy, promote processing of distressing emotions, painful memories, and beliefs about the trauma. Present-focused models emphasize psychoeducation and coping skills training to improve functioning. Examples include cognitive therapy for PTSD, seeking safety, and stress inoculation. Research indicates that these interventions are effective with effect sizes in the moderate to high range (Najavits, 2007). Regarding pharmacotherapy, two antidepressants are approved for PTSD treatment by the US Food and Drug Administration (Stein & Rothbaum, 2018).

Although effective conventional treatments are available for PTSD, several challenges exist. For example, one-third to one-half of veterans receiving exposure-based treatments demonstrate no significant improvement (Steenkamp et al., 2015). Another important issue is utilization. One investigation found that among post-9/11 veterans, only 40% or less of those who benefited from mental health treatment had sought care (Hoge et al., 2004). Further, several studies have reported high attrition rates for both PE and CPT (Kimerling et al., 2010; Watts et al., 2014). For example, a study (Watts et al., 2014) of CPT and PE reported that the median number of sessions attended was 5, which was not an adequate dose. Another study (Maguen et al., 2019) reported that among veterans who had PTSD, only 23% initiated an evidence-based psychotherapy, and of those, only 9% completed treatment. Several factors have been proposed to underlie treatment resistance among this population. These include fear of confronting trauma experiences, stigma, concerns about confidentiality, the number of sessions required, compromised relationships with therapists, and fear of being seen as weak (Fragedakis & Toriello, 2014; Hoge et al., 2014; Hoyt & Candy, 2011).

Regarding pharmacology for PTSD, some patients experience bothersome side effects, do not improve with treatment, and/or discontinue the medication (Puetz et al., 2015). For example, one investigation (Duek et al., 2020) reported that 35% discontinued treatment within 30 days and 72% discontinued within 180 days.

In addition to the above, existing conventional interventions for PTSD may either not be effective at all or only partially effective for other reasons. First, conventional interventions may not address hallmark features and complex aftereffects of MST, which go beyond PTSD (Steenkamp et al., 2015). Further, they may not address disrupted attachment, moral injury, and guilt. Thus, there is a need for interventions that may enhance treatment engagement and/or outcomes to conventional interventions (Imel et al., 2013; Najavits, 2015). Further, there is a need to develop and evaluate novel interventions that might be equally or more effective than existing treatments.

In response to the aforementioned challenges, AAIs are being increasingly used as complementary interventions for trauma survivors in general (Chandler, 2012; Beetz et al., 2019; McCardle et al., 2011) and specifically among veterans (Arnon et al., 2020; Lanning et al., 2018; Burton et al., 2019; Duncan et al., 2014; Ferruolo, 2016; Fisher et al., 2021; Hoopes et al., 2022; Johnson et al., 2018; Lanning et al., 2017; Malinowski et al., 2018; Marchand et al., 2022a, b, 2023; Meyer & Sartori, 2019; Monroe et al., 2019; Romaniuk et al., 2018; Shelef et al., 2019; Steele et al.,

2018; Sylvia et al., 2020; Wharton et al., 2019; Zhu et al., 2021). Among the AAIs, EAS interventions may have the potential to be particularly beneficial for veterans with trauma histories.

Potential Benefits of EAS for Veterans

It is likely that different EAS interventions may result in different outcomes. Further, outcomes may vary between veterans based upon individual diagnostic and demographic characteristics. Nonetheless, it is useful to consider potential benefits that may exist for some veterans and are associated with some EAS interventions.

EAS interventions could benefit veterans by facilitating engagement in conventional psychotherapy and/or psychopharmacological interventions. Also, this population with trauma might be more likely to engage in EAS than conventional treatments. If the latter is true, then it will be essential to conduct rigorous investigations to establish whether EAS interventions have benefits comparable to conventional treatments. The literature regarding this issue is currently limited. However, the non-EAS AAI literature suggests that these interventions augment rapport-building between the client and the therapist (Beetz, 2017; O'Haire et al., 2019) and facilitate the formation of a therapeutic alliance (Beetz & Schöfmann-Crawford, 2019). This could be especially important for veteran trauma survivors who may have trouble trusting others and maintaining relationships (Beetz & Schöfmann-Crawford, 2019; Fry, 2019). Further, AAIs may activate implicit motives and thus promote intrinsic motivation (Beetz & Schöfmann-Crawford, 2019). Intrinsic motivation promotes enjoyment and satisfaction of tasks and may be beneficial for veterans with trauma-related low motivation (Beetz & Schöfmann-Crawford, 2019). As mentioned above, AAIs may induce activation of the oxytocin system, which could potentially facilitate the development of trust toward the therapist, as well as contribute to improved motivation (Beetz & Schöfmann-Crawford, 2019).

Veteran-specific studies provide some evidence that supports treatment engagement. Two studies have reported that participants find EAS interventions to be enjoyable (Marchand et al., 2022b, 2023). Also, a study (Marchand et al., 2023) reported that among participants in a six-session intervention, 58% completed four or more sessions and 24.2% completed all sessions. Another study (Marchand et al., 2022b) of a four-session intervention reported that the mean number of sessions attended was three and that 52% of participants completed all sessions. For comparison, one study of conventional psychotherapy (Mott et al., 2014) reported that only 12% for individual and 34% for group psychotherapy received an adequate dose. Another investigation (Farmer et al., 2020) revealed that among women veterans with PTSD, only 42% received a minimal therapeutic dose. Thus, limited evidence suggests that EAS interventions are comparable favorably with conventional psychotherapy in terms of treatment engagement.

Both the general AAI literature and veteran EAS studies suggest that these interventions are associated with symptom reduction for some psychiatric disorders.

This literature was reviewed above. In addition, there is evidence that AAIs in general and EAS result in trans-diagnostic benefits for some participants.

Evidence in the AAI literature suggests that animals can facilitate decreases in physiological indicators of arousal, such as skin conductance, blood pressure, and heart rate in humans (Friedmann et al., 1983; Nagengast et al., 1997; Odendaal & Meintjes, 2003; Vormbrock & Grossberg, 1988), and have been particularly well studied in this area. For example, a systematic review of canine–human interactions (Rathish et al., 2021) reported reduction of heart rate, blood pressure, and/or cholesterol levels in some studies. Other studies have reported decreased respiratory (Coakley et al., 2021) and heart rates (Clark et al., 2020; Coakley et al., 2021; Krause-Parello et al., 2018; Wolynczyk-Gmaj et al., 2021), as well as lowered blood pressure (Krause-Parello et al., 2018) and increased heart rate variability (Clark et al., 2020). Nonveteran studies have also reported improvements in cognition, quality of life, and well-being (Bachi et al., 2012; Bunketorp-Kall et al., 2017; Cerulli et al., 2014; Fields et al., 2018). Studies of veterans have reported decreased blood pressure (Malinowski et al., 2018), improved functioning (Lanning et al., 2017; Shelef et al., 2019), decreased disability (Lanning et al., 2018), and increased resilience (Burton et al., 2019).

Strategies to Move the Field of EAS for Veterans Forward

The field of EAS for veterans requires rigorous randomized controlled trials of EAS interventions to move the field forward. To proceed beyond the early stages of scientific development, interventions need to be studied that are developed to be manualized to facilitate both replication studies and ultimate dissemination to the field, if shown to be effective. These need to include both psychological and physiological outcome measures and progress to multisite studies. Once convincing evidence of benefits has been established for specific interventions, then mechanisms of action studies can begin to parse which components contribute to benefits for which participants. Several studies (Arnon et al., 2020; Lanning et al., 2018; Marchand et al., 2022b, 2023; Wharton et al., 2019; Zhu et al., 2021) have reported interventions that are manualized or structured to facilitate manual development. Researchers might consider prioritizing investigations of such interventions.

Additional research strategies that may prove valuable include evaluating benefits of mounted versus groundwork and evaluating benefits of psychotherapy incorporating horses versus other EAS interventions.

Conclusions

Currently, the field of EAS interventions for veterans is in the early stages of scientific development. There is a growing literature of pilot studies that indicate promise. Also, AAI studies of non-EAS and nonveteran interventions inform the field.

The path to move the field forward requires rigorous randomized controlled trials of EAS interventions that are developed to be manualized and replicated and which include both psychological and physiological outcome measures. Once convincing evidence of benefits has been established for specific interventions, then mechanisms of action studies can begin to parse which components contribute to benefits for which participants. Additionally, it will be necessary to begin to disambiguate dose–response relationships, as well as the impact of mounted versus unmounted activities, and compare interventions that include only horsemanship skills versus PIH interventions.

References

Alfonso, S. V., Alfonso, L. A., Llabre, M. M., & Fernandez, M. I. (2015). Project stride: An equine-assisted intervention to reduce symptoms of social anxiety in young women. *Explore (New York, N.Y.), 11*(6), 461–467. https://doi.org/10.1016/j.explore.2015.08.003

American Hippotherapy Association. Retrieved from https://americanhippotherapyassociation.org

American Psychiatric Association. (2022). *Diagnostic and statistical manual of mental disorders, text revision*. American Psychiatric Association Publishing.

Anderson, S., & Meints, K. (2016). Brief report: The effects of equine-assisted activities on the social functioning in children and adolescents with autism spectrum disorder. *Journal of Autism and Developmental Disorders, 46*(10), 3344–3352. https://doi.org/10.1007/s10803-016-2869-3

Arnon, S., Fisher, P. W., Pickover, A., Lowell, A., Turner, J. B., Hilburn, A., et al. (2020). Equine-assisted therapy for veterans with PTSD: Manual development and preliminary findings. *Military Medicine, 185*(5–6), e557–e564. https://doi.org/10.1093/milmed/usz444

Bachi, K. (2013). Application of attachment theory to equine-facilitated psychotherapy. *Journal of Contemporary Psychotherapy, 43*(3), 187–196.

Bachi, K., Terkel, J., & Teichman, M. (2012). Equine-facilitated psychotherapy for at-risk adolescents: The influence on self-image, self-control and trust. *Clinical Child Psychology and Psychiatry, 17*(2), 298–312. https://doi.org/10.1177/1359104511404177

Baldwin, A. L., Rector, B. K., & Alden, A. C. (2018). Effects of a form of equine-facilitated learning on heart rate variability, immune function, and self-esteem in older adults. *People and Animals: The International Journal of Research and Practice, 1*(1), 5. Retrieved from https://docs.lib.purdue.edu/paij/vol1/iss1/5

Baldwin, A. L., Walters, L., Rector, B. K., & Alden, A. C. (2023). Effects of equine interaction on mutual autonomic nervous system responses and interoception in a learning program for older adults. *People and Animals: The International Journal of Research and Practice, 6*(1), 3. Retrieved from https://docs.lib.purdue.edu/paij/vol6/iss1/3

Beetz, A. (2017). Theories and possible processes of action in animal assisted interventions. *Applied Developmental Science, 21*(2), 139–149.

Beetz, A., & Schöfmann-Crawford, I. (2019). Clinical objectives for animal-assisted interventions: Physiological and psychological targets in trauma-informed practice. In P. Tedeschi &

M. A. Jenkins (Eds.), *Transforming trauma: Resilience and healing through our connections with animals*. Purdue University Press.
Beetz, A., Julius, H., Turner, D., & Kotrschal, K. (2012a). Effects of social support by a dog on stress modulation in male children with insecure attachment. *Frontiers in Psychology, 3*, 352. https://doi.org/10.3389/fpsyg.2012.00352
Beetz, A., Uvnas-Moberg, K., Julius, H., & Kotrschal, K. (2012b). Psychosocial and psychophysiological effects of human-animal interactions: The possible role of oxytocin. *Frontiers in Psychology, 3*, 234. https://doi.org/10.3389/fpsyg.2012.00234
Beetz, A., Schofmann, I., Girgensohn, R., Braas, R., & Ernst, C. (2019). Positive effects of a short-term dog-assisted intervention for soldiers with post-traumatic stress disorder—A pilot study. *Frontiers in Veterinary Science, 6*, 170. https://doi.org/10.3389/fvets.2019.00170
Biglan, A. (2009). Increasing psychological flexibility to influence cultural evolution. *Behavior and Social Issues, 18*, 15–24.
Borgi, M., Loliva, D., Cerino, S., Chiarotti, F., Venerosi, A., Bramini, M., et al. (2016). Effectiveness of a standardized equine-assisted therapy program for children with autism spectrum disorder. *Journal of Autism and Developmental Disorders, 46*(1), 1–9. https://doi.org/10.1007/s10803-015-2530-6
Branson, S. M., Boss, L., Padhye, N. S., Trotscher, T., & Ward, A. (2017). Effects of animal-assisted activities on biobehavioral stress responses in hospitalized children: A randomized controlled study. *Journal of Pediatric Nursing, 36*, 84–91. https://doi.org/10.1016/j.pedn.2017.05.006
Buck, P. W., Bean, N., & De Marco, K. (2017). Equine-assisted psychotherapy: An emerging trauma-informed intervention. *Advances in Social Work, 18*(1), 387–402.
Bunketorp-Kall, L., Lundgren-Nilsson, A., Samuelsson, H., Pekny, T., Blomve, K., Pekna, M., et al. (2017). Long-term improvements after multimodal rehabilitation in late phase after stroke: A randomized controlled trial. *Stroke, 48*(7), 1916–1924. https://doi.org/10.1161/STROKEAHA.116.016433
Burton, L. E., Qeadan, F., & Burge, M. R. (2019). Efficacy of equine-assisted psychotherapy in veterans with posttraumatic stress disorder. *Journal of Integrative Medicine, 17*(1), 14–19. https://doi.org/10.1016/j.joim.2018.11.001
Carter, C. S. (2022). Oxytocin and love: Myths, metaphors and mysteries. *Comprehensive Psychoneuroendocrinology, 9*, 100107. https://doi.org/10.1016/j.cpnec.2021.100107
Cerino, S., Cirulli, F., Chiarotti, F., & Seripa, S. (2011). Non conventional psychiatric rehabilitation in schizophrenia using therapeutic riding: The FISE multicentre Pindar project. *Annali dell'Istituto Superiore di Sanità, 47*(4), 409–414. https://doi.org/10.4415/ANN_11_04_13
Cerulli, C., Minganti, C., De Santis, C., Tranchita, E., Quaranta, F., & Parisi, A. (2014). Therapeutic horseback riding in breast cancer survivors: A pilot study. *Journal of Alternative and Complementary Medicine, 20*(8), 623–629. https://doi.org/10.1089/acm.2014.0061
Chandler, C. K. (2005). *Animal assisted therapy in counseling*. Routledge.
Chandler, C. K. (Ed.). (2012). *Animal assisted therapy in counseling*. Routledge.
Clark, S., Martin, F., McGowan, R. T. S., Smidt, J., Anderson, R., Wang, L., et al. (2020). The impact of a 20-minute animal-assisted activity session on the physiological and emotional states in patients with fibromyalgia. *Mayo Clinic Proceedings, 95*(11), 2442–2461. https://doi.org/10.1016/j.mayocp.2020.04.037
Coakley, A. B., Annese, C. D., Empoliti, J. H., & Flanagan, J. M. (2021). The experience of animal assisted therapy on patients in an acute care setting. *Clinical Nursing Research, 30*(4), 401–405. https://doi.org/10.1177/1054773820977198
Coetzee, N., Boyce, S., & Masenge, A. (2022). The role of the Eagala model in promoting psychological wellbeing in adolescents: A mixed-methods approach. *Society & Animals, 32*(2), 133–155. https://doi.org/10.1163/15685306-bja10092
Corring, D., Lundberg, E., & Rudnick, A. (2013). Therapeutic horseback riding for ACT patients with schizophrenia. *Community Mental Health Journal, 49*(1), 121–126. https://doi.org/10.1007/s10597-011-9457-y

Currier, J. M., Holland, J. M., Jones, H. W., & Sheu, S. (2014). Involvement in abusive violence among Vietnam veterans: Direct and indirect associations with substance use problems and suicidality. *Psychological Trauma: Theory, Research, Practice, and Policy, 6*(1), 73–82. https://doi.org/10.1016/0022-3956(75)90026-6

Cuypers, K., De Ridder, K., & Strandheim, A. (2011). The effect of therapeutic horseback riding on 5 children with attention deficit hyperactivity disorder: A pilot study. *Journal of Alternative and Complementary Medicine, 17*(10), 901–908. https://doi.org/10.1089/acm.2010.0547

Drinkhouse, M., Birmingham, S. S., Fillman, R., & Jedlicka, H. (2012). Correlation of human and horse heart rates during equine-assisted therapy sessions with at-risk youths: A pilot study. *Journal of Student Research, 1*(3), 22–25. https://doi.org/10.47611/jsr.v1i3.10

Duek, O., Pietrzak, R. H., Petrakis, I., Hoff, R., & Harpaz-Rotem, I. (2020). Early discontinuation of pharmacotherapy in U.S. veterans diagnosed with PTSD and the role of psychotherapy. *Journal of Psychiatric Research, 132*, 167–173. https://doi.org/10.1016/j.jpsychires.2020.10.005

Duncan, C. R., Critchley, S., & Marland, J. (2014). Can praxis: A model of equine assisted learning (EAL) for PTSD. *Canadian Military Journal, 14*(2), 64–69.

Earles, J. L., Vernon, L. L., & Yetz, J. P. (2015). Equine-assisted therapy for anxiety and posttraumatic stress symptoms. *Journal of Traumatic Stress, 28*(2), 149–152. https://doi.org/10.1002/jts.21990

Farmer, C. C., Rossi, F. S., Michael, E. M., & Kimerling, R. (2020). Psychotherapy utilization, preferences, and retention among women veterans with post-traumatic stress disorder. *Womens Health Issues, 30*(5), 366–373. https://doi.org/10.1016/j.whi.2020.06.003

Ferruolo, D. M. (2016). Psychosocial equine program for veterans. *Social Work, 61*(1), 53–60. https://doi.org/10.1093/sw/swv054

Fields, B., Bruemmer, J., Gloeckner, G., & Wood, W. (2018). Influence of an equine-assisted activities program on dementia-specific quality of life. *American Journal of Alzheimer's Disease and Other Dementias, 33*(5), 309–317. https://doi.org/10.1177/1533317518772052

Fisher, P. W., Lazarov, A., Lowell, A., Arnon, S., Turner, J. B., Bergman, M., et al. (2021). Equine-assisted therapy for posttraumatic stress disorder among military veterans: An open trial. *The Journal of Clinical Psychiatry, 82*(5), 21m14005. https://doi.org/10.4088/JCP.21m14005

Fournier, A. K., Letson, E. A., Berry, T. D., & Pasiuk, E. L. (2018). Human-animal interaction and metaphor in equine-assisted psychotherapy: Empirical support for the EAGALA model. *Human-Animal Interaction Bulletin, 6*(1), 47–63. https://doi.org/10.1079/hai.2018.0005

Fragedakis, T. M., & Toriello, P. (2014). The development and experience of combat-related PTSD: A demand for neurofeedback as an effective form of treatment. *Journal of Counseling & Development, 92*(4), 481–488. https://doi.org/10.1002/j.1556-6676.2014.00174.x

Frankfurt, S., & Frazier, P. (2016). A review of research on moral injury in combat veterans. *Military Psychology, 28*(5), 318–330. https://doi.org/10.1037/mil0000132

Frederick, K. E., Ivey Hatz, J., & Lanning, B. (2015). Not just horsing around: The impact of equine-assisted learning on levels of hope and depression in at-risk adolescents. *Community Mental Health Journal, 51*(7), 809–817. https://doi.org/10.1007/s10597-015-9836-x

Friedmann, E., Katcher, A. H., Thomas, S. A., Lynch, J. J., & Messent, P. R. (1983). Social interaction and blood pressure. Influence of animal companions. *The Journal of Nervous and Mental Disease, 171*(8), 461–465. https://doi.org/10.1097/00005053-198308000-00002

Fry, N. E. (2019). Horses in the treatment of trauma. In P. Tedeschi & M. A. Jenkins (Eds.), *Transforming trauma: Resilience and healing through our connections with animals*. Purdue University Press.

Gabriels, R. L., Pan, Z., Dechant, B., Agnew, J. A., Brim, N., & Mesibov, G. (2015). Randomized controlled trial of therapeutic horseback riding in children and adolescents with autism spectrum disorder. *Journal of the American Academy of Child and Adolescent Psychiatry, 54*(7), 541–549. https://doi.org/10.1016/j.jaac.2015.04.007

Garcia-Gomez, A., Guerrero-Barona, E., Garcia-Pena, I., Rodriguez-Jimenez, M., & Moreno-Manso, J. M. (2020). Equine-assisted therapeutic activities and their influence on the heart rate variability: A systematic review. *Complementary Therapies in Clinical Practice, 39*, 101167. https://doi.org/10.1016/j.ctcp.2020.101167

Gehrke, E. K., Baldwin, A., & Schiltz, P. M. (2011). Heart rate variability in horses engaged in equine-assisted activities. *Journal of Equine Veterinary Science, 31*(2), 78–84.

Gehrke, E. K., Myers, M. P., Evans, S., & Garman, K. (2016). Pilot study on impact on balance of autonomic nervous system during equine-assisted coaching: Simultaneous heart rate variability in horses, coach, and client. *International Journal of Human Caring, 20*(1), 12–14.

Gehrke, E. K., Noquez, A. E., Ranke, P. L., & Myers, M. P. (2018a). Measuring the psychophysiological changes in combat Veterans participating in an equine therapy program. *Journal of Military, Veteran and Family Health, 4*(1), 60–69.

Gehrke, E. K., Tontz, P., Bhawal, R., Schiltz, P., Mendez, S., & Myers, M. P. (2018b). A mixed-method analysis of an equine complementary therapy program to heal combat veterans. *Journal of Complementary and Alternative Healthcare, 8*(3), 555739. https://doi.org/10.19080/JCMAH.2018.08.555739

Hallberg, L. (2018). *The clinical practice of equine-assisted therapy: Including horses in human healthcare*. Routledge.

Harris, A., & Williams, J. M. (2017). The impact of a horse riding intervention on the social functioning of children with autism spectrum disorder. *International Journal of Environmental Research and Public Health, 14*(7), 776. https://doi.org/10.3390/ijerph14070776

Harvey, C., Jedlicka, H., & Martinez, S. (2020). A program evaluation: Equine-assisted psychotherapy outcomes for children and adolescents. *Child & Adolescent Social Work Journal, 37*(6), 665–675. https://doi.org/10.1007/s10560-020-00705-0

Hession, C. E., Eastwood, B., Watterson, D., Lehane, C. M., Oxley, N., & Murphy, B. A. (2014). Therapeutic horse riding improves cognition, mood arousal, and ambulation in children with dyspraxia. *Journal of Alternative and Complementary Medicine, 20*(1), 19–23. https://doi.org/10.1089/acm.2013.0207

Hoagwood, K. E., Acri, M., Morrissey, M., & Peth-Pierce, R. (2017). Animal-assisted therapies for youth with or at risk for mental health problems: A systematic review. *Applied Developmental Science, 21*(1), 1–13. https://doi.org/10.1080/10888691.2015.1134267

Hoagwood, K., Vincent, A., Acri, M., Morrissey, M., Seibel, L., Guo, F., et al. (2022). Reducing anxiety and stress among youth in a CBT-based equine-assisted adaptive riding program. *Animals (Basel), 12*(19), 2491. https://doi.org/10.3390/ani12192491

Hockenhull, J., Young, T. J., Redgate, S. E., & Birke, L. (2015). Exploring synchronicity in the heart rates of familiar and unfamiliar pairs of horses and humans undertaking an in-hand task. *Anthrozoös, 28*(3), 501–511. https://doi.org/10.1080/08927936.2015.1052284

Hoge, C. W., Castro, C. A., Messer, S. C., McGurk, D., Cotting, D. I., & Koffman, R. L. (2004). Combat duty in Iraq and Afghanistan, mental health problems, and barriers to care. *The New England Journal of Medicine, 351*(1), 13–22. https://doi.org/10.1056/NEJMoa040603

Hoge, C. W., Grossman, S. H., Auchterlonie, J. L., Riviere, L. A., Milliken, C. S., & Wilk, J. E. (2014). PTSD treatment for soldiers after combat deployment: Low utilization of mental health care and reasons for dropout. *Psychiatric Services, 65*(8), 997–1004. https://doi.org/10.1176/appi.ps.201300307

Holm, M. B., Baird, J. M., Kim, Y. J., Rajora, K. B., D'Silva, D., Podolinsky, L., et al. (2014). Therapeutic horseback riding outcomes of parent-identified goals for children with autism spectrum disorder: An ABA' multiple case design examining dosing and generalization to the home and community. *Journal of Autism and Developmental Disorders, 44*(4), 937–947. https://doi.org/10.1007/s10803-013-1949-x

Hoopes, K. H., Osborne, M., Marchand, W. R., Joubert, K., Nazarenko, E., Black, H., et al. (2022). A pilot observational study of recreational trail riding for Veterans with addictive disorders. *Complementary Therapies in Medicine, 65*, 102813. https://doi.org/10.1016/j.ctim.2022.102813

House Armed Services Committee. (2015). *Equine therapy to treat members of the Armed Forces*. Retrieved from https://www.congress.gov/congressional-report/114th-congress/house-report/102/1
Hoyt, T., & Candy, C. (2011). Providing treatment services for PTSD at an army FORSCOM installation. *Military Psychology, 23*(3), 237–252. https://doi.org/10.1080/08995605.2011.570564
Hyun, G. J., Jung, T. W., Park, J. H., Kang, K. D., Kim, S. M., Son, Y. D., et al. (2016). Changes in gait balance and brain connectivity in response to equine-assisted activity and training in children with attention deficit hyperactivity disorder. *Journal of Alternative and Complementary Medicine, 22*(4), 286–293. https://doi.org/10.1089/acm.2015.0299
Imel, Z. E., Laska, K., Jakupcak, M., & Simpson, T. L. (2013). Meta-analysis of dropout in treatments for posttraumatic stress disorder. *Journal of Consulting and Clinical Psychology, 81*(3), 394–404. https://doi.org/10.1037/a0031474
Jang, B., Song, J., Kim, J., Kim, S., Lee, J., Shin, H. Y., et al. (2015). Equine-assisted activities and therapy for treating children with attention-deficit/hyperactivity disorder. *Journal of Alternative and Complementary Medicine, 21*(9), 546–553. https://doi.org/10.1089/acm.2015.0067
Jennings, M. L., Granger, D. A., Bryce, C. I., Twitchell, D., Yeakel, K., & Teaford, P. A. (2021). Effect of animal assisted interactions on activity and stress response in children in acute care settings. *Comprehensive Psychoneuroendocrinology, 8*, 100076. https://doi.org/10.1016/j.cpnec.2021.100076
Johnson, R. A., Albright, D. L., Marzolf, J. R., Bibbo, J. L., Yaglom, H. D., Crowder, S. M., et al. (2018). Effects of therapeutic horseback riding on post-traumatic stress disorder in military veterans. *Military Medical Research, 5*(1), 3. https://doi.org/10.1186/s40779-018-0149-6
Jones, J. L. (2020). *Horse brain, human brain: The neuroscience of horsemanship*. Trafalgar Square Books.
Jormfeldt, H., & Carlsson, I. M. (2018). Equine-assisted therapeutic interventions among individuals diagnosed with schizophrenia. A systematic review. *Issues in Mental Health Nursing, 39*(8), 647–656. https://doi.org/10.1080/01612840.2018.1440450
Julius, H., Beetz, A., Kotrschal, K., Turner, D., & Uvnäs-Moberg, K. (2013). *Attachment to pets—An integrative view of human-animal relationships with implications for therapeutic practice*. Hogrefe.
Kang, K. D., Jung, T. W., Park, I. H., & Han, D. H. (2018). Effects of equine-assisted activities and therapies on the affective network of adolescents with internet gaming disorder. *Journal of Alternative and Complementary Medicine, 24*(8), 841–849. https://doi.org/10.1089/acm.2017.0416
Kashdan, T. B., & Rottenberg, J. (2010). Psychological flexibility as a fundamental aspect of health. *Clinical Psychology Review, 30*(7), 865–878. https://doi.org/10.1016/j.cpr.2010.03.001
Kashdan, T. B., Barrios, V., Forsyth, J. P., & Steger, M. F. (2006). Experiential avoidance as a generalized psychological vulnerability: Comparisons with coping and emotion regulation strategies. *Behaviour Research and Therapy, 44*(9), 1301–1320. https://doi.org/10.1016/j.brat.2005.10.003
Kashdan, T. B., Disabato, D. J., Goodman, F. R., Doorley, J. D., & McKnight, P. E. (2020). Understanding psychological flexibility: A multimethod exploration of pursuing valued goals despite the presence of distress. *Psychological Assessment, 32*(9), 829–850. https://doi.org/10.1037/pas0000834
Kemp, K., Signal, T., Botros, H., Taylor, N., & Prentice, K. (2014). Equine facilitated therapy with children and adolescents who have been sexually abused: A program evaluation study. *Journal of Child and Family Studies, 23*(3), 558–566. https://doi.org/10.1007/s10826-013-9718-1
Kern, J. K., Fletcher, C. L., Garver, C. R., Mehta, J. A., Grannemann, B. D., Knox, K. R., et al. (2011). Prospective trial of equine-assisted activities in autism spectrum disorder. *Alternative Therapies in Health and Medicine, 17*(3), 14–20. Retrieved from https://www.ncbi.nlm.nih.gov/pubmed/22164808
Kimerling, R., Street, A. E., Pavao, J., Smith, M. W., Cronkite, R. C., Holmes, T. H., & Frayne, S. M. (2010). Military-related sexual trauma among Veterans Health Administration patients

returning from Afghanistan and Iraq. *American Journal of Public Health, 100*(8), 1409–1412. https://doi.org/10.2105/AJPH.2009.171793

Kinney, A. R., Eakman, A. M., Lassell, R., & Wood, W. (2019). Equine-assisted interventions for veterans with service-related health conditions: A systematic mapping review. *Military Medical Research, 6*(1), 28. https://doi.org/10.1186/s40779-019-0217-6

Koch, S. B., van Zuiden, M., Nawijn, L., Frijling, J. L., Veltman, D. J., & Olff, M. (2016). Aberrant resting-state brain activity in posttraumatic stress disorder: A meta-analysis and systematic review. *Depression and Anxiety, 33*(7), 592–605. https://doi.org/10.1002/da.22478

Krause-Parello, C. A., Thames, M., Ray, C. M., & Kolassa, J. (2018). Examining the effects of a service-trained facility dog on stress in children undergoing forensic interview for allegations of child sexual abuse. *Journal of Child Sexual Abuse, 27*(3), 305–320. https://doi.org/10.1080/10538712.2018.1443303

Krause-Parello, C. A., Friedmann, E., Wilson, C., Hatzfeld, J. J., Kolassa, J., Hackney, A., & Morales, K. A. (2019). Relation of post-traumatic stress disorder symptom severity to the efficacy of an animal-assisted intervention for stress reduction after military aeromedical evacuation. *Stress and Health, 35*(4), 480–490. https://doi.org/10.1002/smi.2881

Kubany, E. S. (1994). A cognitive model of guilt typology in combat-related PTSD. *Journal of Traumatic Stress, 7*(1), 3–19. https://doi.org/10.1007/BF02111908

Kubany, E. S., Abueg, F. R., Owens, J. A., Brennan, J. M., Kaplan, A. S., & Watson, S. B. (1995). Initial examination of a multidimensional model of trauma-related guilt: Applications to combat veterans and battered women. *Journal of Psychopathology and Behavioral Assessment, 17*(4), 353–376. https://doi.org/10.1007/BF02229056

Lanata, A., Guidi, A., Valenza, G., Baragli, P., & Scilingo, E. P. (2016). *Quantitative heartbeat coupling measures in human-horse interaction.* Paper presented at the 8th Annual International Conference of the IEEE Engineering in Medicine and Biology Society (EMBC), Orlando, FL, USA.

Lanning, B. A., & Krenek, N. (2013). Guest Editorial: Examining effects of equine-assisted activities to help combat veterans improve quality of life. *Journal of Rehabilitation Research and Development, 50*(8), vii–xiii. https://doi.org/10.1682/JRRD.2013.07.0159

Lanning, B. A., Wilson, A. L., Krenek, N., & Beaujean, A. A. (2017). Using therapeutic riding as an intervention for combat veterans: An international classification of functioning, disability, and health (ICF) approach. *Occupational Therapy in Mental Health, 33*(3), 259–278.

Lanning, B. A., Wilson, A. L., Robert Woelk, A., & Beaujean, A. (2018). Therapeutic horseback riding as a complementary intervention for military service members with PTSD. *Human-Animal Interaction Bulletin, 6*(2), 58–82.

Letica-Crepulja, M., Stevanovic, A., Protuder, M., Grahovac Juretic, T., Rebic, J., & Franciskovic, T. (2020). Complex PTSD among treatment-seeking veterans with PTSD. *European Journal of Psychotraumatology, 11*(1), 1716593. https://doi.org/10.1080/20008198.2020.1716593

Litz, B. T., Stein, N., Delaney, E., Lebowitz, L., Nash, W. P., Silva, C., & Maguen, S. (2009). Moral injury and moral repair in war veterans: A preliminary model and intervention strategy. *Clinical Psychology Review, 29*(8), 695–706. https://doi.org/10.1016/j.cpr.2009.07.003

Machova, K., Souckova, M., Prochazkova, R., Vanickova, Z., & Mezian, K. (2019). Canine-assisted therapy improves well-being in nurses. *International Journal of Environmental Research and Public Health, 16*(19), 3670. https://doi.org/10.3390/ijerph16193670

Maguen, S., Li, Y., Madden, E., Seal, K. H., Neylan, T. C., Patterson, O. V., et al. (2019). Factors associated with completing evidence-based psychotherapy for PTSD among veterans in a national healthcare system. *Psychiatry Research, 274*, 112–128. https://doi.org/10.1016/j.psychres.2019.02.027

Malcolm, R., Ecks, S., & Pickersgill, M. (2018). "It just opens up their world": Autism, empathy, and the therapeutic effects of equine interactions. *Anthropology & Medicine, 25*(2), 220–234. https://doi.org/10.1080/13648470.2017.1291115

Malinowski, K., Yee, C., Tevlin, J. M., Birks, E. K., Durando, M. M., Pournajafi-Nazarloo, H., et al. (2018). The effects of equine assisted therapy on plasma cortisol and oxytocin concentrations and heart rate variability in horses and measures of symptoms of post-traumatic stress disorder in veterans. *Journal of Equine Veterinary Science, 64*, 17–26. https://doi.org/10.1016/j.jevs.2018.01.011

Marchand, W. R. (2023). Potential mechanisms of action and outcomes of equine-assisted services for veterans with a history of trauma: A narrative review of the literature. *International Journal of Environmental Research and Public Health, 20*, 6377. https://doi.org/10.3390/ijerph20146377

Marchand, W. R., Klinger, W., Block, K., VerMerris, S., Herrmann, T. S., Johnson, C., et al. (2018). Safety and psychological impact of sailing adventure therapy among Veterans with substance use disorders. *Complementary Therapies in Medicine, 40*, 42–47. https://doi.org/10.1016/j.ctim.2018.07.013

Marchand, W. R., Andersen, S. J., Smith, J. E., Hoopes, K. H., & Carlson, J. K. (2021a). Equine-assisted activities and therapies for veterans with posttraumatic stress disorder: Current state, challenges and future directions. *Chronic Stress (Thousand Oaks), 5*, 2470547021991556. https://doi.org/10.1177/2470547021991556

Marchand, W. R., Klinger, W., Block, K., VerMerris, S., Nazarenko, E., Curtis, H., et al. (2021b). Mindfulness-based therapeutic sailing for veterans with psychiatric and substance use disorders. *Military Medicine, 187*(3–4), e445–e452. https://doi.org/10.1093/milmed/usab030

Marchand, W. R., Joubert, K., Smith, J., Nazarenko, E., Klinger, W., Sheppard, S., & Hoopes, K. H. (2022a). A pilot observational study of implementing an equine-assisted services program within a VA medical center residential substance use disorder treatment program. *Military Medicine, 188*(7/8), e2175. https://doi.org/10.1093/milmed/usac028

Marchand, W. R., Smith, J., Hoopes, K. H., Osborne, M., Andersen, S. J., Bell, K., et al. (2022b). A pilot observational study of horsemanship skills training for Veterans with posttraumatic stress disorder. *Complementary Therapies in Medicine, 72*, 102910. https://doi.org/10.1016/j.ctim.2022.102910

Marchand, W. R., Lackner, R., Hartquist, A., Finnell, L., & Nazarenko, E. (2023). Evaluation of a mindfulness and self-compassion-based psychotherapy incorporating horses for Veterans who have experienced trauma. *Complementary Therapies in Medicine, 72*, 102914. https://doi.org/10.1016/j.ctim.2023.102914

Marx, B. P., Foley, K. M., Feinstein, B. A., Wolf, E. J., Kaloupek, D. G., & Keane, T. M. (2010). Combat-related guilt mediates the relations between exposure to combat-related abusive violence and psychiatric diagnoses. *Depression and Anxiety, 27*(3), 287–293. https://doi.org/10.1002/da.20659

McCardle, P., McCune, S., Griffin, J. A., & Maholmes, V. (Eds.). (2011). *How animals affect us: Examining the influence of human-animal interaction on child development and human health*. American Psychological Association.

McCraty, R., Atkinson, M., Tomasino, D., & Bradley, R. (2006). *The coherent heart. Heart–brain interactions, psychophysiological coherence, and the emergence of systemwide order*. HeartMath Research Center, Institute of HeartMath.

McCraty, R., Atkinson, M., Tomasino, D., & Bradley, R. T. (2009). The coherent heart: Heart-brain interactions, psychophysiological coherence, and the emergence of system-wide order. *Integral Review, 5*(2), 10–50.

McCullough, L., Risley-Curtiss, C., & Rorke, J. (2015). Equine facilitated psychotherapy: A pilot study of effect on posttraumatic stress symptoms in maltreated youth. *Journal of Infant, Child, and Adolescent Psychotherapy, 14*(2), 158–173. https://doi.org/10.1080/15289168.2015.1021658

Meints, K., Brelsford, V. L., Dimolareva, M., Marechal, L., Pennington, K., Rowan, E., & Gee, N. R. (2022). Can dogs reduce stress levels in school children? Effects of dog-assisted interventions on salivary cortisol in children with and without special educational needs using randomized controlled trials. *PLoS One, 17*(6), e0269333. https://doi.org/10.1371/journal.pone.0269333

Meyer, L., & Sartori, A. (2019). Attachment theory and equine-facilitated psychotherapy for Vietnam veterans. *Society Animals, 27*, 288–306.

Meyer, E. C., Kotte, A., Kimbrel, N. A., DeBeer, B. B., Elliott, T. R., Gulliver, S. B., & Morissette, S. B. (2019). Predictors of lower-than-expected posttraumatic symptom severity in war veterans: The influence of personality, self-reported trait resilience, and psychological flexibility. *Behaviour Research and Therapy, 113*, 1–8. https://doi.org/10.1016/j.brat.2018.12.005

Monroe, M., Whitworth, J. D., Wharton, T., & Turner, J. (2019). Effects of an equine-assisted therapy program for military veterans with self-reported PTSD. *Society & Animals, 29*(5–6), 577–590. https://doi.org/10.1163/15685306-12341572

Mott, J. M., Hundt, N. E., Sansgiry, S., Mignogna, J., & Cully, J. A. (2014). Changes in psychotherapy utilization among veterans with depression, anxiety, and PTSD. *Psychiatric Services, 65*(1), 106–112. https://doi.org/10.1176/appi.ps.201300056

Nagengast, S. L., Baun, M. M., Megel, M., & Leibowitz, J. M. (1997). The effects of the presence of a companion animal on physiological arousal and behavioral distress in children during a physical examination. *Journal of Pediatric Nursing, 12*(6), 323–330. https://doi.org/10.1016/s0882-5963(97)80058-9

Najavits, L. M. (2007). Psychosocial treatments for posttraumatic stress disorder. In P. E. Nathan & J. M. Gorman (Eds.), *A guide to treatments that work* (2nd ed.). Oxford University Press.

Najavits, L. M. (2015). The problem of dropout from "gold standard" PTSD therapies. *F1000Prime Reports, 7*, 43. https://doi.org/10.12703/P7-43

Neria, Y. (2021). Functional neuroimaging in PTSD: From discovery of underlying mechanisms to addressing diagnostic heterogeneity. *The American Journal of Psychiatry, 178*(2), 128–135. https://doi.org/10.1176/appi.ajp.2020.20121727

Nevins, R., Finch, S., Hickling, E. J., & Barnett, S. D. (2013). The Saratoga WarHorse project: A case study of the treatment of psychological distress in a veteran of Operation Iraqi Freedom. *Advances in Mind-Body Medicine, 27*(4), 22–25. Retrieved from https://www.ncbi.nlm.nih.gov/pubmed/24067322

Notgrass, C., & Pettinelli, D. (2014). Equine assisted psychotherapy: The Equine Assisted Growth and Learning Association's model overview of equine-based modalities. *Journal of Experiential Education, 38*(2), 162–174. https://doi.org/10.1177/1053825914528472

Nqwena, Z., & Naidoo, R. (2016). The effect of therapeutic horseback riding on heart rate variability of children with disabilities. *African Journal of Disability, 5*(1), 248. https://doi.org/10.4102/ajod.v5i1.248

Nurenberg, J. R., Schleifer, S. J., Shaffer, T. M., Yellin, M., Desai, P. J., Amin, R., et al. (2015). Animal-assisted therapy with chronic psychiatric inpatients: Equine-assisted psychotherapy and aggressive behavior. *Psychiatric Services, 66*(1), 80–86. https://doi.org/10.1176/appi.ps.201300524

O'Haire, M. E., Tedeschi, P., Jenkins, M. A., Braden, S. R., & Rodriguez, K. E. (2019). The impact of human-animal interaction in trauma recovery. In P. Tedeschi & M. A. Jenkins (Eds.), *Transforming trauma: Resilience and healing through our connections with animals*. Purdue University Press.

Odendaal, J. S., & Meintjes, R. A. (2003). Neurophysiological correlates of affiliative behaviour between humans and dogs. *Veterinary Journal, 165*(3), 296–301. https://doi.org/10.1016/s1090-0233(02)00237-x

PATH Intl. *PATH international statistics 2016*. Retrieved from https://www.pathintl.org/images/pdf/about-narha/documents/2016-fact-sheet-for-web.pdf

Pearlman, L. A., & Courtois, C. A. (2005). Clinical applications of the attachment framework: Relational treatment of complex trauma. *Journal of Traumatic Stress, 18*(5), 449–459. https://doi.org/10.1002/jts.20052

Pichot, T., & Coulter, M. (2007). *Animal-assisted brief therapy: A solution-focused approach*. The Haworth Press.

Puetz, T. W., Youngstedt, S. D., & Herring, M. P. (2015). Effects of pharmacotherapy on combat-related PTSD, anxiety, and depression: A systematic review and meta-regression analysis. *PLoS One, 10*(5), e0126529. https://doi.org/10.1371/journal.pone.0126529

Rathish, D., Rajapakse, R., & Weerakoon, K. (2021). The role of cortisol in the association of canine-companionship with blood pressure, glucose, and lipids: A systematic review. *High Blood Pressure & Cardiovascular Prevention, 28*(5), 447–455. https://doi.org/10.1007/s40292-021-00469-3

Rodriguez, K. E., Bryce, C. I., Granger, D. A., & O'Haire, M. E. (2018). The effect of a service dog on salivary cortisol awakening response in a military population with posttraumatic stress disorder (PTSD). *Psychoneuroendocrinology, 98*, 202–210. https://doi.org/10.1016/j.psyneuen.2018.04.026

Romaniuk, M., Evans, J., & Kidd, C. (2018). Evaluation of an equine-assisted therapy program for veterans who identify as "wounded, injured or ill" and their partners. *PLoS One, 13*(9), e0203943. https://doi.org/10.1371/journal.pone.0203943

Rosing, T., Malka, M., Brafman, D., & Fisher, P. W. (2022). A qualitative study of equine-assisted therapy for Israeli military and police veterans with PTSD-impact on self-regulation, bonding and hope. *Health & Social Care in the Community, 30*(6), e5074–e5082. https://doi.org/10.1111/hsc.13922

Shelef, A., Brafman, D., Rosing, T., Weizman, A., Stryjer, R., & Barak, Y. (2019). Equine assisted therapy for patients with post traumatic stress disorder: A case series study. *Military Medicine, 184*(9–10), 394–399. https://doi.org/10.1093/milmed/usz036

Signal, T., Taylor, N., Botros, H., Prentice, K., & Lazarus, K. (2013). Whispering to horses: Childhood sexual abuse, depression and the efficacy of equine facilitated therapy. *Sexual Abuse in Australia and New Zealand, 5*(1), 24–32.

Silberstein, L., Tirch, D., & Leahy, R. (2012). Mindfulness, psychological flexibility and emotional schemas. *International Journal of Cognitive Therapy, 5*(4), 406–419.

Srinivasan, S. M., Cavagnino, D. T., & Bhat, A. N. (2018). Effects of equine therapy on individuals with autism spectrum disorder: A systematic review. *Review Journal of Autism and Developmental Disorders, 5*(2), 156–175. https://doi.org/10.1007/s40489-018-0130-z

Sripada, R. K., King, A. P., Garfinkel, S. N., Wang, X., Sripada, C. S., Welsh, R. C., & Liberzon, I. (2012). Altered resting-state amygdala functional connectivity in men with posttraumatic stress disorder. *Journal of Psychiatry & Neuroscience, 37*(4), 241–249. https://doi.org/10.1503/jpn.110069

Steele, E., Wood, D. S., Usadi, E. J., & Applegarth, D. M. (2018). TRR's Warrior Camp: An intensive treatment program for combat trauma in active military and veterans of all eras. *Military Medicine, 183*(suppl_1), 403–407. https://doi.org/10.1093/milmed/usx153

Steenkamp, M. M., Litz, B. T., Hoge, C. W., & Marmar, C. R. (2015). Psychotherapy for military-related PTSD: A review of randomized clinical trials. *JAMA, 314*(5), 489–500. https://doi.org/10.1001/jama.2015.8370

Stein, M. B., & Rothbaum, B. O. (2018). 175 Years of progress in PTSD therapeutics: Learning from the past. *The American Journal of Psychiatry, 175*(6), 508–516. https://doi.org/10.1176/appi.ajp.2017.17080955

Suarez-Jimenez, B., Albajes-Eizagirre, A., Lazarov, A., Zhu, X., Harrison, B. J., Radua, J., et al. (2020). Neural signatures of conditioning, extinction learning, and extinction recall in posttraumatic stress disorder: A meta-analysis of functional magnetic resonance imaging studies. *Psychological Medicine, 50*(9), 1442–1451. https://doi.org/10.1017/S0033291719001387

Suris, A., & Lind, L. (2008). Military sexual trauma: A review of prevalence and associated health consequences in veterans. *Trauma Violence Abuse, 9*(4), 250–269. https://doi.org/10.1177/1524838008324419

Sylvia, L., West, E., Blackburn, A. M., Gupta, C., Bui, E., Mahoney, T., et al. (2020). Acceptability of an adjunct equine-assisted activities and therapies program for veterans with posttraumatic stress disorder and/or traumatic brain injury. *Journal of Integrative Medicine, 18*(2), 169–173. https://doi.org/10.1016/j.joim.2020.01.005

Trzmiel, T., Purandare, B., Michalak, M., Zasadzka, E., & Pawlaczyk, M. (2019). Equine assisted activities and therapies in children with autism spectrum disorder: A systematic review and a meta-analysis. *Complementary Therapies in Medicine, 42*, 104–113. https://doi.org/10.1016/j.ctim.2018.11.004

Vormbrock, J. K., & Grossberg, J. M. (1988). Cardiovascular effects of human-pet dog interactions. *Journal of Behavioral Medicine, 11*(5), 509–517. https://doi.org/10.1007/BF00844843

Watts, B. V., Shiner, B., Zubkoff, L., Carpenter-Song, E., Ronconi, J. M., & Coldwell, C. M. (2014). Implementation of evidence-based psychotherapies for posttraumatic stress disorder in VA specialty clinics. *Psychiatric Services, 65*(5), 648–653. https://doi.org/10.1176/appi.ps.201300176

Wharton, T., Whitworth, J., Macauley, E., & Malone, M. (2019). Pilot testing a manualized equine-facilitated cognitive processing therapy (EF-CPT) intervention for PTSD in veterans. *Psychiatric Rehabilitation Journal, 42*(3), 268–276. https://doi.org/10.1037/prj0000359

Wijker, C., Kupper, N., Leontjevas, R., Spek, A., & Enders-Slegers, M. J. (2021). The effects of Animal Assisted Therapy on autonomic and endocrine activity in adults with autism spectrum disorder: A randomized controlled trial. *General Hospital Psychiatry, 72*, 36–44. https://doi.org/10.1016/j.genhosppsych.2021.05.003

Wilson, E. O. (1984). *Biophilia*. Harvard University Press.

Wisco, B. E., Marx, B. P., Wolf, E. J., Miller, M. W., Southwick, S. M., & Pietrzak, R. H. (2014). Posttraumatic stress disorder in the US veteran population: Results from the National Health and Resilience in Veterans Study. *The Journal of Clinical Psychiatry, 75*(12), 1338–1346. https://doi.org/10.4088/JCP.14m09328

Wisco, B. E., Marx, B. P., Miller, M. W., Wolf, E. J., Mota, N. P., Krystal, J. H., et al. (2016). Probable posttraumatic stress disorder in the US veteran population according to DSM-5: Results from the National Health and Resilience in Veterans Study. *The Journal of Clinical Psychiatry, 77*(11), 1503–1510. https://doi.org/10.4088/JCP.15m10188

Wolynczyk-Gmaj, D., Ziolkowska, A., Rogala, P., Scigala, D., Bryla, L., Gmaj, B., & Wojnar, M. (2021). Can dog-assisted intervention decrease anxiety level and autonomic agitation in patients with anxiety disorders? *Journal of Clinical Medicine, 10*(21), 5171. https://doi.org/10.3390/jcm10215171

Wood, W., Alm, K., Benjamin, J., Thomas, L., Anderson, D., Pohl, L., & Kane, M. (2020). Optimal terminology for services in the United States that incorporate horses to benefit people: A consensus document. *Journal of Alternative and Complementary Medicine, 27*(1), 88–95. https://doi.org/10.1089/acm.2020.0415

Yoo, J. H., Oh, Y., Jang, B., Song, J., Kim, J., Kim, S., et al. (2016). The effects of equine-assisted activities and therapy on resting-state brain function in attention-deficit/hyperactivity disorder: A pilot study. *Clinical Psychopharmacology and Neuroscience, 14*(4), 357–364. https://doi.org/10.9758/cpn.2016.14.4.357

Yorke, J., Adams, C., & Coady, N. (2008). Therapeutic value of equine-human bonding in recovery from trauma. *Anthrozoös, 21*(1), 17–30.

Zhu, X., Suarez-Jimenez, B., Zilcha-Mano, S., Lazarov, A., Arnon, S., Lowell, A. L., et al. (2021). Neural changes following equine-assisted therapy for posttraumatic stress disorder: A longitudinal multimodal imaging study. *Human Brain Mapping, 42*(6), 1930–1939. https://doi.org/10.1002/hbm.25360

Equine-Assisted Therapy Programs on the Ground Versus Programs in the Saddle: How Do You Choose?

Jessica Ward, Angela Hovey, and Keith Brownlee

Introduction

Therapeutic activities involving horses can support improved physical and mental well-being. Depending on their focus and population served, therapeutic equine programs are characteristically distinguished by their primary focus on one of these two broad categories,; namely, programs that support improved physical well-being and programs that support improved mental well-being. Riding for persons with disabilities, sometimes referred to as hippotherapy, is an example of a program that supports physical well-being of people who may experience physical health challenges. Programs focused on improved mental well-being are commonly referred to as equine-assisted therapy (EAT) programs. These programs are designed to help clients improve their emotional, social, and behavioral well-being. Although all therapeutic activities involving horses can offer therapeutic value and improved well-being for clients, in order for an EAT program to be considered a form of therapy, the therapist must be a certified or licensed mental health professional. The focus of this chapter is on EAT programs that include mental health therapy as a key component of the program.

EAT programs can be divided into two distinct categories: (1) groundwork-based equine-assisted therapy (G-EAT) and (2) mounted equine-assisted therapy (M-EAT); refer to Fig. 1 for an illustration of types of therapeutic activities involving horses. G-EAT programs are characterized by sessions that specifically focus on groundwork-based activities and *exclude* the mounting, riding, or driving of horses during sessions. The central components of G-EAT sessions consist of various activities that involve working with the horse on the ground, with the horse either at liberty or by using a halter and lead rope. Examples of activities that may be

J. Ward (✉) · A. Hovey · K. Brownlee
School of Social Work, Lakehead University, Orillia, ON, Canada
e-mail: jnward@lakeheadu.ca; ahovey@lakeheadu.ca; kbrownle@lakeheadu.ca

Y. Neria et al. (eds.), *Guide to Equine Assisted Therapy*,
https://doi.org/10.1007/978-3-031-74426-6_3

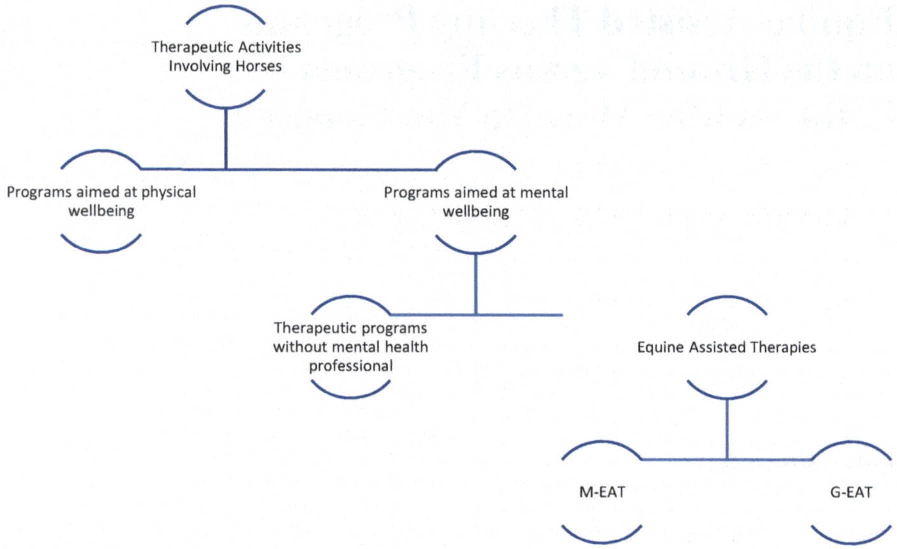

Fig. 1 Types of therapeutic activities involving horses

incorporated into G-EAT programs include, but are not limited to, lunging activities, leading a horse through obstacles, working with the horse in a round pen, observing the horse, or completing grooming/horse-care tasks. Some G-EAT programs may also incorporate strictly limited mounted elements, such as having a celebratory ride to mark the completion of a series of EAT sessions (Lac, 2017; Tsantefski et al., 2017; Vincent et al., 2021) or an opportunity for clients to lie bareback on top of an unmoving horse for a short period of time (Lac, 2017). Comparatively, M-EAT programs encompass both mounted and groundwork-based activities. The central mounted activity may be riding, vaulting, or driving the horse. Groundwork-based elements, such as grooming and tacking/untacking and other essential pre- and post-riding activities, will often be incorporated into the EAT session. Select M-EAT programs may also choose to include additional groundwork-based activities, such as lunging or leading exercises.

These programs share many similarities, for example, therapeutic purposes, client interaction with a horse in therapy sessions, and a therapist to guide the therapy. However, they are also distinct from one another. Just as named (i.e., mounted or groundwork-based), a key distinction is whether the therapy involves substantial time with the client being mounted on or riding the horse versus the therapy being focused primarily, or even exclusively, on groundwork activities with the horse. Determining which program may be better suited to or preferred by clients requires a thorough understanding of the similarities and differences between M-EAT and G-EAT programs. This chapter explores (a) methodological differences between mounted versus groundwork-based EAT, (b) rationales for using the two types of programs, (c) potential differences (or not) in outcomes of mounted and groundwork-based EAT programs, and (d) clinical considerations of these distinctions.

Methodological Differences Between Mounted and Groundwork-Based Programs

The core methodological difference between M-EAT and G-EAT is the inclusion, or exclusion, of mounted activities as a key session element. Although this is a single distinguishing feature, it has important implications for the structure of each session. The inclusion of mounted elements necessitates a moderate amount of pre and post work that must be performed immediately to ensure the horse's well-being. The extent of these pre and post activities is subject to variation among individual horses/riders, but at minimum, proper grooming, tacking/untacking, and warm-up/cool-down procedures need to be completed before and after each ride. For recreational riders, it is typically the rider who performs these tasks before and after their ride. M-EAT programs generally follow this same format (refer to Table 1 for details).

While these tasks are necessities, they are also opportunities for the horse and rider to spend time together and bond. For inexperienced riders, it serves as a first step in being comfortable around their horse prior to riding. Within the equestrian community, taking responsibility for the pre- and post-riding tasks is considered an important element of riding lessons. It develops horsemanship skills and appreciation for the work that goes into caring for the horse. In EAT sessions, there may be some individual variation among therapists who may choose to leave elements out of the session; however, these steps will still need to be performed even if not completed by the client. For example, a therapist may decide not to include grooming in the client session for time management reasons. That horse will still need to be groomed by someone else prior to and after use in the M-EAT session.

For the above reasons, many EAT programs derive their session structure from that of a typical recreational riding lesson and integrate therapeutic conversations within this existing framework. Below is an example of the structure of one M-EAT

Table 1 Stages of a recreational riding lesson

Stage 1: pre-riding responsibilities	Stage 2: mounted activities	Stage 3: post-riding responsibilities
15–30 minutes	*30–60 minutes*	*15–30 minutes*
Retrieve horse from field or stall Secure horse in crossties Groom horse (i.e., curry brush, hard brush, soft brush, mane & tail brush, clean feet, hoof polish) Clean barn aisle Put on rider equipment (i.e., boots, helmet, gloves, chaps) Tack horse Lead horse to arena	Mount Warm up Main riding component Cool down Dismount	Lead horse back to barn Secure horse in crossties Untack horse Bathe horse (if necessary) Groom horse (i.e., curry brush, hard brush, soft brush, mane & tail brush, clean feet, hoof polish) Return horse to field or put in stall Clean barn aisle Clean tack and put away

program called *Reining in Anxiety* designed for adolescents struggling with anxiety (Acri et al., 2021):

1) Weekly review (of homework from previous session)
2) Groom and connect
3) The warm up
4) Session activity
5) Cool down
6) Parent/caregiver psychoeducation
7) Homework instruction (p. 2465)

In their description of this program, Acri et al. (2021) explain how mental health interventions are woven into the existing riding lesson structure. The mental health professional will facilitate opportunities for the client to engage in discussions or activities that are linked to their therapeutic goals, while simultaneously riding their horse and completing groundwork-based tasks when included as part of the lesson. During the mounted aspect of M-EAT, the mental health professional may be riding alongside the client, walking in close proximity to the horse–client duo, or positioned in the center of the area, similar to where many riding coaches position themselves during a recreational lesson. Depending on the size of the arena and the presence of background noise, this may require the mental health professional to factor in acoustics and voice projection into their therapeutic approach.

It is the responsibility of the mental health professional, and the equine professional if present, to balance the focus on mental health and use the experiences of riding and horsemanship to enhance the therapeutic value of the session. This may be done by bringing therapeutic activities and discussions into the riding area and by utilizing time before or after riding to debrief mounted experiences and further explore the client's experience in relation to their identified issues. For example, if the mental health professional observes that their client is nervous to mount their horse, they may prompt their client to take five deep breaths before mounting. This strategy integrates emotional regulation techniques into the mounted experience. Using this same example, the mental health professional may also choose to bring this moment up again later in the session, perhaps asking the client "what was mounting your horse like for you today" or "how might you apply the strategy you used to mount the horse today to other times you are experiencing similar feelings" during the post-ride groom.

G-EAT sessions, on the other hand, do not necessarily resemble a recreational riding lesson structure. Some programs may choose to follow a similar core structure, with grooming/time in the barn before and after working with the horse in the arena, or a client may spend the entire session in the arena with their horse. Some G-EAT sessions might consist entirely of clients and therapists observing horses from afar while the horses are out in the field. Without the mounted component, the necessary horse-care steps before and after a session can be drastically reduced, which enables greater flexibility in how therapists could choose to structure client time with the horse. This potential variability makes it difficult to categorize G-EAT programs solely in terms of session structure; the core activities between M-EAT and G-EAT are distinct from one another and will, therefore, provide different experiences for clients and therapists.

Rationales for Using Mounted Versus Groundwork-Based Approaches

What factors should be considered by mental health professionals when deciding between M-EAT or G-EAT? When comparing rationales for mounted or groundwork-based EAT as a mental health professional, there are three main considerations: first, the resources necessary to provide and participate in mounted or groundwork-based sessions; second, the potential risks inherent to both mounted and grounded approaches; and third, the potential therapeutic value of each respective approach.

Resources

Both M-EAT and G-EAT will require access to the basic facility and amenities necessary for the proper care of horses. This includes a clear and secure field of a reasonable size for turnout, access to appropriate shelter in inclement weather, access to clean water, and sufficient hay/grain to meet the horses' individual dietary needs. Beyond these basic facility features, M-EAT and G-EAT programs may require facilities with additional space and/or equipment in order to safely provide sessions. Both approaches may incorporate additional objects to facilitate certain activities (e.g., pylons, poles, barrels). These can be considered, in general, as optional; however, there are individual activities and exercises that cannot be completed without the supporting equipment (refer to Table 2 for a comparison of required resources for groundwork-based and mounted approaches).

Proper footing for the base of a pen or an arena is always an important consideration when working with horses in general; however, it is exponentially more important when horses are being mounted. The additional weight of carrying a rider has implications for the horses' balance. This means that a proper well-maintained footing is a necessary safety component for both the horse and the rider during mounted sessions. Creating and maintaining proper footing is an expensive and labor-intensive undertaking, placing a greater burden on facilities offering M-EAT programs. Horses will also benefit from proper footing during groundwork exercise; however, the potential risks are much lower when the horse is not mounted. Therefore, it is not considered a safety requirement in the same way.

Horse and client-rider equipment is also more extensive for mounted programs. Complete well-fitting horse tack is required for all mounted activities. Additional tack equipment may be needed depending on the individual horse, and tack must be cared for and maintained meticulously, including regular cleaning when used and

Table 2 Comparison of resources required for specific EAT approaches

Resources	G-EAT	M-EAT
Physical—client	None	Must be fit or able-bodied enough to ride horse. Adaptations possible to meet the needs of all individuals—specialized equipment, training, and/or additional human support (e.g., leaders, side walkers). Weight limit: horses should not carry more than 15–20% of their own body weight (max. 200 lbs.).
Physical—horse	Must be in reasonable health and sound enough for specific activities (i.e., walk short distances for leading activities).	Must be sound and fit to ride for length of lesson duration (30–60 minutes).
Space[a]	Arena can be basic and small (i.e., minimum 30-foot diameter). Footing needs to be reasonably level and safe for both horse and client.	Arena must be large enough to ride (i.e., minimum 60 × 100 feet). Footing must be higher quality, meticulously flat, and regularly maintained.
Equipment—client	Closed toe shoes: ideally boots with heel. Optional: helmet.	Boots with 1–2-inch heel, helmet, long thick pants. Optional: half-chaps/tall boots and gloves.
Equipment—horse	None or minimal (i.e., halter and lead rope).	Full properly fitted tack outfit (i.e., bridle, reins, saddle pad, saddle, and girth).
Equipment—arena	None or may use objects (e.g., barrels, poles, tarps).	None or may use objects (e.g., barrels, poles, tarps).
Experience/training—client	None	None
Experience/training—horse	Polite to be led, groomed, safe on the ground. Variety of temperaments can be utilized as long as reasonably safe to be around/interact.	Polite to be led, groomed, and ridden. Must be exceptionally well trained and well behaved with calm, patient, and generous temperament for beginner riders.
Experience/training—therapist (if not working with additional horse professional)	Minimal horse experience required, knowledge of basic horsemanship and horse handling on ground (e.g., use of crossties, catching/turning out, groundwork safety, basic equipment).	High level of horse experience and horsemanship knowledge. Thorough understanding of instructing beginner riders and all necessary safety precautions.
Insurance/liability	Must cover client engagement with horses on the ground.	Must cover client engagement with horses on the ground and during mounted activities.

[a]The Ultimate Equestrian (2023)

size adjustments as needed as a horse ages. Similarly, client-riders require more specialized equipment to participate in M-EAT compared to G-EAT programs. Working around horses on the ground requires, at minimum, wearing closed toe shoes. Many equestrians also advocate for the wearing of long pants and a helmet when working with horses on the ground due to the possibility of injury, especially when working with people who are new to being around horses or if they are minors (Theodore et al., 2017). When mounted, however, the list of required rider equipment is much longer. Riders must wear closed toe shoes with a 1-inch heel, breeches or long thick-material pants, tall boots or chaps that cover up to the rider's knee, equestrian gloves, and a proper fitting helmet that meets industry safety standards. Most geographic locations will have specific minimum standards that all equestrian facilities are required to meet with regard to government policies as well as insurance policies. These standards may differ between adults and minors and may also vary depending on whether activities are mounted or grounded.

Regardless of which program is selected, both M-EAT and G-EAT involve substantial overheads associated with the maintenance and caring of horses. These expenses inevitably transfer to a greater cost of therapy in comparison to a therapist in their office. M-EAT programs, however, require more resources overall than G-EAT programs, which adds to the relative cost to participate in and run M-EAT programs. Further research is needed to determine if this increase in needed resources impacts the ability to provide a M-EAT program or the choice of program for the client. Further, determining whether EAT programs versus in-office type therapy result in better therapeutic outcomes requires more research-based evidence that examines specific factors pertaining to the impact and therapeutic value of involving horses in the therapy.

Risk Considerations

A crucial consideration of all EAT interventions is the potential danger associated with spending time in the presence of horses, whether on the ground or in the saddle. While the exact number of horse-related injuries in the United States is unknown, it is estimated that in 2022–2023 over 100,000 horse-related accidents occurred, and that 710 of those accidents resulted in death (Mallory, 2023). Approximately 80% of horse-related accidents are associated with mounted activity, mostly from falling off the horse, and about 20% of accidents occur during groundwork (i.e., being kicked, or stepped on; Mayberry et al., 2007). Although the more serious accidents reported pertain to high-level equestrians (Mallory, 2023), these statistics indicate that there are potential risks associated with both horseback riding and groundwork activities, which should be communicated to the client and taken into consideration when offering EAT programs.

Recreational and competitive horseback riding are generally recognized as extreme sports that can be dangerous. However, a wide spectrum of risk exists, depending on the sport or activity of choice, the difficulty level of the riding activity, the age, temperament, and training of the horse, and the person's individual riding level as well as how this ability relates to the particular horse they are on (Mallory, 2023). Horseback riding disciplines that include jumping, racing, rodeo sports, and other high speed/high intensity activities have much higher risk levels compared with disciplines such as dressage or pleasure riding.

The rationale for the increased risk would essentially be for the sake of the sport and discipline and/or the riders' enjoyment. No equestrian activity is free from risk; however, there are many ways that risks can be mitigated, depending on where priority is placed. For example, 66% of reported horse-related accidents may have been preventable by addressing one of the three following concerns: (1) broken tack, (2) slipped saddle, or (3) absent safety check (Camargo et al., 2018). The main variable that can be used to minimize risk is through comparable horse and rider pairing (Camargo et al., 2018).

In the contexts of therapeutic riding, where safety should be prioritized above all else, the margin for risk can be substantially reduced when compared to recreational or competitive riding contexts. Steps like being in a controlled environment, using suitable well-trained animals, being under the direct supervision of a trained horse professional, multiple tack/equipment checks, and using proper safety equipment can produce an environment that has fewer risks than other mounted equestrian activities. One can look at the field of hippotherapy and riding programs geared toward physical therapy as an example of how risk associated with being around and riding horses can be minimized. In hippotherapy programs, additional safety procedures and equipment, beyond what would be used in typical recreational equestrian environments, are implemented to ensure horseback riding is accessible and safe for children and adults with complex physical and developmental challenges (Peters et al., 2020). These additional safety policies and procedures are credited with reducing physical injuries during hippotherapy sessions that require basic first aid to less than 1% and a tiny fraction of those injuries requiring off-site care (Peters et al., 2020).

The risk of injury to a client or a mental health professional will always be present in G-EAT and M-EAT approaches, with M-EAT programs having a higher risk of injury, and this risk is an important consideration for anyone interested in participating in EAT programs. Both M-EAT and G-EAT approaches present greater risk to a client compared with in-office therapy appointments. However, the benefits of G-EAT or M-EAT may possibly be so unique for an individual client that it would be impossible to replicate in a traditional office setting or with a smaller animal. This could underpin the rationale for engaging in a therapeutic modality that is inherently dangerous or risky.

Therapeutic Value

A key rationale for both M-EAT and G-EAT is rooted in the therapeutic benefits of the horse–client relationship. The horse–client relationship distinguishes EAT from other forms of therapy (e.g., talk therapy in an office setting). Physical interaction with horses is an intrinsic part of both mounted and unmounted contexts and is an element of EAT interaction that distinguishes it from other therapeutic approaches. Professional boundaries make physical touch between clients and therapists inappropriate in traditional contexts; however, horses are not subject to these same restrictions. Both M-EAT and G-EAT models provide opportunity for tactile stimulation and affectionate physical touch.

EAT sessions utilize the experiential nature of being around horses and the relationship that develops between horses and humans as a way for clients to gain insight about their emotions, behaviors, and relationships with others, and to develop new skills that can be translated into other areas of their life. EAT sessions typically involve one horse, one client, one equine professional, and one mental health professional who work together to facilitate a therapeutic experience. The dynamic that develops in these sessions has been conceptualized as a *Diamond Model* of therapeutic interaction (Brooks & McCullough, 2008). The Diamond Model symbolizes the web of relational interconnectedness that develops between all beings present in an EAT session, with an emphasis on the client–therapist alliance and the horse–equine professional alliance (McCullough et al., 2015). This dynamic has been compared to group therapy in the sense of allowing for a group dynamic to develop but with distinct benefit of the client not having to share the focus with other group members (Parish-Plass, 2008). The Diamond Model results in multiple interactions, between all individuals and the horse, and that the collective of these interactions allows the client to experience and witness several relationships occurring simultaneously (Brooks & McCullough, 2008). The multifaceted dynamic within this Diamond Model is considered to create opportunities for relational experiences of significant therapeutic value to participants (Chandler, 2018).

Chandler (2018) developed the Human Animal Relational Theory (HART), which identifies the relational processes that occur in therapeutic interventions involving animals and explains how emerging processes or "moments" become therapeutically significant for the client. In addition to highlighting the potential therapeutic value of interactions between the client and the animal, the HART framework also draws attention to the important role EAT therapists play in balancing the experiential nature of EAT with intentionally therapeutic dialogue. The HART framework distinguishes between (a) relational moments that a client processes internally without direct intervention or dialogue and (b) relational moments that are processed externally through direct facilitation by the mental health professional (Chandler, 2018). It is left up to the judgment of the therapist to balance internal and external processing moments and choose if, and how, to directly involve themselves. In this way, the HART framework recognizes not only the occurrence of relational moments in EAT but also acknowledges the responsibility of

EAT-licensed therapists to be knowledgeable and skilled in their therapeutic approach, thus distinguishing EAT from recreational activities involving horses (Karol, 2007). The resulting impact of these relational experiences occurs when the client feels an internal change emerging from their relational experience. Specifically, the client is able to create new meaning and insights about themselves and develop new skills and understandings that can be transferred to other areas of their life.

To illustrate how a relational moment could be processed internally or externally, consider a scenario where a client approaches a horse quickly, and the horse greets them by pinning their ears back and swishing their tail, indicating unease. In this example, the client has approached their horse in an aggressive way, presumably unintentionally. If the client demonstrates a positive adjustment in their own actions and body language, this suggests internal processing has occurred and resulted in the client regulating their own behavior appropriately. A therapist's decision to externalize this processing may be unnecessary, or even harmful to the client should they feel reprimanded or that their self-correction was unnoticed. Alternatively, the therapist may choose to acknowledge or congratulate the client for the self-correction to reinforce the internal processing that resulted.

Conversely, if the client appears to have *not* noticed their horses' body language, or if they seem distressed, fearful, or unsure of how to proceed, initiating external processing may be needed. In this moment, the therapist might ask a question such as "What do you think caused your horse to swish their tail like that?" This question would serve to facilitate external processing by prompting a dialogue between the client and the mental health therapist. The impact of this experience and processing could be that the client develops new meaning surrounding nonverbal communication. They may recognize increased value or importance in body language and begin intentionally practicing, being aware of both their own and their horses' body language. It is then possible that this new sense of body awareness when working with horses will evolve to improved interpersonal and communication skills more generally.

In summary, the dynamic that occurs between the client, horse, therapist, and equine professional is well illustrated within the Diamond Model. This relational model for understanding how a horse is involved in the therapeutic relationship demonstrates the multifaceted relational dynamics that are at play in EAT (Brooks & McCullough, 2008). Chandler's (2018) HART framework outlines the processes and exchanges that occur during EAT and within the Diamond Model (Brooks & McCullough, 2008), along with how processing relational experiences with animals is impactful to clients. Integrating these theoretical concepts provides some explanation to understand and fully appreciate the robustness of the clients' relational experience and processes at work across various EAT models and approaches.

M-EAT and G-EAT approaches both present with opportunities for relational interactions between the horse and the client, and the subsequent processing of these moments. What separates mounted from groundwork-based approaches, however, is the "language" used to build the horse–rider relationships and to experience and engage with relational moments as they happen. Groundwork-based approaches rely predominantly on body language communicated visually and orally, while a mounted approach draws on the additional capacity of the horse and the client-rider to communicate far more extensively via physical, tactile sensations.

Horse–Client Communication on the Ground

Groundwork with horses is commonly recognized as an important aspect of horsemanship in recreational or competitive equestrian environments, both for the horses' training, referred to as ground manners, and for the opportunity it provides for the horse and rider to spend time together, get to know each other, and, ultimately, bond. Some approaches to EAT have chosen to exclusively use groundwork-based activities and exercises due to a belief that this context of horse–human interaction provides superior therapeutic value. No known comparative evidence exists to support this claim, but theoretical frameworks have been offered by organizations that promote G-EAT approaches. The largest and most predominate of these organizations is the Equine-Assisted Growth and Learning Association (EAGALA, 2018).

G-EAT approaches use a theoretical framework that does not include mounting of horses at any time during EAT sessions, and sometimes also does not permit the use of equipment or tack of any kind that is placed directly on the horses' body (e.g., halter, lead rope, bridle). G-EAT assumes that working with horses at liberty allows the horse to be more freely and authentically themselves, and that this level of freedom and autonomy on the part of the horse is imperative to the success of EAT interventions (Thomas et al., 2006). The rationale provided for this belief is the idea that EAT is successful only when horses are free to act in whatever they want to in a given moment, rather than act in a way that they have been trained to do (Thomas et al., 2006). Those who adhere to the G-EAT model believe that incorporating mounted activities into EAT sessions adds a layer of complexity that impedes the therapeutic nature/value of the experience and posit that mounted activities are, at best, unnecessary and do not add therapeutic value of any kind, and at worst, diminish the therapeutic value of EAT (Thomas et al., 2006).

In G-EAT, body language is the primary means of communication between the horse and the client. Information is exchanged between each other through often subtle body movements and/or facial expressions. This requires the participant to be present and observant of both their own and their horses' body language. Horses are flight animals and, as such, are very attuned to the environments they are in, making them sensitive and responsive to even the smallest changes or cues in human body language. Horses will not only notice these changes in human body language, but they will also respond according to how they have interpreted the human behavior. The meaning that a horse takes from human behavior is not the same as the meaning that another human would take, meaning that some behaviors generally considered unremarkable to humans can be upsetting to a horse. This requires an individual to be astutely aware of their own vocal sounds and body movements when working with horses in order to avoid unintentionally spooking or upsetting the horse.

For example, fast movements are interpreted as a sign of danger to most horses, whether it is a quick movement of a body limb (e.g., waving hands) or a fast movement of the whole body (e.g., running). Imagine the scenario of a child being in the arena who has forgotten their water bottle in the barn. They may have an instinctive reaction to turn and run back to the barn to quickly get their water bottle. In other sporting environments, such as on a soccer field or a baseball pitch, running to retrieve a forgotten item would be common and likely go unnoticed. In an equestrian environment, however, running could very likely result in the horse reacting to this behavior (i.e., spooking or even beginning to run themselves). This is one example of a situation where an individual working on the ground with a horse must begin to see their own body language through the perspective of their horse, thus, requiring them to become aware of their own body movements in a deeper way.

Through this process of increased awareness and intentionality regarding body language and nonverbal communication, clients can learn how to interact with their horse in a way that builds trust and rapport, while simultaneously developing the ability to read, understand, and respond appropriately to their horses' body language. Through these ongoing exchanges between the horse and the client, meaningful relational moments occur, and a relationship is fostered.

Horse–Client Communication in the Saddle

In M-EAT, the concepts of body language and facial communication are utilized during the groundwork-based elements; however, during the mounted exercises, clients begin to communicate with their horse in a different way—through tactile communication. The language of tactile communication is integrated into the process of learning to ride and is therefore, learned through direct instruction in gradual steps that build upon one another. For example, the first two methods of tactile communication that a new rider learns are commonly: (1) squeeze the horse's sides with both legs to signal the horse to move forward and (2) pull gently back on the reins to signal the horse to stop. As an individual builds their riding skills, they will learn increasingly sophisticated ways of utilizing and understanding tactile communication. In M-EAT, this instruction and gradual skill development is integrated into the session structure. Tactile communication can be taught by verbal instruction, demonstration, and/or experiential learning.

It is essential for the rider to understand the elevated importance of physical touch as a means of tactile communication when working with horses from a mounted position. Riding a horse cannot occur without constant physical contact. Ongoing intimate physical connection between the horse and the rider is inherent to horseback riding and requires that the rider be physically connected with their horse from the moment they mount. The physicality of this bond is unique to this relational context and introduces a new level of connection and shared experience between the horse and the rider. Developing a partnership with a horse from the mounted perspective is a distinct experience from that which is formed when interacting with horses on the ground.

Once mounted, the horse and the rider become linked to one another through a physical connection that can be characterized by two qualities, *physical unity* and the *tactile communication loop* (Ward, 2020). The concept of physical unity is described as the shared experience of movement that occurs between the horse and the rider. The tactile communication loop refers to the unfolding communication and shared information between the horse and the rider through physical touch. The combination of physical unity and the tactile communication loop creates a relational dynamic that is presented in this chapter as the *Mounted Connection* (Ward, 2020).

The act of mounting a horse establishes physical unity between the horse and the rider and can be understood as a symbolic expression of mutual trust (Ward, 2020). Both the horse and the rider are exposed to increased levels of vulnerability as their individual well-being becomes inextricably linked to the behavior of each partner. After being mounted, horses are susceptible to any pain or discomfort that may be intentionally or unintentionally inflicted through the rider's bodily movements. Conversely, riders open themselves up to the possibility of injury or physical danger that could be caused by the behavior of the horse.

Prior to mounting, a rider must understand that they are knowingly putting themselves in a state of heightened physical vulnerability and must decide whether their trust in their horse outweighs this risk. In this way, the rider's relationship with their horse is a pivotal factor in mastering initial feelings of apprehension related to mounting. It is through the rider's willingness to mount despite fear and possible risks, and the horse's acceptance of the rider on their back, that both parties demonstrate their mutual trust, and by so doing intensifying the contexts of their bond. After the rider has successfully mounted, this can feel like a meaningful bonding moment for the rider. Rather than resulting in a feeling of autonomous accomplishment of "I did it," the feelings a rider has after mounting may be more accurately described as "we did it together" or "I did it with my horse." Mounting marks the beginning of establishing physical unity between the horse and the rider, and as they progress from a static state into an active riding state, the physical unity between them deepens as their movement becomes intertwined (Ward, 2020).

The act of horseback riding is dependent on a fundamental exchange occurring between the horse and the rider, where the rider adopts the horse's stride as a temporary replacement for their own and in exchange assumes responsibility for all cognitive decision-making and leadership within the partnership. In essence, the horse provides their feet, and the rider decides where their feet will go. The result of this exchange is a phenomenon that could be described as *sharing steps* (Ward, 2020). Through sharing steps, the horse and rider become capable of moving as a cohesive unit continuously linked through this ongoing shared physical experience. By completing tasks as a unified whole, the horse–rider physical connection is deepened, and they become capable of completing tasks as a team that they would not be capable of completing independently.

The combined abilities of a horse and rider sharing steps are greater than the sum of two separate parts. The horse–rider team forms a distinct entity that allows both parties to accomplish tasks beyond their individual abilities. This partnership is only effective, however, when both parties support each other, communicate, and rely on each other. The horse–rider partnership can be seen as a symbolic representation of how positive, growth-fostering relationships mutually empower both individuals. Thus, sharing steps allows the horse and rider to complete tasks in a unified way and gain access to a new world and a new set of tasks that are possible to complete. To gain access to these opportunities, however, the horse and rider require a mutual language from which to communicate. This language is conceptualized as a tactile communication loop (Ward, 2020).

Mounting a horse not only initiates physical unity, it also establishes a continuous tactile communication loop between the horse and the rider (Ward, 2020). Once in the saddle, riders instantly begin communicating with their horse through the giving and receiving of tactile stimulation. This physical feedback loop becomes the medium through which horse–rider partnerships engage in direct communication with each other. The strength of the tactile communication loop is not dependent on the rider or the horse's ability level; it is a quality that is equal across all equestrian partnerships and integral to the horseback riding experience. Although it can be conducted with various levels of skill, it is always inherently present when a rider is in the saddle. Unlike forms of nonverbal communication that rely on visual and auditory engagement of discrete moments, without dismounting, it is not possible to interrupt the tactile communication loop.

The continuous nature of this loop makes it a phenomenon that functions to tether the rider to the present moment (Ward, 2020). Physical stimulation, transmitted through the feedback loop, holds the rider's attention, retaining them in the present moment. In in this way, within M-EAT contexts, the tactile communication loop becomes a method of engaging participants in the therapeutic process (Ward, 2020). From a relational perspective, the tactile communication loop becomes a gentle, continuous pull into the moment, into the therapeutic process, and into the relationship, without any additional effort on the part of the rider, therapist, or horse. The horse and the rider do have the power to choose how much they will focus on the information being shared in this loop; however, regardless of cognitive engagement, their body remains firmly engaged in this communication. The therapist's role facilitates the external processing of this experience.

If the horse and the rider do choose to engage with this information, as is the case in willing equestrian partnerships, the tactile communication loop then becomes the binding force between them, which facilitates the internal processing of this experience. This loop becomes the foundation from which the horse and rider can create a shared understanding of meaning associated with various physical sensations. The horse and rider become able to give and receive information through symbolic tactile stimulation. Equestrian sports describe the rider as having four natural aids at their disposal to communicate in this way; these are the rider's seat, leg, hands, and voice. Three out of the four aids correspond to points of physical contact between the horse and the rider, which is reflective of how significant physical contact is in the horse–rider relationship. As an individual develops as a rider, they must learn how to use these aids in more sophisticated ways to both listen and speak to their horse, and ultimately be able to engage in more complicated "conversations." This method of communication has been described as physical sign language (Edgette, 1996).

There are some elements of this language that are universal among equestrian sports or within a given equestrian discipline. For example, squeezing your horse with equal pressure from both legs is universally the physical sign meaning "walk on." At other times, an individual horse–rider team may develop meaning around a feeling that is unique to them or their relationship. For example, if a horse has an old injury in one of their legs, when they are feeling pain from this injury, their gate may be affected in a particular way due to weakness in a given area. A person who is familiar with riding that horse will begin to recognize when their horse is becoming tired and being affected by that old injury based on a particular feeling they recognize through their aids.

The above two examples also illustrate how the information transmitted in the tactile communication loop can be the information that was both intentionally and unintentionally transmitted. This is reflective of the continuous nature of the feedback loop. As this connection is never paused or broken, the horse and the rider will communicate to each other the physical manifestation of their subjective states. For example, riders may feel the sensations of a horse stomping their feet or swishing their tail if they become irritated. Equally, riders communicate unintentionally via the feedback loop subjective states such as nervousness or insecurity as a rider by holding tension in their body or by being unclear in their use of communication aids. From this perspective, an important aspect of a rider's learning is to engage with the feedback loop and learn how to manage the information they contribute to the loop. This is achieved through the development of increased body awareness and control.

The tactile communication loop is indicative of the distinctive relational experience that occurs between the horse and the rider. This loop, and the way it is used in combination with physical unity, is what makes the experience of bonding with a horse through riding fundamentally different from the way other relationships are formed, including G-EAT experiences (Ward, 2020). For individuals who may have struggled to establish growth-fostering relationships in their lives through conventional ways, M-EAT presents the opportunity to build a relationship in a different way. The foundational qualities of mutual empathy and relational authenticity are still essential parts of the horse–rider relationship; however, the skills and tools that are used to reach such a relationship are unique and differ from the groundwork-based relationship.

Outcomes

Both M-EAT and G-EAT approaches have preliminary evidence suggesting they are therapeutically valuable to a wide range of client populations and presenting mental health issues. M-EAT and G-EAT approaches have demonstrated positive outcomes across all age groups (Aviv et al., 2020; Cerulli et al., 2014; Dunlop & Tsantefski, 2018; Zhu et al., 2021), in different settings (Arnon et al., 2020; Dell et al., 2011; Mueller & McCullough, 2017; Tsantefski et al., 2017), and with individual and group formats (Collingwood et al., 2021; Fisher et al., 2021; Schultz et al., 2007).

Beneficial outcomes that have been identified include improvements in self-esteem, emotional regulation, communication, assertiveness, understanding of the impact of their actions on others, body awareness, problem-solving, and general symptom reduction for various mental health diagnoses (Kersten & Thomas, 2000; Ward et al., 2022). Table 3 outlines some of the key areas that have been studied.

No studies have compared the outcomes between G-EAT and M-EAT approaches. A key consideration when comparing the outcomes associated with M-EAT and G-EAT approaches is the lack of research that has isolated the mounted and groundwork-based variables and examined the explicit contribution that each element makes. Due to the fact that most M-EAT programs consist of a combination of both mounted and groundwork-based elements, without explicitly distinguishing the variables, it is impossible to know if positive results are due to experiences while mounted or during groundwork-based activities. A primary distinguishing factor is physical interaction between the horse and the client. Arena groundwork with horses at liberty is based on communicating through noncontact body language, which limits opportunities for touching a horse while doing this kind of work and never involves mounting a horse or communicating physically while mounted. Even when manually leading a horse on the ground, the horse and human are typically linked through a lead rope and halter, which also limits direct physical connection.

In their literature review, Ward et al. (2022) reported some preliminary evidence of the specific contribution that mounted activities make to the EAT experience.

Table 3 M-EAT and G-EAT studies with positive results by the client group

Client group	Studies
Substance use	Atherton et al. (2020), Gatti et al. (2020), and Kern-Godal et al. (2015)
Veterans with PTSD	Fisher et al. (2021) and Johnson et al. (2018, 2021)
Persons diagnosed with schizophrenia	Corring et al. (2013) and Nurenberg et al. (2015)
Children with histories of trauma	Kemp et al. (2014) and Naste et al. (2018)
Youth at risk	Bachi et al. (2012) and Frederick et al. (2015)
Persons with symptoms of depression	Frederick et al. (2015) and Lutter and Smith-Osborne (2011)
Persons with symptoms of anxiety	Wilson et al. (2017) and So et al. (2017)

Based on a review of qualitative M-EAT research, Ward et al. were able to isolate quotes and descriptions reported by participants that directly associated a given outcome with a moment or experience that happened while they were mounted. Key themes that were reported in this review included the following:

- The normalizing aspect of mounted activities and taking on the identity of a rider contribute to the overall therapeutic experience
- The physicality of being up high on a horse
- The importance and value of physical touch
- The sense of partnership and one-ness with their horse
- The increased body awareness and attunement with their horse
- A feeling of success
- A sense of accomplishment
- The overcoming of fears (Ward et al., 2022)

Further research is needed to explicitly examine the contribution of mounted and groundwork-based activity in isolation, to better understand how outcomes differ between M-EAT and G-EAT approaches. In addition, these outcomes should be examined with a focus on horse-specific variables to determine whether or how EAT programs may be superior to or more effective than in-office type therapy.

Clinical Considerations

Based on the existing evidence, rather than asking the question of which approach is better overall, perhaps the more relevant questions to consider pertain to which approach is better suited to an individual client's needs, wants, or therapeutic goals and/or a therapist's preference and/or comfort with a particular therapeutic approach. If you are a client or a clinician wondering whether you would like to pursue therapeutic activities involving horses and what would be best suited to your needs, here are some questions to consider or ask yourself.

Questions for Therapists

1. *Am I a trained and certified mental health professional?*

   Regardless of whether using mounted or groundwork-based EAT approaches, it is essential that every session be facilitated by a trained and licensed mental health professional without exceptions. Programs that are not facilitated by a qualified mental health professional may be therapeutic but cannot be considered equine therapy.
2. *Do I have the resources necessary for mounted or groundwork-based EAT?*

   Both mounted and groundwork-based EAT require the appropriate facility in which to hold sessions. The requirements are more extensive for mounted programs. Ensuring you have the appropriate environment and equipment to accommodate each respective approach is critical.

3. *Do I know how to ride? Do I have the skill set to be a riding instructor?*

   M-EAT and G-EAT programs are best facilitated by individuals with an equestrian background, and mounted programs in particular require an experienced rider who is able to teach the beginner riding lessons, ideally is a certified equestrian coach. A team approach can also be used, where one individual is a mental health professional and one individual is a horse professional. However, in a mounted program, the therapist should have reasonable enough knowledge and experience with horsemanship and horseback riding.

4. *Do I want to do training with a professional association? Do I have a particular association in mind?*

   If you plan on registering with a professional association, ensure that you select an organization that endorses groundwork-based or mounted work, depending on your interest. If you are already certified/interested with a particular organization, ensure that you are selecting an approach (i.e., mounted or groundwork-based) based on their model. Refer to Table 4 for a list of popular certification organizations in North America and EAT programs.

Questions for Clients

1. *Am I interested in being near horses or do I prefer the idea of riding a horse?*

   If the idea of riding a horse is appealing to you, M-EAT may be a better fit for you. If you are uninterested in riding but like the idea of being near horses, G-EAT may be your preferred option.

2. *Am I comfortable with mounting a horse?*

Table 4 Predominate EAT training and certification organizations in North America

Professional association	Mental health program descriptor	M-EAT	G-EAT
Canadian Therapeutic Riding Association (CanTRA)	Equine Facilitated Wellness	X	X
Cartier Farms Equine Assisted Learning	Equine Assisted Learning Building Block Certification Program		X
Equine Assisted Growth and Learning Association (EAGALA)	Equine Assisted Psychotherapies & Personal Development		X
Professional Association of Therapeutic Horsemanship International (PATH Intl.)	Equine Assisted Activities and Therapies	X	X
Natural Lifemanship	Trauma-Focused Equine Assisted Psychotherapy and Trauma-Informed Equine Assisted Learning	X	X
Horse Spirit Connections	Facilitated Equine Experiential Learning (FEEL) Certification Program		X

Riding a horse may not be for every client and can elicit fear in some individuals; however, the M-EAT approach can support therapeutic goals such as facing one's fear. Alternatively, the G-EAT approach may be a way to become more comfortable to someday mount a horse while addressing other therapeutic goals.

3. *Do I meet the physical requirements of mounted work?*

   As demonstrated by organizations that provide therapeutic riding or hippotherapy for persons with disabilities, it is possible for horseback riding to be adapted to suit the physical needs of any and all abilities. In some situations, however, additional equipment and/or support personnel are needed to facilitate these accommodations (i.e., side-walker, accessible mounting block). Not all facilities focused on mental health will have the necessary resources. There is also a weight limit for riding, usually about 200 lbs.

4. *Do I think it would be more therapeutic for me to incorporate riding or not?*

   This is a personal preference. Brainstorm some personal therapeutic goals. Try to link them with the thought of being near horses and interacting with horses on the ground; then try to link the therapeutic goals with the thought of being mounted on a horse. Consider which approach may be more therapeutic for you.

5. *What services are offered by licensed and trained mental health professionals in my geographical area?*

   Refer to Table 4 for North American Associations to determine programs in your area.

Conclusion

This chapter reviewed the similarities and differences between M-EAT and G-EAT approaches with regard to their methodology, rationale, outcomes, and clinical considerations. The nature of the relational dynamics that occur in both mounted and groundwork-based approaches was explored using HART (Chandler, 2018) and the Diamond Model of therapeutic interaction between the client, horse, therapist, and horse professional (Brooks & McCullough, 2008). The idea of the mounted connection was introduced as a conceptualization of how the physicality involved in riding a horse makes the relational experience distinct from that which can be had when working with horses on the ground (Ward, 2020). Therapeutic outcomes appear to be positive for M-EAT and G-EAT, although both approaches could benefit from further research about the contribution that specific mounted and groundwork-based elements offer to the EAT experience. Therapists and clients who are interested in EAT, but are unsure of whether a mounted or groundwork-based approach is best suited to their needs and preferences, were provided with a number of questions to facilitate decision-making. Finally, further exploration is recommended to learn more about the therapeutic benefits and differences between mounted and groundwork-based approaches.

References

Acri, M., Morrissey, M., Peth-Pierce, R., Seibel, L., Seag, D., Hamovitch, E., Guo, F., Hoagwood, K. (2021). An equine-assisted therapy for youth with mild to moderate anxiety: Manual development and fidelity. *Journal of Child and Family Studies, 30*(10), 2461–2467. https://doi.org/10.1007/s10826-021-02011-4

Arnon, S., Fisher, P. W., Pickover, A., Lowell, A., Turner, J. B., Hilburn, A., Jacob-McVey, J., Malajian, B. E., Farber, D. G., Hamilton, J. F., Hamilton, A., Markowitz, J. C., & Neria, Y. (2020). Equine-assisted therapy for veterans with PTSD: Manual development and preliminary findings. *Military Medicine, 185*(5–6), e557–e564. https://doi.org/10.1093/milmed/usz444

Atherton, W. L., Meola, C. C., & Pritchard, K. S. (2020). Innovative equine facilitated psychotherapy intervention for adolescent addiction treatment: A pilot study. *International Journal of HighRisk Behaviors and Addiction, 9*(3), e103877. https://brief.land/ijhrba/articles/103877.html

Aviv, T. L. M., Katz, Y. J., & Berant, E. (2020). The contribution of therapeutic horseback riding to the improvement of executive functions and self-esteem among children with ADHD. *Journal of Attention Disorders, 25*(12), 1743–1753. https://doi.org/10.1177/1087054720925898

Bachi, K., Terkel, J., & Teichman, M. (2012). Equine-facilitated psychotherapy for at-risk adolescents: The influence on self-image, self-control and trust. *Clinical Child Psychology and Psychiatry, 17*(2), 298–312. https://doi.org/10.1177/1359104511404177

Brooks, S., & McCullough, L. M. (2008). The diamond model. In S. Brooks, M. Hogan, L. M. McCullough, & M. Stuart (Eds.), *Equine specialist workshop faculty manual* (pp. 43–47). North American Riding for the Handicapped Association.

Camargo, F., Gombeski, W. R., Barger, P., Jehlik, C., Wiemers, H., Mead, J., & Lawyer, A. (2018). Horse-related injuries: Causes, preventability, and where educational efforts should be focused. *Cogent Food & Agriculture, 4*(1), 1432168. https://doi.org/10.1080/23311932.2018.14321681432168

Cerulli, C., Minganti, C., De Santis, C., Tranchita, E., Quaranta, F., & Parisi, A. (2014). Therapeutic horseback riding in breast cancer survivors: A pilot study. *The Journal of Alternative and Complementary Medicine, 20*(8), 623–629. https://doi.org/10.1089/acm.2014.0061

Chandler, C. K. (2018). Human-animal relational theory: A guide for animal-assisted counseling. *Journal of Creativity in Mental Health, 13*(4), 429–444. https://doi.org/10.1080/15401383.2018.1486258

Collingwood, E., Messina, A., Dam, A., Bernard, T., Cockburn, L., & Penney, S. (2021). Experiences of recovery for Canadian forensic mental health patients and staff participating in a horse stables program. *The Journal of Forensic Psychiatry & Psychology, 32*, 641–657. https://doi.org/10.1080/14789949.2021.1881582

Corring, D., Lundberg, E., & Rudnick, A. (2013). Therapeutic horseback riding for ACT patients with schizophrenia. *Community Mental Health Journal, 49*(1), 121–126. https://doi.org/10.1007/s10597-011-9457-y

Dell, C., Chalmers, D., Bresette, N., Swain, S., Rankin, D., & Hopkins, C. (2011). A healing space: The experiences of first nations and Inuit youth with equine-assisted learning (EAL). *Child & Youth Care Forum, 40*(4), 319–336. https://doi.org/10.1007/s10566-011-9140-z

Dunlop, K., & Tsantefski, M. (2018). A space of safety: Children's experience of equine-assisted group therapy. *Child & Family Social Work, 23*(1), 16–24. https://doi.org/10.1111/cfs.12378

Edgette, J. S. (1996). *Heads up! Practical sports psychology for riders, their families, and their trainers*. Doubleday.

Equine Assisted Growth and Learning Association [EAGALA]. (2018). *Equine Assisted Growth and Learning Association*. https://www.eagala.org/index

Fisher, P. W., Lazarov, A., Lowell, A., Arnon, S., Turner, J. B., Bergman, M., Ryba, M., Such, S., Marohasy, C., Zhu, X., Suarez-Jimenez, B., Markowitz, J. C., & Neria, Y. (2021). Equine-assisted therapy for posttraumatic stress disorder among military veterans: An open trial. *The Journal of Clinical Psychiatry, 82*(5), 21m14005. https://doi.org/10.4088/JCP.21m14005

Frederick, K. E., Ivey Hatz, J., & Lanning, B. (2015). Not just horsing around: the impact of equine-assisted learning on levels of hope and depression in at-risk adolescents. *Community Mental Health Journal, 51*(7), 809–817. https://doi.org/10.1007/s10597-015-9836-x

Gatti, F., Walderhaug, E., Kern-Godal, A., Lysell, J., & Arnevik, E. A. (2020). Complementary horse-assisted therapy for substance use disorders: A randomized controlled trial. *Addiction Science & Clinical Practice, 15*, 1–11. https://doi.org/10.1186/s13722-020-0183-z

Johnson, R. A., Albright, D. L., Marzolf, J. R., Bibbo, J. L., Yaglom, H. D., Crowder, S. M., Carlisle, G. K., Willard, A., Russell, C. L., Grindler, K., Osterlind, S., Wassman, M., & Harms, N. (2018). Effects of therapeutic horseback riding on post-traumatic stress disorder in military veterans. *Military Medical Research, 5*(3), 3. https://doi.org/10.1186/s4077901801496

Johnson, R. A., Albright, D. L., Marzolf, J. R., Bibbo, J. L., Yaglom, H. D., Crowder, S. M., Carlisle, G. M., Grindler, K., Harms, N., Willard, A., Wassman, M., & Russell, C. L. (2021). Experiences of military veterans in a therapeutic horseback riding program. *Clinical Nursing Research, 30*(7), 923–933. https://doi.org/10.1177/10547738211003580

Karol, J. (2007). Applying a traditional individual psychotherapy model to equine-facilitated psychotherapy (EFP): Theory and method. *Clinical Child Psychology and Psychiatry, 12*(1), 77–90. https://doi.org/10.1177/1359104507071057

Kemp, K., Signal, T., Botros, H., Taylor, N., & Prentice, K. (2014). Equine facilitated therapy with children and adolescents who have been sexually abused: A program evaluation study. *Journal of Child and Family Studies, 23*(3), 558–566. https://doi.org/10.1007/s10826-013-9718-1

Kern-Godal, A., Arnevik, E., Walderhaug, E., & Ravndal, E. (2015). Substance use disorder treatment retention and completion: A prospective study of horse-assisted therapy (HAT) for young adults. *Addiction Science & Clinical Practice, 10*(1), 21. http://ascpjournal.biomedcentral.com/articles/10.1186/s13722-015-0043-4

Kersten, G., & Thomas, L. (2000). *Equine assisted psychotherapy: Training manual*. Equine Assisted Growth and Learning Association.

Lac, V. (2017). Amy's story: An existential-integrative equine-facilitated psychotherapy approach to anorexia nervosa. *Journal of Humanistic Psychology, 57*(3), 301–312. https://doi.org/10.1177/002216781562790

Lutter, C., & Smith-Osborne, A. (2011). Exercise in the treatment of eating disorders: An alternative view. *Best Practices in Mental Health: An International Journal, 7*(2), 42–59.

Mallory, B. (2023, May 17). *Horse riding accident statistics in 2023 (latest U.S. data)*. Horses Only. https://horsesonly.com/horse-riding-accidents/

Mayberry, J. C., Pearson, T. E., Wiger, K. J., Diggs, B. S., & Mullins, R. J. (2007). Equestrian injury prevention efforts need more attention to novice riders. *Journal of Trauma: Injury, Infection, and Critical Care, 62*(3), 735–739. https://doi.org/10.1097/ta.0b013e318031b5d4. PMID: 17414356.

McCullough, L., Risley-Curtiss, C., & Rorke, J. (2015). Equine facilitated psychotherapy: A pilot study of effect on posttraumatic stress symptoms in maltreated youth. *Journal of Infant, Child, and Adolescent Psychotherapy, 14*(2), 158–173. https://doi.org/10.1080/15289168.2015.1021658

Mueller, M. K., & McCullough, L. (2017). Effects of equine-facilitated psychotherapy on posttraumatic stress symptoms in youth. *Journal of Child and Family Studies, 26*(4), 1164–1172. https://doi.org/10.1007/s10826-016-0648-6

Naste, T. M., Price, M., Karol, J., Martin, L., Murphy, K., Miguel, J., & Spinazzola, J. (2018). Equine facilitated therapy for complex trauma (EFF-CT). *Journal of Child & Adolescent Trauma, 11*(3), 289–303. https://doi.org/10.1007/s40653-017-0187-3

Nurenberg, J. R., Schleifer, S. J., Shaffer, T. M., Yellin, M., Desai, P. J., Amin, R., Bouchard, A., & Montalvo, C. (2015). Animal-assisted therapy with chronic psychiatric inpatients: Equine-assisted psychotherapy and aggressive behavior. *Psychiatric Services, 66*(1), 80–86. https://doi.org/10.1176/appi.ps.201300524

Parish-Plass, N. (2008). Animal-assisted therapy with children suffering from insecure attachment due to abuse and neglect: A method to lower the risk of intergenerational transmission of abuse? *Clinical Child Psychology and Psychiatry, 13*(1), 7–30. https://doi.org/10.1177/1359104507086338

Peters, B. C., Fields, B. E., & Erdman, E. A. (2020). Hippotherapy practice and safety patterns in the United States: A descriptive survey study. *The Journal of Alternative Complementary Medicine, 26*(8), 743–749. https://doi.org/10.1089/acm.2020.0039

Schultz, P. N., Remick-Barlow, G., & Robbins, L. (2007). Equine-assisted psychotherapy: A mental health promotion/intervention modality for children who have experienced intra-family violence. *Health & Social Care in the Community, 15*(3), 265–271. https://doi.org/10.1111/j.1365-2524.2006.00684.x

So, W. Y., Lee, S. Y., Park, Y., & Seo, D. (2017). Effects of 4 weeks of horse- back riding on anxiety, depression, and self-esteem in children with attention deficit hyperactivity disorder. *Journal of Men's Health, 13*(2), e1–e7. https://doi.org/10.22374/1875-6859.13.2.2

The Ultimate Equestrian. (2023). *The ultimate guide to horse riding arenas & equestrian facilities*. https://theultimateequestrian.com/the-ultimate-guide-to-horse-riding-arenas-equestrian-facilities/

Theodore, J. E., Theodore, S. G., Stockton, K. A., & Kimble, R. M. (2017). Paediatric horse-related trauma. *Journal of Paediatrics and Child Health, 53*(6), 543–550. https://doi.org/10.1111/jpc.13471

Thomas, L., Lytle, M., & Damman, B. (2006). *Transforming therapy through horses: Case stories teaching the EAGALA model in action*. Equine Growth and Learning Association.

Tsantefski, M., Briggs, L., Griffiths, J., & Tidyman, A. (2017). An open trial of equine-assisted therapy for children exposed to problematic parental substance use. *Health & Social Care in the Community, 25*(3), 1247–1256. https://doi.org/10.1111/hsc.12427

Vincent, A., Ballard, I., & Farkas, K. J. (2021). Mind full or mindful? A cohort study of equine-facilitated therapy for women veterans. *Journal of Creativity in Mental Health, 18*(3), 367–382, 1–16. https://doi.org/10.1080/15401383.2021.1984353

Ward, J. (2020). *Equine assisted therapy: Understanding the mounted connection* (Unpublished master's project). Lakehead University.

Ward, J., Hovey, A., & Brownlee, K. (2022). Mental health benefits of mounted equine-assisted therapies: A scoping review. *Health & Social Care in the Community, 30*(6), e4920–e4935. https://doi.org/10.1111/hsc.13904

Wilson, K., Buultjens, M., Monfries, M., & Karimi, L. (2017). Equine-assisted psychotherapy for adolescents experiencing depression and/or anxiety: A therapist's perspective. *Clinical Child Psychology and Psychiatry, 22*(1), 16–33. https://doi.org/10.1177/135910451557237

Zhu, X., Suarez-Jimenez, B., Zilcha-Mano, S., Lazarov, A., Arnon, S., Lowell, A. L., Bergman, M., Ryba, M., Hamilton, A. J., Hamilton, J. F., Turner, J. B., Markowitz, J. C., Fisher, P. W., & Neria, Y. (2021). Neural changes following equine-assisted therapy for posttraumatic stress disorder: A longitudinal multimodal imaging study. *Human Brain Mapping, 42*(6), 1930–1939. https://doi.org/10.1002/hbm.25360

Equine-Assisted Therapy Development: Methodology and Rationale

Merav Moshe-Grodofsky

Introduction

Equine-assisted interventions that promote learning, growth, and especially psychotherapeutic processes are increasingly recognized in professional practice. Over the last two decades, there has been a significant increase in the development, study, and implementation of equine-assisted modalities (Carlsson, 2016; Gehtmane-Hofmane, 2019). A growing body of literature has explored equine-assisted therapy, equine-assisted psychotherapy, equine-assisted social work, and the theoretical frameworks that reinforce each approach.

Concurrently, there has been a growth in the application and study of equine-assisted approaches with diverse client populations including children, adults, populations with special needs and developmental challenges, individuals with chronic illness, populations that have experienced trauma, law violators, and more (Kemp et al., 2013; Lac, 2017; Nurenberg et al., 2014; Townsend & Hood, 2019). The expansion of equine-assisted therapy (EAT) methodologies with such a wide variety of populations and the development of equine-assisted training models have enhanced the ability of practitioners including psychologists, psychiatrists, counselors, and social workers to integrate EAT into their professional work with individuals, families, and groups (Bachi & Parish-Plass, 2017; Bailey & Bailey, 2019; Carlsson, 2016; Dunlop & Tsantefski, 2017; Johns et al., 2016).

Despite these developments, there is a paucity of literature that examines the impact of EAT on treatment providers, service provider training, the experiences of service providers in EAT workshops, and the clinical and professional implications that EAT has for therapists. In addition, the literature has paid little attention to the economic costs of equine-assisted therapies, raising issues of access based on

M. Moshe-Grodofsky (✉)
The School of Social Work, Sapir Academic College, D.N. Ashkelon, Israel
e-mail: meravmo@sapir.ac.il

Y. Neria et al. (eds.), *Guide to Equine Assisted Therapy*,
https://doi.org/10.1007/978-3-031-74426-6_4

socioeconomic class and financial subsidies. This chapter addresses those gaps in the literature. This chapter begins with a discussion of EAT and its significance in promoting the therapeutic process. A short review of the populations most closely aligned with EAT interventions and the theoretical frameworks that are used to guide the therapeutic process are presented. This chapter then focuses on the perceptions and impact of EAT on treatment providers, the experience of providing equine workshops to mental health professionals, and the clinical and professional implications that EAT has for therapists. Finally, this chapter discusses some of the limitations entailed in equine-assisted interventions.

Equine-Assisted Therapy (EAT)

Equine-assisted therapy, also referred to as equine-assisted psychotherapy, has received growing attention in the literature (Frederick, 2019; Gehtmane-Hofmane, 2019). Equine-assisted therapy (EAT) engages horses as an integral component of the therapeutic process. It is described as an alternative or a complementary approach to traditional talk therapy, is experiential in nature, and focuses on emotional growth and learning through experience and action.

Within the overriding term of equine-assisted therapy, a number of additional terms can be found in the literature including equine-assisted mental health, equine-assisted counseling, and equine-assisted services (Hallberg, 2018). Two more specific names have been documented in the literature: equine-assisted psychotherapy (EAP) and equine-assisted social work (EASW) (Bachi, 2013b; Rambo, 2016; Carlsson et al. 2014). Equine-assisted psychotherapy (EAP) is defined as "a form of animal-assisted therapy that employs horses in and around the natural surroundings of the stables used to treat human psychological problem" (Bachi, 2013b, p. 187). Carlsson et al. (2014) define equine-assisted social work (EASW) as "an alternative or supplement to conventional treatment and social work and involves a triangular relationship between staff, client and horse" (p. 21).

While differences among the terms and approaches exist, common to EAT, EAP, and equine-assisted social work (EASW) is the incorporation of horses into the therapeutic setting with a trained mental health expert. In some models, a mental health expert and an equine specialist work together as a team. The approaches recognize that the horse is quintessential to differentiating this form of therapy from other experiential therapies. In other words, this form of therapy cannot be conducted without horses (EAGALA, 2006).

As an experiential approach to treatment, EAT invites action and immersion in the therapeutic process and entails movement, response, problem-solving, inquiry, and reflection (Bilginoglu, 2021; Thomas & Lytle, 2016). It takes place outside of the traditional clinical office setting, most often at an equestrian/riding center, a horse ranch or farm, and centers around horse-related activity. Working with horses challenges clients to remain focused and "present" when engaging with the horses. The horses' feedback, combined with a reflective process, facilitated by the EAT therapist, provides opportunities for the client to try or do something to elicit desired responses from the horses. These may then benefit real-life situations as they unfold outside of the arena.

Why EAT?

There is overwhelming support in the literature for the fact that horses can be agents of therapeutic change. A plethora of studies have identified the impact of the human–horse relationship in promoting the therapeutic process. As described below, researchers and service providers engaged in EAT suggest five predominant themes that characterize the unique contribution of the horses to the therapeutic process as it impacts on both clients and the therapeutic team.

Relationship and Connection

Bailey and Bailey (2019) and Bachi et al. (2012) address the horses' unique ability to elicit a range of emotional responses in the client. Emotional responses are prompted through observation, touching, and grooming and walking side by side with the horses at eye level. These interactions provide opportunities for what Bachi et al. (2012) refer to as deep emotional connections that support meaningful relationships between the horses and humans. This bond and the range of emotions that it stimulates can contribute to the client's interpersonal skills as well as the therapeutic alliance. Some suggest that in the presence of horses, individuals experience a boost in oxytocin. Oxytocin is referred to as (Hallberg, 2017) the "love" hormone (https://www.health.harvard.edu/mind-and-mood/oxytocin-the-love-hormone), a hormone that facilitates feelings of trust and attachment (https://my.clevelandclinic.org/health/articles/22618-oxytocin).

Horses have an innate ability to read their environment. They are prey animals, and this has protected them from danger and enabled their survival. In the context of the human–horse interaction, horses use this innate ability to read verbal and nonverbal messages (Thomas & Lytle, 2016). As herd animals, horses are especially aware of social bonding (Brandt, 2013). Buck et al. (2017) suggest that "observing equine behaviors provides humans the opportunity to think differently about the value of connectedness, especially in times of stress, anger and fear as they process these emotions while interacting with the herd" (p. 390). As connection with the horses deepens, additional opportunities arise to address issues such as trust, boundaries, self-concept, assertiveness, and more (Masini, 2010).

The Horse–Human Relationship as a Metaphor for Client Realities

Lac (2017) suggests that the horse–human interaction helps clients move from an intrapersonal focus to an interpersonal domain and as such to identify metaphors for problematic and unresolved human relationships. Kakacek and Ottens (2008) note that clients oftentimes label or interpret horses' behavior in ways analogous to the presenting problems that brought them to therapy. The dynamics of horse interactions in the herd can mirror human interaction that clients themselves experience in their own lives. Clients might observe horse exchanges that resemble friendship, rejection, courting, fighting, hierarchy, and more. These provide opportunities to address these topics as they relate to client interactions and relationships (Bachi et al., 2012).

Gaining a horse's cooperation requires congruence between one's inner thoughts and feelings and what one conveys through body posture and voice. When such congruence exists, the horse is likely to respond to human directives. When these are incongruent, the horse is more likely to disregard what is that the human wants from him. Experiencing this in "real time" provides opportunities for the client to explore the link between his inner thoughts and emotions and how these are conveyed. He can then experiment with new strategies to ensure greater alignment between the two (Carlsson, 2016) so as to receive the kind of interaction that he is seeking.

As Brandt (2013) notes, clients will often relate to the horses in a manner that reflects their own relational experiences. For example, a client may exhibit overly affectionate or, alternatively, aggressive behavior with the horse. In either of these situations, the horse will ultimately disengage, establishing a clear boundary between himself and the client. Using this "here and now" experience, the therapist can engage the client in performing a structured task with the horse that focuses on methods of relating, boundaries, and recognition of the experience of the other. These can then be extrapolated to the client's interactions outside of the arena. The horse, then, can "serve as a powerful means of transference learning" (Bennett & Woodman, 2019, p. 1047).

Thomas and Lytle (2016) maintain that anything that occurs in the arena has a parallel in life. As such, everything that is present in the arena can potentially become a metaphor that the client can explore through his or her interpretation of each representation. Moreover, the experience in the arena invites clients to experiment with new behaviors that may ultimately enhance clients' abilities to be their best selves (Buultjens et al., 2015).

Contributions to the Therapeutic Alliance

Stapleton and Grimmett (2021) suggest that equine-assisted intervention reduces reliance on verbal communication and in general lends to less intrusive interactions between the therapist and the client. The bulk of the work in EAT is conducted between the client and the horses. Much of the discourse in the arena focuses on what is happening with the horses, and hence the discomfort that oftentimes accompanies the discourse about the self is mitigated. Similarly, processes of transference are limited as the horses occupy the space between the therapist and the client. Scopa et al. (2019) note that the presence of the horses in the therapeutic setting serves as a "social lubricant" (p. 9) fostering the connection between the client and the therapist.

The therapeutic alliance is recognized as one of the most important factors in the psychotherapeutic process (Bachi & Parish-Plass, 2017). Even in an optimal therapeutic alliance, the client may lack some ability or willingness to work with the therapist. Winnicott (1968, in Oren & Parish-Plass, 2013) suggested that in such cases, establishing a neutral area between the therapist and the client that "unites [us] but which at the same time keeps us safely apart, because it does not involve direct exchange between us" (Oren & Parish-Plass, 2013; p. 10) can facilitate a process of sharing ideas, opinions, and feelings. This neutral or "third thing is outside of the therapist-client relationship and can be looked at and observed by both, because it does not belong to, or come from inside of, either" (p.10). Rather, it serves as a bridge for communication between the two.

In equine-assisted therapy, the horse becomes the "third thing"—the neutral area external to the therapist–client relationship that can be observed by both and can serve as a bridge of communication between the two, especially when it is difficult for the client to communicate an inner experience. Research has shown that in addition to the physiological benefits of the human–animal relationship, the presence of an animal can contribute to the client's sense of safety and trust (Bachi et al., 2012). As Oren and Parish-Plass (2013) note, this is "likely to lead to an increase in the client's emotional ability for the therapy process to occur and also in his or her ability to deal with anxiety-producing content" (p. 19).

Creation of a Holding Environment

Notions of a holding space and safe space were fundamental to Winnicott's (1965) psychoanalytical work, where he focused on the concept of a "holding environment" within the context of the parent–infant relationship. This was later adapted by and incorporated into experiential learning theories aligned with EAT (Moshe-Grodofsky & Allassad Alhouzail, 2021). Within a holding environment, the client can experience a secure base that makes self-exploration possible. Bachi (2013a, b) suggests that the horse–human relationship creates a range of opportunities "for the provision of a secure base and a haven of safety through a holding environment" (p. 190). Trust and rapport can flourish in such a context, and as Bachi (2013a, b) and later Mandrell (2014) note, the ability of the horses to accept the client as is, in a nonjudgmental manner, reinforces a sense of holding, critical to enabling the client to become more open to self-discovery and revealing himself to himself. It is within such an environment that change and growth can occur. Within this space, Scopa et al. (2019) contend that the horse represents the "catalyst of the healing process" (p. 12). Through both physical and emotional interplay, the client and horse come to interact as a joint holding ground, promoting cognitive, emotional, and social development (Notgrass & Pettinelli, 2015).

Support for the Therapeutic Team

In any psychotherapeutic intervention, the therapeutic process may include periods in which the therapist experiences an impasse and a sense of helplessness (Oren & Parish-Plass, 2013). As an integral part of the therapeutic team, the horse offers the therapist and the therapeutic process additional opportunities to breakthrough such impasses. Carlsson et al. (2014) suggest that the client–therapist interaction in the horse farm is quite different from that which develops in a traditional clinical setting. They note that "the relationship between the staff and the clients in the presence of the horse was less strict and based more on mutual respect" (p. 28). This can lead to a more collaborative effort. Moreover, observing the horses provides the therapeutic team with important information regarding both verbal and nonverbal human messages. By observing the horse behavior, the team can gain insight into what the client is experiencing.

Taken together, the abovementioned themes provide a framework to articulate the significance of EAT for the therapeutic process. Lee and Makela (2015) sum it up in their work by noting that the horses promote positive change in therapy simply by being present with their natural characteristics. The opportunities that they present to practice new skills and to assist in identifying and accessing one's own inner abilities for healing are critical in mending intrapersonal distress, social relationships, and behavioral dysfunction. The range of populations that have been treated within the EAT context suggests that it is an approach to therapy that can be easily transferred and adapted to meet the needs of diverse populations throughout the various stages of the life cycle as well as amidst the range of situations that humans encounter throughout their lives.

Who Benefits? Populations Served by EAT and Theoretical Frameworks That Guide EAT Intervention

Equine-assisted therapeutic interventions are expanding and have been adapted for and used with a wide variety of populations (Boyd, 2013; EAGALA, 2012; Hayes, 2015; Notgrass & Pettinelli, 2015). According to Hallberg (2017), over 50 countries around the world provide equine-assisted therapy; EAT has been provided to individuals with mental illness (Corring et al., 2013), psychiatric patients (Nathans-Barel et al., 2005), adults including war veterans with PTSD (Earles et al., 2015; Arnon et al., 2019), at-risk children and youth (Bachi & Parish-Plass, 2017; Boshoff et al., 2015; Burgon, 2011), youth with PTSD (Mueller & McCullough, 2017), children and young adults with autism (Bass et al., 2009), Indigenous peoples (Bennett & Woodman, 2019), prison inmates (Bachi, 2013b, 2014), patients with substance-abuse disorders (Kern-Godal et al., 2016), and people with dementia (Dabelko-Schoeny et al., 2014).

The theoretical frameworks and the clinical approaches that guide EAT intervention are also quite varied. While it is beyond the scope of this chapter to address the breadth and depth of the theoretical approaches and models that have accompanied EAT with these populations, a short synopsis of some of the overarching theories is in order. Burgon et al. (2017) suggest that person-centered and relationship-based approaches have been at the forefront of the field of EAT. Others have highlighted the relevance of attachment theory as a basis to support the benefits of the horse–human relationship, noting that the presence of horses is significant in advancing the ability of the client to create relationships as they evoke client feeling, thoughts, and behaviors (Bachi, 2013a; Vincent & Farkas, 2017; Zilcha-Mano et al., 2012). Psychodynamic therapy (Parish-Plass, 2013), intersubjectivity (Parish-Plass & Oren, 2013), Rogerian theory and person-centered approaches (Chardonnens, 2009), and eye movement desensitization and reprocessing (EMDR), and mindfulness practice (Burgon et al., 2017) have also been associated with the psychosocial benefits of EAT for a variety of client populations.

Family and Group Interventions

The bulk of existing literature on EAT has focused on treatment with individual clients. Some studies, however, have explored EAT in family and group settings. For example, Romaniuk et al. (2018) conducted EAT group interventions with individual veterans as well as with veterans and their partners. They found that participants in both programs showed significantly higher levels of happiness and quality of life and significantly fewer psychological symptoms following group treatment. However, only the participants in the couple EAT group intervention continued to show reduced psychological symptoms at the three-month program follow-up. Willmund et al. (2020) studied equine-assisted psychotherapy treatment with soldiers and their partners who experienced severe relationship problems. Study results showed significant improvement in communication and partnership quality for the program participants (Willmund et al., 2020).

Steele et al. (2018) studied a treatment program for soldiers and veterans who experienced combat trauma. Equine-assisted psychotherapy was one component of the overall treatment program. Program outcomes showed significant improvement in psychological symptoms; however, the study was unable to determine the specific level of contribution of the equine therapy to these results. Nevertheless, the authors suggested that "the equine element of treatment may help to establish safety, and development of trust, self-esteem and increased self-efficacy" (p. 405).

Equine-assisted group therapy has been found to be effective with additional populations, including adolescents (Carlsson et al., 2014) and women survivors of interpersonal violence (Porter-Wenzlaff, 2007; Schroeder et al., 2018). In their qualitative study of women survivors of interpersonal violence, the authors identified cognitive, affective, and behavioral benefits of equine-assisted group therapy among the study participants. These included increased insight and self-awareness, emotional validation, instillation of hope, sharing needs, and altruistic experiences. Carlsson et al. (2014) conducted semi-structured interviews with adolescents who participated in equine-assisted group therapy. They reported that the experiences with the horses made the clients more aware of their own emotions, intentions, and attitudes. Clients spoke of experiencing a greater sense of calm, feelings of trust and respect, and an ability to share their authentic selves.

Treatment Providers' Perceptions and AAT and EAT Impact and Implementation

Despite advancements in research and practice in the field of animal-assisted interventions, few studies have focused on the perceptions and impact of animal-assisted therapy (AAT) in general, or of equine-assisted therapy (EAT) on treatment providers. Research points to the fact that studies that seek to identify the contribution of AAT and EAT to the treatment goals usually lack the methodological rigor necessary to evaluate the therapeutic effectiveness of AAT and EAT. This includes using standardized (replicable) treatment protocols, ample sample sizes, consistent validated measures, and comparison groups (Flynn et al., 2020; Stewart et al., 2013). Lack of methodological rigor makes it difficult to conclude that AAT and EAT are actually effective.

An additional limitation relates to mental health providers' understanding and misconceptions about what AAT actually is, with some believing that it is merely a matter of bringing an animal into the therapy session (Bachi & Parish-Plass, 2017; Flynn et al., 2020). This misunderstanding may limit the ability of mental health providers to recognize how the human–animal bond can create unique opportunities to explore emotion and relational issues and hence contribute to the therapeutic process (Flynn et al., 2020). Furthermore, Hediger and Hund-Georgiadis (2017) note the lack of long-term data that focuses on changes in mental health provider perspectives over time as well as the concerns that they share about animal-assisted interventions.

Despite these limitations, mental health providers who incorporate AAT and EAT into their clinical practice are uniquely situated to address the human–animal interaction in the therapeutic process. Current studies, both quantitative and qualitative, focus on mental health providers' perceptions of AAT and mental health providers' perceptions of EAT and EAT implementation and their impact on the therapeutic process (Bachi & Parish-Plass, 2017; Berget et al., 2013; Buultjens et al., 2015; Flynn et al., 2020; Hediger & Hund-Georgiadis, 2017; Stewart et al., 2013). These will be elaborated upon in the following sections.

Mental Health Providers' Perceptions of AAT

Flynn et al. (2020) used a phenomenological approach to assess how mental health providers regarded AAT as a complementary approach to traditional psychotherapy with youth experiencing complex psychosocial health challenges. Study results revealed five themes that addressed clinicians' perceptions of the contribution of AAT as a complementary approach with these youth: (1) opportunities for contribution, (2) sense of safety, (3) self-regulation, (4) engagement, and (5) facilitating relationships. Each of the themes included subthemes that provide an in-depth account of how the clinicians perceived the impact of the animal–human bond to the therapeutic process. For example, the theme *opportunities for contribution* addressed the clinicians' sense that incorporating animals into the therapeutic process provided the youth with a sense that they were doing something important as they engaged in nurturing and caring actions toward the animals. This was then translated to what the clinicians identified as a sense of self-efficacy and competence among the youth, an experience of equity with the therapist and other adults and an increase in a sense of self-worth. The second theme, *sense of safety*, also included two subthemes expressed through a safe environment and a less stressful therapy environment. Clinicians noted that the youth appeared to feel safe in their relationships with the animals and that the farm itself became a haven for the youth in times of crisis. Moreover, the safety that the youth experienced with the animals contributed to their experience of the farm as a relaxed environment and hence led to a less stressful therapeutic encounter.

Clinicians noted that the interaction with the animals enhanced the youths' ability to self-regulate the third theme. This *self-regulation* was expressed through what the clinicians identified as reduced hypervigilance and anxiety. The clinicians also noted youths' heightened self-awareness of their internal state. The fourth theme, addressing the clinicians' perspectives that the animal–human interaction enhanced youth *engagement*, was illustrated through greater cooperation. Finally, the fifth theme addressed the notion of *facilitating relationships*. Here, the clinicians noted that the work with the animals presented "more opportunities to build rapport and use positive reinforcement when working towards treatment goals" (p. 637). Facilitating relationships was expressed through the building of interpersonal skills and improved boundaries and communication skills.

In an earlier study, Stewart et al. (2013) interviewed 14 mental health professionals who reported using AAT in clinical settings to gain an understanding of how clinicians perceived AAT as a therapeutic intervention. Four overarching themes impacting the utilization of AAT were identified: (a) AAT implementation requires a unique set of skills and competencies, (b) treatment providers incorporate a highly developed working relationship with the therapeutic animal, (c) AAT has an impact on the therapeutic process, and (d) the traditional professional–client relationship is enhanced by AAT. The overall findings of the study were that mental health providers recognized that the incorporation of AAT as a meaningful approach to the therapeutic process requires appropriate training to ensure that practitioners implement and interpret the animal–human relationship in a manner that is therapeutically meaningful.

In a study conducted in Norway among 400 psychiatrists, 300 psychologists, and 400 general practitioners, the majority of whom *had no*t practiced AAT, a total of 89% of the participants in the study deemed that animal-assisted interventions (AAIs) should be more widely used in psychiatric treatment and expressed motivation to learn more and adapt it to their own therapeutic work (Berget et al., 2013). An earlier study of 60 Norwegian therapists employed in psychiatric departments and municipal health services also reported positive attitudes among study participants regarding the engagement of farm animals in the therapeutic setting (Berget et al., 2008).

In their study of healthcare staff members in a rehabilitation clinic in Basel, Hediger and Hund-Georgiadis (2017) reported that staff members shared overall positive attitudes toward animal-assisted therapy. The authors noted that most negative attitudes about the approach that had been held prior to actual experience nearly disappeared after the staff engaged in animal-assisted therapy. In other words, their actual experiences were more positive than their expectations. They attributed this finding to what researchers have pointed to as the lack of a clear picture of what AAT involves (Bachi & Parish-Plass, 2017; Flynn et al., 2020).

Legge (2016) researched the role of animal-assisted intervention (AAI) in anti-oppressive social work practice. She identified three themes and corresponding subthemes to support the notion that social work practitioners identified congruency between AAI and anti-oppressive social work practice. The first theme addressed the *theoretical parallels between AAI and anti-oppressive practice*. Study participants noted that service users, some of whom lacked shelter and had experienced oppression in their own lives, had rescued animals in similar situations. Similarly, they reported that service users were able to relay their stories more easily when an animal was present to provide support. Moreover, social workers who participated in the study suggested that AAI was useful in challenging "dominant discourses and problematic social constructions of oppressed people…." (p. 7), noting that service users who live in poverty and maintain the company of an animal companion have been subject to both personal and institutional oppression. Social workers reported that the animal–human relationship was significant in shifting the professional-service users' power dynamic. For example, one participant noted, "it is basically directed by them, and the horses, and I'm actually in a position where I'm just allowing it to unfold, so there's a real letting go. And there is no controlling it" (p. 7).

Legge's second theme related to *barriers and benefits*. In general, the benefits of the animals in the therapeutic process were seen to outweigh the barriers. Among the barriers reported were fear and allergies. Among the benefits noted was the experiential nature of AAI and hence its unique results. In addition, social work participants recognized that the animal–human relationship is nonjudgmental and therefore lends to a type of "anti-oppressive interaction" (p. 8), or a more level playing field. In such cases, the social workers noted that this made it easier to establish rapport with service users and helped them refrain from more judgmental interactions. Moreover, the social workers noted that the animal–human interaction enabled service users to make positive changes in their lives.

The final theme that emerged was the *novelty* of animal-assisted practice with the field of anti-oppressive social work. On the one hand, Legge (2016) noted that both social workers and service users alike were unaware of the possibility of incorporating AAI into the therapeutic setting. The social workers reported that despite its proven benefits, AAI is less credible than other forms of intervention. They had trouble in receiving referrals from other service providers for this type of therapy. On the other hand, novel aspects of the therapy were also expressed in relation to the therapeutic environment which differed from the conventional clinical context making it easier for service users to seek support in a less stigmatized setting. Study participants reported that the nontraditional environment made it easier to talk in ways that they did not experience in the office setting. Moreover, practitioners noted that since equine-assisted intervention allows them to be less central to the intervention, they had the opportunity to observe more. Finally, study participants noted that the simple fact that the animal was part of the therapeutic relationships offered opportunities for service users' life shifts.

Mental Health Providers' Perceptions of EAT and EAT Implementation

Some studies have focused specifically on mental health service providers' perceptions of the incorporation of horses into the therapeutic process. For example, Johns et al. (2016) interviewed 14 South African therapists, among them, psychologists, social workers, and a registered counsellor, to identify their experiences and perceived benefits of equine-assisted practice. Study participants identified a variety of benefits to EAT as opposed to the traditional talk therapy in an office-bound environment. These included exposure to an outdoor, relaxed context, intervention flexibility, the horses' contribution to the building of trust in the therapeutic relationship, and the instant nonverbal feedback that clients receive from the horses. Clinicians noted that their clients learned that in order to change the horse's behavior, they needed to be aware of and often change their own thoughts, feelings, and behaviors. This proved to be therapeutically valuable as these were then transferred to their relationships outside of the therapeutic experience.

Harbeson (2019) interviewed 19 EAGALA-certified psychotherapists to discern how they perceived the role of projection in EAT and how they use projection in EAT therapy. Study participants identified the role of projection in EAT in three areas: self-awareness, insight into situations, and as practice for new skills. The psychotherapists reported that the project was useful for clinical assessment.

Buultjens et al. (2015) study included Australian equine-assisted psychotherapists working under the EAGALA model and examined their perceptions, views, and experiences of EAP for adolescents. Their findings point to the significance that mental health professionals attribute to the incorporation of horses into the therapeutic setting as well as to the experiential nature of the therapy that enables adolescents to see "the visual representation of things in and about their life" (p. 7). The mental health professionals who participated in the study also referred to the clinical implications of the therapy. Most cited were the improvements in confidence, self-esteem, and assertiveness among the adolescents in their care. They also indicated that the therapy was significant in aiding their clients to achieve greater control of their behavior.

In her study of equine-assisted social work (EASW) and the therapeutic relationship between social work professionals and self-harming youth, Carlsson (2016) found that when horses were incorporated into the therapeutic setting, three types of triads, central to the therapeutic process, emerged. In each of the triads, both the client and the mental health provider described the functions of the horses within the therapeutic relationship. The three triads that were identified were "triads based on trust in the dyad between the staff member and client-indirect relation to the horse"; "triads based on trust in double dyads between the staff member and client as well as between the client and horse"; and "triads based on trust in the dyad between the client and horse—necessary to form a relationship between the staff member and client" (p.5). According to the author, the three types of triads were found to be qualitatively different in regard to the notion of attachment, an issue that is oftentimes at the heart of self-harming behaviors (Ashrafi et al., 2021; Wingenfeld et al., 2011). Unpacking the different types of triads and their roles in the therapeutic setting can assist therapists in developing more precise types of interaction and in understanding how each of the triads works independently and yet are interwoven.

For example, in regard to the first triad, while the role of the horses was indirectly related to the staff–client relationships, the staff perceived of them as an entity that assisted in reducing performance anxiety, reducing problems in the staff–client relationship. In the second triad, staff members reported feeling calmer and more stable when in cooperation with the horses. Moreover, staff reported that equine-assisted social work (EASW) added a strong dimension of emotional connection to the client–staff relationship. Finally, in the third triad, the horse provided a linking function. Staff reported greater attunement to clients' nonverbal cues. Through the linking function of the horse, staff reported that their impressions of the client changed. They viewed clients as more empathetic, related to them with greater respect and noted that "first impressions should not determine a relationship" (p. 7).

Carlsson's study (2016) came on the heels of an earlier study of EASW with self-harming adolescents focused on the functioning of both service providers and clients with the horses (Carlsson et al., 2015). Four themes that emerged from the research illustrate service provider functions: *doing and performing with the horse as an object, being and feeling with the horse as an object, doing and performing with the horse as a subject and being and feeling with the horse as a subject* (pp. 333–334). When the equine-assisted session focused on *doing and performing with the horse as an object,* the client–staff relationship was characterized by less interpersonal communication. The absence of communication about emotions and the fact that the horse was seen as an object limited the horse's ability to serve as a mirror for the client's emotions, ultimately limiting the impact of EASW. In the second theme that emerged from the study, *being and feeling with the horse as an object*, staff members addressed the client's emotions however were oblivious to the emotions expressed by the horses. Here, the full potential of EASW was left unmet in that opportunities to observe and relate to the emotions of another, in this case the horses were left untapped. The third theme, *doing and performing with the horse as a subject,* summarized the work that the staff conducted jointly with the clients to communicate both on the horse's emotions and behaviors as well as on how the horse was able to learn about the client's emotions and behaviors. The staff encouraged clients to be attentive to the horses, encouraging them to look into the horse's eyes in order to understand what he might be feeling. Actions to assist the horse were encouraged to assist the clients to develop empathy for the horses. Finally, the fourth theme, *being and feeling with the horse as a subject*, focused on the horse's emotions and on expressions of empathy. Staff offered meaning for the horse's behavior assisting clients to view them as subjects within their relationship. They invited the clients to inquire about what the horse might be experiencing.

The research points to the fact that AAT and EAT are gaining ground among mental health professionals. While there is a good deal of anecdotal support for this unique type of intervention (Lanning & Krenek, 2013), and while qualitative studies have shown evidence of mental health practitioner support, there is still a need for research that can provide evidence as to both the short-term and long-term benefits of this form of intervention (Diaz et al., 2022). Moreover, the expanding interest in EAT interventions among mental health professionals requires appropriate training opportunities.

EAT Workshops and Mental Health Professionals

Incorporating horses into the therapeutic setting with a wide variety of populations through activities that involve horsemanship skills focused on handling and riding the horse is well known. The benefits of this type of use of horses in therapeutic setting have been documented extensively (Corring et al., 2013; Lanning et al., 2017). Less well known than this type of horse–human interaction are those activities with horses that are ground-based and that do not include horse mounting or handling skills. Here, all of the activity that is conducted with horses is done from the ground.

Ground-based activity encourages eye-to-eye contact and human–horse relationship building on equal terrain. In ground-based human–horse interaction, the client cannot direct the horse through the equipment used while on the horse's back, such as the reins, a mouthpiece, and the saddle, but rather must enlist other types of resources in order to gain the horse's cooperation. As noted earlier, these resources are more often, than not, internal resources and their expression in the horse–human interaction becomes the focus of the EAT intervention (Buck et al., 2017).

As a new field, EAT is still in the process of developing a comprehensive theoretical framework. Equine-assisted therapy training programs for mental health professionals are available in countries around the world; among them are the United States, England, Ireland, South Africa, and Australia. Some of the programs are university-based, some are part of animal-assisted therapy institutes, and finally, others are based in nonprofit organizations. Acri et al. (2016) identified seven programs that offer a structured certification program for equine-assisted training. The authors detail eligibility requirements for enrollment, program requirements and programmatic components for credit, type of certification, level of horse experience required, and program costs. Brandt (2013) identified four central US-based organizations, some of which are international, that provide training and certification for mental health professions.

Among the EAT programs that focus on ground-based EAT activity and that provide training for mental health professionals is the Equine Assisted Growth and Learning Association (EAGALA) model. The Association has over 4500 members in 50 countries around the world and is recognized as the leading equine-assisted psychotherapeutic model. A more recent development that has emerged in regard to EAT workshops and mental health professional training and that is an outgrowth of the EAGALA model is the Arenas for Change (ARCH) framework (www.arenasforchange.com). The framework and training are offered to mental health professionals and like the EAGALA model are based in experiential practice and learning. The ARCH approach also adopts a narrative theoretical approach encouraging clients to tell their stories through the work with the horses and the equipment available in the EAT arena.

Equine Workshops and Social Work Professionals

Within the social work literature, there has been a significant growth in work that focuses on equine-assisted activity (Buck et al., 2017; Mandrell, 2006; Smith-Osborne & Selby, 2010; Cody et al., 2011; Carlsson et al., 2015; Carlsson, 2016; Burgon et al., 2017; Moshe-Grodofsky & Allassad Alhouzail, 2021). Within this body of literature, one can find work that focuses on the value of EAT for social work clients (Carlsson, 2016) and the importance of the EAT intervention as a complementary form of social work practice (Smith-Osborne & Selby, 2010). Carlsson et al (2015) coined the term equine-assisted social work (EASW) as an alternative or supplemental form of conventional social work treatment. The authors refer to EASW as activities that "involve care of the horse, training with the horse, riding, carriage driving, and vaulting" (p.21) and note that EASW differs from other equine-assisted interventions in that it is not based upon a program or manual but rather will depend upon the staff involved, the client, and the horse.

EAT, EASW, and, in particular, the EAGALA model and social work are a good fit. They are based on common theoretical frameworks. They share a strengths-based approach. The EAGALA model and social work integrate post-modern standpoints, and both are guided by specific ethical codes (Moshe-Grodofsky & Allassad Alhouzail, 2021). However, despite growing interest within the social work profession in equine-assisted activity, few studies have explored the experiences of social workers who either have participated in equine-assisted workshops or, alternatively, have reported on their experience when employing EAT.

Moshe-Grodofsky and Allassad Alhouzail (2021) interviewed 14 Bedouin Arab social workers in Israel who participated in a three-day equine workshop based upon the EAGALA model. The workshop was designed to assist the social work participants to overcome obstacles that were hindering their professional performance. Study findings identified three themes that embodied participant experience. The notion of space was central to each of the themes as was expressed as a space to "meet" myself, the significance of maintaining space in relationships, and in particular in relationships with clients and space as a location for teamwork (Moshe-Grodofsky & Allassad Alhouzail, 2021). The significance of equine-assisted interventions as reported by the professionals who participated in the workshop suggests that this may be a unique method to promote professional growth and learning among social workers.

One additional study conducted with social work professionals explored the cognitive activities and strategies employed by eight mental health practitioners in therapeutic setting with horses (Lee & Makela, 2018). The researchers identified two themes and eight subthemes that the social work practitioners who participated in the study discussed. The first theme addressed the concrete strategies that the social work professionals used in order to meet the clients' needs and included two subthemes. The first focused on choosing an appropriate setting to hold the client–therapist–horse interaction. This could mean determining whether to use a round pen or a larger arena or a pasture for example. A second subtheme centered on the choice of horses for therapy sessions. The social workers described the importance of incorporating specific horses in order to provide different levels of challenge for the clients. This could be addressed by including horses of different sizes and personalities into the therapeutic process. A second theme that arose from the interviews with the social workers focused on how the participants used themselves in order to apply cognitive thoughts or ideas into the therapeutic process. This theme was defined in six subthemes. The first subtheme addressed the notion of synchronicities and the fact that the mental health professional must be aware of these as they occur in the therapeutic process. Synchronicities occur in psychotherapy and refer to "a meaningful coincidence unexplained by causality-based science" (Lee & Makela, 2018, p. 126). Synchronicities can be quite common in EAT, and the ability of the mental health professional to notice these can then be used to advance the therapeutic process. Social work professionals also addressed the importance of adaptation in the equine-assisted process in order to ensure that if it would meet the needs of the individual client. In addition, a third subtheme that they discussed referred to the amount of structure that was needed for the sessions. Different levels of structure were recommended depending upon the client's age, functional level, and the level of rapport that the client had developed with the therapist. Managing risk was also determined to be influential for the therapeutic process and was determined in line with the unique characteristics of the client. The two final subthemes addressed the importance of aiding the client to observe the horses' behavior and to interpret and reinterpret the meaning of their behaviors in an objective manner and asking important questions to challenge the client.

The increasing focus of the social work profession on the field of EAT suggests that the profession has expanded its view of the importance of EAT to those clients often served by social work professionals. The ability of the profession to identify the parallels between the values and goals of the profession and those of EAT means that we may see an increase in the number of professionals that are joining the EAT field and incorporating it into their clinical practice. The same case can be made for additional mental health professionals as well.

Clinical and Professional Implications for EAT Providers

The benefits of EAT as a form of therapy for a wide variety of populations have been documented (Kemp et al., 2013; Lac, 2017; Nurenberg et al., 2014; Townsend & Hood, 2019). As the field has grown and the research in its outcomes recorded (Bachi & Parish-Plass, 2017; Berget et al., 2013; Buultjens et al., 2015; Flynn et al., 2020; Hediger & Hund-Georgiadis, 2017; Stewart et al., 2013), new questions arise as to what it will take to ensure that EAT standards for practice are being developed for mental health professionals and that EAT is in fact accessible to a wide variety of populations. Furthermore, the need for greater evidence-based research in the field of EAT is evident (Fine & Anderson, 2021).

Ensuring EAT training and practice standards will require the development of standards that monitor the field and ensure professional competency (Fine et al., 2019) as well as the development of an agreed among curriculum that can be supported by mental health professional associations. These will ultimately elevate the field and develop its credibility (Fine & Anderson, 2021). Furthermore, once developed, the curriculum will need to be offered by institutions and meet licensing requirements.

Moreover, if EAT is to move from the mental health field periphery to mainstream service, it will need to be made more accessible. Currently, there are a number of obstacles preventing this goal. EAT is often expensive. It is defined by a team approach requiring payment for both a mental health practitioner and an equine specialist together with providing for the cost of the horses. In some countries, some forms of EAT, such as EAT based on groundwork only, are not yet recognized by healthcare insurance, the social service system, or private insurance. As such, the client is left to bear the brunt of the cost or such programs must rely on philanthropic support or consistently participate in fund-raising. Ballard et al. (2020) note that insurance companies have both historically and currently neglected to cover equine-assisted interventions and "without coverage, the cost of participating…is a financial barrier to accessing the intervention" (p. 657). Furthermore, while insurance will cover the costs for traditional psychotherapy, EAT costs are often higher than typical psychotherapy costs making this type of intervention less accessible to individuals and families who do not have the economic means to pay for it.

EAT requires a particular setting. Oftentimes, horse farms or ranches are in areas that are inaccessible to clients who are dependent upon public transportation and are hence unable to reach the EAT setting. Finally, EAT requires a setting that is conducive to changing weather seasons. This may require an indoor arena during the rain or snow seasons, a shaded round pen for the summer, heat in the winter, and more. These can be costly for a farm or ranch yet are absolutely necessary to ensure that EAT is available year-round.

The unique contributions of EAT as a form of psychotherapy that qualitatively differs from the traditional clinical setting has yet to be recognized. Among the existing horseback riding and boarding facilities, EAT is simply viewed as one additional avenue to generate revenue and not as a unique stand-alone form of therapy.

Conclusion

EAT is an expanding field within the larger arena of mental health services. While the documentation of the horse–human interaction only began officially in the 1950s, the role of horses and their importance to humans is historically much older (Nelson et al., 2016; Fine & Anderson, 2021). More recently, the role that horses can play in assisting humans to cope with the circumstances that arise throughout the different stages of the lifespan has been the focus of mental health research, theory, and practice (Fine & Anderson, 2021).

This chapter has aimed at presenting an overview of the development of EAT and the rationale beyond this type of therapy. In addition, this chapter has identified some of the challenges that continue to face EAT as professionals and clinicians forge their way in the field.

References

Acri, M., Hoagwood, K., Morrissey, M., & Zhang, S. (2016). Equine-assisted activities and therapies: Enhancing the social worker's armamentarium. *Social Work Education, 35*(5), 603–612.

Arenas for Change (ARCH). https://arenasforchange.com

Arnon, S., Fisher, P. W., Pickover, A., Lowell, A., Turner, J. B., Hilburn, A., Jacob-McVey, J., Malajian, B. E., Farber, D. J., Hamilton, J. F., Hamilton, A., Markowitz, J. C., & Neria, Y. (2019). Equine-assisted therapy for veterans with PTSD: Manual development and preliminary findings. *Military Medicine, 00*(0/0), 1. 1–8.

Ashrafi, E., Karami, J., & Nasori, M. (2021). The mediating role of difficulties in emotion regulation in the correlation between attachment styles and childhood trauma with self-harming behaviors in adolescents. *Journal of Kermanshah University of Medical Sciences, 25*(4), e119094. https://doi.org/10.5812/jkums.119094

Bachi, K. (2013a). Application of attachment theory to equine-facilitated psychotherapy. *Journal of Contemporary Psychotherapy, 43*, 187–196. https://doi.org/10.1007/s10879-013-9232-1

Bachi, K. (2013b). Equine-facilitated psychotherapy: Practice, theory and empirical knowledge. In N. Parish-Plass (Ed.), *Animal-assisted psychotherapy: Theory, issues and practice* (pp. 221–244). Purdue University.

Bachi, K. (2014). *An equine-facilitate prison-based program: Human –horse relations and effects on inmate emotions and behaviors*. City University of New York ProQuest Dissertations Publishing. 3615012.

Bachi, K., & Parish-Plass, N. (2017). Animal-assisted psychotherapy: A unique relational therapy for children and adolescents. *Clinical Child Psychology and Psychiatry, 22*(1), 3–8. https://doi.org/10.1177/1357104516672549

Bachi, K., Terkel, J., & Teichman, M. (2012). Equine-facilitated psychotherapy for at-risk adolescents: The influence on self-image, self- control and trust. *Clinical Child Psychology and Psychiatry, 17*(2), 298–312. https://doi.org/10.1177/1359104511404177

Bailey, R. F., & Bailey, E. (2019). The transitioning families equine-assisted model for the treatment of anxiety. In K. Sudekum Trotter & J. N. Baggerly (Eds.), *Equine-assisted mental health interventions: Harnessing solutions to common problems*. Routledge.

Ballard, I., Vincent, A., & Collins, C. (2020). Equine facilitated psychotherapy with young people: Why insurance coverage matters. *Child and Adolescent Social Work Journal, 37*, 657–663. https://doi.org/10.1007/s10560-020-00712-1

Bass, M. M., Duchowny, C. A., & Llabre, M. M. (2009). The effect of therapeutic horseback riding on social functioning of children with autism. *Journal of Autism and Developmental Disorders, 39*, 1261–1267. https://doi.org/10.1007/s10803-009-0734-3

Bennett, B., & Woodman, E. (2019). The potential of equine-assisted psychotherapy for treating trauma in Australian Aboriginal Peoples. *British Journal of Social Work, 49*, 1041–1058. https://doi.org/10.1093/bjsw/bcz053

Berget, B., Ekeberg, O., & Braastad, B. O. (2008). Animal-assisted therapy with farm animals for persons coping with psychiatric disorders : effects on self-efficacy, coping ability and quality of life, a randomized controlled trial. *Clinical Practice and Epidemiology*. https://doi.org/10.1186/1745-0179-4-9

Berget, B., Grepperud, S., Aasland, O. G., & Braastad, B. O. (2013). Animal- assisted interventions and psychiatric disorders: Knowledge and attitudes among general practitioners, psychiatrists, and psychologists. *Society and Animals, 21*, 284–293. https://doi.org/10.1163/15685306-12341244

Bilginoglu, E. (2021). Equine-assisted experiential learning on leadership development. *International Journal of Organizational Leadership, 10.*, (Special Issue), 3–16.

Boshoff, C., Grobler, H., & Nienaber, A. (2015). The evaluation of an equine- assisted therapy programme with a group of boys in a youth care facility. *Journal of Psychology in Africa, 25*(1), 86–90. https://doi.org/10.1080/14330237.2015.1007611

Boyd, K. J. (2013). *The language of Equus: Exploring equine-assisted psychotherapy (EAP) using the Equine Assisted Growth and Learning Association (EAGALA) model*. Theses, Dissertations, and Projects. Paper 587. http://scholarworks.smith.edu/theses

Brandt, C. (2013). Equine-facilitated psychotherapy as a complementary treatment intervention. *The Practitioner Scholar: Journal of Counseling and Professional Psychology, 2*, 23–42.

Buck, P. W., Bean, N., & de Marco, K. (2017). Equine-assisted psychotherapy: An emerging trauma-informed intervention. *Advances in Social Work, 18*(1), 387–402. https://doi.org/10.18060/21310

Burgon, H. L. (2011). 'Queen of the world': Experiences of 'at-risk' young people participating in equine-assisted learning/therapy. *Journal of Social Work Practice, 25*(02), 165–183. https://doi.org/10.1080/02650533/2011.561304

Burgon, H. L., Gammage, D., & Hebden, J. (2017). Hoofbeats and heartbeats: Equine-assisted learning and therapy with young people with psychosocial issues-theory and practice. *Journal of Social Work Practice, 1*, 3–16. https://doi.org/10.1080/02650533.2017.1300878

Buultjens, M., Monfries, M., & Karimi, L. (2015). Equine-assisted psychotherapy for adolescents experiencing depression and/or anxiety: A therapist's perspective. *Clinical Child Psychiatry and Psychology, 22*, 1–18. https://doi.org/10.1177/1359104515572379

Carlsson, C. (2016). Triads in equine-assisted social work enhance therapeutic relationships with self-harming adolescents. *Clinical Social Work Journal, 45*, 320. https://doi.org/10.1007/s10615-016-0613-2

Carlsson, C., Ranta, D. N., & Traeen, B. (2014). Equine assisted social work as a means for authentic relations between clients and staff. *Human-Animal Interaction Bulletin, 2*(1), 19–38.

Carlsson, C., Ranta, D., & Traeen, B. (2015). Mentalizing and emotional labor facilitate equine-assisted social work with self-harming adults. *Child and Adolescent Social Work Journal, 32*, 329–339. https://doi.org/10.1007/s10560-015-0376-6

Chardonnens, E. (2009). The use of animals as co-therapists on a farm: The child-horse bond in person-centered equine-assisted psychotherapy. *Person Centered and Experiential Psychotherapies, 8*(4), 318–332.

Cody, P., Holleran Steiker, L., & Szymandera, M. L. (2011). Equine therapy: Substance abusers' 'healing through horses'. *Journal of Social Work Practice in the Addictions, 2*, 198–204. https://doi.org/10.1080/1533256X.2011.571189

Corring, D., Lundberg, E., & Rudnick, A. (2013). Therapeutic horseback riding for ACT patients with schizophrenia. *Community Mental Health Journal, 49*, 121–126. https://doi.org/10.1007/s10597-011-9457-y

Dabelko-Schoeny, H., Phillips, G., Darrough, E., DeAnna, S., Jarden, M., Johnson, D., & Lorch, G. (2014). Equine-assisted intervention for people with dementia. *Anthrozoös, 27*(1), 141–155. https://doi.org/10.2752/175303714X13837396326611

Diaz, L., Gormley, M. A., Coleman, A., Sepanski, A., Corley, H., Perez, A., & Litwin, A. H. (2022). Equine-assisted services for individuals with substance use disorders: A scoping review. *Substance Abuse Treatment, Prevention and Policy, 17*, 81. https://doi.org/10.1186/s13011-022-00506-x

Dunlop, K., & Tsantefski, M. (2017). A space of safety: Children's experience of equine-assisted group therapy. *Child and Family Social Work*. https://doi.org/10.1111/cfs.12378

EAGALA. (2006). *Fundamentals of The Eagala Model: Becoming an Eagala certified professional*. EAGALA.

EAGALA. (2012). *Fundamentals of The Eagala Model: Becoming an Eagala certified professional*. EAGALA.

Earles, J. L., Vernon, L. L., & Yetz, J. P. (2015). Brief report: Equine-assisted therapy for posttraumatic stress symptoms. *Journal of Traumatic Stress, 28*, 1–4. https://doi.org/10.1002/jts.21990

Fine, A. H., & Anderson, S. J. (2021). A commentary on the contemporary issues confronting animal assisted and equine assisted interactions. *Journal of Equine Veterinary Science, 100*, 1–7. https://doi.org/10.1016/j.jevs.2021.103436

Fine, A. H., Tedeschi, P., Morris, K. N., & Elvov, E. (2019). Forward thinking: The evolving field of human-animal interactions. In A. H. Fine (Ed.), *Handbook on animal-assisted therapy: Foundations and guidelines for animal-assisted interventions* (5th ed.). Academic Press.

Flynn, E., Gandenberger, J., Mueller, M. K., & Morris, K. N. (2020). Animal- assisted interventions as an adjunct to therapy for youth: Clinician perspectives. *Child and Adolescent Social Work Journal, 37*, 631–642. https://doi.org/10.1007/s10560-020-00695-z

Frederick, K. (2019). An Eagala Model approach to using equine- assisted counseling with teens suffering from depression. In K. Sudekum Trotter & J. N. Baggerly (Eds.), *Equine-assisted mental health interventions: Harnessing solutions to common problems*. Routledge.

Gehtmane-Hofmane, I. (2019). The unique characteristics of the horses for humans learning purposes in equine assisted learning practice. *International Journal of Smart Education and Urban Society, 10*(3), 35–42.

Hallberg, L. (2017). *The clinical practice of equine-assisted therapy: Including horses in human healthcare*. New York: Routledge. First Edition.

Hallberg, L. (2018). *The clinical practice of equine-assisted therapy: Including horses in human healthcare*. Routledge.

Harbeson, L. R. M. (2019). *Psychotherapists perceptions and use of projection in equine-assisted interventions: A phenomenological study*. Northcentral University ProQuest Dissertations Publishing, 13427544.

Hayes, T. (2015). *The power of horses to heal: Riding home*. St. Martin's Griffin.

Hediger, K., & Hund-Georgiadis, M. (2017). Animal-assisted therapy in the view of staff members before and after implementation in a rehabilitation center. *Human-Animal Interaction Bulletin, 5*(2), 61–73.

Johns, L., Bobat, S., & Holder, J. (2016). Therapist experiences of equine-assisted psychotherapy in South Africa: A qualitative study. *Journal of Psychology in Africa*. https://doi.org/10.1080/14330237.2016.1167333

Kakacek, S. L., & Ottens, A. J. (2008). An arena for success: Exploring equine- assisted psychotherapy. *Michigan Journal of Counseling: Research, Theory and Practice, 35*(1), 14–23. https://doi.org/10.22237/mijoc/1217548920

Kemp, M., Signal, T., Botros, H., Taylor, N., & Prentice, K. (2013). Equine facilitated therapy with children and adolescents who have been sexually abused: A program evaluation study. *Journal of Child and Family Studies, 23*, 558–566.

Kern-Godal, A., Brenna, I. H., Arnevik, E. A., & Ravndal, E. (2016). More than just a break from treatment: How substance use disorder patients experience the stable environment in horse-assisted therapy. *Substance Abuse: Research and Treatment, 10*, 99–108. https://doi.org/10.4137/SART.S40475

Lac, V. (2017). Amy's story: An existential-integrative equine-facilitated psychotherapy approach to anorexia nervosa. *Journal of Humanistic Psychology, 57*(3), 301–312.

Lanning, B. A., & Krenek, N. (2013). Examining effects of equine-assisted activities to help combat veterans improve quality of life. *Journal of Rehabilitation Research and Development, 50*, 8.

Lanning, B. A., Wilson, A. L., Krenek, N., & Beaujean, A. A. (2017). Using therapeutic riding as an intervention for combat veterans: An international classification of functioning, disability and health (ICF) approach. *Occupational Therapy in Mental Health, 3*, 259–278. https://doi.org/10.1080/0164212X.2017.1283282

Lee, P. T., & Makela, C. (2015). Horses' roles in equine-assisted psychotherapy: Perspectives of mental health practitioners. *Journal of Psychology and Behavioral Science, 3*(1), 78–95. https://doi.org/10.15640/jpbs.v3n1a9

Lee, P. T., & Makela, C. (2018). Mental health practitioners' strategies in equine-assisted psychotherapy: Implications for social work. *Social Work Education, 37*(1), 119–135.

Legge, M. M. (2016). The role of animal-assisted interventions in anti- oppressive social work practice. *The British Journal of Social Work, 46*(7), 1926–1941.

Mandrell, P. (2006). *Introduction to equine-assisted psychotherapy:A comprehensive overview*. Maitland, FL: Xulon Press.

Mandrell, P. J. (2014). *Introduction to equine-assisted psychotherapy: A comprehensive overview*. Xulon Press.

Masini, A. (2010). Equine-assisted psychotherapy in clinical practice. *Journal of Psychosocial Nursing, 48*(10), 30–34.

Moshe-Grodofsky, M., & Allassad Alhouzail, N. (2021). The significance of space: Experiences of Arab social work professionals with EAGALA equine-assisted learning. *British Journal of Social Work, 00*, 1–19. https://doi.org/10.1093/bjsw/bcab113

Mueller, M. K., & McCullough, L. (2017). Effects of equine-facilitated psychotherapy on post-traumatic stress symptoms in youth. *Journal of Child and Family Studies, 26*, 1164–1172. https://doi.org/10.1007/s10826-016-0648-6

Nathans-Barel, I., Feldman, P., Berger, B., Modai, I., & Silver, H. (2005). Animal-assisted therapy ameliorates anhedonia in schizophrenia patients. *Psychotherapy and Psychosomatics, 74*(1), 31–35. https://doi.org/10.1159/000082024

Nelson, A., Signal, T., & Wilson, R. (2016). Equine assisted therapy and learning: A survey of methodologies in Australia. *Society and Animals, 24*, 337–357.

Notgrass, C. G., & Pettinelli, J. D. (2015). Equine-assisted psychotherapy: The Equine-Assisted Growth and Learning Association's model overview of equine-based modalities. *The Journal of Experimental Education, 38*(2), 162–174. https://doi.org/10.1177/1053825914528472

Nurenberg, J. R., Schleifer, S. J., Shaffer, T. M., Yelling, M., Desai, P. J., Amin, R., Bouchard, A. B., & Montalvo, C. R. (2014). Animal-assisted therapy with chronic psychiatric in-patients: Equine-assisted psychotherapy and aggressive behavior. *Psychiatric Services in Advance*. https://doi.org/10.1176/appi.ps201300524

Oren, D., & Parish-Plass, N. (2013). The integration of animals into the therapy process and its implications as a unique medium in psychotherapy. In N. Parish-Plass (Ed.), *Animal-assisted psychotherapy: Theory, issues and practice* (pp. 3–46). Purdue University.

Parish-Plass, N., & Oren, D. (2013). The animal as a relational medium: An object relations approach to the therapy triangle in animal-assisted psychotherapy. In N. Parish-Plass (Ed.), *Animal-assisted psychotherapy: Theory, issues and practice* (pp. 47–64). Purdue University.

Parish Plass, N. (2013). The contribution of animal-assisted psychotherapy to the potential space in play therapy. In N. Parish Plass (Ed.). *Animal-assisted psychotherapy: Theory, issues and practice* (pp. 79–110). Purdue University

Porter-Wenzlaff, L. (2007). Finding their voice: Developing emotional, cognitive, and behavioral congruence in female abuse survivors through equine-facilitated therapy. *Nursing, 3*, 529–534.

Rambo, A. (2016). About animal-assisted family therapy. In A. Rambo (Ed.), *The marriage and family therapy career guide*. Routledge.

Romaniuk, M., Evans, J., & Kidd, C. (2018). Evaluation of an equine-assisted therapy program for veterans who identify as 'wounded, injured or ill' and their partners. *PLoS One, 13*(9), 1–15. https://doi.org/10.1371/journal.pone.0203943

Schroeder, K., Stroud, D., Sherwood, D. M., & Udell, M. A. R. (2018). Therapeutic factors in equine-facilitated group psychotherapy for women survivors of interpersonal violence. *The Journal for Specialists in Group Work, 43*(4), 326–348. https://doi.org/10.1080/01933922.2018.1516707

Scopa, C., Contalbrigo, L., Greco, A., Lanata, A., Scilingo, E. P., & Baragli, P. (2019). Emotional transfer in human-horse interaction: New perspectives on equine assisted interventions. *Animals, 9*, 1030. https://doi.org/10.3390/ani9121030

Smith-Osborne, A., & Selby, A. (2010). Implications of the literature on equine-assisted activities for use as a complementary intervention in social work practice with children and adolescents. *Child and Adolescent Social Work Journal, 27*, 291–307. https://doi.org/10.1007/s10560-010-0201-1

Stapleton, P., & Grimmett, K. T. (2021). Australian community and health professionals perceptions of equine-assisted psychotherapy. *Evidence-based Complementary and Alternative Medicine, 2021*, 1. https://doi.org/10.1155/2021/2217761

Steele, E., Wood, D. S., Usadi, E. J., & Applegarth, D. M. (2018). TRR's Warrior Camp: An intensive treatment program for combat trauma in active military and veterans of all eras. *Military Medicine, 183*(3/4), 403.

Stewart, L. A., Chang, C. Y., & Rice, R. (2013). Emergent theory and model of practice in animal-assisted therapy in counseling. *Journal of Creativity in Mental Health, 8*(4), 329–348. https://doi.org/10.1080/15401383.2013.844657

Thomas, L., & Lytle, M. (2016). *Transforming therapy through horses: Case stories teaching the EAGALA model in action*. EAGALA.

Townsend, R., & Hood, M. (2019). Horse talk: Equine based learning programs and their engagement with individuals. *Australian Journal of Adult Learning, 2*, 254–368.

Vincent, A., & Farkas, K. J. (2017). Application of attachment theory to equine- facilitated therapy. *Society Register, 1*(1), 7–22. https://doi.org/10.14746/sr.2017.1.1.02

Willmund, G., Zimmermann, P., Alliger-Horn, C., Varn, A., Fischer, C., Parent, I., Sobottka, A., Bering, R., Rose, C., Strohle, A., & Kohler, K. (2020). Equine-assisted psychotherapy with traumatized couples- improvement of relationship quality and psychological symptoms. *Journal of Marital and Family Therapy, 47*, 925–944. https://doi.org/10.1111/jmft.12485

Wingenfeld, K., Schaffrath, C., Rullkoetter, N., Mensebach, C., Schlosser, N., Beblo, T., et al. (2011). Associations of childhood trauma, trauma in adulthood and previous-year stress with psychopathology in patients with major depression and borderline personality disorder. *Child Abuse & Neglect, 35*(8), 647–654. [PubMed ID: 21855143]. https://doi.org/10.1016/j.chiabu.2011.04.003

Winnicott, D. (1965). *The maturational processes and the facilitating environment*. International University Press.

Winnicott, D. W. (1968). Playing: its theoretical status in the clinical situation. *The International Journal of Psychoanalysis, 49*(4):591–599.

Zilcha-Mano, S., Mikulincer, M., & Shaver, P. R. (2012). Pets as safe havens and secure bases: The moderating role of pet attachment orientations. *Journal of Research in Personality, 46*(5), 571–580. https://doi.org/10.1016/j.jrp.2012.06.005

The Equus Effect: Somatic Experiencing with Horses

Jane Strong, David Sonatore LCSW, and Elizabeth E. Lloyd-Richardson

Overview of The Equus Effect Program

The Equus Effect (TEE) program was developed in 2008 by Jane Strong and David Sonatore as an alternative, complementary therapeutic approach to assist veterans in navigating the personal and social struggles often faced during the transition from military to civilian life. The program has since expanded to include work with a range of populations, including, but not limited to, first responders and those in recovery from addictions and sexual trauma. TEE does not focus on "treatment goals" but aims simply to support and develop stronger emotional and mental foundations on which participants can build healthy, authentic relationships. The goal is to cultivate physical, emotional, and mental fitness skills that allow them to move beyond their habitual patterns of thinking, feeling, and behaving toward others. The program consists of four group sessions meeting weekly, typically with four to six participants and four horses. Each four-hour session provides dynamic, real-time opportunities to cultivate self-awareness, practice emotion regulation and interpersonal skills, and includes time for participants to debrief about what they learned that day. They are also encouraged to identify how they might apply this knowledge to manage their mental health concerns and become more adept at navigating personal and professional relationships. TEE uses a manualized curriculum, offering a semi-structured format that allows facilitators specific yet flexible guidelines for delivering the program content. The program is fully unmounted and typically co-facilitated by two individuals trained and certified in TEE delivery.

J. Strong (✉) · D. Sonatore
The Equus Effect, Inc., Sharon, CT, USA

E. E. Lloyd-Richardson
University of Massachusetts Dartmouth, Department of Psychology, Dartmouth, MA, USA
e-mail: erichardson@umassd.edu

Y. Neria et al. (eds.), *Guide to Equine Assisted Therapy*,
https://doi.org/10.1007/978-3-031-74426-6_5

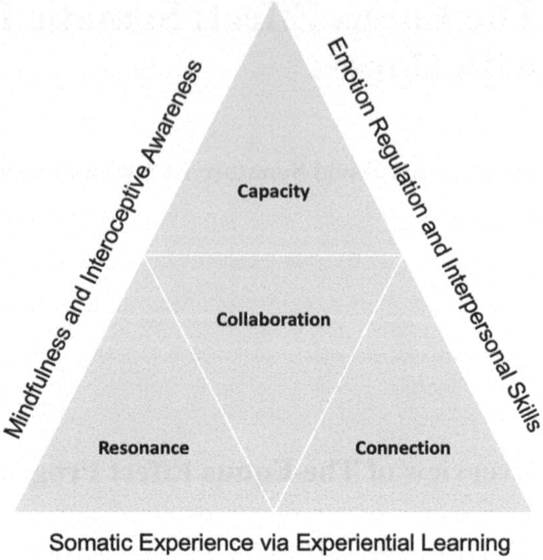

Fig. 1 An overview of the core experiential concepts and key theorized principles of The Equus Effect program

Figure 1 illustrates the three-core experiential and educational concepts implemented throughout the four sessions: mindfulness/interoceptive awareness, emotion regulation and interpersonal skills, and somatic experience via experiential learning. Underlying these, there are four key principles at the heart of TEE, all theorized to drive change: resonance, connection, collaboration, and capacity. Each of these core concepts and key theoretical principles are discussed further.

The Equus Effect Core Experiential Concepts: Key Influences and Applications

An overview of the session content is included in Table 1. For each of the three core experiential concepts, key influences are reviewed that have shaped curriculum development. These have been derived from pioneers in the fields of horse–human relationships, horsemanship, nonmedical forms of trauma healing, and the mental and spiritual impacts of war. Illustrations of how these concepts are applied in sessions are also included.

Mindfulness and Interoceptive Awareness

TEE's experiential learning and somatic experiencing practices with horses are designed to help participants cultivate physical, emotional, and mental fitness skills that allow them to move beyond habitual patterns of thinking, feeling, and behaving

Table 1 Session overview of The Equus Effect program

Session	Experiential and educational concepts	Content/activities
1	Overview/orientation/why horses?	Prey dynamics/horse–human history
	Mindfulness/interoceptive awareness	Joint fluidity/body scan in horse barn
	Emotion regulation and interpersonal skills education	Fear and vulnerability video, discussion with parallels to horses, application to relevant situations in life
	Somatic experience via experiential learning activities	Real-time exploration of fear and vulnerability as it arises with horse-related experiences. Setting healthy boundaries, grounding practices for more effective communication, grooming, yielding, backing up, and circling with horses using minimum essential pressure
2	Mindfulness/interoceptive awareness	Joint fluidity/body scan in horse barn. Reflections, insights, and observations around the impact of prior week's session
	Emotion regulation and interpersonal skills education	Anger, frustration, and agitation video, discussion with parallels drawn to experiences with horses, applications to personal and professional lives
	Experiential learning activity	Real-time exploration of anger and frustration that can arise when learning how to work with horses, boundary setting, as well as agitation observed in horses reacting to incongruence in humans. Attunement and collaboration, grooming, and obstacle course with horses
3	Mindfulness/interoceptive awareness	Joint fluidity/body scan in horse barn. Reflections, insights, and observations regarding impact of prior week's session
	Emotion regulation and interpersonal skills education	Sadness and grief/video, discussion with parallels to horses and distinctions in life/situations away from barn
	Experiential learning activity	Real-time exploration of sadness and grief as it arises in the presence of horses. Attunement and collaboration, grooming, navigating labyrinth, or trail walk with horses
4	Mindfulness/interoceptive awareness	Joint fluidity/body scan in horse barn. Reflections, insights, and observations regarding prior week's session
	Emotion regulation and interpersonal skills education	Review of emotional states/video, discussion with parallels drawn to horses, and challenges related to personal and professional relationships
	Experiential learning activity	Collaboration and capacity, grooming, working with horses at liberty (unrestrained) in a round pen to widen the window of tolerance for sympathetic nervous system responses. Practice effective energy management

toward others. Often referred to as resilience, this is commonly defined as one's ability to positively adapt to stress, trauma, and adversity (Luthar et al., 2000). Substantial research indicates that the development of mindfulness is crucial to building individual resilience levels in the face of adversity (e.g., O'Connor et al., 2021; Bajaj et al., 2022).

Inherent to mindfulness approaches is interoceptive awareness, or direct experience of the body's internal state and possible stressors impacting this state, which then allows for goal-directed action that can serve to restore the homeostatic balance of the body (Gibson, 2019; Paulus et al., 2009). Haase et al. (2016) found that individuals with low levels of resilience demonstrate lower levels of interoceptive awareness and body responsiveness than those with normal or high levels of resilience, indicating that these individuals have significantly less awareness and responsiveness to interoceptive signals which points to the potential for interventions that improve this kind of sensitivity to one's own state.

Levine's somatic experiencing approach (1997, 2010) and van der Kolk's (2014) description of mind–body processes are both perspectives that incorporate mindfulness and interoceptive awareness to facilitate emotional development. Van der Kolk (2014) describes this:

> In my practice I begin the process by helping my patients to first notice and then describe the feelings in their bodies—not emotions such as anger or anxiety or fear but the physical sensations beneath the emotions: pressure, heat, muscular tension, tingling, caving in, feeling hollow, and so on. I also work on identifying the sensations associated with relaxation or pleasure. I help them become aware of their breath, their gestures and movements. (p.117)

The program incorporates exercises at the start of each weekly session that are designed to recognize and strengthen interoceptive awareness, thereby improving mindfulness and ability to notice and articulate internal emotional experiences. Learning to set boundaries, collaborating with horses in activities that require mutual cooperation, and working with horses at liberty are all elements designed to engage and "thaw" the whole body from the ground up, inviting participants to once again regulate their own nervous systems. Tasks are broken down into small steps designed to both identify and "meet" resistance in the body. By focusing on the somatic aspects of resistance rather than historically based stories, the participant–facilitator interaction centers around "what" participants notice rather than "why" they feel a certain way.

Consistent with this, reported results of equine-assisted learning and therapy studies to date indicate improvements in mindfulness, engagement in the present moment, and acceptance, noted across various populations, such as veterans (e.g., Reive, 2019), prison inmates (e.g., Robinson-Edwards et al., 2019), and women with a history of abuse (e.g., Schroeder et al., 2018).

Interpersonal Skills and Emotion Regulation

At its core, the program recognizes the value to individuals—and the collective—when they operate interdependently. In 2023, the US Surgeon General issued an advisory on the epidemic of loneliness and isolation, outlining the numerous ways that physical and mental health are affected by loneliness, and calling for greater efforts to develop social connection solutions (Office of the Surgeon General, 2023).

Military veterans present unique experiences of loneliness and social isolation, described both in the popular press (Junger, 2017) and documented in the scientific literature. For instance, Wilson et al. (2018) conducted a systematic narrative review that describes the high prevalence of loneliness in the veteran subpopulation, particularly among older veterans, and the heavy toll that loneliness exerts on mental health, particularly depression and as a risk factor for suicide.

Military units operate much the same way that collectivist societies or a herd of horses does. The parallels between the two species and orientation to life are a natural fit for one another. Like each other or not, they both know that the survival of individuals depends on the survival of the unit, with emphasis placed on mutual support, cooperation, and shared commitment, all of which are critical to military performance, combat motivation, and social support (Flack & Kite, 2021; Human Performance Resources, 2022). In a study of 358 Australian Defence Force veterans, Flack and Kite (2021) found evidence for the protective aspects of military identity (e.g., not feeling like an outsider), but also noted that maintaining strong military identity as core to one's personal identity was negatively related to building and maintaining helpful social connections.

Unlike horses, however, military veterans and first responders have commonly been trained to override the body's natural instinct to preserve life and to minimize response to fear and vulnerability through historic practices of hazing during military training. These practices were designed to serve three primary functions—socialization, cohesion-building, and eliminating those deemed unfit or unwilling to serve—but certainly come with costs to the individual (DiRosa & Goodwin, 2014; Sherin & Nemeroff, 2011). Further, mental health challenges are prevalent in these groups, with 14–16% of US service members deployed in the past 20 years affected by post-traumatic stress disorder (PTSD) or depression, and still others impacted by suicide, traumatic brain injury, substance use disorder, interpersonal violence, and other emotional and behavioral challenges (Inoue et al., 2023).

TEE activities and experiences are designed to expand participants' ability to tolerate challenging situations and build their capacity to return to healthy emotional functioning. Siegel (1999) terms this the "window of tolerance," proposing that everyone has a range of intensities of emotions which they can comfortably experience, process, and integrate. When pushed outside of our window of tolerance, the nervous system can respond with feeling overwhelmed and other *hyper-arousal* reactions, or by shutting down and other *hypo-arousal* reactions.

Individuals' windows of tolerance can be narrow or wide and can vary at different times in life (Ogden et al., 2006). Figure 2 (Foundation for Human Enrichment,

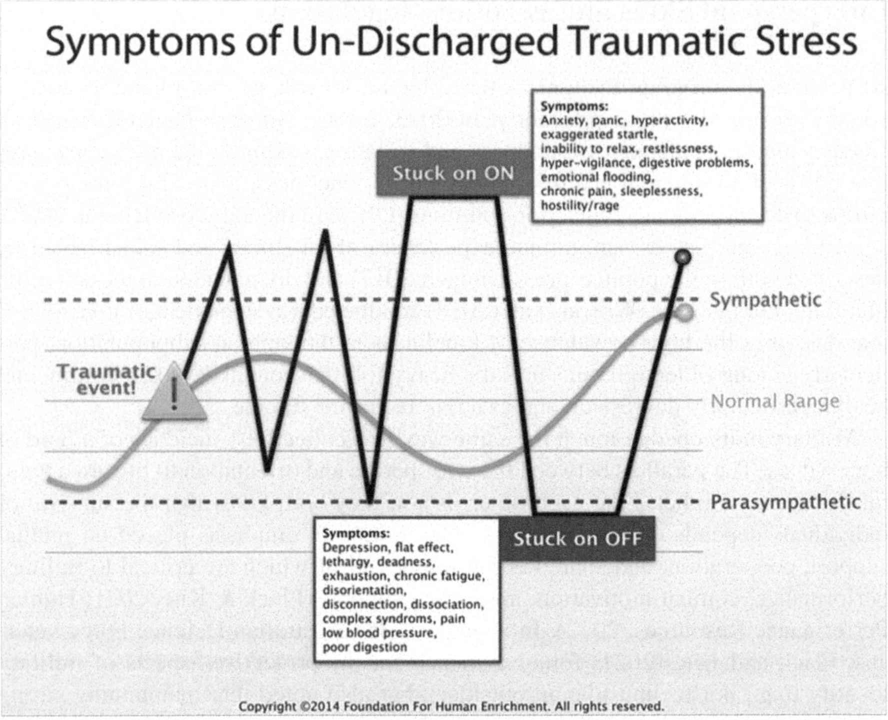

Fig. 2 The window of tolerance and symptoms of un-discharged traumatic stress

2014) reflects graphically the window of tolerance and is used to help participants understand how their emotional responses can become "stuck" as a result of trauma. Thus, the program focuses on participants' real-time experiences with the horses with an aim to address nervous systems that may be "stuck" in states of hyper- or hypo-arousal rather than what are considered to be healthy responses to activation and settling.

Recognizing and interrupting habitual dynamics along with offering new choices promotes healthier interactions. For instance, among participants in recovery from substance abuse, emotion regulation and interpersonal skills often appear along a spectrum of two extremes: They are either terrified to ask for what they want or they have no regard for the reactions from the horses to their advances. Some can barely touch a horse with grooming tools, while others walk up to the horses as if they intend to push them around and demand what they want. Neither of these extremes is healthy for the horses and both present an opportunity to interrupt the process and invite participants to redirect their approaches through revisiting the mindfulness and interoceptive tools presented at the outset of sessions. Since displays of bravado or anxiety masked with stoicism are often met with signs of agitation in the horses, it also becomes obvious that horse–human interactions have the potential to reveal a great deal about how humans interact with one another. Scopa and colleagues

(2019) describe this as emotional transfer in horse–human interaction, although they clearly indicate that there is great need for additional scientific understanding of this process.

In her early studies of shame, Brown (2006) contextualized shame as a psycho-socio-cultural construct and proposed the shame resilience theory, which emphasized the importance of acknowledging vulnerability and building mutually empathic relationships through such strategies as psychoeducational group support. Given the size and power of horses, as well as the fact that most participants have little to no horse experience, it would appear logical that vulnerability is an important component of the initial contact and connection between participants and horses, as well as for the development of healthy, authentic relationships in participants' lives.

Similarly, Porges (2017) speaks of the need for working with feelings of shame that often follow such incidents where fight or flight may not be an option. For instance, tonic immobility is a body-based survival strategy in which some animals experience paralysis or loss of muscle tone, a state of "freeze," thus significantly reducing their capacity for fight or flight (Schlote, 2017). Humans, however, tend to judge this inherent inactivity as a failure to "do" something. As Porges (2017) suggests:

> There is no such thing as a bad response. There are only adaptive responses. The primary point is that our nervous system is trying to do the right thing for us to survive, and we need to respect what it has done. When we respect our body's responses, we move from this more evaluative state and become more respectful of ourselves, this functionally contributes to the healing process. (p. 85)

When someone has survived sexual assault, that individual may have prevailed because they froze (Porges, 2011). Working with horses can bring about a thaw from this freeze, slowly inviting sensation back into the body through ground-based horsemanship skills. Reflective grooming using co-regulating touch, learning to set boundaries, collaborating, and working at liberty with horses are all elements designed to engage the whole body from the ground up, inviting trauma survivors to once again regulate their own nervous systems and then move forward in whatever types of counseling or healing work they choose.

Participants frequently remark that in learning to respect their fear and vulnerability, they are less fearful, more patient, more empathetic, and more tolerant of sharing responsibility and control in situations. They also describe having an increased ability to recognize what is happening in their bodies and use it as information to observe and interrupt habitual ways of thinking, feeling, and behaving. Mental health providers have anecdotally noted that participants become more focused, less agitated, and move through issues more quickly, assuming responsibility and agency in situations that had seemed insurmountable. While limited empirical examination of these phenomena exists as related to equine-assisted learning, there are interesting parallels to be drawn to studies employing a 12-week exercise program (Mehling et al., 2018) and a 9-day sports training program (Belrose et al.,

2021) targeting veterans with chronic post-traumatic stress disorder (PTSD) and designed to improve mindfulness, interoceptive awareness, and positive self-image.

The Essential Role of Horses: Somatic Experiencing via Experiential Learning

Based on the work of Kohanov (Kohanov, 2001), founder of the Eponaquest School in Tucson, Arizona, and Brannaman (Brannaman & Brannaman, 2001), their extensive knowledge of equine behavior and horsemanship has contributed to our understanding that horses are essential to this work and must not be perceived simply as "tools," or metaphors. Indeed, horses do much of the heavy lifting when it comes to the learning, healing, and growth that take place during TEE sessions. Horses are recognized by the program as sentient beings, each of whom offer distinct forms of support or challenge for participants at various points in time.

As prey animals, their survival depends on an accurate read of anything in their environments that could mean danger. They live in herds or bands for safety, reinforcing the need for, and benefits of, interdependence. Horses do so in order to increase their chances of survival by covering larger sectors of the landscape for potential threats, but also because the less time they spend scanning for danger, the more time they have to graze and reproduce (Rubenstein, 2024). Their reactions to their environments are grounded in their instincts for individual, reproductive, and herd survival, responding to reality simply as they perceive it in the moment (Kohanov, 2001, pp. 160–161). In addition, horses are known to develop strong social relationships. Noting a similar pattern to humans, Rubenstein (2024, p. 10) describes them as neolocal, meaning their sons and daughters commonly leave the herd when they mature, such that many social relationships that develop among adults are with nongenetic members. As Rubenstein (2024) suggests, this socialization process may create an affinity for horses to form bonds with people as well.

While horses show comparable neuroanatomy with humans and other mammals, there are some neuroanatomical differences in structure that may help to explain differences in species functioning, and resulting differences in how they express and experience their environments (Schlote, 2017). Horses react to the various sources of information conveyed by participants, such as body posture, gestures, facial expressions, use of the breath, and levels of attentiveness, aggression, or submission displayed (see Merkies & Franzin, 2021 for review).

Further, horses remember previous experiences with humans, where positive experiences with humans tend to promote a generalization to all human interactions. In addition, if not fully present, participants may be confronted with their emotional incongruence as reflected in the horse's reactions. Participants have the opportunity to recognize whether they are too aggressive, impatient, unclear, or unsure in their interactions with horses. In the face of these real-time insights, not only do facilitators provide coaching to shift the body and mind to operate from a more grounded, congruent, and regulated state, but participants describe being able to make connections between their actions and reactions in the round pen and habitual patterns in other areas of their lives.

Nearly three-quarters of each weekly session is devoted to teaching participants how to engage with the horses through developing basic horsemanship skills. The curriculum starts in the barn aisle, outside the horses' stalls, with exercises that cultivate interoceptive awareness and teach participants the value of presence in working with the horses' natural way of being. By noticing the settling that occurs when participants become more present and inhabit their own bodies, they tend to become aware of the impact that presence and groundedness has on others in their surroundings. Rather than facilitators trying to convey the value of presence to participants, it is the horses themselves who demonstrate the impact of this settling and greater presence. Touching a horse helps us tap into some of the deepest natural resources we have—the ground under our feet, the ability our bodies have to attune to, and comfort and care for a sentient being whose trust is transparent. Consistent with this, van der Kolk (2014) describes:

> Touch, the most elementary tool we have to calm down, is proscribed from most therapeutic practices. Yet, you can't fully recover if you don't feel safe in your own skin. Mindful touch and movement grounds people and allows them to discover tensions they may have held for so long, they are not even aware of them any longer. (p. 234)

Participants learn very quickly where to put their feet, how to move away from a horse who spooks, and how to read the signs of appreciation when respectful touch is used to connect with a horse. Facilitators point this out so that participants recognize the inherent wisdom in the body.

Since most participants are novices around horses, teaching them how to handle horses respectfully and fairly is key to the well-being of both. Horses' honest responses and expressions of willingness, or not, offer lessons for participants to experience creativity, innovation, patience, and compassion for themselves, staff and other participants, and for the horses. For instance, by introducing participants to horsemanship exercises that are increasingly complex, participants experience for themselves that excitement is not always linked to danger, finesse is more powerful than force, vulnerability is not a sign of weakness but rather an opportunity to learn and grow, and collaboration is more effective than control. Further, participants commonly demonstrate learning to manage their own levels of energy and to regulate their emotional responses in order to stay present and connected with the horses, while also navigating more complex tasks. These experiences culminate with an at-liberty exercise in the round pen that demands integration of previously learned skills while managing the space, speed, and direction the horse is traveling.

Preliminary Pilot Data

The Equus Effect curriculum and methods were developed over time to meet the imminent needs of the original target population—US veterans and active-duty personnel. While TEE has now been used across a variety of populations (e.g., veterans, substance abuse recovery, first responders, at-risk youth, sexual assault survivors), development of a standardized curriculum has allowed for consistent and successful delivery of TEE through working with over 700 veterans. Between 2016 and 2019, program evaluation data was collected assessing the perceived value of the program for participants and improvements in participants' abilities to manage their emotions and handle daily interactions with others. Based on this feedback, minor modifications to the program, such as length of sessions, were made to imrove accessiblity and usefulness to some of these other populations.

Since 2022, program evaluations are also routinely completed by individuals at two large addiction-recovery centers who elect to participate in the TEE program, one optional aspect of these comprehensive 12-step, immersive recovery programs. It is noteworthy that there is a waiting list for participating in TEE program at these recovery centers, and TEE is consistently recognized by these agencies as one of the most helpful programs, attesting to its acceptability and impact with participants. Over 330 anonymous evaluations have been collected since 2022, with example survey items and their average ratings below:

> Overall, The [TEE] program was more helpful than I expected. (mean rating: 4.9/5)
>
> Learning about horses and how they see the world helped me understand more about how I respond to people in my life. (mean rating: 4.79/5)
>
> I was surprised at how easy it was to connect with the horses once I understood how sensitive they are to the energy I was bringing to them and to others in my life. (mean rating: 4.83/5)
>
> Learning how to 'identify and interpret' the horses' body language helped me understand how my body language will affect others. (mean rating: 4.72/5)
>
> I feel that I have gained insight into the importance of feeling my emotions in the present moment and in responding more appropriately to them. (mean rating: 4.85/5)
>
> I feel that I have gained practical tools I can use in my relationships with others in my life. (mean rating: 4.74/5)
>
> Others have noticed that I seem calmer and clearer since working with the horses. (mean rating: 4.43/5)
>
> I have learned to be more in tune with my emotions and do a body scan to see where I am holding tension. (mean rating: 4.86/5)

Ratings are positive and offer insight into potential mechanisms of change. Of note, participants were able to relate to—and connect with—the horses and draw parallels between their experiences with the horses and how they engage with others in their lives. Participants also indicated that they learned how to better recognize their own emotional states in the present moment and to respond to them in a calmer, clear manner. While these program evaluation results yield positive feedback from participants, they also offer suggestions on how and why TEE may help participants. A scientific lens brought by controlled experimental research is needed to better understand and evaluate intervention efforts such as TEE. As Kazdin (2008) outlines in his seminal work, in order for clinical work and scientific research to benefit fully from one another, we must explore clinical interventions to ask (and answer) questions such as these: What components of the program contribute to change? How does TEE compare relative to other treatments for these particular challenges? What participant, facilitator, treatment, and contextual factors are related to behavioral or cognitive outcomes of interest? Recent research efforts designed to examine TEE's efficacy and mechanisms are now underway. A small randomized controlled pilot study has recently been completed testing the feasibility and acceptability of TEE's manualized curriculum with a cohort of 31 veterans receiving VA mental health services and randomized to either weekly TEE or attention control sessions over 4 weeks. Attention control sessions were time-matched and included somatic exercises and emotional agility presentations, with no inclusion of horses. Key informant interviews with veterans and their clinicians are also underway to examine the perceptions of the program's acceptability, usefulness, and satisfaction and the ways in which it might complement standard mental health care (Aim 3). We expect results from this study will be available by year end 2024 and will be foundational to the growth and scalability of the program as we continue to train facilitators at centers across the United States.

Proposed Mechanisms of Change: Four Key Principles and Case Examples

The Equus Effect is a combination of body-based experiencing, coaching, and learning in a way that invites mutual respect and partnerships between human and horse to enhance the health, wholeness, and well-being of both. While continued research is needed for exploring the mechanisms of change of equine-assisted learning interventions generally, TEE curriculum is based on four key principles, which we assert are foundational to improvements in responses to stress and overall healing. These four principles are generally progressive, beginning with the development of resonance and connection, and then putting both into action through collaboration. Immersion in these principles, as well as didactic lessons on emotional agility, all serve to build capacity.

Given the nature of developing awareness and skill capacities, each of these is dynamic, such that when someone falls back to a state of dysregulation, participants are encouraged to "return to the basics" of resonance and connection, which allow them to then continue work progressing to build collaboration and capacity. Additional description of each of these processes is provided, along with brief case examples (names have been altered for privacy).

Resonance

Resonance is conceptualized as the ability to attune to another through unspoken empathy, identification, and understanding. In her positivity resonance theory, Fredrickson (2016) defined positivity resonance as a momentary experience that occurs when an interpersonal connection is characterized by three features: shared positive affect, mutual care and concern, and behavioral and biological synchrony. Major et al. (2018) evaluated this theory of resonance and found perceived positivity resonance to be associated with flourishing mental health, lower depressive symptoms, loneliness, and illness symptoms.

TEE program works to establish resonance between participants and horses. Initially, participants learn about the evolution of horses, survival mechanisms of prey animals, and the power of the herd. Once participants get over their initial fear and vulnerability that comes with being close to a large animal, participants typically express curiosity about how horses operate and the role they have played in our lives for thousands of years. Participants are then open to cultivating both the nuance and assuredness it takes to work with horses, which helps to shape and inform their own abilities to read nonverbal cues and improve their communication abilities with the horses and other human beings.

Resonance Case Illustration

Robert is a first responder from the New York City Fire Department who was 22 years old when 9/11 took place, and he experienced the horrific loss of 343 fellow firefighters. Since then, he has spent his career trying to serve the needs of this tight-knit brotherhood of fellow firefighters and has found himself exhausted and depleted from seeing himself as the "strong, resourceful one" who feels guilty about asking for any kind of help. He wants to know who he is outside of feeling responsible for everyone and everything in his life. He found meaning in learning about horses, the role of the herd, and the relationship horses and humans have shared for thousands of years. As Robert shared:

> When you mentioned that we have known horses for 6,000 years, that it has only been 110 or 120 [years] since they were not an integral part of our lives and that we were here to remember something we'd lost touch with, I wanted to do everything I could to reach into that part of myself that knows how to be with the horses. There was something about remembering that was different from you giving us instructions or telling us how to "be". It was like I was the me I knew before everyone else started demanding things from me. This was more satisfying to me than anything I've done in a long time. That horse didn't need me to be any particular way, except clear, purposeful, and confident. He needed me to be what worked for both of us, not just him.

Connection

Once resonance is built between the horses and participants, thus aiming to develop greater presence and emotional calm and regulation, we proceed with developing a hands-on relationship with the horse. For most, proximity to this large sentient being is an act of true vulnerability. By slowing things down, participants can gain a better sense of their capacity for connection at their own pace. Informed by the real time and nonverbal response of the horse, hands-on grooming activities create opportunities for interactions between the participant and the horse which lead to reciprocal exchanges of respect, appreciation, and co-regulating touch. Even something as simple as regulating one's breath can become a heightened experience as participants notice a perceptible change in the horses when they take more oxygen into the diaphragm.

The keys to authentic relationships, such as patience and trust, emerge as participants touch the horses. This promotes a series of physiological benefits to the heart and lungs that, in turn, invites more trust and connection. First, oxytocin is released and both the horse and the participant seem more attuned to one another. And, since the horse's resting heart rate is slightly more than half of a human's, the participant starts to notice that their heart rate also slows. All of this is relaxing, reciprocal, and often very moving to people who are used to being in charge or on guard. Many participants who are used to high stress situations will report that they no longer believed it would ever be possible to return to this state.

Connection Case Illustration

Cliff, a Vietnam veteran, was fit, strong, and healthy, except for his darting eyes, leg that bounced when he sat down, and his startle reflex that was apparent to all of us in the barn. He had not slept the night before coming to the barn because he was worried that he wouldn't find us and mapped his route several times before leaving very early to reach us by 10:00 AM. He listened carefully to our instructions and then chose to groom Tango. He put his hands on Tango's side and stood silently for a long time. His back was facing the rest of us, and we gave him some time to have his own experience. When we returned to the cottage for lunch, he started to cry and said:

> I feel terrible saying this because you all are my brothers in arms, but it has been 49 years since I have stood down. I never, ever turn my back on anyone—ever—but when I put my hands on that horse, I felt my shoulders come down and I knew I was safe. I'm so embarrassed to cry like this but I've carried this tension in my body for so long, I hardly know what to do without it.

Collaboration

Veterans and first responders often tackle many of life's challenges with force, control, and dominance. However, force and control have no place in engaging with horses when the goal is to develop collaboration between horse and human through engagement and mutual trust. Participants are taught to use their embodied presence to create movement through clarity, direction, and feel. As prey animals, horses respond to subtle differences in participants' energy and intention that are derived from gestures and postures that indicate dominance, submissiveness, and attunement, based on shifts in body weight distribution, alterations in breathing, and overall confidence (Merkies & Franzin, 2021). So, in order to work with horses trained to attune to those types of signals, participants must learn to shift the management of their energy from an on/off switch to an attenuator that increases or decreases incrementally and *always* returns to the lowest set point once the goal or task is performed. Willingness on the part of the horse is also a key factor in true collaboration because a horse that feels included and interested in any activity is one that feels safe and supported. It is this awareness and consideration of the other being in the interaction (horse or human) that prompts a felt sense of how defensive rigidity can shift into greater attunement and experience of fluidity. Participants are taught to start with minimum essential pressure on the horse to achieve the target goal and use more as needed to evoke the desired response from each horse. The ability to raise and lower one's energy and intensity is a valuable life skill, allowing for a more nuanced ability to navigate tricky and provocative situations in life. In a world that presents us with a wide range of people whose sensitivities, levels of congruence and range of awareness vary significantly, helping participants to comfortably modulate their energy and intensity levels will assist them in fostering collaborations and handling challenging interpersonal exchanges. Further, working with the unique temperaments and responses from each of the horses involved provides participants with valuable insights around navigating relationships with different types of people. It also helps participants to take responsibility for their own self-management when learning to adapt to a horse that is more sensitive or more resistant than another.

Collaboration Case Illustration

Rebecca is an Iraq veteran whose rank indicated her level of responsibility for others, where she expected immediate responses to her commands. She had been wounded, however, and retired from active duty in 2012. She was in the process of a divorce, had just lost her mother, and her two daughters who lived at home with her were also grieving. Rebecca was nervous about asking Dutch to circle the round pen with no lead line and no tools other than a flag to get him to move forward. "I feel like I don't have any authority with him," she told us. Since we prefer that participants remain silent unless they need their voices to bring their own energy up, she felt that she had little, if any, power. It was clear to us, however, that she did not need any kind of support because he clearly felt her presence and intention. After making a few rounds and turning in both directions at a canter and trot in the 70′-diameter round pen, she pulled back, lowered her gaze and shoulders, thus lowering the pressure she had been putting on Dutch and drew him toward her.

Dutch willingly followed her around and when she exhaled deeply, he stopped on the mark Rebecca had identified. She then came to the edge of the pen with tears in her eyes. The next week, she returned with an interesting story about Dutch and how this experience impacted her life at home.

> I can't believe he did what I wanted without me raising my voice or demanding that he listen to me. I was silent and used my body to influence him and he just seemed to know what I wanted. When I got home, I used this same thing with my kids. Instead of chasing them down and insisting that they tell me how they felt (which is exactly what I would have done before), I waited at the kitchen table and let them come to me. Instead of putting pressure on them, I waited and it worked. I can't believe it.

Capacity

Development of participants' abilities to work with horses and use ground-based horsemanship skills is an important component of the program. These activities are designed to activate participants by pushing them to the edges of their windows of tolerance. This serves to both build their capacity for stronger emotional self-management and show them they have control over returning to a settled state of nervous system regulation. Indeed, one of the key distinctions between this equine-assisted intervention versus many traditional therapeutic approaches may be that TEE is not centered on recounting of the trauma itself but rather addresses resistance and barriers in the body to widen the window of tolerance between the sympathetic and parasympathetic nervous system (Mittly et al., 2023). Coaching participants to navigate this terrain in real time allows them to have the direct experience of both activated and settled states and to notice the difference. In that process, not only do participants have the opportunity to sense these states in their own bodies, but they also learn how this is done naturally by horses, who model activation and settling with fluidity and grace.

Vulnerability and activation in the face of these potential emotional triggers do not imply brokenness but rather opportunities to explore the edges of what is considered "tolerable." As participants observe and then learn to experience and interpret the movement of their own nervous systems from activation to settling firsthand, they naturally learn to trust their experience. This is a journey that unfolds over the course of the four-week curriculum, so that participants have the chance to unwind and explore without limits on time or pressure to learn new things quickly. Vulnerability often evokes a sense of resistance or urgency, so the pace we create takes this pressure off and invites experimentation and the ability to break skills down into steps that are easier for adults to learn and practice. Across the structured didactic material, the reflective aspects of the work with horses, and the ground-based horsemanship techniques, participants regain agency and emotional agility by experiencing both dysregulation and then the liberation and expansion that is inherent in the ability to move to a place of presence, authenticity, and the absence of self-consciousness. The program focus is not on "treatment goals" per se but is simply to build sturdier foundations on which individuals from all walks of life can rebuild healthy, authentic relationships.

Capacity Case Illustration

Chris served two tours in Afghanistan before being medically discharged for PTSD. He was ashamed of himself for not being able to stay in the service and finish his career in the Army. He told us about the dark days he experienced before coming to us and that he did not respond well to programs where people sit and talk about their experiences. Then, he said:

> While I do see the value of some programs offered at the VA, I realized that picking up the memories of traumatic events from Afghanistan was like picking up pieces of broken
>
> glass that cut my hands again and hurt. I realize that I had made some progress because I was able to get here, but after working with these horses for four weeks in a row, I look at my hands and instead of seeing broken shards that cut me, I see pieces of sea glass. They're still fragmented, but I can hold them and can even see some beauty in them. I think it was the presence-based skills, the insights and connection to the horses that's making me able to put the memories into perspective.

Facilitator Training Curriculum

Along with having a herd of healthy horses who like their jobs, it is essential to provide participants with the sense that they are in confident and competent hands. There is a *vast* difference between teaching and facilitating. Facilitators and horse handlers who assist in the program must understand exactly what they are capable of and what they are not. A rigorous four-module training curriculum for facilitator candidates has been developed that allows facilitators to learn how to safely and effectively deliver the program, as well as to determine whether they are capable of delivering it with competence. Facilitator trainings are taught by the creators of TEE, who not only deliver the concepts but also relate the myriad experiences and scenarios they have derived from a dozen years of delivering the curriculum.

During the 9-month training, TEE facilitators and horse handlers learn how to read the horses' body language and recognize signs of overwhelm or shut down in participants. Facilitators-in-training spend a great deal of time working with each other and with a variety of participants in the apprenticeship and mastery sessions in order to give them a wide range of opportunities to develop self-mastery and competence with participants. We provide follow-up questions and scripts from the TEE facilitator's guide around somatic practices and didactic material to support them, but ultimately, they are required to demonstrate through videos they upload to our academic site that they have mastered the material and themselves in real time before they are able to graduate.

Trainees are expected to cultivate keen observation skills and be competent with horses. It is often the horse that provides essential clues that a participant may not have noticed in themselves, so facilitators also rely on horses as guides for cultivating interoceptive awareness among participants. Since it is the horses that are most capable of regulating a participant's nervous system, facilitators are encouraged to direct participants back to the horses to notice their equine partners' innate response to participants' mental or emotional states. In addition, when participants get into stories about the past, facilitators guide them back to the present with an invitational, somatically-informed question (e.g., "what are you noticing right now?") designed to increase interoceptive awareness and facilitate connection.

Facilitators are not required to be mental health practitioners. All elements in the training curriculum for new facilitators are intended to cultivate the following qualities and skills in teams who will ultimately be working with participants: Emotional intelligence and maturity, resilience, horsemanship skills that focus on attunement, the ability to collaborate with each other as a team and the capacity to understand the differences between teaching and facilitating.

Candidates are first asked to participate in an introductory weekend that invites them to experience the work as a participant and creates an opportunity to evaluate whether or not TEE is a good fit for them. A second introductory weekend then helps trainees identify their own strengths and blind spots as they pertain to their roles as facilitators. During this session, facilitators in training are asked to complete the Chestnut Paes Sullivan Enneagram Compass Assessment (CPEnneagram.com). There are several Enneagram tests available and most of them commonly measure nine personality strategies characterizing an individual's worldview and how they relate to self and others (Alexander & Schnipke, 2020). For TEE training purposes, the CPR Enneagram Compass Report is used to provide potential facilitators with insight into their own personality patterns that uncover specific triggers and blind spots that may come up for them in real sessions with participants. It is important to note that while the Enneagram is reported to have demonstrated usefulness and comprehensiveness and has comparable validity to other personality models, such as the Big Five or Myers-Briggs (Alexander & Schnipke, 2020), there remains mixed evidence for its reliability and validity according to a recent systematic review of 104 studies (Hook et al., 2021).

Trainees also spend a great deal of time and energy integrating the somatic awareness practices required to recognize and manage their own potential triggers, regulate their nervous systems and learn how to support each other as a team in real time. It is extremely important that facilitators are able to do this since the horses, facilitators, and participants are all working in the same physical space, and thus have the ability to impact one another. Horses do not make a distinction between facilitators, participants, or horse handlers.

Hence, if a facilitator is dysregulated or distracted, the horse will respond to them in the same way as he or she would if a participant is being incongruent and needs support.

Facilitator trainees are asked to practice and embody scripted material and all other elements of the curriculum at their own facilities; create and upload demonstration videos of their skill delivery to the training platform; complete and discuss an extensive reading list; and take advantage of facilitators' feedback both at the training site and in separate meetings to hone their skills. While the training program is relatively time intensive, many facilitators indicate that the nine months they spent acquiring and integrating the materials and practices has a positive impact on their own lives. They are not just delivering something to others but have also reported to TEE staff that they are learning how to improve their own relationships with partners, children, and co-workers. This unique feature of facilitating in a participatory way can also serve to mitigate burnout as there is always something to observe about oneself. Given the horse's absence of discernment between the facilitator and the participant from an embodiment perspective, facilitators must "walk the talk" in order to effectively model for participants how to engage with the horses.

In sum, facilitator training is designed to build facilitators' capacity for curiosity, calm, creativity, compassion, and congruence in the face of many challenging situations by helping them become more congruent and grounded in themselves. Only facilitators who meet TEE criteria for the congruence, sensitivity, and skills outlined in the facilitator's training manual are able to become certified facilitators. Others are given the opportunity to apprentice and continue with coaching until they are ready. The aim is to ensure that no matter where TEE is delivered, participants, horses, and facilitators will always feel safe, supported, and treated with professionalism and dignity.

Summary and Next Research Steps

The shift of attention from the outside-in to the inside-out, from the top-down to the bottom-up, that comes about through resonance, connection, and collaboration with a horse can feel like a homecoming for many participants—a welcome home to the wisdom of their own bodies and to their own humanity. As one veteran who served in five wars beginning with Vietnam described, "This is the transition from war to peace that we never got." To that end, the bridge back to the body can easily emerge from interacting with horses, the very species whose nature is based—as it has been for some 55 million years—on somatic experience. As reflected in this chapter, TEE program integrates mindfulness/interoceptive awareness, capacity building, emotion regulation and interpersonal skills development, and somatic experiencing, all through real-time engagement and processing with equines.

The Equus Effect core curriculum concepts have remained consistent over the past 11 years. Minor additions or changes to the content have been made in response to comments from veterans and other populations who express interest in knowing more about the mechanisms that keep them stuck in old patterns. Therefore, the didactic material has been augmented to include more robust explanations of how triggers turn into reactivity that is detrimental to individuals' mental health, well-being, and significant personal and professional relationships. TEE facilitators welcome the opportunity to include more insight and information so that participants will realize that barriers to engagement with others in the present arise from what has *happened* to them rather than what is *wrong* with them.

Future research efforts in the field of equine-assisted learning, and with TEE more specifically, must incorporate quantitative and qualitative methods that both acknowledge participants' perceptions and also capture potential bio-psycho-social changes taking place that speak to how the program impacts participants in the short and long term. TEE offers a paradigm containing many hands-on, scaffolded exercises designed to raise somatic awareness and develop horsemanship skills, as well as structured emotional agility content. Thus, while firmly grounded in the real world, it is immensely testable from a scientific perspective. For instance, measurement of key theoretical concepts, such as interoceptive awareness, is necessary for examining both support for the effectiveness of TEE programs and advancing theoretical understanding of how equine-assisted learning interventions work.

To assist in this process of evaluation, new tools are continually being developed that could significantly enhance the assessment of factors contributing to change in participants' mental health and well-being and allow for modeling the underlying processes involved. For instance, in addition to incorporation of physiological assessments of bodily reactions, the 24-item multidimensional assessment of interoceptive awareness (Brief MAIA-2; Rogowska et al., 2023) consists of eight scales assessing awareness of bodily sensations, distraction, worry, attention regulation, emotion awareness, self-regulation, body listening, and trusting in bodily sensations as an important source of information on one's needs. These subscales directly align with the somatic experience framework incorporated in TEE. As another example, the 12-item trait perceived positivity resonance measure (Major et al., 2018) is designed to assess the extent to which a person's typical interpersonal connections are characterized by shared positivity, mutual care and concern, and behavioral and biological synchrony. This scale was designed to assess perceptions of "momentarily shared experiences during typical interpersonal encounters" and the degree to which a participant perceived this affective experience was shared with the partner in question (whether this be with a horse or human). This could be incorporated as a way to explore the role of resonance as a mediator or moderator of change.

Also of note is the limited incorporation of comparison conditions or control groups in the extant literature. This is essential for moving knowledge forward and should include activities designed to evoke emotions and experiences in a similar environment, and engage in somatic practices, but without inclusion of the horses.

References

Alexander, M., & Schnipke, B. (2020). The Enneagram: A primer for psychiatry residents. *The American Journal of Psychiatry Residents Journal, 15*, 2–5.
Bajaj, B., Khoury, B., & Sengupta, S. (2022). Resilience and stress as mediators in the relationship of mindfulness and happiness. *Frontiers in Psychology*. Sec. Positive Psychology, *13*, 771263.
Belrose, C., Duffaud, A., Levy, D., Beji, A., Jacob, S., Lorion, G., Martin-Krumm, C., & Trousselard, M. (2021). Self-representations of military veterans suffering from chronic post-traumatic stress disorder: The role of sport. *Frontiers in Psychiatry*. Sec. Psychopathology, *12*, 766515.
Brannaman, B., & Brannaman, W. (2001). *The faraway horses*. The Lyons Press.
Brown, B. (2006). Shame resilience theory: A grounded theory study on women and shame. *Families in Society, 87*(1), 43–52.
DiRosa, G. A., & Goodwin, G. F. (2014). Moving away from hazing: The example of military initial entry training. *AMA Journal of Ethics, 16*(3), 204–209.
Figure 1 Foundation for Human Enrichment ©2014.
Flack, M., & Kite, L. (2021). Transition from military to civilian: Identity, social connectedness, and veteran wellbeing. *PLoS One, 16*(12), e0261634.
Fredrickson, B. L. (2016). Love: Positivity resonance as a fresh, evidence-based perspective on an age-old topic. In L. F. Barrett & J. M. Haviland (Eds.), *Handbook of emotions* (4th ed., pp. 847–858). Guilford Press.
Gibson, J. (2019). Mindfulness, Interoception, and the body: A contemporary perspective. *Frontiers in Psychology*. Sec. Neuropsychology, *10*, 2012.
Haase, L., Stewart, J. L., Youssef, B., May, A. C., Isakovic, S., Simmons, A. N., Johnson, D. C., Potterat, E. G., & Paulus, M. P. (2016). When the brain does not adequately feel the body: Links between low resilience and interoception. *Biological Psychology, 113*, 37–45.
Hook, J. N., Hall, T. W., Davis, D. E., Van Tongeren, D. R., & Conner, M. (2021). The Enneagram: A systematic review of the literature and directions for future research. *Journal of Clinical Psychology, 77*(4), 865–883.
Human Performance Resources by CHAMP (2022, September 6). Building team cohesion in military units. Uniformed Services University. https://www.hprc-online.org/total-force-fitness/gotmysix/resources/building-team-cohesion-military-units
Inoue, C., Shawler, E., Jordan, C. H., et al. (2023). Veteran and military mental health issues. [Updated 2023 Aug 17]. In *StatPearls [Internet]*. StatPearls Publishing. Available from: https://www.ncbi.nlm.nih.gov/books/NBK572092/
Junger, S. (2017). *Tribe*. Fourth Estate.
Kazdin, A. E. (2008). Evidence-based treatment and practice: New opportunities to bridge clinical research and practice, enhance the knowledge base, and improve patient care. *American Psychologist, 63*(3), 146–159.
Kohanov, L. (2001). *The Tao of Equus*. New World Library.
Levine, P. A. (1997). *Waking the tiger: Healing trauma: The innate capacity to transform overwhelming experiences*. North Atlantic Books.
Levine, P. A. (2010). *In an unspoken voice: How the body releases trauma and restores goodness*. North Atlantic Books.
Luthar, S. S., Cicchetti, D., & Becker, B. (2000). The construct of resilience: A critical evaluation and guidelines for future work. *Child Development, 71*(3), 543–562.
Major, B. C., Le Nguyen, K. D., Lundberg, K. B., & Fredrickson, B. L. (2018). Well-being correlates of perceived positivity resonance: Evidence from trait and episode-level assessments. *Personality & Social Psychology Bulletin, 44*(12), 1631–1647.
Mehling, W., Chesney, M., Metzler, T., Goldstein, L., Maguen, S., Geronimo, C., et al. (2018). A 12-week integrative exercise program improves self-reported mindfulness and interoceptive awareness in war veterans with posttraumatic stress symptoms. *Journal of Clinical Psychology, 74*(4), 554–565.

Merkies, K., & Franzin, O. (2021). Enhanced understanding of horse-human interactions to optimize welfare. *Animals: an Open Access Journal from MDPI, 11*(5), 1347. https://doi.org/10.3390/ani11051347

Mittly, V., Farkas-Kirov, C., Zana, Á., et al. (2023). The effect of animal-assisted interventions on the course of neurological diseases: A systematic review. *Systematic Reviews, 12*, 224. https://doi.org/10.1186/s13643-023-02387-y

Moore, C. G., Carter, R. E., Nietert, P. J., & Stewart, P. W. (2011). Recommendations for planning pilot studies in clinical and translational research. *Clinical and Translational Science, 4*(5), 332–337.

O'Connor, M., O'Reilly, G., Murphy, E., Connaughton, L., Hoctor, E., & McHugh, L. (2021). Resilience mediates the cross-sectional relationship between mindfulness and positive mental health in early adolescence. *Journal of Contextual and Behavioral Science, 21*, 171–175.

Office of the Surgeon General (OSG). (2023). *Our epidemic of loneliness and isolation: The U.S. Surgeon General's Advisory on the healing effects of social connection and community*. US Department of Health and Human Services.

Ogden, P., Minton, K., & Pain, C. (2006). *Trauma and the body: A sensorimotor approach to psychotherapy*. Norton.

Paulus, M. P., Potterat, E. G., Taylor, M. K., Van Orden, K. F., Bauman, J., Momen, N., & Swain, J. L. (2009). A neuroscience approach to optimizing brain resources for human performance in extreme environments. *Neuroscience & Biobehavioral Reviews, 33*(7), 1080–1088.

Porges, S. W. (2011). *The polyvagal theory: Neurophysiological foundations of emotions, attachment, communication, and self-regulation*. W Norton &.

Porges, S. W. (2017). *The pocket guide to the polyvagal theory: The transformative power of feeling safe*. W W Norton & Co..

Reive, C. A. (2019). *The effects of equine assisted psychotherapy on mindfulness, self-reflection, insight, and psychological well-being in veterans* [Doctoral dissertation/Florida Atlantic University].

Robinson-Edwards, S., Kewley, S., Riley, L., & Fisher, D. (2019). Examining prisoner experience of an equine assisted psychotherapy. *Therapeutic Communities: The International Journal of Therapeutic Communities, 40*(3–4), 111-124(14).

Rogowska, A. M., Tataruch, R., & Klimowska, K. (2023). Validation of the shortened 24-item multidimensional assessment of interoceptive awareness, version 2 (Brief MAIA-2). *Scientific Reports, 13*, 21270.

Rubenstein, D. (2024). Introduction to part one. In M.A. Simonds (Ed.), A Horse by nature: Managing emotional and mental stress in horses for improved welfare (p. 10). Vermont: Trafalgar Square Books.

Schlote, S. (2017). Applying a trauma lens to equine welfare. In I. Parent (Ed.), *A horse is a horse, of course: Compendium from the first international symposium of equine welfare and wellness*. Createspace Independent Publishing Platform.

Schroeder, K., Stroud, D., Sherwood, D. M., & Udell, M. A. R. (2018). Therapeutic factors in equine-facilitated group psychotherapy for women survivors of interpersonal violence. *The Journal for Specialists in Group Work, 43*(4), 326–348. https://doi.org/10.1080/01933922.2018.1516707

Scopa, C., Contalbrigo, L., Greco, A., Lanatà, A., Scilingo, E. P., & Baragli, P. (2019). Emotional transfer in human-horse interaction: New perspectives on equine assisted interventions. *Animals: An Open Access Journal From MDPI, 9*(12), 1030. https://doi.org/10.3390/ani9121030

Sherin, J. E., & Nemeroff, C. B. (2011). Post-traumatic stress disorder: the neurobiological impact of psychological trauma. *Dialogues in Clinical Neuroscience, 13*(3), 263–278. https://doi.org/10.31887/DCNS.2011.13.2/jsherin

Siegel, D. J. (1999). *The developing mind: How relationships and the brain interact to shape who we are*. Guilford Press.

Van der Kolk, B. A. (2014). *The body keeps the score: Brain, mind, and body in the healing of trauma*. Viking.

Wilson, G., Hill, M., & Kiernan, M. D. (2018). Loneliness and social isolation of military veterans: Systematic narrative review. *Occupational Medicine, 68*(9), 600–609.

Equine-Facilitated Cognitive Processing Therapy (EF-CPT) for Psychotherapy with Adults

Tracy Wharton, James Whitworth, and Marguerite Malone

Introduction

Equine-facilitated cognitive processing therapy (EF-CPT) is a therapy model that has demonstrated evidence of success with individuals seeking help for trauma, particularly those who have not had success in office-style settings. The intervention adapts the CPT model of therapy, an established and well-researched approach. CPT is a cognitive behavioral therapy-based (CBT) approach largely based on the cognitive model, which asserts that an individual's perception of a situation influences his or her emotional response to it. This type of therapy is commonly used with military veterans, first responders, and has also been used successfully with survivors of sexual assault.

EF-CPT is one of many types of equine-assisted activities and therapies (EAT). EF-CPT is a manualized intervention, based on a modification of the well-established cognitive processing therapy (CPT) model (see, e.g., Monson et al., 2006; Resick et al., 2002; VA/DoD Clinical Practice Guideline, 2023). The manual created for EF-CPT (Wharton et al., 2015) is intended to be used as a supplement to the basic CPT manual. The authors of the manual used the U.S. Department of Veterans Affairs (VA) version during the design, but any core (non-VA) CPT manual should work as well. The rationale for the combination of equine activities with CPT and

T. Wharton (✉)
National Network of Public Health Institutes, Washington, DC, USA
e-mail: twharton@nnphi.org

J. Whitworth
School of Social Work, University of Central Florida, Orlando, FL, USA
e-mail: jwhitworth@ucf.edu

M. Malone
Psychological Associates, Tuscaloosa, AL, USA

Y. Neria et al. (eds.), *Guide to Equine Assisted Therapy*,
https://doi.org/10.1007/978-3-031-74426-6_6

for the creation of a supplement rather than a new manual will be discussed later in this chapter.

The format of the intervention involves 12 sessions that are structured with a flexible curriculum that brings the client through the identification of their thoughts, skills development for the management of symptoms, and development of new frameworks for understanding responses and actions. Manualized interventions are not intended to be cookbooks. A good manual provides guidelines for decision-making both within and between sessions so that adaptations can be made to meet the unique needs of each client, while still covering the components of the intervention.

The EF-CPT model involves homework between sessions—observations and documentation of patterns of thinking and behavioral responses. The difference between the standard CPT model and EF-CPT is that the activities in session for EF-CPT are physically active and engage an equine partner. For clarity, physical activity is possible regardless of style or supports needed for movement (e.g., wheelchair, walker, and cane), since activities may involve a range of horse interactions, rather than only riding. Additionally, the horse is viewed as an equal, thinking partner in this approach, rather than a tool, so we use the term equine partner for this reason. This therapeutic approach has elements of externalization, active behavioral engagement, and observation. While EF-CPT, and indeed other forms of CPT and CBT models, can be used with a range of issues that bring people to therapy, this approach has had success with traumatic issues in therapy, with those who carry a diagnosis of post-traumatic stress disorder (PTSD), and with those who have had little or no success in office-based therapies. Estimates of CPT dropout rates when used for PTSD treatment range from 29% to 36% with even higher rates among military veterans (Edwards-Stewart et al., 2021; Goetter et al., 2015; Kline et al., 2018). The known predictors of CPT dropout include client hesitancy to reexperience their trauma, pretreatment avoidance, higher levels of anger, and hyperarousal symptoms (Alpert et al., 2020), as well as documented concerns of stigma or distrust (Tanielian & Jaycox, 2008). This type of therapy can be especially powerful because of the interaction and relationship with the horse(s), which can support re-evaluation of trauma that occurred in the context of power dynamics, hierarchical settings such as the military, or in situations where the client was or feels to have been disempowered. This dynamic will be discussed later in the chapter, when we discuss the rationale for the EF-CPT model.

The Growing Background About EAT

EAT is a well-established intervention for which there is a growing body of evidence. The EAT category includes a range of activities that involve horses, ranging from adaptive and therapeutic riding to equine-facilitated educational activities to trauma-centered psychotherapy. While there is benefit in many types of activities, EF-CPT engages CPT, a variant of CBT models, and addresses trauma in a specific and structured format that must be delivered by a trained and qualified mental health provider.

Hippotherapy similarly involves licensed professionals, who deliver physical (rehabilitative), occupational, or speech and language therapy. Hippotherapy has also demonstrated successful outcomes with children, such as improvement in spasticity in cerebral palsy, for example (Macauley & Gutierrez, 2004; Hallberg, 2017; Wood et al., 2021). Therapeutic or adaptive riding, on the other hand, is focused on inclusive engagement in horse activities (e.g., riding, carriage driving, or grooming) that provide opportunities for the social and active engagement of individuals who need supportive accommodation of some kind, rather than outcomes such as physical rehabilitation or psychotherapy. This type of activity requires riding instructors with specialized training and expertise in the physical and emotional needs of the specific types of riders that they serve (e.g., special needs youth, riders with cerebral palsy, and disabled veterans), as the accommodations needed may be different across groups and the overall goal is to provide inclusive activities. Facilitators for these types of interventions should have experience with horses and an understanding of horse communication and herd behavior, as this is a substantial component of the dynamic in any equine activity. See Table 1 for a comparison of types of EAT.

Each of these types of activities requires horses that have received specialized training with equipment, tools, rider needs, and trainer commands that enable the horse handler to keep both the horses and humans safe during sessions. Horses that are used for EAT programs of any kind must have a baseline of standard riding training and calm demeanor. From that baseline, additional training is tailored to the type of needs of the program but may include desensitization to adaptive equipment and unexpected rider movements, training to voice commands, or different types of cues such as where and how the horse handler may be holding the lead rope. Horses also generally receive training in a "stop or freeze" command of some kind. For example, at Therapeutic Riding of Tuscaloosa in Alabama, horses are trained that if a rider comes off-balance and begins to fall, they are to take their last step in reverse, plant their feet and put their head down at the hip of the horse handler, and remain still until another cue is given, so that the rider can be safely reoriented. Such training may require up to 6 months of work but is essential for safety.

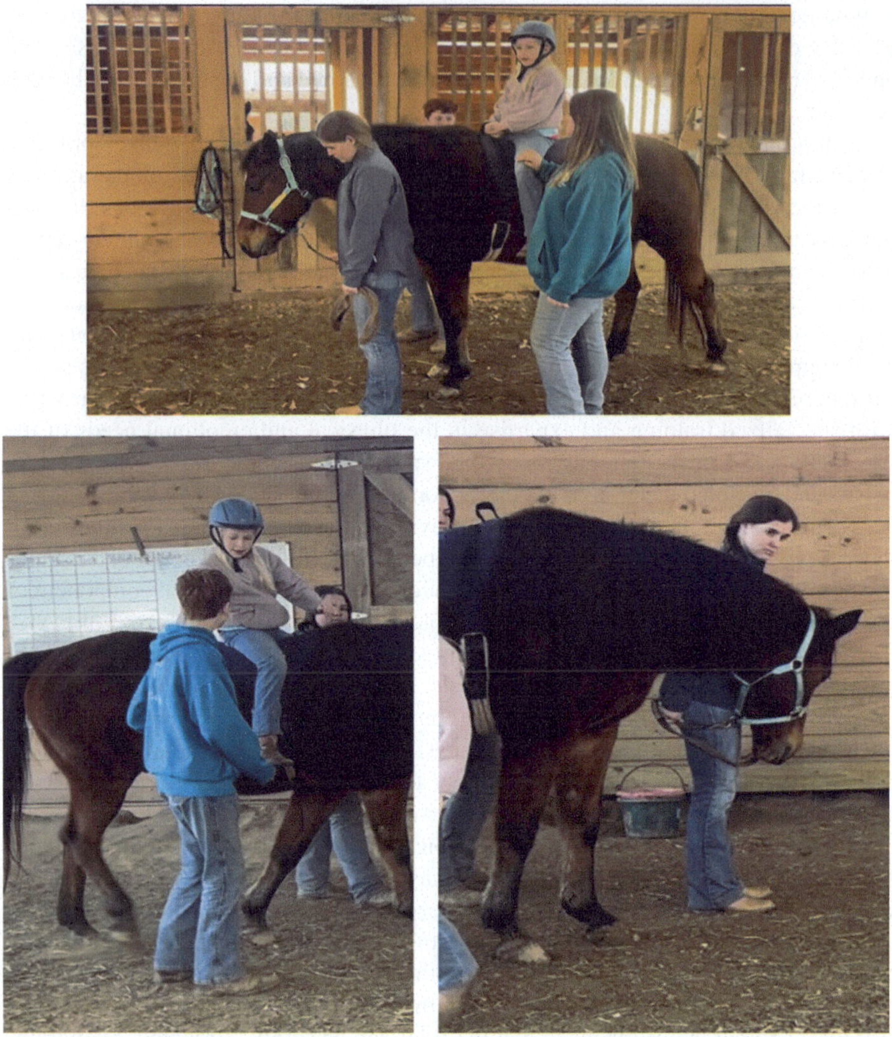

Top photo: a rider with side walkers and a horse walker; Left photo: rider becomes unbalanced; Right photo: horse freezes with head down and feet planted, waiting for a cue from the horse walker. (Photos courtesy of Therapeutic Riding of Tuscaloosa)

Some of these types of activities are specifically psychotherapy approaches, which require an appropriately licensed and trained mental health professional, compliant with the state where services are being provided. It is also important to have a horse handler in every session. Their presence is for safety—both for human and animal participants. Therapy can be intense, and the focus of any mental health or health professional must remain on the person and the therapy dynamic. It is therefore the important role of the horse handler to monitor the well-being of the horse and intervene if risk to either humans or horses emerges in any situation.

Table 1 A comparison of some types of EAT

Model	Population of focus	Requirements
EF-CPT	Individuals with a history of trauma or a diagnosis of PTSD; military or service personnel with hyperarousal symptoms; individuals who have not met goals or felt comfortable in office-based psychotherapy	Licensed mental health provider trained in cognitive therapy approaches; horse handler; horse partner
Equine-assisted therapy groups for adults (EAT)	Individuals who prefer not to engage in office-based programs; individuals who thrive with a group cohort	Licensed mental health provider; horse handler; horse partners for each group member
Equine-assisted therapy (EAT) groups for youth, such as Stable Moments	Foster or legal involved youth; children with special needs	Licensed mental health provider; horse handler; horse partners for each group member
Hippotherapy (speech and language therapy, physical therapy, occupational therapy)	Speech and language, PT or OT clients who would prefer a therapy context other than office-based; those who struggle with attention related issues	Licensed speech/language professional, PT or OT; horse handler; horse partners trained with adaptive commands and equipment
Therapeutic or adaptive riding	Youth or adults with special needs or a need for extra emotional, social, or physical support	Trained horse-riding instructor with specialized training in TR; adaptive equipment; horse partners trained with adaptive commands and equipment

Providers and horse-staff must have a collaborative working relationship and a system of communication that will maintain safety while not disrupting the therapeutic process (Table 1).

Rationale for Developing EF-CPT for PTSD

CPT is one of the commonly used research-based trauma-focused interventions used to treat PTSD (Reisman, 2016; Resick et al., 2017). There is a substantial volume of evidence supporting the use of CPT with civilians, veterans, and survivors of sexual assault and individuals with a diagnosis of PTSD, including four meta-analyses consisting of all of these population groups summarizing the strong efficacy of this treatment (Asmundson et al., 2019; Cusack et al., 2016; Forbes et al., 2012; Haagen et al., 2015; Monson et al., 2006; Resick et al., 2017; Taylor & Harvey, 2009; Watts et al., 2013). One meta-analysis identified 11 published trials with a total of 1130 participants comparing CPT against an inactive control condition or other active treatment for PTSD in adults with the average participant treated with CPT having fewer PTSD symptoms compared to 89% of those in inactive control conditions at post-treatment and 82% at follow-up (Asmundson et al., 2019).

CPT is endorsed by the U.S. Department of Defense (DoD) and the VA as a best practice for the treatment of PTSD as well as the International Society of Traumatic Stress Studies (National Center for PTSD, 2023; VA/DoD clinical practice guideline, 2023).

Dropout (attrition) among veterans with PTSD remains a persistent problem with both office-based CPT and another frequently used therapy type, prolonged exposure therapy, despite their known efficacy with this population (Edwards-Stewart et al., 2021; Goetter et al., 2015). Dropout rates for veterans involved in these trauma-focused interventions range from 5.0% to 78.2% (Edwards-Stewart et al., 2021; Goetter et al., 2015). Several studies have theorized that veterans' concerns about privacy and stigma along with negative perceptions of mental health care and providers account for such poor treatment engagement (Kehle-Forbes et al., 2016; Kim et al., 2010; Seal et al., 2010; Tanielian & Jaycox, 2008). Other explanations for this underutilization include the frequency and number of sessions required for CPT, a desire by veterans to not be perceived as being "weak" when asking for help, and high levels of avoidance in confronting their trauma experiences, a necessary part of therapy (Fragedakis & Toriello, 2014; Hoge et al., 2015; Tanielian & Jaycox, 2008).

Innovative approaches addressing veterans' concerns are needed to boost their treatment utilization and decrease dropout rates. Veterans with PTSD may be more likely to seek alternative care options such as EAT and EF-CPT (Cohen et al., 2010; Monroe et al., 2019; Wharton et al., 2019). They may prefer "activity-based" approaches where the focus of the treatment is less centered on themselves and more focused on interaction with the horse. Involvement with EAT, in an environment distinct from common prevailing treatment settings that use activities not usually included in office-based CPT, may increase veterans' comfort level, overcome some of their stigma concerns, and reduce resistance to care. Dropout rates for EAT are considerably lower compared to traditional office-based forms of PTSD treatment (Shelef et al., 2019).

Horses possess unique behavioral characteristics that appear to make them particularly well suited for assisting humans to recover from traumatic experiences as a contributing factor in therapy. The sheer size of horses commands nearly instantaneous respect from humans that are interacting with them. As prey animals, they are remarkably sensitive to changes in their environment including the actions and responses of humans or other animals. Horses are often compatible as models of hyperarousal since they are prey animals whose main defense is to flee. They will often seek to run away (i.e., flight) when sensing threats. Horses are especially aware of agitation, issues of affective incongruity, and elevated autonomic arousal in others (Gehrke et al., 2018). They often mirror the responses they perceive in others including their behaviors and emotions. If an individual in reasonable proximity to them is upset, agitated, anxious, or angry, they will most likely react in a similar manner (Monroe et al., 2019).

Horses possess both a pronounced flight instinct along with a strong desire for connection. This desire for connection may allow them the potential to develop a human–animal bond that permits veterans and others to form a relationship "connection where both can feel some level of trust. Human-animal bonds are defined as mutually beneficial and dynamic relationships between people and animals" (American Veterinary Medical Association, 2023). EAT as an intervention is also conducted outside and not in confined office spaces, where veterans often feel more comfortable and may experience decreased hypervigilance, feeling less as closed in by their environment. Additionally, this engagement with a large animal has the potential to reestablish feelings of empowerment for individuals who have lost that personal sense of power.

Humans participating in EF-CPT can with guidance and practice start to recognize their own physiological and emotional reactions due to forming a bonding relationship with the horse, which requires them to focus more on the present moment and situation (Shelef et al., 2019). Horses are social herding mammals that establish a specific hierarchical structure, similar to a family or workplace, with relationships that require leadership, closeness, affection, and setting boundaries (Shelef et al., 2019). Being around such animals who transparently and nonjudgmentally communicate as part of the intervention may allow humans who have experienced trauma to feel safe and free to examine their own post-traumatic stress responses (Marchand et al., 2021; Shelef et al., 2019).

The Process of Developing EF-CPT

The process of creating the manual for EF-CPT involved mapping the topics in the standardized CPT protocol, identifying how each topic could be facilitated by equine partnership, and linking appropriate equine-facilitated activities to the sessions and homework worksheets. For example, session two of the standard CPT protocol focuses on the meaning of an activating event (an event that cues symptoms to appear). The planned work that should happen in that session includes addressing the client's ability to identify and name emotions that come up, and identifying the connections between the event, thoughts, and feelings using the A-B-C strategy (a behavioral concept that is part of the standard CPT/CBT model). An office-based session would usually involve talking through an event, teaching the A-B-C concept, and working through the emotions and connections verbally, using guided imagery, dialogue, and imagination, drawing on the cognitive abilities of the client to interpret and re-interpret.

A session with the EF-CPT model would apply the same concepts, but would add an activity that involves, for example, observation of a herd dynamic involving an alpha horse and several other herdmate horses alone in a paddock with one pile of hay. The client and therapist would observe the behavior and discuss what is perceived to be happening, how the client feels about it, and how this type of behavior might reflect similar dynamics in the client's life. The element of externalization (discussing a group of horses rather than the client's self and family) can make the identification of emotional content or response easier for the client to initiate. The approach requires that the activity get to the heart of the concept being discussed and create a context in which the client can observe a similar cue for their own emotions (e.g., bullying for aggressive horse behavior in getting to a single pile of hay). The resulting conversation can engage issues of hierarchy and pecking order, appropriate responses, instinctual responses, logic, and interpretation, giving a lot of fertile ground for addressing the kinds of symptoms that the client may be experiencing. The model effectively replaces the office-based activities with farm-based activities that are conceptually similar and activate the responses of the client through the externalization process, while still relying on the cognitive-processing part of the model.

The new protocol was always meant to be used in conjunction with the established VA-endorsed *CPT Patient Workbook*, Veteran/Military Version (Resick et al., 2010), including the framework, worksheets, and handouts. While combining the protocols into one manual may have seemed efficient, we had several concerns which led us to create a protocol addendum manual, rather than an entire new manual. Firstly, we were wary of untrained persons having access to the complete protocol without adequate training. There have been instances that we were aware of where accomplished equestrian professionals felt that they could apply psychotherapeutic interventions, using their skills and insight into horses. Some people sought out training that was created for horse handlers that work with therapists and then felt that they could do the intervention themselves.

Psychotherapy, particularly when it focuses on trauma, can be of great benefit to those who suffer, but it can also do tremendous harm. Trauma interventions rely on the observations, skill, and depth of knowledge of the therapist to ensure psychological safety and prevent unintended consequences such as psychiatric emergencies. Secondly, experienced clinicians will be familiar with the standardized CPT workbook, so making a shift to an addendum would be minimal effort, while preserving and emphasizing the centrality of the CPT concepts and importance of preserving the overall model. We did not want to make this a cookbook that anyone could pick up without appropriate training or necessary structures in place. While therapists will learn many different approaches to the work throughout their career, even the most manualized approach is never as simple, straightforward, or risk-free as a recipe card. The skill of the therapist is the secret ingredient that makes things come together, regardless of model. In the case of EF-CPT, the skill of the therapist also includes the ability to work seamlessly with a horse handler and equine partner to support a safe therapy context. When this happens, clients can access the most challenging of memories and emotions and re-learn how to manage and interpret them with the support of positive regard from not only the therapist, but also from a large animal.

The process of creating the new protocol involved the steps shown in Fig. 1. As described in the previous example, each standard session goal was clearly identified so that activities could be matched to elicit the target behaviors, cues, and emotional content. Suggested activities were identified for each session, and guidance was created for the introduction of the content and activities, and also for debriefing the activities to ensure that therapeutic goals remain at the forefront. Because working with horses and other humans can sometimes involve unexpected things such as

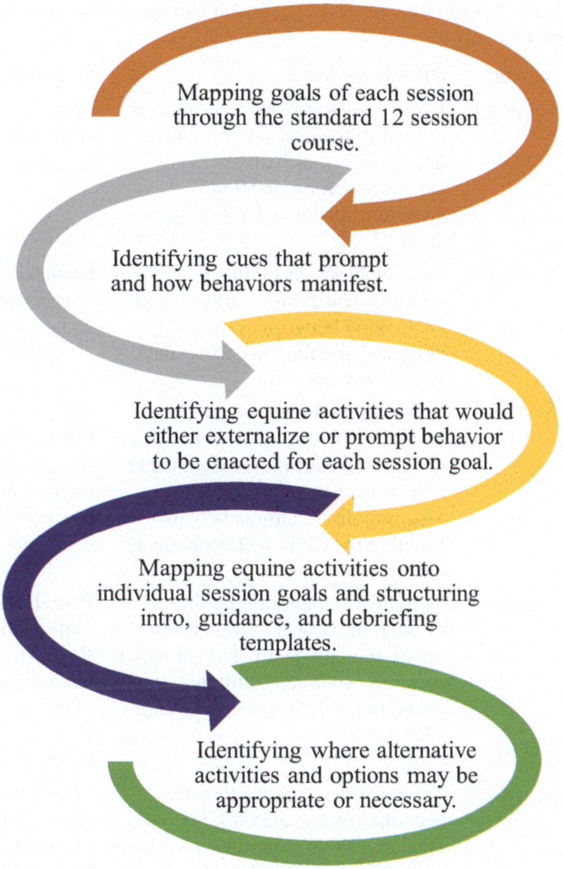

Fig. 1 The process of creating the new protocol

staffing changes, unanticipated needs of the horse, or other unexpected shifts in plans, alternative exercises and options were identified for each session, to provide the therapist with several options to best meet the needs of the therapeutic relationship. These might be, for example, a riding-involved activity instead of an observation, or a teamwork-based activity with the horse handler instead of a discussion-based activity.

The initial session, as with any therapy model, involves an introduction to the process and expectation setting with the client. Additionally, EF-CPT requires some introduction to the facility and basic safety around horses. For this reason, either a longer session must be scheduled for this first encounter, or a separate orientation for the facility must be scheduled. The session then proceeds along the CPT framework to identify self-soothing approaches and begin the introduction of Stuck Points in thinking about trauma. Therapy sessions then proceed as demonstrated in Table 2, moving the client through a mapped process of identifying thought patterns, cognitive distortions, and learned responses, challenging and examining each of these in turn.

Table 2 Overview of EF-CPT session foci and activities (excerpted and adapted for this text from the manual)[a]

Session	Overall session focus	Example activities
Session 1	*Initial session* involves orientation to facility policies and basic horse–human safety, as well as psychoeducation on PTSD symptoms and how CPT addresses them.	Selection of equine partner; safety orientation; soothing techniques instruction and enactment.
Session 2	*Session 2* focuses on the meaning of trauma, identifying emotions, and connection between events, thoughts, and feelings, using the A-B-C strategy	Equine activities focus on identifying the connection between events, perceptions, consequences, and feelings.
Session 3	*Session 3* continues coaching related to identification of thoughts and feelings, using horse choice to springboard to beliefs and assumptions. Additional details found in the CPT workbook, under "Session 3."	The participant chooses a horse to groom. Dasalaar and Cabeza (2004) suggest that movement in R or L directions and attentional focus stimulate cross-brain hemispheric function and facilitate memory recall.
Session 4	*Session 4* involves telling the story of the trauma, with as much sensory detail, thought detail, and emotional recall as possible. Additional details found in the CPT workbook, under "Session 4."	Participant grooms using a curry in circular motion and brush in lengthwise strokes. Evidence suggests that different physical movements have an effect on the recall of emotional memories (Barsalou, 1999; Casasanto, 2009; Casasanto & Dijkstra, 2010; Dijkstra et al., 2007).
Session 5	*Session 5* involves reading the account of trauma aloud; Socratic-style questions regarding self-blame and other cognitive distortions; use client's A-B-C worksheets (see above) as guides.	The participant chooses horse, identifies the emotional basis for the choice, cognitions involved, and distortions that surface. Participant leads horse through obstacles in a pattern.
Session 6	*Session 6* involves challenging questions and finding examples of problematic thinking patterns.	Activities address building self-confidence in actions, in creating thought processes, and in decision-making.

(continued)

Table 2 (continued)

Session	Overall session focus	Example activities
Session 7	*Session 7* addresses patterns of thought, issues of safety, and expansion of Socratic questioning to include challenging current cognitions and also beliefs.	Activities address challenging assumptions and beliefs.
Session 8	*Session 8* addresses trust and continues work on challenging beliefs and stuck points; concepts related to trust of both self and others ("Session 8" of CPT manual)	Activities focus on trust between the participant and the horse, and build on exercises related to leadership, perceptions, and boundaries.
Session 9	*Session 9* integrates challenging beliefs dialogue with material about power and control. Focus on beliefs and/or expectation about problem-solving, issues of power, and association with capacity for self-growth.	Discussion about thought processes and emotional choices that occur in activities.
Session 10	*Session 10* involves reviewing power and control issues that have been raised and initiating discussion about esteem.	Focus on esteem and self-worth, and build on work related to power/control, trust, leadership, boundaries, and safety.
Session 11	*Session 11* involves review of esteem, power, and control issues and expands focus to address issues of intimacy.	Observations of horse behavior springboard into the discussion of how boundaries and relationships have been impacted by trauma.
Session 12	*Session 12* involves review of successes, worksheets and concepts, and work with equine partners, and preparing for termination of the therapeutic relationship.	Significant anthropomorphizing is used to identify areas of success and areas that need continued work, as the therapeutic relationship comes to a close.

[a]All sessions also include material from appropriate sessions found in the VA-endorsed CPT manual

The Clinical Benefits of EF-CPT for PTSD Treatment

Disruptive events can occur in the daily lives of individuals experiencing symptoms of PTSD. For example, a particular type of weather, presence of an object, sound, or smell may trigger PTSD symptoms. These symptoms may include physiological dysregulation and increased autonomic function (such as heart rate or sweat gland activity, or increased perceived physical impairment and pain), functional impairment in areas such as trust, ability to tolerate mistakes and frustration, and inability to feel emotions (APA, 2013; Brewin et al., 2000; Hoge, 2011). The task of the mental health professional engaging in treatment with these individuals is to address the cognitive processing and reactions underlying these symptoms which have become patterned as a result of the traumatic experience(s) and challenge the assumptions that people make in current circumstances about themselves, their life, and the world (Monson et al., 2006).

EF-CPT is a specific type of cognitive-processing therapy, where the focus on cognition has been noted to be particularly successful with military veterans (Monson et al., 2005, 2006; Department of Veterans Affairs, 2017). CPT has been established as effective in both randomized controlled trials and in clinical settings, where substantial improvement can be made in relatively short intervention times (Forbes et al., 2012; Bradley et al., 2005; Resick et al., 2008). A meta-analysis of studies of PTSD interventions found effect sizes, suggesting that cognitive-based psychotherapies have a substantial impact and that substantial improvement in outcomes related to the PTSD Symptom Checklist (PCL) are seen consistently (Bradley et al., 2005). Evidence suggests that CPT has larger effect sizes in outcomes and post-treatment functioning than any other intervention tested to date and that this intervention has a better impact on issues of guilt, shame, and self-blame when compared to prolonged exposure (PE) therapy, the alternative treatment recommended by the VA (Resick et al., 2002). Dropout rates for PE, as noted previously, can be significant, and alternatives that avoid triggering feelings of guilt and shame among potential clients have tremendous potential for helping the many individuals who continue to struggle.

This intervention was created with an explicit intent to leverage the impact of the environment of the farm/ranch, the distraction to the participant of the horse as a partner in the session, and the associations that exist between the abstract states of emotions such as helplessness or guilt and concrete stimuli that can be introduced through active sessions. Horses are prey animals and are trained to engage safely with their human partners while also remaining sensitive to issues of affective incongruity, agitation, or threat. Trained horse handlers and experienced clinicians are able to identify signals of confusion or concern in the horse and reflect these signals back verbally to the human client as a way of reflecting and challenging behavior. For example, a person might insist that they are not upset and are "fine," while a horse may be exhibiting ear flattening or side-eye type of behavior, indicating that they are seeing something different. The therapist can raise this observation with the client as an objective measure of their mood state and bring the discussion into the therapy. Working with horses can provide opportunities to address issues of trust, intolerance of mistakes and low frustration tolerance, and issues of self-efficacy, through matching activities that cue these challenges and provide opportunity to enact the challenge in session and work through with support, addressing emotional flooding and hyperreactivity while they occur. Combined with CPT, which is focused on cognitive reframing, this is a powerful approach. The model also provides a set structure and endpoint that can be reassuring for some clients.

EF-CPT is grounded in a well-established manual and the addendum manual contains activities and guidance (as described in Table 2) to expand the skill sets of experienced therapists. While the intervention is manualized, such frameworks are always intended as a guide, rather than a cookbook approach. Each client is unique and manualized interventions are generally embedded with varying levels of flexibility so that topics can be addressed out of order, issues raised by clients can be addressed in real time, and activities can be moved around in the order of sessions as needed. Provided that the overall progress toward the therapy goals remains intact, such modifications are expected and are guided by the skill of the clinician. The EF-CPT and CPT manuals have been tested repeatedly and few changes to the order of things have been seen in the studies, but clinicians should not be concerned if such a thing arises, as such adaptations are completely normal.

Studies of equine-facilitated psychotherapy have found very low dropout rates and significantly reduced rates of trauma symptoms, including hyperarousal, distress, and guilt among both older and younger veterans (Monroe et al., 2019; Wharton et al., 2019). The 12-session EF-CPT protocol was tested using a pre-test, post-test design with a single psychologist and consistent horse handler (Wharton et al., 2019). The study engaged 27 veterans (78% male) who all met the VA criteria for diagnosis of PTSD, and most of the participants indicated that they struggled with a mood disorder, as well. Of these, 21 identified their index trauma as being combat-related; four identified their index trauma as being a sexual assault, seven identified their index trauma as being a physical trauma of some kind, and five indicated more than one kind of trauma. The study hypothesized improvement of all the measures, low attrition, and good model fidelity. The outcomes demonstrated that the validated PTSD Checklist (PCL) scores significantly reduced from pre- to post ($M1 = 68.25$, $M2 = 35.96$, $p < 0.001$), indicating a reduction in symptoms that is both clinically evidenced and statistically significant. Similarly, scores on the validated Trauma Related Guilt Inventory demonstrated significant improvement ($p < 0.001$). The study used two measures to attempt to capture the quality of the working relationship within the therapy sessions: the validated Working Alliance Index and the Human-Animal Bond Scale (HABS). These indicated positive therapeutic alliance with the psychologist and high rates of bonding with the horses, although the HABS is not a validated measure. The study had a 7% attrition (dropout) rate, with two individuals dropping out after their first session. Fidelity to the manual by the treating psychologist was high and was verified through audio-recording review. The psychologist understood the areas where flexibility was built into the protocol and points where there was less flexibility in order to maintain true fidelity to the intervention and indicated satisfaction with the ease of applying the manualized protocol in real-life clinical practice (Wharton et al., 2019).

Another equine therapy study, examining a similar intervention that was delivered in a group format by a licensed mental health provider and a horse trainer engaged 60 military veterans who self-identified as having a diagnosis of PTSD, although only 48 consented to allow their assessments to be used in research (Monroe et al., 2019). This format involved the same material and exercises but used longer and fewer overall sessions. Participants represented all military branches and ranged in age from 24 to 71 years old. Scores at post-test on validated measures of trauma symptoms (the PCL, military version), depression (Beck Depression Inventory II), and anxiety (Burns Anxiety Inventory) all indicated improvement ($p < 0.05$), and an assessment of overall quality of life using the validated Quality of Life Inventory (QOLI) indicated significant improvement ($p = 0.002$). The study had an 88% retention rate (12% attrition), with reasons for dropout listed as issues with childcare or transportation, and conflicts with other doctor appointments, especially at the VA.

While outcomes have been shown to be slightly better than office-based studies in terms of PTSD-related symptoms, dropout rates below 15% are a dramatic and important improvement. For those who are not inclined or cannot tolerate the pressures of trauma therapy in an office-based environment, EF-CPT applies a well-established model to ground an alternative approach that works just as well and may feel more accessible to therapy hesitant clients.

Future Directions

One of the challenges in establishing the evidence for any therapeutic intervention is the need for studies with large enough sample sizes to enable generalization. It is hard to draw a conclusion about whether something works for a particular client if there was no one similar written about in the available published evidence. Similarly, while there are many ways to gather evidence and evaluate data, medical systems generally seek out evidence produced by randomized controlled trials, a notoriously challenging method of research in human therapy studies. Randomizing people to different therapy styles involves consent and provision of care that still meets minimum standards and further requires staff for the study who understand the research concepts of contamination and fidelity in order to ensure a rigorous study. While such studies are possible, they can be expensive, so many of the studies of animal therapies tend to be smaller, pragmatic trials that rely on methods such as wait-list comparison groups or delayed treatment groups. Large sample sizes are a further challenge in animal-facilitated studies due to the overall capacity of practitioners to have enough clients for the study. In our trials of EF-CPT, we were able to get a large enough sample size by gathering data over the course of a year, as the therapist was able to intake people. Due to the specialty nature of this therapy, capacity issues for research show up in both available therapists and available space, as well as in availability of appropriately trained horses and horse handlers. Work has continued over the last decade to expand the available evidence base regarding equine-facilitated therapies and interventions, and ever more promising findings continue to emerge.

A question that continues to arise is whether the magic ingredient of therapy is actually the horse, or whether similar outcomes can be found with dogs or even with other outdoor activities. Positive outcomes have been demonstrated in other active therapies and overlapping variables may be at play (Whitworth et al., 2019). There are certainly a number of advantageous elements of any outdoor or actively engaged therapy and many of the same principles discussed here will continue to apply. Horses, however, have a particular presence and size that make them unique as therapy partners. Their generally gentle disposition provides an opportunity to leverage the size and intelligence of a larger animal as a therapeutic aspect and their highly communicative and responsive nature offers an opening for dialogue in unique ways.

There is a cost differential related to animals in therapy. Horses require additional staff and maintenance expenses, while dogs require somewhat less cost but do still require specialized training. There have not been cost–benefit analyses that we are aware of at this point that unpack the overhead costs of the various approaches relative to their expense versus justification. However, where such approaches are feasible and trained staff are available, there appears to be an enticement of this type of therapy that holds some level of appeal for participants who may be resistant to engage in office-based therapy. The justification of cost must, of course, be balanced by increased access and opportunity for therapy among potential participants, and this is mitigated heavily by the resources available to a therapist who wishes to approach this type of practice. Nonetheless, the field would benefit from research that examines outcomes and engages cost–benefit analyses across therapy types and more clearly examines the variables involved in different approaches.

Conclusions

EF-CPT does, to be sure, involve more training and resources per client than office-based therapy models do, but once established, equine practices tend to be popular and as sustainable as any other private practice. Therapists should bear in mind that this type of intervention is a psychotherapy with the same high stakes and risk to the well-being of the participant as any other trauma therapy approach. Therapy for PTSD should only be conducted by appropriately trained mental health providers. Additionally, therapists who seek to work with horses should have a solid working knowledge of equine behaviors and communication and should have a strong working relationship with at least one horse handler partner. This type of therapy can be stressful for the animals, due to the strong emotions that may be present in the human participant, so training and ongoing attention to the rest and comfort of the horse partner are critical components of a successful therapy practice (Wharton et al., 2005).

Available evidence to date for animal assisted interventions has shown excellent outcomes that are remarkably consistent across studies, with consistently low dropout rates. Criticisms of equine-facilitated interventions have argued that more traditional therapy approaches have reliable and consistent outcomes. Such critics have argued that these more traditional (office-based) approaches should be the first line of treatment for clients. Office-based CPT works and the outcomes are notably consistent when a client completes the series of sessions for treatment. In the end, however, how much does consistency of outcomes matter if participants are more likely to drop out and never complete the treatment? For individuals who would benefit from professional support but are hesitant to engage in office-based therapies, equine-facilitated therapy provides an approach that can seem less intimidating, more accessible, and with more incentive to complete a series of sessions.

References

Alpert, E., Hayes, A. M., Barnes, J. B., & Sloan, D. M. (2020). Predictors of dropout in cognitive processing therapy for PTSD: An examination of trauma narrative content. *Behavior Therapy, 51*(5), 774–788. https://doi.org/10.1016/j.beth.2019.11.003

American Veterinary Medical Association. (2023). *Human-animal bond.* https://www.avma.org/one-health/human-animal-bond

APA. (2013). *Diagnostic and statistical manual of mental disorders* (5th ed., (DSM-5)). American Psychiatric Association.

Asmundson, G. J. G., Thorisdottir, A. S., Roden-Foreman, J. W., Baird, S. O., Witcraft, S. M., Stein, A. T., Smits, J. A. J., & Powers, M. B. (2019). A meta-analytic review of cognitive processing therapy for adults with posttraumatic stress disorder. *Cognitive Behaviour Therapy, 48*(1), 1–14. https://doi.org/10.1080/16506073.2018.1522371

Barsalou, L. (1999). Perceptual symbol systems. *Behavioral Brain Science, 22*, 577–660.

Bradley, R., Greene, J., Russ, E., Dutra, L., & Westen, D. (2005). A multidimensional meta-analysis of psychotherapy for PTSD. *American Journal of Psychiatry, 162*, 214–227.

Brewin, C., Andrews, B., & Rose, S. (2000). Fear, helplessness, and horror in posttraumatic stress disorder: Investigating DSM-IV criterion A2 in victims of violent crime. *Journal of Trauma and Stress, 13*(3), 499–509.

Casasanto, D. (2009). Embodiment of abstract concepts: Good and bad in right- and left-handers. *Journal of Exploratory Psychology, 138*, 351–367.

Casasanto, D., & Dijkstra, K. (2010). Motor action and emotional memory. *Cognition, 115*, 179–185.

Cohen, B., Gima, K., Bertenthal, D., Kim, S., Marmar, C., & Seal, K. (2010). Mental health diagnoses and utilization of VA non-mental health medical services among returning Iraq and Afghanistan veterans. *Journal of General Internal Medicine, 25*(1), 18–24. https://doi.org/10.1007/s11606-009-1117-3

Cusack, K., Jonas, D. E., Forneris, C. A., Wines, C., Sonis, J., Middleton, J. C., Feltner, C., Brownley, K. A., Olmsted, K. R., Greenblatt, A., Weil, A., & Gaynes, B. N. (2016). Psychological treatments for adults with posttraumatic stress disorder: A systematic review and meta-analysis. *Clinical Psychology Review, 43*, 128–141. https://doi.org/10.1016/j.cpr.2015.10.003

Dasalaar, S., & Cabeza, R. (2004). Age-related changes in hemispheric organization. In R. Cabeza, L. Nyberg, & D. Park (Eds.), *Cognitive neuroscience of aging: Linking cognitive and cerebral aging*. Oxford Publishing. ISBN: 9780195156744.

Department of Veterans Affairs and Department of Defense. (2017). *VA/DOD clinical practice guideline for the management of posttraumatic stress disorder and acute stress disorder.* Retrieved from www.healthquality.va.gov/guidelines/MH/ptsd/VADoDPTSDCPGFinal012418.pdf

Dijkstra, K., Kaschak, M., & Zwaan, R. (2007). Body posture facilitates retrieval of autobiographical memories. *Cognition, 102*, 139–149.

Edwards-Stewart, A., Smolenski, D. J., Bush, N. E., Cyr, B. A., Beech, E. H., Skopp, N. A., & Belsher, B. E. (2021). Posttraumatic stress disorder treatment dropout among military and veteran populations: A systematic review and meta-analysis. *Journal of Traumatic Stress, 34*(4), 808–818. https://doi.org/10.1002/jts.22653

Forbes, D., Lloyd, D., Nixon, R. D. V., Elliot, P., Varker, T., Perry, D., Bryant, R. A., & Creamer, M. (2012). A multisite randomized controlled effectiveness trial of cognitive processing therapy for military-related posttraumatic stress disorder. *Journal of Anxiety Disorders, 26*(3), 442–452. https://doi.org/10.1016/j.janxdis.2012.01.006

Fragedakis, T. M., & Toriello, P. (2014). The development and experience of combat-related PTSD: A demand for neurofeedback as an effective form of treatment. *Journal of Counseling & Development, 92*(4), 481–488. https://doi.org/10.1002/j.1556-6676.2014.00174.x

Gehrke, E. K., Noquez, A. E., Ranke, P. L., & Myers, M. P. (2018). Measuring the psychophysiological changes in combat veterans participating in an equine therapy program. *Journal of Military, Veteran and Family Health, 4*(1), 60–69. https://doi.org/10.3138/jmvfh.2017-0015

Goetter, E. M., Bui, E., Ojserkis, R. A., Zakarian, R. J., Brendel, R. W., & Simon, N. M. (2015). A systematic review of dropout from psychotherapy for posttraumatic stress disorder among Iraq and Afghanistan combat veterans. *Journal of Traumatic Stress, 28*(5), 401–409. https://doi.org/10.1002/jts.22038

Haagen, J. F., Smid, G. E., Knipscheer, J. W., & Kleber, R. J. (2015). The efficacy of recommended treatments for veterans with PTSD: A metaregression analysis. *Clinical Psychology Review, 40*, 184–194. https://doi.org/10.1016/j.cpr.2015.06.008

Hallberg, L. (2017). *The clinical practice of equine-assisted therapy: Including horses in human healthcare*. Taylor & Francis Group. ISBN: 97811347931.

Hoge, C. (2011). Interventions for war-related posttraumatic stress disorder: Meeting veterans where they are. *Journal of the American Medical Association, 306*(5), 549–551. https://doi.org/10.1001/jama.2011.1096

Hoge, C. W., Grossman, S. H., Auchterlonie, J. L., Riviere, L. A., Milliken, C. S., & Wilk, J. E. (2015). PTSD treatment for soldiers after combat deployment: Low utilization of mental health care and reasons for dropout. *Psychiatric Services, 65*(8), 997–1004. https://doi.org/10.1176/appi.ps.201300307

Kehle-Forbes, S. M., Meis, L. A., Spoont, M. R., & Polusny, M. A. (2016). Treatment initiation and dropout from prolonged exposure and cognitive processing therapy in a VA outpatient clinic. *Psychological Trauma: Theory, Research, Practice and Policy, 8*(1), 107–114. https://doi.org/10.1037/tra0000065

Kim, P. Y., Thomas, J. L., Wilk, J. E., Castro, C. A., & Hoge, C. W. (2010). Stigma, barriers to care, and use of mental health services among active duty and National Guard soldiers after combat. *Psychiatric Services, 61*(6), 582–588. https://doi.org/10.1176/ps.2010.61.6.582

Kline, A. C., Cooper, A. A., Rytwinksi, N. K., & Feeny, N. C. (2018). Long-term efficacy of psychotherapy for posttraumatic stress disorder: A meta-analysis of randomized controlled trials. *Clinical Psychology Review, 59*, 30–40. https://doi.org/10.1016/j.cpr.2017.10.009

Macauley, B. L., & Gutierrez, K. M. (2004). The effectiveness of hippotherapy for children with language-learning disabilities. *Communication Disorders Quarterly, 25*(4), 205–217. https://doi.org/10.1177/15257401040250040501

Marchand, W. R., Andersen, S. J., Smith, J. E., Hoopes, K. H., & Carlson, J. K. (2021). Equine-assisted activities and therapies for veterans with posttraumatic stress disorder: Current state, challenges and future directions. *Chronic Stress, 5*. https://doi.org/10.1177/2470547021991556

Monroe, M., Whitworth, J. D., Wharton, T., & Turner, J. (2019). Effects of an equine-assisted therapy program for military veterans with self-reported PTSD. *Society & Animals, 29*(5–6), 577–590. https://doi.org/10.1163/15685306-12341572

Monson, C. M., Price, J. L., & Ranslow, E. (2005). Treating combat PTSD through cognitive processing therapy. *Federal Practitioner, 22*, 75–83.

Monson, C. M., Schnurr, P. P., Resick, P. A., Friedman, M. J., Young-Xu, Y., & Stevens, S. P. (2006). Cognitive processing therapy for veterans with military-related posttraumatic stress disorder. *Journal of Consulting and Clinical Psychology, 74*(5), 898–907. https://doi.org/10.1037/0022-006X.74.5.898

National Center for PTSD. (2023). *Cognitive processing therapy for PTSD*. https://www.ptsd.va.gov/professional/treat/txessentials/cpt_for_ptsd_pro.asp

Reisman, M. (2016). PTSD treatment for veterans: What's working, what's new, what's next. *P&T, 41*, 623–634. https://www.ncbi.nlm.nih.gov/pmc/articles/PMC5047000/

Resick, P., Nishith, P., Weaver, T., Astin, M., & Feuer, C. (2002). A comparison of cognitive-processing therapy with prolonged exposure and a waiting condition for the treatment of chronic posttraumatic stress disorder in female rape victims. *Journal of Consulting and Clinical Psychology, 70*(4), 867–879. https://doi.org/10.1037/0022-006X.70.4.867

Resick, P., Galovski, T., O'Brien Uhlmansiek, M., Scher, C., Clum, G., & Young-Xu, Y. (2008). A randomized clinical trial to dismantle components of cognitive processing therapy for posttraumatic stress disorder in female victims of interpersonal violence. *Journal of Consulting and Clinical Psychology, 76*(2), 243–258. https://doi.org/10.1037/0022-006X.76.2.243

Resick, P. A., Monson, C. M., & Chard, K. M. (2010). *CPT patient workbook, veteran/military version*.

Resick, P. A., Wachen, J. S., Dondanville, K. A., Pruiksma, K. E., Yarvis, J. S., Peterson, A. L., Mintz, J., and the STRONG STAR Consortium, Borah, E. V., Brundige, A., Hembree, E. A., Litz, B. T., Roache, J. D., & Young-McCaughan, S. (2017). Effect of group vs. individual cognitive processing therapy in active-duty military seeking treatment for posttraumatic stress disorder: A randomized clinical trial. *JAMA Psychiatry, 74*(1), 28–36. https://doi.org/10.1001/jamapsychiatry.2016.2729

Seal, K. H., Maguen, S., Cohen, B., Gima, K. S., Metzler, T. J., Ren, L., Bertenthal, D., & Marmar, C. R. (2010). VA mental health services utilization in Iraq and Afghanistan veterans in the first year of receiving new mental health diagnoses. *Journal of Traumatic Stress, 23*(1), 5–16. https://doi.org/10.1002/jts.20493

Shelef, A., Brafman, D., Rosing, T., Weizman, A., Stryjer, R., & Barak, Y. (2019). Equine assisted therapy for patients with post traumatic stress disorder: A case series study. *Military Medicine, 184*(9–10), 394–399. https://doi.org/10.1093/milmed/usz036

Tanielian, T., & Jaycox, L. (2008). *Invisible wounds of war: Psychological and cognitive injuries, their consequences, and services to assist recovery*. RAND Center for Military Health Policy Research. ISBN: 9780833044549.

Taylor, J. E., & Harvey, S. T. (2009). Effects of psychotherapy with people who have been sexually assaulted: A meta-analysis. *Aggression and Violent Behavior, 13*(5), 273–285. https://doi.org/10.1016/j.avb.2009.03.006

VA/DoD Clinical Practice Guideline. (2023). *Management of posttraumatic stress disorder and acute stress disorder work group. Version 4.0*. U.S. Government Printing Office.

Watts, B. V., Schnurr, P. P., Mayo, L., Young-Xu, Y., Weeks, W. B., & Friedman, M. J. (2013). Meta-analysis of the efficacy of treatments for posttraumatic stress disorder. *The Journal of Clinical Psychiatry, 74*(6), e541–e550. https://doi.org/10.4088/JCP.12r08225

Wharton, T., Sercu, C., Malone, M., & Macauley, B. (2005). An analysis of equine stress levels after participation in therapy sessions. *Scientific and Educational Journal of Therapeutic Riding*, 25–30.

Wharton, T., Scogin, F., & Malone, M. (2015). *Equine-facilitated cognitive processing therapy: An addendum to the CPT patient workbook, veteran/military version*.

Wharton, T., Whitworth, J. D., Macauley, E., & Malone, M. (2019). Pilot testing a manualized Equine-Facilitated Cognitive Processing Therapy (EF-CPT) intervention for PTSD in veterans. *Psychiatric Rehabilitation Journal, 42*(3), 268–276. https://doi.org/10.1037/prj0000359

Whitworth, J. D., Scotland-Coogan, D., & Wharton, T. (2019). Service dog training programs for veterans with PTSD: Results of a pilot controlled study. *Social Work in Health Care, 58*(4), 412–430. https://doi.org/10.1080/00981389.2019.1580238

Wood, W., Alm, K., Benjamin, J., Thomas, L., Anderson, D., Pohl, L., & Kane, M. (2021). Optimal terminology for services in the United States that incorporate horses to benefit people: A consensus document. *Journal of Alternative and Complementary Medicine, 27*(1), 88–95. https://doi.org/10.1089/acm.2020.0415

Part II
Equine Assisted Therapies for Adults

Equine-Assisted Therapy for PTSD (EAT-PTSD): The Man O' War Protocol

Prudence W. Fisher, Allan J. Hamilton, and Yuval Neria

Introduction

Posttraumatic stress disorder (PTSD) is a prevalent debilitating mental health disorder that develops after exposure to a traumatic event that involves actual or threatened death, serious injury, or sexual violence. Exposure can be by experiencing a traumatic event directly (i.e., happening to oneself), witnessing a trauma happen to someone else, learning about a trauma experienced by a close family member or friend, and/or repeated or extreme exposure to grotesque or aversive of a traumatic event, as can happen with first responders or emergency medical personnel (American Psychiatric Association, 2022). Exposure to trauma might be to a single event, or to multiple traumas.

Individuals with PTSD experience symptoms across four primary domains: *intrusion/re-experiencing* (e.g., thinking about the trauma when they don't want to, having nightmares or flashbacks where it feels like it's happening again, or getting very upset or feel sick when something makes them think about what happened); *avoidance* (e.g., avoids going places, people, or doing things that make them think about the trauma); *changes in cognition or mood* (e.g., feeling that the world is unsafe, people are not trustworthy; detachment from others; emotional numbness, inappropriate self-blame; depression or other strong negative emotions; diminished interest in activities); and *changes in arousal and reactivity* (e.g., irritable or angry

P. W. Fisher (✉) · Y. Neria
Department of Psychiatry and the New York State Psychiatric Institute, Columbia University Irving Medical Center, New York, NY, USA
e-mail: prudence.fisher@nyspi.columbia.edu; yuval.neria@nyspi.columbia.edu

A. J. Hamilton
Department of Neurosurgery, Artificial Intelligence Division of Health Sciences, University of Arizona, Tucson, AZ, USA
e-mail: allan@surgery.arizona.edu

Y. Neria et al. (eds.), *Guide to Equine Assisted Therapy*,
https://doi.org/10.1007/978-3-031-74426-6_7

behavior, difficulty sleeping, hypervigilance, exaggerated startle response, problems with concentration, reckless or self-destructive behavior). These symptoms cause significant distress or interfere with a person's social, occupational, or other major area of functioning (American Psychiatric Association, 2022). The effect of PTSD on daily functioning is often extreme. Individuals with PTSD commonly report high levels of anxiety with the expectation that danger can strike at any moment. Benign experiences are often interpreted as dangerous or threatening and, driven by fear, individuals with PTSD commonly become easily frustrated and angry. They try to suppress uncomfortable emotions and avoid reminders of the trauma, two effortful and ultimately futile tasks. Individuals with PTSD frequently describe disrupted relationships, inability to function at work, and difficulty thinking clearly when fear cues have been activated.

In the United States, the estimated lifetime prevalence of PTSD ranges from 6.1% to 8.3%, with a 12-month prevalence rate of about 4.7% (Goldstein et al., 2016; Kilpatrick et al., 2013; American Psychiatric Association, 2022). Prevalence rates for women (8.0–11.0%) are higher than those for men (4.1–5.4%) (Goldstein et al., 2016; Kilpatrick et al., 2013). As military personnel face increased risk for exposure to trauma, through combat, injury, captivity, and sexual assault (Hoge et al., 2004; Murdoch et al., 2004; Suris & Lind, 2008), with one study finding nearly all (up to 95%) of post-9/11 service member had experienced ambushes, attacks, or seeing human remains (Hoge et al., 2004), the rates of PTSD in veteran populations are especially high (10–30%).

PTSD can persist for years. Although several therapies have been developed to address PTSD (Foa et al., 2000; Bradley et al., 2005; Schneier et al., 2012; Steckler & Risbrough, 2012; Sullivan & Neria, 2009; Vereecken & Corso, 2024; Markowitz, 2016), over one-third of the treated patients do not achieve full remission, with a median illness duration of 3–5 years despite treatment (Difede et al., 2014; Kessler et al., 1995). Even, the "gold standard" PTSD treatment, prolonged exposure (PE) treatment, which requires patients to engage with their traumatic reminders and process traumatic memories (Rauch et al., 2012) doesn't benefit approximately half of the patients who have PTSD, with many dropping out before completing treatment (Gros et al., 2013; Imel et al., 2013; Najavits, 2015; Szafranski et al., 2017). In addition, many individuals with PTSD avoid or reject treatment altogether (Schneier et al., 2012; Stecker et al., 2013). Military veterans, in particular, face weaker treatment effectiveness and higher dropout rates (Kehle-Forbes et al., 2016; Steenkamp et al., 2015, 2020) and are more likely to avoid seeking treatment due to stigma, mistrust, logistical challenges, or because their experiences with nonspecific or ineffective treatments have demoralized them (Ouimette et al., 2011; Stecker et al., 2013).

Given that many individuals with PTSD do not benefit from standard treatments, only partially remit, find standard treatments aversive, or avoid treatment altogether, the development of additional acceptable primary or complementary treatments for PTSD is important. Equine-assisted therapy (EAT) (also referred to as equine-assisted psychotherapy (EAP)), practiced across the United States and around the world, is an alternative treatment approach for many mental health disorders, including PTSD. EAT offers individuals with PTSD an opportunity to receive treatment in a less traditional and possibly more palatable format, potentially yielding less treatment attrition relative to prevalent exposure-based treatments.

The interest in and enthusiasm for applying EAT with trauma-exposed populations, particularly military service members, has burgeoned. In 2006, the International Horses for Heroes initiative was formalized by the Professional Association of Therapeutic Horsemanship, International (PATH Intl) to serve veterans returning from post-9/11 conflicts; in 2011, this became "PATH International Equine Services for Heroes®" with a more explicit focus on veteran mental health and wellness. The Equine-Assisted Growth and Learning Association (Eagala) introduced a "Military Services Designation" training for its members in 2013. In 2017, the Bob Woodruff Foundation hosted a "high-impact convening" to explore equine-assisted activities and therapies and in 2018, the U.S. Department of Veterans Affairs was mandated by Congress to set aside funds for EAT from its Adaptive Sports Program (U.S. Department of Veterans Affairs).

Why EAT? Why Horses?

Advocates for EAT assert that horses are inherently conducive to this treatment as they are herd animals, naturally hypervigilant, and sensitive to verbal and nonverbal cues, so that they provide immediate feedback during horse–human interactions, which, in turn, affords opportunities to foster emotional awareness, reflection, and attunement to thoughts, behaviors, and forms of communication (Anestis et al., 2014; Schultz et al., 2007; Selby & Smith-Osborne, 2013). Horses are thought to partially resemble humans in their behavior, particularly in social contexts (Schultz et al., 2007) and bring specific attributes to the therapeutic environment including patience, receptiveness, and cooperation (Selby & Smith-Osborne, 2013). Finally, and of relevance to PTSD, horses are also large, potentially intimidating animals that may evoke fear in humans interacting with them. Thus, the experiential EAT approach could also potentially help patients develop awareness of arousal cues, utilizing this in therapy to promote anxiety and stress tolerance.

The Man O' War Project

In 2015, the Man O' War Project (MOW Project) at Columbia University Irving Medical Center/New York State Psychiatric was initiated through a generous gift from the Earle I. Mack Foundation. Led by PWF and YN, faculty in the Department of Psychiatry at Columbia, the lofty goal of the MOW Project was to establish the efficacy and effectiveness of equine-assisted therapy for military veterans who suffer from PTSD. Although PWF and YN both had life experience with horses, neither had experience with EAT, so the project began with their own education about

EAT through visiting websites, visiting and observing programs (including AH's Rancho Bosque Equestrian Center in Tucson, AZ), attending meetings and conferences (including the Eagala Conference), and consulting the literature. Although EAT had grown in popularity (and continues to grow) and there were exuberant proponents (Masini, 2010), they found that EAT, like most complementary and alternative treatments, lacked standardization and rigorous testing. Programs, practitioners, and approaches varied widely. At that time, there were no well-specified treatment manuals and little safety, feasibility, and efficacy research. EAT research that focused on mental health conditions, including PTSD, was scarce and usually poorly designed, with small samples, inconsistent assessments, unstandardized treatment procedures, and researcher conflicts of interest. These difficulties, reiterated in several reviews (Anestis et al., 2014; Bachi et al., 2012; Kendall et al., 2015; Kinney et al., 2019; Selby & Smith-Osborne, 2013; Smith-Osborne & Selby, 2010; Staudt & Cherry, 2017), caused some (Anestis et al., 2014) to raise ethical concerns about the use of and funding for EAT as an empirically unsupported therapy. Indeed, it was often not clear what EAT comprises or means, let alone whether it works. Methodologically sound and rigorous research, which includes the use of a well-specified, standardized EAT, was needed to determine whether EAT should be considered a complementary and/or alternative treatment for PTSD (Kinney et al., 2019; Marchand et al., 2021).

Accordingly, given that there was no well-specified EAT manual/protocol, the next step for the MOW Project was to develop a well-specified EAT treatment protocol (and manual) for PTSD ("EAT-PTSD") that could be tested. Manualizing a treatment with sufficient clarity and accuracy is necessary so that adherence to the treatment protocol can be monitored and the efficacy and effectiveness of a treatment can be evaluated. This requires treatment developers to define what the treatment is (and what it is not), allows training of treatment providers, allows testing of specific treatment elements, and, should the treatment prove promising, allows dissemination to the field.

From the outset, PWF and YN agreed on the following parameters for the protocol: group format, due to cost and potential benefits of the group modality (social engagement; facilitating trust and interpersonal skills [Sloan et al., 2012]); eight 90-minute, once-weekly sessions (similar to how other group psychotherapy protocols are structured); all activity would be "on the ground"—i.e., no riding—both for safety concerns and the different equine-patient relationship; sessions to be led by a treatment team comprising a *licensed* mental health professional (as this was a treatment for PTSD) and an "equine specialist" (trained horse expert); sessions would take place in a confined activity space (small paddock, "round pen"—this enclosed space can be thought of as comparable to a room where more traditional group therapy might take place, as opposed to in an open arena or field, which would be more comparable to an auditorium); and sessions would be progressive—build on one another. In addition, as this was to be an experimental treatment, with the focus being on interactions with the horses in the "here and now," the treatment sessions would *not* include any sharing of, talking about or discussion/focus on the traumatic events experienced by the participants. Instead, the focus of treatment would be to increase affective awareness of oneself and others, improve communication, help regulate emotional response, improve critical thinking/problem-solving, and increase self-confidence/self-efficacy through engaging with the horses. A growing body of literature had demonstrated that exercises involving reciting traumatic experiences are not always a critical component of recovery (Markowitz, 2016; Resnick et al., 2008). The lack of focus on the PTSD-associated trauma could also make this form of treatment more palatable for individuals with PTSD.

Taking account of these parameters, PWF, YN, Ari Lowell, Ph.D. (a psychologist with experience treating veterans with PTSD), and John Markowitz, MD (a psychiatrist with experience with PTSD and development and testing of psychotherapy manuals) developed the treatment protocol, with substantial input from Allan J. Hamilton and Jane F. Hamilton and Eagala-certified EAT providers and in consultation with other Columbia University psychiatry faculty. Development was an iterative process, drawing first on Allan Hamiltn's and Jane Hamilton's experience delivering EAT at Rancho Bosque; they prepared an outline, which served as a starting point for developing the protocol and demonstrated and trained the team on exercises that might be considered.

It was quickly decided that groups would comprise four to six veterans, with two or three horses included in each session and participants would get to know and interact with both horses during sessions, rather than forming a "special bond" with a single horse, as is encouraged by some EAT programs. Also, sessions would begin with an "opening circle" and end with a "closing circle," a structure common to many group therapies. As a primary goal was for developing a manualized treatment for *PTSD*, special consideration was given to the relevance of each exercise/activity for PTSD patients—all potential exercises/activities were reviewed by clinicians with PTSD expertise and those deemed as unsuitable or being of limited benefit were dropped. For example, early on it was decided that, in contrast to what transpires in many EAT programs, horses would never be "at liberty" (i.e., without halter or lead rope) until very late in the treatment progression, as this could be overwhelming for individuals with PTSD. The exercises were also reviewed with the experienced EAT providers, who suggested additional exercises and activities based on their own experiences. Suggestions incorporated into the protocol included an introductory barn "tour" and beginning each session with a "grounding exercise;" a relaxation exercise using perceptual sensations to focus attention on the present moment. The treatment also incorporated a "join-up" activity (adapted from Roberts [1997]), wherein participants summon a horse "at liberty" from a trotting or cantering position as a focal point of treatment progression. After many meetings, a testable protocol was crafted of eight 90-minute sessions, each with a clear agenda and goals, with sessions building upon one another as the treatment progressed. Finally, mock sessions, led by the EAT providers, were held with the developers in patient roles, with session feedback used to refine and revise treatment elements.

Pilot Study of EAT-PTSD

During June to December 2016, the eight-session EAT-PTSD protocol was piloted with two groups of four veterans each (a total of eight veterans: six men and two women, mean age 45 years, range 30–61 years, six in concurrent mental health treatment) all of whom had a diagnosis of PTSD (Arnon et al., 2020). All participants in the first group were men and the second group had two men and two women. The pilot study served three purposes: (1) to check for timing, order, and flow in sessions and identify any parts of the EAT-PTSD protocol that should be revised or dropped, (2) to pilot the research procedures that would be implemented in a larger research project (e.g., recruitment and screening procedures, measures/assessments and practical issues such as transportation, use of the barn facility), and (3) to obtain information on probable treatment effects (symptom improvement and safety, feasibility, and acceptability). The study was reviewed and approved by the Institutional Review Board at New York State Psychiatric Institute and registered (ClinicalTrials.gov: identifier: NCT03068325).

Veterans with PTSD were recruited through clinical referrals and advertisement and were screened by telephone to determine probable eligibility using the PTSD Checklist for Diagnostic and Statistical Manual of Mental Disorders-5 (PCL-5 [Weathers et al., 2013]). Those potentially eligible (PCL-5 score ≥30, and information gathered by the screener about other eligibility obstacles, including physical limitations, and substance problems) were scheduled for in-person clinical assessment visit at the research office (at New York State Psychiatric Institute) with a PhD- or MA-level psychologist (trained to ≥85% reliability with a senior experienced clinician) to determine study eligibility. Inclusion criteria for the pilot were: (a) DSM-5 diagnosis of PTSD (assessed with the Structured Clinical Interview for DSM-5 (SCID [First et al., 2015]. and score ≥50 on the Clinician-Administered PTSD Scale (CAPS-IV [Weathers et al., 2013]); (b) age 18–65 years; (c) military experience; and (d) English fluency. Exclusion criteria were: (a) history of psychotic disorder or unstable bipolar disorder (SCID-5); (b) elevated depression impeding treatment engagement, and/or 17-item Hamilton Rating Scale for Depression (HAM-D [Hamilton, 1960]) score >25 (indicating severe depression and potential risk the EAT protocol was not designed to address); (d) elevated suicide risk, determined by clinical interview; (e) severe substance or alcohol use disorder within the past 6 months, or moderate substance or alcohol use disorder within the past 2 months (SCID-5); (f) phobia of horses or large animals; and (g) physical limitations impeding participation. Concurrent ongoing mental health treatment was allowed if the participant agreed not to alter it during the eight-session EAT-PTSD treatment period. At this visit, self-report questionnaires, including the PCL (Bovin et al., 2016; Weathers et al., 2013) and Beck Depression Inventory (BDI-II; Beck et al., 1996; Dozois et al., 1998), were also completed.

Veterans who participated in the EAT-PTSD groups were clinically reassessed mid-treatment (after session four), post-treatment (after session 8), and at 3-month follow-up. (The initial eligibility assessment provided baseline ratings of symptom severity.) These reassessments, done by a PhD or MA-level psychologist, included the CAPS-5 and Ham-D, and the participant completed self-reports. Participants received $100 compensation per assessment.

The EAT-PTSD sessions took place at Bergen Equestrian Center in Leonia, New Jersey, a full-service equestrian center, and were held in a private indoor space. (Transportation and boots were provided.) As per the protocol, sessions were led by a team comprising a licensed mental health professional (licensed professional counselor or licensed social worker) and a qualified equine specialist, assisted by a "wrangler"—an experienced horse handler to assure safety. All sessions were videotaped and observed by members of the development team who monitored protocol adherence and took notes on aspects of the protocol that looked awkward or didn't seem to "work" well so might warrant a revision or change to the protocol. The development team also held weekly supervision calls with the treatment team. After the first group, one exercise (a "trust walk") was dropped because it made little sense when it was observed. During the first group, it also decided that it was important that the same two horses be used for all eight sessions (this had not been decided earlier) as they clearly were an important part of the "treatment team" and this requirement was added to the protocol.

Results The pilot study confirmed that the research methods (recruitment, screening, assessments, transportation, videotaping) one might use in a larger investigation were sound. Regarding the initial effects of the EAT-PTSD treatment, clinician-assessed PTSD (CAPS-5) and depressive (HAM-D) symptoms significantly decreased from pre- to post-treatment and from pre-treatment to 3-month follow-up. Five participants achieved "response status" defined as ≥30% decrease in severity/frequency of PTSD symptoms post-treatment and one remitted. However, at 3-month follow-up, both PTSD and depression symptoms had increased slightly compared to post-treatment (but had not returned to baseline). At follow-up, two of the five "responders" (one was the remitter) no longer met that designation. One participant who was a "non-responder" at post-treatment had remitted by follow-up. Symptom changes on self-report questionnaires for PTSD and depression showed trends in the same direction as those for clinician assessment but were not significant. There were no adverse events, no treatment dropouts, and high patient satisfaction (Arnon et al., 2020). These encouraging initial findings led to further refinement of the treatment protocol, which was converted into a formal treatment manual.

Open Trial Examining EAT-PTSD

The EAT-PTSD manual was then tested in a rigorous, moderately large open trial with military veterans who were diagnosed with PTSD (Fisher et al. 2021a). The research methods that had been used in the earlier pilot study—screening process, inclusion/exclusion criteria, well-validated measures (SCID-5, CAPS-5, HAM-D,

PCL-5, BDI-II), experienced evaluators, treatment location, observed and videotaped sessions, clinical supervision—were used in this trial with one exception—the upper age limit for participants was 70. Much effort went toward recruitment; these included meetings with veteran-focused organizations and service providers, presentations at community meetings, local colleges, online and print advertising, attending public events (e.g., street fairs, parades), and distributing information and flyers about the project; hosting open houses at the equestrian center for service providers, veterans, and the community; media involvement (radio interviews, local news stories). These efforts resulted in 186 phone-screened veterans of whom 97 were invited for clinical intake, which resulted in a final sample of 63 veterans with PTSD (*mean age 50,* range = 27–70; 23 [37%] female); 48 (76%) participants had at least one comorbid psychiatric disorder (two-thirds had a depression diagnosis). Nearly three-quarters of participants were receiving concurrent mental health treatment (psychotherapy or pharmacotherapy, with half receiving both). Of note, no participant was receiving a well-defined manualized treatment for PTSD; the psychotherapy received was long-term, stable supportive talk therapy in various settings. Between October 2016 and October 2019, the manualized EAT-PTSD protocol was implemented with 16 groups, most comprising four veterans and all but one was mixed in terms of gender (there were no all-female groups). The groups were mixed in type of trauma(s) experienced—some occurred during their time in the military, some before enlistment or during childhood, some after discharge, and many had more than one trauma.

Results Only five participants (7.9%) did not complete the EAT-PTSD protocol; of these, one of these dropped out between baseline and starting EAT-PTSD due to an accidental injury. There were no adverse events or safety concerns.

On the primary outcome in this study, clinician-rated PTSD severity as measured by the CAPS-5, there was significant pre- to post-treatment reduction in PTSD severity, which persisted at 3-month follow-up. Moreover, this decrease was evident at the midpoint assessment and there was a further (trend level) decrease between posttest and the follow-up. At post-treatment, over half of the participants met the criteria for a “clinically significant response” based on the CAPS-5 and slightly more met this at the 3-month follow-up. The decrease in symptom levels of PTSD assessed by self-report (using the PCL-5) was also significant and maintained at follow-up; again, this was evident at midpoint with additional reduction at post-treatment. Decreases in depression, as assessed by clinicians using the HAM-D, were also significant from baseline to post-treatment and persisted at the follow-up. This decrease in depression was evident at midpoint and did not further decrease between midpoint and the end of treatment. Self-reported depression (using the BDI-II) significantly decreased from baseline to midpoint and again from midpoint to end of treatment and was maintained at follow-up.

Taken together, these findings suggest that EAT-PTSD is an acceptable, well-tolerated, and safe protocol, showing promise as an effective treatment for PTSD and thus might be an effective primary intervention or adjunctive therapy for PTSD or PTSD symptoms. The very low dropout stands in stark contrast to the roughly

20% treatment dropout rates reported for PTSD patients broadly (Imel et al., 2013) and the 30–40% rates reported for veterans specifically (Kehle-Forbes et al., 2016; Goetter et al., 2015; Olatunji et al., 2009). Indeed, most participants seemed excited or eager to try the EAT-PTSD treatment, pleased at the opportunity to interact with horses. Many remarked that they looked forward to coming to the EAT sessions, some saying it was the "highlight" of their week, and most wished that the treatment had more than eight sessions, and that the treatment didn't have to end. EAT-PTSD might engage avoidant individuals, resistant to more formal treatment modalities, encouraging subsequent openness to additional therapy. Using experienced evaluators and well-validated measures, this open trial found significant reductions in the severity of symptoms of PTSD (the main focus of the study) and severity of depression, based on clinical evaluation and self-reports. While an open trial is appropriate for this preliminary stage of treatment development, open trials have inherent limitations—observed symptom change could conceivably reflect passage of time and evaluators can't be "blinded" to treatment received—and the absence of a control condition precludes testing the clinical efficacy of EAT. The very positive findings warrant further testing of EAT-PTSD in randomized controlled trials, widely considered the "gold standard" for judging the efficacy of a treatment intervention and a standard part of health research (Riegelman, 2012).

Overview of EAT-PTSD Protocol

EAT-PTSD is well-specified, manualized, group treatment for individuals with PTSD or significant trauma-related symptoms. It is based on the premise that horses can provide an emotional bond as other higher mammals who reflect anxious feelings, entail cooperation for effective interaction, and may be imposing. All activities in EAT-PTSD are "on the ground"—there is no riding. Participants become attuned to the reactions of the horses, as horses provide clear and steady feedback to participants reflecting the mood and messages the participants are projecting. Interacting with horses in a safe, controlled, often bucolic environment removed from daily life may help participants to reflect on their own feelings and behaviors and on their interactions with other people, develop greater awareness of their own internal emotional cues, communicate more effectively, and develop more self-confidence. Direct interventions by the (human) treatment staff should be sparing and pithy, so as to enhance participants' engagement with the horses and their own processes rather than interfere with or supplant it. Although from time-to-time discussion may address topics that extend beyond the treatment sessions, the goal in EAT-PTSD is always to return to the "here and now" and what is happening between participants and the horses. In addition, as a group treatment, EAT-PTSD has the benefit of involving teamwork and camaraderie with other treatment participants. This can bolster feelings of self-efficacy, self-esteem, and safe connection with others, important clinical issues for individuals suffering from PTSD. Participation in group treatment with other participants may help to combat stigma and feelings of doubt and shame.

EAT-PTSD also taps into many of what are known as the "common factors of psychotherapy," general qualities of psychotherapy that may account for as much as 50 percent of the benefit of mainstream psychotherapies (Frank, 1971). These factors include developing a framework for understanding; benefiting from professional expertise; having a therapeutic procedure; developing optimism for improvement; feeling understood by the "therapist"; affective arousal (encouraging and allowing emotional connection is particularly important for those with PTSD who experience emotional numbing or who are afraid of anxious and angry feelings); and having success experiences.

While the participants in both the pilot and the full open trial were all veterans who had the diagnosis of PTSD, there is nothing in the EAT-PTSD protocol that makes the treatment specific to veterans or for traumas arising out of military experience. Indeed, the participants in both studies had experienced a wide variety of traumas, many not part of their military experience. Unlike many EAT programs, especially those who focus on veterans, and many psychotherapies aimed at treating PTSD, talking about trauma is specifically not part of the EAT-PTSD protocol, and participants should be gently steered away from doing so.

EAT-PTSD takes place in eight, 90-minute sessions (typically once a week). Sessions are led by a (human) team comprising a licensed mental health professional (MHP) and an equine specialist (ES) each with specific roles, who (ideally) are assisted by a knowledgeable and experienced horse wrangler (HW). Two or three horses, depending on the size of the group, participate in each session and are integral members of the treatment team. Barring some unforeseen situation (e.g., a horse becomes unavailable due to illness), the same horses are used for all the eight treatment sessions.

Each session follows an established agenda although team members use their judgment to balance adherence to the structure with the organic flow of therapy and meeting the needs of the group; thus, EAT-PTSD is flexible within a larger structure. (See Table 1 for an outline of the sessions.) The first session focuses on psychoeducation and orientation; participants are oriented to the setting and EAT-PTSD treatment (rationale, description, possible benefits), receive psychoeducation (common reactions to trauma, development and maintenance of PTSD), and take a tour where they observe horses and horse behavior and the MHP and ES observe them (level of anxiety and apprehension, behavior, interactions with others). The session ends in the round pen (or small paddock), where they meet the horses who will be working with the group and learn the "grounding exercise," focusing attention on current physical sensations to draw attention to present moment, which is included as part of the *Opening Circle* in subsequent sessions.

Sessions two through eight all take place entirely in the round pen. Each session starts with an *Opening Circle* "and ends with a *Closing Circle*." The primary purpose is of the Opening Circle is to help process relevant clinical matters, such as lingering concerns or worries from the previous session or thoughts that may have arisen during the week regarding using new skills/insights, as well as to orient participants to the day's session. The MHP addresses the former and then turns responsibility over to the ES, who sets the day's agenda. The MHP completes the *Opening Circle* by leading participants in the grounding exercise. *Closing Circle* provides an opportunity to review the day's activities, process the experience with the participants, and generate some discussion. Participants are encouraged to talk about their feelings, what they have noticed, and to comment on each other's observations and relate to one another. They are invited to ask questions about anything they feel uncertain about or reflect about their progress. After the *Opening Circle*, participants move on to greeting and grooming the horses, followed by specific activities and encounters with the horses that build upon each other from session to

Table 1 Equine-assisted therapy for PTSD: treatment outline

	Activites	Goals, focus of session
1.	Welcome/introductions Set agenda, discuss "group rules," confidentiality Tour of facility/"Walk About" Psychoeducation: PTSD, PTSD-EAT Grounding exercise Observe and meet "team" horses Closing circle	Orienting to facility, treatment framework of sessions Becoming acquainted with (human) treatment team, horse(s), participants. Learning grounding exercise (using sensory cues to attend to present moment. This is used in all subsequent sessions)
2.	Opening circle Horse greeting/grooming Lead walking Lead/walk/stop Four feet Closing circle	"Normalizing" experience of therapy: Mindful awareness Improving self-awareness Awareness of others (other's intentions, nonverbal cues) Awareness of arousal cues Frustration tolerance (if horse not conforming) Self-efficacy (engaging in activity while feeling anxious) Setting boundaries Communication (being assertive, not aggressive or passive) Adapting to changes, thinking flexibly Team building
3.	Opening circle Horse greeting/grooming A leg up (cleaning hoof) Lead/walk/stop Introduction to wand Fly fishing Closing circle	Further mastery and comfort with horses Mindful awareness Improving self-awareness Awareness of others (other's intentions, nonverbal cues) Awareness of arousal cues Frustration tolerance (if horse not conforming) Self-efficacy (engaging in activity while feeling anxious) Trust Setting boundaries Self-regulation Communication Adapting to changes, thinking flexibly Learning to use the wand (power, without being dangerous) Team building

(continued)

Table 1 (continued)

	Activites	Goals, focus of session
4.	Opening circle Horse greeting/grooming A leg up (cleaning hoof) Four feet Fly fishing Send away Closing circle	Further mastery and comfort with horse(s) Mindful awareness Improving self-awareness Awareness of others (other's intentions, nonverbal cues) Awareness of arousal cue and self-regulation Frustration tolerance (if horse not conforming) Self-efficacy (engaging in activity while feeling anxious) Trust Setting boundaries Communication skills Adapting to changes, thinking flexibly Increase comfort with the wand Not being afraid to be emotional and energetic Recognizing legitimacy of and expressing personal needs Team building
5.	Opening circle Horse greeting/grooming/leg up Fly fishing Wand walking Send away Demo/abbreviated join-up1 (all participants) Closing circle (begin conversation about approaching termination)	Further mastery and comfort with horse(s) Completion of more advanced exercises Mindful awareness Improving self-awareness Awareness of others (other's intentions, nonverbal cues) Awareness of arousal cues and self-regulation Self-efficacy (engaging in activity while feeling anxious) Trust Setting boundaries Frustration tolerance (if horse not conforming) Communication skills Adapting to changes, thinking flexibly Increase comfort with the wand Not being afraid to be emotional and energetic Recognizing legitimacy of and expressing personal needs Team building Begin processing thoughts, feelings about impending termination
6.	Opening circle Horse greeting/grooming/leg up Obstacle course Join-up (1/2 of participants) Closing circle	Completion of more advanced exercises Mastery, consolidating skills from earlier exercises Confirmation of relationship with horse(s) Mindful awareness (using sensory cues to attend to present moment) Improving self-awareness Awareness of others (other's intentions, nonverbal cues) Awareness of arousal cues and self-regulation Self-efficacy (engaging in activity while feeling anxious) Trust Setting boundaries Frustration tolerance (if horse not conforming) Communication skills (being assertive, not aggressive or passive) Adapting to changes, thinking flexibly Recognizing legitimacy of and expressing personal needs Team building Processing thoughts, feelings about impending termination

(continued)

so that they might easily share observations of the interactions of the horses and the humans, and quietly check in with each other while the participants are performing activities. Before each session, they should review the manual chapter together and after each s session, the MHP and ES should debrief—discussing participant (and horse) behaviors and reactions, what worked, what didn't, and what should be stressed/addressed/reviewed at the next session. If a HW is available, it is helpful to include them in planning and debriefing discussions.

Horse wrangler (HW) The role of the horse wrangler (HW) is to provide an additional layer of safety and protection for participants and to assist the ES in conducting exercises as needed. The HW should not provide direct instruction or treatment but can always act spontaneously if a safety concern arises.

Horses The horses involved in EAT-PTSD are the most important members of the treatment team, as it is the participants' experiences working with and relating to the horses that forms the crux of the treatment. Thus, in selecting horses for EAT-PTSD, it is important to consider their individual personalities and characteristics. The horses should be relatively calm and well-mannered, and accustomed to and appropriate for working with people who may not be comfortable with or familiar with horses. At the same time, they should not be excessively docile or non-reactive (as might be desirable for therapeutic riding or trail riding), as their interactions and reactions are a key part of the therapy. The horses should also "know" one another before being included in EAT-PTSD so that an excessive number of horse-to-horse interactions do not inadvertently become the focus of sessions. It is desirable that the horses differ from one another in noticeable way, such as their size, personality, energy, level of reactivity, etc. The ES and HW (and ideally, the MHP) should get to know the horses, their personalities, quirks, and energy levels, and should be aware of the relationship between them before the first session. In addition, the horses should be given some experience/training in the specific tasks they will do during the sessions such as the "Send Away," "Join-Up," and "Tarp Exercise," which can also give the (human) treatment team an indication of where "problems" might arise for the participants in undertaking a particular activity.

The detailed EAT-PTSD manual (Fisher et al., 2021b) contains clear instructions to allow the treatment teams to deliver EAT-PTSD consistently, emphasizing keeping the treatment as experiential as possible. The manual clearly delineates each team member's role and includes an outline, detailed descriptions of activities, and an example "script" for each session. It also provides guidance on how to manage challenges, clinical contingencies, and difficult situations that might arise during treatment. Finally, the manual includes recommendations for standardized measures that can be used in assessing participants and tracking change.

Although EAT-PTSD is not an "Eagala" program, it is consistent with the general Eagala guidelines promulgated at the time the project began (Kersten & Thomas, 2000; Notgrass & Pettinelli, 2015), which emphasize experiential learning and exploration through interactive equine ground exercises. A licensed mental health professional and equine specialist jointly lead treatment, promoting reflection and ensuring safety (Kersten & Thomas, 2000; Notgrass & Pettinelli, 2015; Professional Association of Therapeutic Horsemanship International, 2013). All the individuals on the treatment teams for both the pilot study and the open trial were "Eagala certified," and they continue to work with the MOW Project to provide services for veterans using the EAT-PTSD protocol.

EAT-PTSD and MOW Project: Present and Future

Further research on EAT-PTSD The results from the moderately large open trial indicate that EAT-PTSD holds promise as an effective and efficacious adjunctive or stand-alone treatment for individuals with PTSD- or trauma-related symptoms. However, much more work remains. A logical next step is to undertake a large randomized controlled trial (RCT), but such a study would require substantial funding. An RCT would also be most efficiently carried out in collaboration with other centers, trained by the MOW Project to deliver the protocol with fidelity, with the MOW Project providing a centralized clinical assessment team. A lesson learned during the COVID-19 pandemic was that quality clinical research assessments could be done remotely, and having a single team perform this function could obviate the problem of site differences in how participants are evaluated. This trial would have a control condition and would not necessarily be confined to veterans, although that might depend on the funding source. Until such a trial is mounted, much can be learned by small replication studies, where the manual is implemented by other groups, using similar assessment methods to those used in the earlier research.

In addition, the MOW team is undertaking a small project piloting and adaptation of the EAT-PTSD protocol for anxious adolescents and consulting with a program who will be piloting its implementation with youth who have experienced bullying.

Training and dissemination Despite the absence of a definitive RCT, many have expressed interest in being trained to use the EAT-PTSD protocol. In 2018–2021, the MOW Project worked with PATH Intl to develop a training curriculum for the EAT-PTSD using the EAT-PTSD manual using the funding received by PATH Intl. from the Bob Woodruff Foundation. This curriculum comprised three parts: (1) a two-day in-person training at a premier PATH center in Colorado, which, in addition to didactics, provided demonstrations and "hands-on" activities; (2) supervision calls with the MOW team (PF, AL, and treatment team members) as trainees implemented the protocol with two groups; and (3) onsite observation visits by MOW Project to the trainees to observe their implementation with two groups. Teams from four PATH Intl. centers were selected to be trained and attended the in-person training, which was videotaped and edited by PATH Intl. Unfortunately, because of the COVID-19 pandemic, some of the planned groups and observation visits could not be carried out. This first foray into training revealed changes and additions that should be made to the curriculum, including more instruction about "working as a team," experiential treatment, and group management and the training curriculum and manual were revised accordingly.

During the COVID-19 pandemic (2020–2022), the MOW project also trained an Israeli team of very experienced Eagala-certified providers to administer the EAT-PTSD protocol via Zoom. This included six 2-hour zoom sessions with PF and MOW treatment team members. Between sessions, the trainees would try out and videotape various activities to be reviewed and follow-up meetings/check-ins as they implemented the program in Israel. In addition, the MOW Team has trained several groups via Zoom (for didactics and in-depth manual review) followed by a full day in-person hands-on training at Bergen Equestrian Center.

Based on these training experiences, the MOW Project has refined the training curriculum, now divided into three steps (or levels) that would assure competency/proficiency in implementation the EAT-PTSD protocol as intended: (1) Completion of a sequential state-of-the-art, online training module with accompanying materials in which that interested users review the EAT-PTSD protocol and manual; this will incorporate videotapes of specific techniques, animation, interactive exercises and quizzes and be available in 2025; (2) in-person demonstrations and "hands-on" exercises with the MOW team (1.5 days), offered two to three times per year; and (3) "supervision" by the MOW team via Zoom/conference calls, including observation visits or review of taped sessions by the MOW team as users implement the protocol at their own sites. By moving a portion of the training online, which can be assessed at the learner's convenience, it will be more accessible to a greater number of interested EAT providers, and significantly reduce costs (in terms of travel, lodging, time away from work/home). The MOW team anticipates that some who complete Step 1 will not take the more advanced training, but that the online training and manual together will have much value to EAT providers. Those who successfully complete all the three levels could possibly be included as sites in future research endeavors.

Conclusion

PTSD is a debilitating, frequently comorbid disorder for which effective "out of the box" treatments are highly needed, particularly for individual for whom current treatments have been found to be effective. EAT-PTSD, an emerging treatment approach described in this chapter, is one alternative, experiential, and effective treatment approach, although more controlled studies are needed to establish its efficacy. As evident across this volume, EAT might be a powerful intervention across psychiatric disorders, which may suggest that its benefits and mechanisms are not disorder specific. The brain results presented in the following chapter (Neria et al., this book) suggest that the brain areas that showed the most change among individuals who participated in EAT-PTSD open trial were not necessarily fear or trauma related, but are mood related; this may explain why interest in EAT treatment is has grown and is highly sought and loved by patients.

Acknowledgments The Man 'O War Project was the brainchild of Earle I Mack, who provided generous financial support for our work. Ari Lowell, Ph.D., and John C. Markowitz were part of the core development team for the EAT-PTSD protocol and coauthored the treatment manual; Debra G. Farber, MA, LPC, Jody Jacob-McVey Bonnie E. Malajian, LCSW, April Neumann, all Eagala-certified EAT providers, provided invaluable input on the EAT-PTSD protocol and manual, served on the treatment teams for the pilot and open trial studies, and have helped in training efforts; Jane F. Hamilton, Ph.D., was invaluable in our thinking about the structure of the protocol and, with AJH, was incredibly generous in providing an outline we could use as a starting point, Amit Lazarov, Ph.D., was responsible for analyzing data from the project and a major contributor to publications. We are especially grateful to the participants in the pilot study and open trial—71 veterans with PTSD—who willingly engaged in what was, at the time, an untested and still developing treatment.

References

American Psychiatric Association. (2022). *Diagnostic and statistical manual of mental disorders* (5th ed Text Revision ed.). American Psychiatric Association Press.

Anestis, M., Anestis, J., Zawilinski, L., Hopkins, T., & Lilienfeld, S. (2014). Equine-related treatments for mental disorders lack empirical support: A systematic review of empirical investigations. *Journal of Clinical Psychology, 70*, 1115–1132. https://doi.org/10.1002/jclp.22113

Arnon, S., Fisher, P. W., Pickover, A. M., Pini, K., Pollock, J. A., & Schechter, M. (2020). Equine-assisted therapy for veterans with PTSD: Manual development and preliminary findings. *Military Medicine, 185*(9–10), e1484–e1492. https://doi.org/10.1093/milmed/usaa119

Bachi, K., Terkel, J., & Teichman, M. (2012). Equine-facilitated psychotherapy for at-risk adolescents: The influence on self-image, self-control, and trust. *Clinical Child Psychology and Psychiatry, 17*(2), 298–312. https://doi.org/10.1177/1359104511404177

Beck, A. T., Steer, R. A., & Brown, G. K. (1996). *Beck depression inventory-II*. The Psychological Corporation.

Bovin, M. J., Marx, B. P., Weathers, F. W., Gallagher, M. W., Rodriguez, P., Schnurr, P. P., & Keane, T. M. (2016). Psychometric properties of the PTSD checklist for diagnostic and statistical manual of mental disorders-fifth edition (PCL-5) in veterans. *Psychological Assessment, 28*(11), 1379–1391. https://doi.org/10.1037/pas0000254

Bradley, R., Greene, J., Russ, E., Dutra, L., & Westen, D. (2005). A multidimensional meta-analysis of psychotherapy for PTSD. *American Journal of Psychiatry, 162*(2), 214–227. https://doi.org/10.1176/appi.ajp.162.2.214

Difede, J., Olden, M., & Cukor, J. (2014). Evidence-based treatment of post-traumatic stress disorder. *Annual Review of Medicine, 65*, 319–332. https://doi.org/10.1146/annurev-med-052812-112919

Dozois, D. J. A., Dobson, K. S., & Ahnberg, J. L. (1998). A psychometric evaluation of the Beck Depression Inventory-II. *Psychological Assessment, 10*(2), 83–89. https://doi.org/10.1037/1040-3590.10.2.83

First, M. B., Williams, J. B. W., Karg, R. S., & Spitzer, R. L. (2015). *Structured clinical interview for DSM-5 research version (SCID-5 for DSM-5, Research Version; SCID-5-RV)*. American Psychiatric Association.

Fisher, P. W., Lazarov, A., Lowell, A., Arnon, A., Turner, J. B., Bergman, M., Ryba, M., Such, S., Morahasy, C., Zhu, X., Suarez-Jimenez, B., Markowitz, J. C., & Neria, Y. (2021a). Equine-assisted therapy for posttraumatic stress disorder among military veterans: An open trial. *Journal of Clinical Psychiatry, 82*(5), 21m14005. https://doi.org/10.4088/JCP.21m14005

Fisher, P. W., Lowell, A., Markowitz, J. C., & Neria, Y. (2021b). *Equine-assisted therapy for posttraumatic stress disorder (EAT-PTSD) treatment manual*. The Man O' War Project, Research Foundation for Mental Hygiene, Inc. & New York State Psychiatric Institute.

Foa, E. B., Keane, T. M., & Friedman, M. J. (Eds.). (2000). *Effective treatments for PTSD: Practice guidelines from the International Society for Traumatic Stress Studies*. The Guilford Press.
Frank, J. D. (1971). Therapeutic factors in psychotherapy. *American Journal of Psychotherapy, 25*(3), 350–361.
Goetter, E. M., Bui, E., Ojserkis, R. A., Zakarian, R. J., Brendel, R. W., & Simon, N. M. (2015). A systematic review of dropout from psychotherapy for posttraumatic stress disorder among Iraq and Afghanistan combat veterans. *Journal of Trauma & Stress, 28*(5), 401–409. https://doi.org/10.1002/jts.22059
Goldstein, R. B., Smith, S. M., Chou, S. P., et al. (2016). The epidemiology of DSM-5 posttraumatic stress disorder in the United States: Results from the National Epidemiologic Survey on Alcohol and Related Conditions–III. *Social Psychiatry and Psychiatric Epidemiology, 51*(8), 1137–1148. https://doi.org/10.1007/s00127-016-1217-6
Gros, D. F., Price, M., Yuen, E. K., & Acierno, R. (2013). Predictors of completion of exposure therapy in OEF/OIF veterans with posttraumatic stress disorder. *Depression and Anxiety, 30*(12), 1107–1113. https://doi.org/10.1002/da.22207
Hamilton, M. (1960). A rating scale for depression. *Journal of Neurology, Neurosurgery, and Psychiatry, 23*, 56–62. https://doi.org/10.1136/jnnp.23.1.56
Hoge, C. W., Castro, C. A., Messer, S. C., McGurk, D., Cotting, D. I., & Koffman, R. L. (2004). Combat duty in Iraq and Afghanistan, mental health problems, and barriers to care. *New England Journal of Medicine, 351*(1), 13–22. https://doi.org/10.1056/NEJMoa040603
Imel, Z. E., Laska, K., Jakupcak, M., & Simpson, T. L. (2013). Meta-analysis of dropout in treatments for posttraumatic stress disorder. *Journal of Consulting and Clinical Psychology, 81*(2), 394–404. https://doi.org/10.1037/a0031474
Kehle-Forbes, S. M., Meis, L. A., Spoont, M. R., & Polusny, M. A. (2016). Treatment initiation and dropout from prolonged exposure and cognitive processing therapy in a VA outpatient clinic. *Psychological Trauma: Theory, Research, Practice, and Policy, 8*(1), 107–114. https://doi.org/10.1037/tra0000077
Kendall, E., Maujean, A., Lakhani, A., Macfarlane, K., Downes, M., & Byrne, J. (2015). A systematic review of the efficacy of equine-assisted interventions on psychological outcomes. *European Journal of Psychotherapy & Counselling, 17*(1), 57–79. https://doi.org/10.1080/13642537.2014.986806
Kersten, G., & Thomas, L. (2000). *Equine assisted psychotherapy: Training manual*. Equine Assisted Growth and Learning Association.
Kessler, R. C., Sonnega, A., Bromet, E., Hughes, M., & Nelson, C. B. (1995). Posttraumatic stress disorder in the National Comorbidity Survey. *Archives of General Psychiatry, 52*(12), 1048–1060. https://doi.org/10.1001/archpsyc.1995.03950240066012
Kilpatrick, D. G., Resnick, H. S., Milanak, M. E., Miller, M. W., Keyes, K. M., & Friedman, M. J. (2013). National estimates of exposure to traumatic events and PTSD prevalence using DSM-IV and DSM-5 criteria. *Journal of Traumatic Stress, 26*(5), 537–547. https://doi.org/10.1002/jts.21848
Kinney, A. R., Eakman, A. M., Lassell, R., & Wood, W. (2019). Equine-assisted interventions for veterans with service-related health conditions: A systematic mapping review. *Military Medicine, 184*(5–6), e168–e177. https://doi.org/10.1093/milmed/usz037
Marchand, W. R., Andersen, S. J., Smith, J. E., Hoopes, K. H., & Carlson, J. K. (2021). Equine-assisted activities and therapies for veterans with posttraumatic stress disorder: Current state, challenges, and future directions. *Chronic Stress, 5*, 1–11. https://doi.org/10.1177/24705470211010852
Markowitz, J. C. (2016). *Interpersonal psychotherapy for PTSD*. Oxford University Press.
Masini, A. (2010). Equine-assisted psychotherapy in clinical practice. *Journal of Psychosocial Nursing and Mental Health Services, 48*(10), 30–34. https://doi.org/10.3928/02793695-20101001-06
Murdoch, M., Polusny, M. A., Hodges, J., & O'Brien, N. (2004). Prevalence of in-service and post-service sexual assault among combat and noncombat veterans applying for Department of Veterans Affairs posttraumatic stress disorder disability benefits. *Military Medicine, 169*(5), 392–395. https://doi.org/10.7205/MILMED.169.5.392

Najavits, L. M. (2015). The problem of dropout from "gold standard" PTSD therapies. *F1000Prime Reports, 7*, 43. https://doi.org/10.12703/P7-43

Notgrass, C. G., & Pettinelli, J. D. (2015). Equine-assisted psychotherapy: The Equine Assisted Growth and Learning Association's model overview of equine-based modalities. *The Journal of Experimental Education, 38*(2), 162–174. https://doi.org/10.1177/1053825914528472

Olatunji, B., Deacon, B. J., & Abramowitz, J. S. (2009). The cruelest cure? Ethical issues in the implementation of exposure-based treatments. *Cognitive and Behavioral Practice, 16*(2), 172–180. https://doi.org/10.1016/j.cbpra.2008.09.002

Ouimette, P., Vogt, D., Wade, M., Tirone, V., Greenbaum, M. A., Kimerling, R., et al. (2011). Perceived barriers to care among Veterans Health Administration patients with posttraumatic stress disorder. *Psychological Services, 8*(3), 212–223. https://doi.org/10.1037/a0024360

Professional Association of Therapeutic Horsemanship International. (2013). *What is equine-facilitated psychotherapy and equine-facilitated learning*. http://www.pathintl.org/resources-education/resources/eaat/201-what-is-efpl

Rauch, S. A., Eftekhari, A., & Ruzek, J. I. (2012). Review of exposure therapy: A gold standard for PTSD treatment. *Journal of Rehabilitation Research and Development, 49*(5), 679–687. https://doi.org/10.1682/JRRD.2011.12.0232

Resnick, P. A., Galovski, T. E., Uhlmansiek, M. O., Scher, C. D., Clum, G. A., & Young-Xu, Y. (2008). A randomized clinical trial to dismantle compenents of cognitive processing therapy for posttraumatic stress disorder in female victims of interpersonal violence. *Journal of Consulting and Clinicial Psychology, 76*(2), 243–258. https://doi.org/10.1037/0022-006X.76.2.243

Riegelman, R. K. (Ed.). (2012). *Studying a study & testing a test: Reading evidence-based health research* (6th ed.). Wolters Kluwer/Lippincott Williams & Wilkins.

Roberts, M. (1997). *The man who listens to horses: The story of a real-life horse whisperer*. Random House.

Schneier, F. R., Neria, Y., Pavlicova, M., et al. (2012). Combined prolonged exposure therapy and paroxetine for PTSD related to the World Trade Center attack: A randomized controlled trial. *American Journal of Psychiatry, 169*(1), 80–88. https://doi.org/10.1176/appi.ajp.2011.11030435

Schultz, P., Remick-Barlow, A. G., & Robbins, L. (2007). Equine-assisted psychotherapy: A mental health promotion/intervention modality for children who have experienced intra-family violence. *Health & Social Care in the Community, 15*(3), 265–271. https://doi.org/10.1111/j.1365-2524.2007.00720.x

Selby, A., & Smith-Osborne, A. (2013). A systematic review of the effectiveness of complementary and adjunct therapies and interventions involving equines. *Health Psychology, 32*(4), 418–432. https://doi.org/10.1037/a0030283

Sloan, D. M., Bovin, M. J., & Schnurr, P. P. (2012). Review of group treatment for PTSD. *Journal of Rehabilitation Research and Development, 49*(5), 689–701. https://doi.org/10.1682/JRRD.2011.07.0123

Smith-Osborne, A., & Selby, A. (2010). Implications of the literature on equine-assisted activities for use as a complementary intervention in social work practice with children and adolescents. *Child and Adolescent Social Work Journal, 27*(4), 291–307. https://doi.org/10.1007/s10560-010-0204-5

Staudt, M., & Cherry, D. (2017). Equine-facilitated therapy and trauma: Current knowledge, future needs. *Advances in Social Work, 18*(1), 233–245. https://doi.org/10.18060/21392

Stecker, T., Shiner, B., Watts, B., Jones, M., & Conner, K. (2013). Treatment-seeking barriers for veterans of the Iraq and Afghanistan conflicts who screen positive for PTSD. *Psychiatric Services, 64*(3), 280–283. https://doi.org/10.1176/appi.ps.001372012

Steckler, T., & Risbrough, V. (2012). Pharmacological treatment of PTSD: Established and new approaches. *Neuropharmacology, 62*(2), 617–627. https://doi.org/10.1016/j.neuropharm.2011.07.014

Steenkamp, M. M., Litz, B. T., Hoge, C. W., & Marmar, C. R. (2015). Psychotherapy for military-related PTSD: A review of randomized clinical trials. *JAMA, 314*(5), 489–500. https://doi.org/10.1001/jama.2015.8370

Steenkamp, M. M., Litz, B. T., & Marmar, C. R. (2020). First-line psychotherapies for military-related PTSD. *JAMA, 324*(6), 619–620. https://doi.org/10.1001/jama.2020.13957

Sullivan, G. M., & Neria, Y. (2009). Pharmacotherapy in post-traumatic stress disorder: Evidence from randomized controlled trials. *Current Opinion in Investigational Drugs, 10*(1), 35–45.

Suris, A., & Lind, L. (2008). Military sexual trauma: A review of prevalence and associated health consequences in veterans. *Trauma, Violence, & Abuse, 9*(4), 250–269. https://doi.org/10.1177/1524838008325913

Szafranski, D. D., Smith, B. N., Gros, D. F., & Resick, P. A. (2017). High rates of PTSD treatment dropout: A possible red herring? *Journal of Anxiety Disorders, 47*, 91–98. https://doi.org/10.1016/j.janxdis.2017.02.001

Vereecken, S., & Corso, G. (2024). Revisiting eye movement desensitization and reprocessing therapy for post-traumatic stress disorder: A systematic review and discussion of the American Psychological Association's 2017 recommendations. *Cureus, 16*(4), e58767. https://doi.org/10.7759/cureus.58767

Weathers, F. W., Litz, B. T., Keane, T. M., Palmieri, P. A., Marx, B. P., & Schnurr, P. P. (2013). *The PTSD checklist for DSM-5 (PCL-5)*. National Center for PTSD.

Discovering Brain-Based Mechanisms and Predictors of Clinical Outcomes of EAT for Patients with PTSD

Yuval Neria, Xi Zhu, Prudence W. Fisher, Neal Prasad, and Allan J. Hamilton

Introduction

Equine-assisted treatment (EAT), also known as equine psychotherapy, is a therapeutic approach that involves interactions between humans and horses, aiming to promote well-being and mental health (Anestis et al., 2014; Nisar et al., 2020). The roots of equine-assisted therapy can be traced back to ancient civilizations (Anestis et al., 2014), where horses were admired for their intuitive capacity to inflict a range of psychological responses among humans, from tranquility to excitement, and happiness (Anestis et al., 2014).

Modern approaches to utilize horses as therapeutic allies started to evolve in the mid-twentieth century (Stafford, 2023), due to an increasing number of reports describing beneficial physical and emotional outcomes due to interaction with horses (Anestis et al., 2014). For example, when Liz Hartel, an Olympic equestrian who had contracted polio-related partial paralysis, demonstrated significant physical and emotional benefits associated with horseback riding; she advanced this approach among individuals with disabilities (Stafford, 2023). This groundbreaking

Y. Neria (✉) · P. W. Fisher
Department of Psychiatry and the New York State Psychiatric Institute, Columbia University Irving Medical Center, New York, NY, USA
e-mail: yuval.neria@nyspi.columbia.edu; prudence.fisher@nyspi.columbia.edu

X. Zhu · N. Prasad
New York State Psychiatric Institute, Columbia University Irving Medical Center, New York, NY, USA
e-mail: xi.zhu@nyspi.columbia.edu; neal.prasad@nyspi.columbia.edu

A. J. Hamilton
Department of Neurosurgery, Artificial Intelligence Division of Health Sciences, University of Arizona, Tucson, AZ, USA
e-mail: allan@surgery.arizona.edu

Y. Neria et al. (eds.), *Guide to Equine Assisted Therapy*,
https://doi.org/10.1007/978-3-031-74426-6_8

work laid a foundation for further and more systematic exploration into the potential emotional benefits of equine-human interactions across a range of psychological needs and psychiatric diagnoses. During the 1970s, organizations such as the North American Riding for the Handicapped Association (now known as the Professional Association of Therapeutic Horsemanship International) were established to promote the use of horses in therapeutic settings.

Over the years, equine-assisted therapy gained recognition across multiple fields, including mental health, physical rehabilitation, education, and personal development (Anestis et al., 2014). As the field continues to expand, professionals in psychiatry, social work, psychology, counseling, occupational therapy, and physical therapy developed, tested, and eventually began implementing equine-assisted interventions into practice. Today, equine therapy programs are offered in a wide range of settings, including therapeutic riding farms and centers, counseling practices, schools, universities, hospitals, and residential treatment facilities.

Equine-assisted therapy (EAT) is widely practiced as an alternative treatment for various physical and mental health conditions (Anestis et al., 2014; Nisar et al., 2020), including substance use disorders (Dell et al., 2008), eating disorders (Christian, 2005; Cumella, 2003; Lac et al., 2013; Lutter & Smith-Osborne, 2011), mood and anxiety disorders (Wilson et al., 2017), and distress associated with terminal illness (Haylock & Cantril, 2006). EAT studies report patient gains in global psychological functioning (Schultz et al., 2007), emotional regulation, self-esteem (Wilson et al., 2017), and self-efficacy (Haylock & Cantril, 2006). Experientially oriented, EAT uses horses to facilitate communication and mindful awareness of thoughts and behaviors (Anestis et al., 2014; Nisar et al., 2020). Non-riding, on-the-ground exercises interacting with horses have been found to foster regulation, reflection, and verbal and nonverbal communication (Anestis et al., 2014; Selby & Smith-Osborne, 2013).

The expansion of research in the field contributed to better understanding of the role emotional and physical proximity to the horses may play in the therapeutic benefits. Numerous reports have pointed to the unique bond and trust that are developed between the two species during therapy. Horses, being a herd animal, highly social and perceptive, have a superb ability to interact with humans, to respond and to mirror emotions, to provide nonverbal feedback, and create an opportunity for humans to observe, explore, and own their thoughts and feelings (Hamilton, 2011). Yet, the mechanisms underlying therapeutic benefits of equine therapies are yet to be systematically identified. The current chapter aims to close this gap by offering a number of hypotheses regarding brain-based mechanisms of clinical change following EAT-PTSD.

The Brain and EAT-PTSD Changes

Efforts to determine whether psychological treatments might be associated with brain changes have increased in the last decade. For example, in patients with PTSD, magnetic resonance imaging (MRI) has been used to assess neural treatment-related changes, including structural alteration (Helpman et al., 2016), task-based functional activity (Fonzo et al., 2017a; Helpman et al., 2016), and resting-state functional connectivity (Zhu et al., 2018). Studies have explored these brain changes following prolonged exposure (PE), the first-line treatment for PTSD (Fonzo et al., 2017a; Helpman et al., 2016; Suarez-Jimenez et al., 2020; Zhu et al., 2018), affect-focused interpersonal psychotherapy (IPT; Suarez-Jimenez et al., 2020), eye movement desensitization and reprocessing (EMDR; Laugharne et al., 2016), cognitive behavioral therapy (CBT; Levy-Gigi et al., 2013), brief eclectic psychotherapy (BEP; Lindauer et al., 2005), and trauma-focused therapy (van Rooij et al., 2015).

Only one study to date has utilized neuroimaging methods to identify neural-related changes following EAT and to determine brain-based mechanisms of clinical outcomes (Zhu et al., 2018).

Nineteen treatment-seeking American service members with PTSD participated in this study. They underwent multimodal MRI before and after EAT. EAT for PTSD comprised 8 weekly 90-minute group sessions held at an equestrian center. Each group was led by a licensed mental health professional, an equine specialist, and an extra horse wrangler to enhance safety. All sessions began with a grounding exercise, focusing attention on current physical sensations. The first session oriented patients to EAT (rationale, description, possible benefits), provided safety guidelines, psychoeducation (common reactions to trauma, development and maintenance of PTSD), and a barn tour, and ended with meeting two horses in a round-pen. Subsequent sessions were built upon previous ones, by reviewing previous session content and introducing increasingly complex encounters and interactions with horses, coupled with team feedback and direction. Each session ended with an opportunity for participants to review and discuss their experiences. The final session included a graduation ceremony celebrating patients' treatment progress and accomplishments (for more information on this treatment, see Arnon et al., 2020; Fisher et al., JCP).

This multimodal MRI study of neural mechanisms and predictors of treatment response to EAT for patients with PTSD revealed several key findings. First, a significant increase in caudate connectivity within the basal ganglia network after treatment; second, a reduction in the regional gray matter volume (GMV) of the thalamus and the caudate; third, increased caudate connectivity following treatment was associated with greater symptom reduction. Fourth, higher levels of baseline caudate connectivity were predictive of greater symptomatic reduction at the end of EAT and were even more strongly correlated with sustained improvement seen at the 3-month follow-up after the conclusion of EAT.

The findings suggest for the first time that the limbic-basal ganglionic reward system may be successfully engaged and modified by a relatively short (8-week-long) EAT employed for patients undergoing treatment for PTSD.

Previous resting-state fMRI studies have implicated the basal ganglia/limbic network, including the striatum, thalamus, and amygdala (Cole et al., 2012; Moussa et al., 2012), in dopaminergic reward and learning processes (Sesack & Grace, 2010). The caudate nucleus is involved in reward anticipation and response. Abnormal functioning within the caudate has been documented not only in PTSD (Elman et al., 2009; Sailer et al., 2008), but also in depression (Eshel & Roiser, 2010) and substance abuse (Volkow et al., 2011). Moreover, increased connectivity of the bilateral nucleus accumbent to the right dorsomedial prefrontal cortex was previously associated with higher levels of anhedonia in trauma-exposed individuals (Olson et al., 2018). This evidence suggests that connectivity abnormalities within the basal ganglia/limbic network may contribute to aberrant reward processing (Schmidt et al., 2015) in PTSD. The findings from this study suggest that these abnormalities may be successfully targeted by EAT.

The results further show that baseline rsFC within the BGN predicted clinical treatment outcomes. Specifically, baseline caudate rsFC was positively correlated with improvement in PTSD scores after treatment, and at the 3-month follow-up. This suggests that the level of baseline striatal connectivity—and rsFC in the caudate nucleus, in particular—may be a stronger predictor of EAT outcome. Furthermore, EAT is changing the rsFC of the caudate, which in turn improves the symptoms of the patient.

Structural MRI findings show a reduction in regional GMV of the caudate. Together with the pre- to post-treatment connectivity changes, these results suggest a pruning effect in the caudate over the course of treatment. In depression, decreased caudate volume has been associated with anhedonia and greater depressive severity (Pizzagalli et al., 2009). Felmingham et al. (2014) suggested that impaired recruitment of the striatum may partially mediate the anhedonia characteristic of depression, addictive disorders, and PTSD (Felmingham et al., 2014). Studies have reported significantly increased GMV in the left caudate in individuals with PTSD (Yang et al., 2009). In addition, our study also found a reduction in the regional GMV of the thalamus. The thalamus, along with the caudate and putamen, comprises an essential part of the limbic cortico-striatal-thalamocortical circuit, which is involved in fear and anxiety. Dysfunction in this circuit appears to compromise cognitive control, behavioral self-regulation, and emotion. Thalamus volume abnormalities are consistently reported across depression studies (Espinoza Oyarce et al., 2020). Our findings of decreased GMV of the caudate and thalamus at post-treatment support the idea that patients with PTSD might have a disrupted, dysfunctional reward circuitry, including cortico-striatal-thalamocortical circuits, that might be alleviated through EAT.

Taken together, this study demonstrated that a brief, structured 8-week EAT was associated with significant changes in resting-state reward networks in the caudate and volume changes in the thalamus and caudate. Furthermore, baseline caudate connectivity significantly correlated with clinical improvement, suggesting enhanced reward responsiveness may underlie the improvements seen in subjects with PTSD after EAT treatment. Given that PTSD is commonly associated with diminished reward circuitry responsivity, patients with PTSD experience disturbed emotional responses, social functioning, and a general capacity to seek and experience pleasurable activities. Therefore, improving reward circuitry via human–equine interactions might be a significant step to finding new and enhanced treatment methods for people with PTSD and depression.

References

Anestis, M. D., Anestis, J. C., Zawilinski, L. L., Hopkins, T. A., & Lilienfeld, S. O. (2014). Equine-related treatments for mental disorders lack empirical support: A systematic review of empirical investigations. *Journal of Clinical Psychology, 70*(12), 1115–1132. https://doi.org/10.1002/jclp.22113

Arnon, S., Fisher, P. W., Pickover, A., Lowell, A., Turner, J. B., Hilburn, A., Jacob-McVey, J., Malajian, B. E., Farber, D. G., Hamilton, J. F., Hamilton, A., Markowitz, J. C., & Neria Y. (2020). Equine-assisted therapy for veterans with PTSD: Manual development and preliminary findings. Military Medicine, 185(5–6):e557–e564. https://doi.org/10.1093/milmed/usz444. PMID: 32034416; PMCID: PMC7282489.

Christian, J. E. (2005). All creatures great and small: Utilizing equine-assisted therapy to treat eating disorders. *Journal of Psychology and Christianity, 24*, 65–67.

Cole, D. M., Beckmann, C. F., Searle, G. E., Plisson, C., Tziortzi, A. C., Nichols, T. E., et al. (2012). Orbitofrontal connectivity with resting-state networks is associated with midbrain dopamine D3 receptor availability. *Cerebral Cortex, 22*(12), 2784–2793. https://doi.org/10.1093/cercor/bhr354

Cumella, E. J. (2003). Is equine therapy useful in the treatment of eating disorders? Eating disorders. *The Journal of Treatment & Prevention, 11*, 143–147. https://doi.org/10.1080/10640260390199325

Dell, C. A., Chalmers, D., Dell, D., Suave, E., & MacKinnon, T. (2008). Horse as healer: An examination of equine assisted learning the healing of First Nations youth from solvent abuse. *Pimatisiwin: A Journal of Aboriginal and Indigenuous Community Health, 6*, 81–106.

Elman, I., Lowen, S., Frederick, B. B., Chi, W., Becerra, L., & Pitman, R. K. (2009). Functional neuroimaging of reward circuitry responsivity to monetary gains and losses in posttraumatic stress disorder. *Biological Psychiatry, 66*(12), 1083–1090. https://doi.org/10.1016/j.biopsych.2009.06.006

Eshel, N., & Roiser, J. P. (2010). Reward and punishment processing in depression. *Biological Psychiatry, 68*(2), 118–124. https://doi.org/10.1016/j.biopsych.2010.01.027

Espinoza Oyarce, D. A., Shaw, M. E., Alateeq, K., & Cherbuin, N. (2020). Volumetric brain differences in clinical depression in association with anxiety: A systematic review with meta-analysis. *Journal of Psychiatry & Neuroscience, 45*(6), 406–429. https://doi.org/10.1503/jpn.190156

Felmingham, K. L., Falconer, E. M., Williams, L., Kemp, A. H., Allen, A., Peduto, A., & Bryant, R. A. (2014). Reduced amygdala and ventral striatal activity to happy faces in PTSD is associated with emotional numbing. *PLoS One, 9*(9), e103653. https://doi.org/10.1371/journal.pone.0103653

Fonzo, G. A., Goodkind, M. S., Oathes, D. J., Zaiko, Y. V., Harvey, M., Peng, K. K., et al. (2017b). Selective effects of psychotherapy on frontopolar cortical function in PTSD. *The American Journal of Psychiatry, 174*(12), 1175–1184. https://doi.org/10.1176/appi.ajp.2017.16091073

Hamilton, A. J. (2011). *Zen mind, Zen horse: The science and spirituality of working with horses*. Storey Publishing.

Haylock, P. J., & Cantril, C. A. (2006). Healing with horses: Fostering recovery from cancer with horses as therapists. *EXPLORE, 2*, 264–268. https://doi.org/10.1016/j.explore.2006.03.013

Helpman, L., Papini, S., Chhetry, B. T., Shvil, E., Rubin, M., Sullivan, G. M., et al. (2016). PTSD Remission after prolonged exposure treatment is associated with anterior cingulate cortex thinning and volume reduction. *Depression and Anxiety, 33*(5), 384–391. https://doi.org/10.1002/da.22471

Lac, V., Marble, E., & Boie, I. (2013). Equine-assisted psychotherapy as a creative relational approach to treating clients with eating disorders. *Journal of Creativity in Mental Health, 8*, 483–498. https://doi.org/10.1080/15401383.2013.852451

Laugharne, J., Kullack, C., Lee, C. W., McGuire, T., Brockman, S., Drummond, P. D., & Starkstein, S. (2016). Amygdala volumetric change following psychotherapy for posttraumatic stress disorder. *The Journal of Neuropsychiatry and Clinical Neurosciences*, appineuropsych16010006. https://doi.org/10.1176/appi.neuropsych.16010006

Levy-Gigi, E., Szabo, C., Kelemen, O., & Keri, S. (2013). Association among clinical response, hippocampal volume, and FKBP5 gene expression in individuals with posttraumatic stress disorder receiving cognitive behavioral therapy. *Biological Psychiatry, 74*(11), 793–800. https://doi.org/10.1016/j.biopsych.2013.05.017

Lindauer, R. J., Vlieger, E. J., Jalink, M., Olff, M., Carlier, I. V., Majoie, C. B., et al. (2005). Effects of psychotherapy on hippocampal volume in out-patients with post-traumatic stress disorder: A MRI investigation. *Psychological Medicine, 35*(10), 1421–1431. https://doi.org/10.1017/S0033291705005246

Lutter, C., & Smith-Osborne, A. (2011). Exercise in the treatment of eating disorders: An alternative view. *Best Practices in Mental Health: An International Journal, 7*, 42–59.

Moussa, M. N., Steen, M. R., Laurienti, P. J., & Hayasaka, S. (2012). Consistency of network modules in resting-state FMRI connectome data. *PLoS One, 7*(8), e44428. https://doi.org/10.1371/journal.pone.0044428

Nisar, S., Bhat, A. A., Hashem, S., Syed, N., Yadav, S. K., Uddin, S., et al. (2020). Genetic and neuroimaging approaches to understanding post-traumatic stress disorder. *International Journal of Molecular Sciences, 21*(12). https://doi.org/10.3390/ijms21124503

Olson, E. A., Kaiser, R. H., Pizzagalli, D. A., Rauch, S. L., & Rosso, I. M. (2018). Anhedonia in trauma-exposed individuals: Functional connectivity and decision-making correlates. *Biological Psychiatry: Cognitive Neuroscience and Neuroimaging, 3*(11), 959–967. https://doi.org/10.1016/j.bpsc.2017.10.008

Pizzagalli, D. A., Holmes, A. J., Dillon, D. G., Goetz, E. L., Birk, J. L., Bogdan, R., et al. (2009). Reduced caudate and nucleus accumbens response to rewards in unmedicated individuals with major depressive disorder. *The American Journal of Psychiatry, 166*(6), 702–710. https://doi.org/10.1176/appi.ajp.2008.08081201

Sailer, U., Robinson, S., Fischmeister, F. P., Konig, D., Oppenauer, C., Lueger-Schuster, B., et al. (2008). Altered reward processing in the nucleus accumbens and mesial prefrontal cortex of patients with posttraumatic stress disorder. *Neuropsychologia, 46*(11), 2836–2844. https://doi.org/10.1016/j.neuropsychologia.2008.05.022

Schmidt, A., Denier, N., Magon, S., Radue, E. W., Huber, C. G., Riecher-Rossler, A., et al. (2015). Increased functional connectivity in the resting-state basal ganglia network after acute heroin substitution. *Translational Psychiatry, 5*, e533. https://doi.org/10.1038/tp.2015.28

Schultz, P. N., Remick-Barlow, G. A., & Robbins, L. (2007). Equine-assisted psychotherapy: A mental health promotion/intervention modality for children who have experienced intra-family violence. *Health & Social Care in the Community, 15*, 265–271. https://doi.org/10.1111/j.1365-2524.2006.00684

Selby, A., & Smith-Osborne, A. (2013). A systematic review of effectiveness of complementary and adjunct therapies and interventions involving equines. *Health Psychology, 32*(4), 418–432. https://doi.org/10.1037/a0029188

Sesack, S. R., & Grace, A. A. (2010). Cortico-Basal Ganglia reward network: Microcircuitry. *Neuropsychopharmacology, 35*(1), 27–47. https://doi.org/10.1038/npp.2009.93

Stafford, C. Throwback Thursday: No obstacle was too great for Lis Hartel. *The Chronicle of the Horse*. Retrieved September 20, 2023.

Suarez-Jimenez, B., Zhu, X., Lazarov, A., Mann, J. J., Schneier, F., Gerber, A., et al. (2020). Anterior hippocampal volume predicts affect-focused psychotherapy outcome. *Psychological Medicine, 50*(3), 396–402. https://doi.org/10.1017/S0033291719000187

van Rooij, S. J., Kennis, M., Sjouwerman, R., van den Heuvel, M. P., Kahn, R. S., & Geuze, E. (2015). Smaller hippocampal volume as a vulnerability factor for the persistence of post-traumatic stress disorder. *Psychological Medicine, 45*(13), 2737–2746. https://doi.org/10.1017/S0033291715000707

Volkow, N. D., Baler, R. D., & Goldstein, R. Z. (2011). Addiction: Pulling at the neural threads of social behaviors. *Neuron, 69*(4), 599–602. https://doi.org/10.1016/j.neuron.2011.01.027

Wilson, K., Buultjens, M., Monfries, M., & Karimi, L. (2017). Equine-Assisted Psychotherapy for adolescents experiencing depression and/or anxiety: A therapist's perspective. *Clinical Child Psychology and Psychiatry, 22*, 16–33.

Yang, C., Wu, S., Bai, Y., Hou, C., & Gao, H. (2009). Voxel based morphometric study of brain structure in patients with posttraumatic stress disorder. *Sheng Wu Yi Xue Gong Cheng Xue Za Zhi, 26*(1), 30–33. Retrieved from https://www.ncbi.nlm.nih.gov/pubmed/19334548

Zhu, X., Suarez-Jimenez, B., Lazarov, A., Helpman, L., Papini, S., Lowell, A., et al. (2018). Exposure-based therapy changes amygdala and hippocampus resting-state functional connectivity in patients with posttraumatic stress disorder. *Depression and Anxiety, 35*(10), 974–984. https://doi.org/10.1002/da.22816

Therapeutic Riding for Patients With Schizophrenia

Stefania Cerino

Introduction

Mental health, as documented by the WHO in 2014, is defined as "a state of well-being, in which an individual realizes his or her own abilities, can cope with the normal stress of life, can work productively and is able to make a contribution to his or her community" (World Health Organization, 2014). Good mental health is a critical part of individual well-being, and the foundation for happy, fulfilled, productive lives. Psychiatric disorders represent disturbances to a person's mental health that are often characterized by a combination of troubled thoughts, emotions, behavior, and relationships with others (World Health Organization, 2013). Mental disorders are increasing considerably in our society, especially following the COVID-19 pandemic with teenagers and young people being particularly affected, UNICEF data had already pointed out that one in seven adolescents worldwide between the ages of 10 and 19 live with a diagnosed mental disorder, and 40% of these are anxiety and depression. In Western Europe, suicide is the second leading cause of death among 15- to 19-year-olds, (4/100,000) (UNICEF, 2021). In addition, the UNICEF report "Life in Lockdown—Child and adolescent mental health and well-being in the time of COVID-19" highlights how changing living conditions during the lockdown following the COVID-19 pandemic have affected adolescents' mental health. The report analyzes 50 peer-reviewed studies on this topic and details the consequences of COVID-19 on teen mental health (UNICEF Office of Research, 2021). Poor mental health has many consequences. Psychiatric patients are at a higher risk of developing addictions (drugs, cigarette smoking) and partaking in risky behaviors (unhealthy diets, alcohol abuse, sexual promiscuity). Mental illness is strongly associated with exposure to major cardiovascular risk factors (Coen, 2017).

S. Cerino (✉)
Centro di Riabilitazione Equestre G. de Marco, Rome, Italy

Y. Neria et al. (eds.), *Guide to Equine Assisted Therapy*,
https://doi.org/10.1007/978-3-031-74426-6_9

Studies conducted in the United States estimate that cardiovascular risk increases from 10% to 30% in patients with bipolar disorder, schizophrenia, and schizoaffective disorder compared with the general population. Thirty years after receiving the psychiatric diagnosis, the cardiovascular risk is at 25% among psychiatric patients compared with 11% among those without mental disorders (Rossom et al., 2022).

Colton and Manderscheid (2006) studied causes of death among public mental health clients in eight US states (Arizona, Missouri, Oklahoma, Rhode Island, Texas, Utah, Vermont, and Virginia) between 1997 through 2000. He writes:

> In all eight states, we found that public mental health clients had a higher relative risk of death than the general populations of their states. Deceased public mental health clients had died at much younger ages and lost decades of potential life when compared with their living cohorts nationwide. Clients with major mental illness diagnoses died at younger ages and lost more years of life than people with non-major mental illness diagnoses. Most mental health clients died of natural causes like the leading causes of death found nationwide, including heart disease, cancer, and cerebrovascular, respiratory, and lung diseases.

In 2022, WHO published "World Mental Health Report: Transforming Mental Health for All" assessing that more than 14% of the global burden of disability consists of mental disease. Moreover, one death in 100 is caused by suicide, with 58% of these cases occurring in younger people, or people under 50 years of age. The report revealed that over a billion people (one in eight people) suffer from a mental disease, with 52% being women (World Health Organization, 2022).

Mental disease is accompanied by a strong stigma based on stereotypes, fear, and shame (Martinez Zambrano et al., 2013). This is occasionally followed by rights violations. In most countries, pharmacologic treatment remains the treatment of choice, but this ends up increasing discrimination and social exclusion.

The stigma of being labeled as suffering from a mental health (MH) disorder often results in the affected individual being shunned, isolated, or bullied. In many countries, the access to treatment is limited and expensive (Loch et al., 2014). Globally, most interventions for MH disorders are pharmacologic and only 30% of countries can implement psychosocial interventions (World Health Organization, 2014). It follows that the importance of prevention and rehabilitation actions in order to improve the social functioning and inclusion of people with mental health problems is clear. Among the various therapeutic rehabilitative opportunities since the late 1900s, interventions with animals and horses, in particular, have begun to be considered as valuable operational tools (Cerino, 2022). A discrete scientific literature has also developed to support the effectiveness of therapeutic riding (TR) in the field of mental health. As will be seen later, it is particularly metacognitive and relational work that yields the most interesting results.

Schizophrenia

Among mental disorders, schizophrenia is one of the most complex and severe. Approximately one billion people in the world are affected by mental disorders, and 2.4% of them suffer from schizophrenia.

From a nosographic point of view, schizophrenia is classified among "psychoses," diseases characterized by distortions in thinking, perception, emotions, language, sense of self, and behavior. Common psychotic experiences include hallucinations (hearing, seeing, or feeling things that are not there) and delusions (fixed false beliefs or suspicions that are firmly held, even when there is evidence to the contrary). The disorder can make it difficult for people to work or study effectively (World Health Organization, 2014). Schizophrenia is particularly characterized by a loss of contact with reality, hallucinations, delusions, disorganized language and behavior, flattening of emotions, cognitive impairments, and social malfunctioning. The causes are unknown, but there is strong evidence of genetic and environmental components. Men and women are affected in similar percentages. The symptoms are categorized into positive (hallucinations and delusions), negative (normal functions and emotions decreased or lost), disorganized (thought disorder and bizarre behavior), and cognitive (memory, information processing, and problem-solving deficits).

Patients can exhibit symptoms of one or more categories. Treatment is based on drug therapy, cognitive therapy, psychosocial rehabilitation, and animal-/horse-assisted intervention (therapeutic riding). Schizophrenia is certainly the most serious and disabling chronic psychiatric pathology, where deep emotional-affective deficits, cognitive distortion, and lack of disease awareness contribute to profoundly altering the mental and social functioning of the person. One of the diagnostic criteria for schizophrenia is a deficit in social functioning, which refers to a number of aspects, such as an individual's ability to fulfill the main roles expected of him or her in a defined social sphere (as worker, student, housewife, spouse, friend, etc.), to take care of himself and his living environment, and to involve himself positively in recreational and leisure activities.

From peacox dementia (1904) by Kraepelin to today's DSM-V (American Psychiatric Association, 2017), the concept of schizophrenia has changed significantly. The disease, known as one of the most "familiar" mental illnesses, has undergone numerous revisitations, to the point of suggesting that the concept of schizophrenia should not refer to a specific type of psychiatric disorder, identified by a unitary etiopathogenetic process. The boundaries of the disease have from time to time widened and/or narrowed according to the diagnostic tools possessed, different cultural approaches, and dominant scientific paradigms (Tandon & Maj, 2008).

Osview writes, "In my opinion, current data, including the neuropsychiatric data, indicate that psychotic disorders are best understood not categorically but dimensionally, comprising parameters that vary continuously and can appear in various combinations—a 'mix-and-match' nosology. From these combinations can certainly emerge the classic clinical pictures described by Kraepelin and seen in daily practice" (Ovsiew, 2000).

We do not know how much and whether the pathology in its essence has changed: it is still, if not "incomprehensible," as Jaspers said, surely much still unknowable (Jaspers, 1965).

Theraputic Riding and Schizophrenia

In addition to pharmacological interventions that have surely facilitated the approach to treating individuals with schizophrenia over the years, great attention is paid to bio-psycho-social rehabilitation, a mode of approach to the psychotic patient based on encouraging his or her return to society. The interventions of bio-psycho-social rehabilitation include psychological, relational, and behavioral support. The concept of rehabilitation in medicine is quite recent. It was around 1938 in the United States that Krusen began to use physical therapies for rehabilitation purposes (Alvarez, 1964). These interventions have then developed significantly after World War II to become nowadays one of the most important branches of medicine.

The same concept of recovery and implementing residual skills was extended to mental illness, an area in which it was considered that no matter how severe the pathology, still some functionality was preserved. In the 1960s in the United Kingdom, as a direct consequence of the great changes occurring in the approach to mental health in the nineteenth century, community psychiatry developed to be used as a "base" for the recovery of psychic dysfunctionality, which sought to help the sick person in social integration (Lieberman, 1997).

In Italy, with the final closure of asylums in 1978, to facilitate the reintegration of the sick into their families, people began to think about specific paths of "Psychiatric Rehabilitation." This period saw the emergence of various forms of community-based and outpatient care, where pathways to social reintegration were aviated to rebuild social functioning that would allow the patient not to be excluded from social life.

This is a process implemented through music therapy, social farming, cognitive interventions, and interventions with animals, whose goals are to identify, prevent, and reduce the causes of incapacity and to help the person develop and use his or her own resources and abilities to gain more self-confidence and increase the level of self-esteem. This work is done by specialized staff who leverage what is healthy in the patient and not the pathology. With psychotic patients, rehabilitation aims at first-person participation in activities (such as sport, horticulture, and computer-based activities) to gain the best possible access to autonomy, quality interpersonal relationships, self-determination, and to be able to meet both concrete and emotional needs.

A good rehabilitation program reduces the risk of recurrence, acting also as prevention. It is clear that the main aim of psychiatric rehabilitation is to give the patient a satisfactory and dignified "quality of life." This work involves the patient's life at all levels and cannot be developed if the patient himself is not willing to participate. Once the pharmacological treatment has solved the acute states of illness, it is the newfound health condition the point on which to leverage to undertake a wide-ranging rehabilitation project.

Therapeutic riding is among the various rehabilitation activities that can improve the social functioning and emotional well-being of psychotic patients. The presence and communicative nature of the horse enable therapists to interact more effectively with patients, helping them take charge of their distress and build a rehabilitation and treatment pathway.

The presence of an animal in the therapeutic setting evokes play and experimental ideas typical of early childhood, which play a crucial role in psychotherapy and rehabilitation for children, adults, and the elderly. Winnicott emphasized the therapeutic importance of play and relationships with transitional objects—objects that hold special significance for the child, existing in a space between internal and external reality (Winnicott, 1975). Play unleashes creativity and imagination, while transitional objects facilitate contact with the symbolic spaces of the mind. In this context, horses serve as living, sentient transitional objects, fully integrating into the therapeutic relationship and fostering its development.

Therapeutic riding also enhances nonverbal communication. When verbal communication is not possible, therapists can propose games on horseback, establishing a different form of interaction with the patient. Horses embody various symbolic values that help distinguish the "ego" from the "Otherness," aid in behavioral organization, and promote emotional and cognitive development. Therapeutic riding thus holds significant potential as an unconventional psychiatric rehabilitation method for schizophrenic patients.

The theoretical assumption of therapeutic riding as a non-conventional psychiatric rehabilitation method is based on the hypothesis that it can positively influence metacognition, relationship building, and social integration. This, in turn, enhances the quality of life for both the patient and their caregiver. Specifically, for young patients experiencing the onset of schizophrenia, it helps mitigate the painful stigma associated with social isolation and emotional relationship deficits.

In the psychiatric rehabilitation of a schizophrenic patient, it is crucial to rebuild the empathetic relationship between the "ego" and "Otherness," and between the inner and outer worlds disrupted by the disease. Psychosis creates a rift between the individual and others, making communication and relationships challenging and leading to a dimension of isolation. Identifying a "mental space" where the patients can perceive their condition is essential. This space, internal to ourselves, contains our memories, thoughts, and representations of the world. When the patient becomes aware of this mental space and reconnects with the deeper parts of their "Self," it becomes possible to work on reconstructing their identity.

Therapeutic riding offers both a physical and mental space where an encounter with Otherness is possible. The horse, representing the "Other," introduces the patient to a new environment, provides novel communication channels, and helps them find a different social dimension. Conducting equestrian rehabilitation in open, green spaces, away from typical medicalized settings, allows the patient to detach from the often-marginalizing healthcare circuit.

To interact with the horse in this new environment, the patient must learn new skills and rebuild connections with the outside world. This process serves as the starting point for integration, rehabilitation, and an improved quality of life.

Previous Research on Therapeutic Riding for People with Schizophrenia

This section will present insights from various scholars on the impact of therapeutic riding on participants with schizophrenia. Although there are few recent articles on this topic, historical and scientific papers provide valuable context. The first scientific papers on "Hippotherapy" or "Therapeutic Horseback Riding" appeared in the literature in the late 1970s, addressing various disabilities and considering therapeutic horseback riding as a useful means to counteract physical deficits.

Throughout its long history, medical literature has included numerous texts highlighting the benefits of horseback riding on physical and mental health. Since Greek-Roman times, horseback riding has been recognized for its therapeutic value in various pathological conditions. After a long period of medieval obscurity, Girolamo Mercuriale, an Italian physician (1530–1606), was the first to specify how physical activity can positively affect overall health (Mercuriale, 2008).

According to Mercuriale, riding a horse is part of real gymnastic, that is, exercises having the same purpose of therapy. Also, Thomas Syndenham, the "English Hippocrates" (Payne, 1900), speaks about the beneficial psychophysical effects of riding a horse. Also Georg Stahl (1660–1743) considers the gymnastic exercises on horseback essential for wellness (Stahl, 1733). In the work *Grundliche Anweisungen wie ein Mensch durch ernuftigen Gebrauch der Leibesbewegungen seine Gesundheit erhalten und sichvon schweren krannkheiten befrein kann* (In-depth instructions about how a person can mantain his health and get rid of serious diseases through the reasonable practice of physical exercises) of 1719 by Hoffmann (1719), one chapter is dedicated to *Reiten und der selbe herrliche Nutzen* (Horse riding and its huge benefits). The walking pace is defined as the most healthy one. Another Italian doctor, Giuseppe Benvenuti, in 1772, published *Considerations on the Effects of Riding* (Benvenuti, 1760), a dissertation about riding benefits which describes the positive effects of blood circulation, the elasticity of muscle fibers, and the arterial and lymphatic vessels.

R. Pickenbach in 1909 publishes *Einfluss des Reitsports auf den meschlichen Organismus* (The impact of horse riding on human body) (Pickenbach, 1909), where he considers "horse riding as a remedy for relapsing pathological states (…) this sport will play the most important role among all the physical exercises." In his opinion, horseback riding acted as a prevention of potential relapse in several disease states.

Max Senator is the author in 1930 (Senator, 1930) of a study entitled *Der gesundheithliche Wert es Reitens* (The Healthy Value of Horse Riding). All these papers get close to the "birth" of modern therapeutic riding. In European countries with more equestrian culture, they have began to deepen the studies concerning the horse as a therapeutical means, to face a big range of physical, psychic, behavioral, and sensorial disabilites.

The first publication on the use of horses for therapeutic purposes in the German language was Ernst Druschky's book *Gymnastik zu Pferde, ein Weg zur Heilung* (*Horseback Gymnastics, a Way to Recovery*) in 1961. Druschky advocated for a range of gymnastic exercises, such as equestrian vaulting, that could be performed with horses to complement traditional physiotherapy. He believed this approach could improve motor disorders, including gait difficulties and infant cerebral palsy. Subsequent publications by Reichenbach (1965), Geldmacher (1968), Nedelmann (1967), Hengst (1968), and Ledermann (1968) further explored these ideas.

In 1962, de Lubersac and Lallery wrote *Reeducation par l'équitation* (*Rehabilitation through Horse Riding*), which remains a foundational text for understanding therapeutic riding. This work systematized the approach to equestrian rehabilitation from a modern perspective, advancing beyond previous publications.

The first modern peer-reviewed scientific works on "hippotherapy" or "therapeutic horseback riding" appeared in the literature at the end of the 1970s, addressing various physical disabilities. However, research specifically focusing on mental health, particularly schizophrenia, has been less extensive.

In 1986, German psychiatrist and psychotherapist Michaela Scheidhacker began using horses in group therapy with an analytic orientation for schizophrenic patients. Drawing on observations about nonverbal communication by Watzlawick (Watzlawick et al., 1967) and Bateson (Bateson, 1977), Scheidhacker developed an intervention methodology and published her initial findings. Her protocol involves several stages: initially, patients engage in feeding and grooming the horse to foster physical contact and a sense of responsibility. The second stage includes rope leading, where patients ride the horse without a saddle, addressing issues of corporeality, sexuality, and mobility. In the final stage, patients ride with a saddle and are confronted with a "barrier" or "border" that helps them redefine their sensations and identity. At this point, the reins are handed to the patients, allowing them to take control of the horse and, symbolically, their own identity (Scheidhacker, 1998; Scheidhacker and Kupsch, 2010). Following are some sessions of group horseback riding, where the patients mostly experience their autonomy and self-determination, to end with horse trek and:

> Now nobody can leave the group, while the single members depend directly on each other for trekking time, about one hour or two. The patients learn, controlling their anxiety and needs, to be interested in Others' needs and anxiety and handle it, here and now, in unexpected situations.

Over the last 20 years, numerous studies have emerged with more defined experimental protocols, the presence of control groups, and efficacy evaluations. In 2003,

Bizub et al. published a study involving five patients with longstanding psychiatric disabilities, including chronic schizophrenia, who participated in a 10-week therapeutic horseback riding program. The authors concluded that "the riders reported success in learning basic horsemanship and, in doing so, also reported additional psychosocial benefits, including an augmented sense of self-efficacy and self-esteem. In sum, this adjunctive therapy can facilitate the recovery process."

In 2009, a new scientific paper focused on therapeutic riding with schizophrenic patients was released. Thirty participants took part in a weekly animal-assisted activity program for 2 months. The study aimed to assess self-esteem, self-determination, social support, and psychiatric symptoms using a self-administered questionnaire given the week before and after the activity. The results showed significant clinical improvements in inpatients with schizophrenia, particularly in mitigating negative symptoms and enhancing relational abilities (Chu et al., 2009).

In 2011, Cerino et al. published a paper on therapeutic riding as a nonconventional psychiatric rehabilitation. This research involved 24 subjects diagnosed with schizophrenia who participated in a year-long therapeutic horseback riding program, with sessions held once a week, totaling 40 sessions per patient. Each session included grooming and harnessing the horse, riding, and a final phase of cleaning and rewarding the animal. The sessions began individually and progressed to small group activities. Patients showed improvement in negative symptoms, disease remission, and a reduced rate of hospitalization. However, the study's limitations included the absence of a control group and long-term follow-up.

In 2012, Banszky et al. published a review examining the effectiveness of therapeutic riding in easing symptoms of specific psychiatric disorders, including schizophrenia, depression, and anxiety. The review concluded that animal-assisted therapies improve social and communication skills, ease anxiety, enhance mood, support independent living, and develop empathetic skills.

In 2013, Corring et al. demonstrated the benefits of horseback riding for patients with schizophrenia at various levels of psychiatric disability. Their study, conducted with a small group of six psychiatric outpatients, suggested that therapeutic horseback riding is a promising tool in psychiatric rehabilitation. However, the authors emphasized the need for studies with larger sample sizes to verify these results. They highlighted the importance of further research in this field.

In 2015, Nurenberg et al. published a study involving 90 inpatients diagnosed with schizophrenia, schizoaffective disorder, affective disorders, or other psychiatric conditions. The sample included patients with aggressive or regressive behavior and persistent social isolation. The patients were randomly enrolled in a rehabilitation program of either equine-assisted psychotherapy (EAP) or canine-assisted psychotherapy. In the EAP program, the horses were not ridden. The authors concluded that EAP might be an effective therapeutic modality for long-term psychiatric patients at risk of violence. Nurenberg also emphasized the necessity of study replications using similar and disparate intervention models and populations, noting that the canine-assisted activity did not produce significant results.

In 2018, Jormfeldt and Carlsson published a review on equine-assisted therapeutic interventions among individuals diagnosed with schizophrenia. The review indicated that these interventions could be beneficial for individuals with severe mental illness such as schizophrenia or schizophrenia-like disorders.

In 2023, Cappelen et al. published a paper discussing the effects of an equine-assisted therapeutic (EAT) intervention on the well-being of individuals diagnosed with schizophrenia. Twenty adults participated in a 12-week EAT intervention, with sessions held every 14 days by a licensed mental health nurse. Two validated self-rated questionnaires, HSCL-25 and SHIS, were used as outcome measurements at baseline and post-treatment. The 25-item Hopkins Symptom Checklist (HSCL-25) assesses anxiety and depression symptoms, while the Salutogenic Health Indicator Scale (SHIS) measures health indicators from a salutogenic perspective. Additionally, the self-rated Positive and Negative Symptoms Scales (PANSS) questionnaire was completed twice a week, starting 1 week before the 12-week EAT intervention. The PANSS includes three subscales: Positive Scale, Negative Scale, and General Psychopathology Scale, with scores ranging from 7 to 49 for the Positive and Negative Scales and 16 to 112 for the General Psychopathology Scale.

Only 6 of the 20 participants managed to complete the validated questionnaires. Despite the low response rate of approximately 30%, a significant difference was found between pre- and post-intervention scores for positive affect and well-being. Effect sizes, ranging from small to large, indicated less depression and anxiety, more positive affect, less negative affect, and reinforced well-being. The results suggest that EAT interventions may have beneficial effects for individuals with schizophrenia and that a varied range of research methods is needed to create a solid evidence base for EAT interventions.

Overall, while further scientific data are needed to more clearly establish the benefits of human–animal companionships, understanding the mechanisms underlying our continuous seeking for pet companionship may help shed new light on the processes of emotional regulation for the promotion of mental health.

The Clinical Benefits of Therapeutic Riding for Schizophrenia

Although qualitative observations allow us to appreciate positive results by employing therapeutic riding as an unconventional psychiatric rehabilitation in schizophrenia, the mechanisms of action are still being investigated and deepened.

Therapeutic riding, like any other animal-assisted intervention, assumes that there is a relationship between man and horse. In the latter animal's home, the relationship with humans begins about 6000 years ago with domestication (Galli, 2002).

Contact with the horse evokes an emotional response from humans, which leads to the building of a bond of affiliation, similar to what takes place in family ties (Berry et al., 2013). These bonds have also been investigated at the neuroendocrine level. This is not the place to delve into these aspects, we will simply point out how the neurobiological substrate underlying social ties has highlighted the primary role of two neuroendocrine systems: oxytocin (OT) and vasopressin (AVP). The effects of the two hormones are related to the brain areas where their receptors are present.

Those for OT (OTRs) are found in the limbic, olfactory, spinal, and brainstem systems, highlighting the role of this peptide in mnestic-type functions, regulation of reproductive behavior and sensory and emotional processing (Carter, 1998).

From the perspective of social interaction, the basic cornerstones for building a therapeutic relationship with the horse are communication and affective exchange (Vygotskij, 1980). All this takes place within the space-setting in which the intervention with the horse materially takes place. The interaction between patient and therapist, mediated by the horse, activates specific metacognitive work for the former. In this way, patients are able to "observe" the animal by reflecting on its communication and relationship codes, being able to gain greater awareness also with respect to their own modes of interaction with others.

To date, a psychoanalytic theory has not yet been developed to explain in what precise way equestrian rehabilitation works in schizophrenia. However, one can refer to some elements of Freudian and post-Freudian theory to gain insights, which will then have to be systematized, as knowledge progresses, into a specific construct.

As mentioned earlier, in the rehabilitation setting, the horse can be considered a transitional object in the sense in which Winnicott understood it. For the English psychoanalyst, the transitional object is something that has a calming and relaxing effect on the child. These are objects that refer to an area of the child's experience that is located in the place that connects and separates internal and external reality and will later become a permanent function of the psyche (Winnicott, 1975).

Typically, in psychotics, experiences of detachment are experienced as catastrophic, leading to avoidance of contact and relationships with the outside world. A therapeutic setting, with a different and non-disturbing presence such as that of the animal, helps to approach this situation from a less traumatic perspective, and helps the patient develop new resources to reconnect with the reality from which he wanted to escape (Cerino, 2015).

Another important aspect to consider with respect to schizophrenic patients is that of corporeality. As Freud mentioned, "The ego is essentially a corporeal ego" (Freud, 1977). What of the psychotic subject relates to the Other is the "expressive body" as a whole consisting of verbal and nonverbal parts. A physical body as well, which must recognize and have awareness of its own limitations. The body is also an intermediary with the world (Resnik et al., 1982).

Generally, psychotics have a rather rigid corporeality, tending to close in on themselves, avoiding eye contact with others. The presence of the horse in the therapeutic/rehabilitation setting inevitably prompts a redefinition of one's body structure, which must relate to that specific and defined situation, to the stimuli coming from the horse's gait. After a number of TR sessions with psychotic patients, it is possible to observe a change in body positions, such as a higher head, a more upright posture, and an expansion of one's movements in space.

The first contact with the animal often occurs with a caress; tactile communication is the one most easily understood in the intraspecific relationship (Amiot & Bastian, 2015). Thus the encounter between two "skins," two "boundaries," takes place, which can be seen as closeness, acquaintance, separation, and communication (Amati, 2012).

The horse is thus the mediator of the relationship between therapist and patient. Generally, the encounter with the Other (whether human or animal) makes us reflect on who the Other really is. In the psychotic world, this encounter becomes difficult, and problems are manifested in interacting with the world of reality. This situation is referred to as social cognition disorder. To overcome this condition, the patient and the therapist must identify a space of communication, where it is possible to interact without fear. The specific setting of therapeutic riding offers the possibility for this to happen and for the relationship with the patient to begin to develop.

Work Tools

For a therapeutic riding intervention to be effective, it is essential that, during the planning phase, both the methodology to apply and the efficacy evaluation to be used for performance measurement are well defined. It is complex work, not comparable to a "riding lesson." In fact, it is not the horse "itself" to be "therapeutical." It is the animal presence in the setting and the relationship that, skillfully managed, gives the therapist the possibility to deepen experiences, stimulate reactions, create investments on external objects, move libidinal energies, and aid the metacognition to build an effectively "therapeutic" space for the patient.

Methodological Experiences

Social cognition is our way to "think about the world." The psychotic state of mind makes this cognition "other" compared to that of most individuals; from this follows a "fracture" in the communication and in establishing personal relationships. The task of therapeutic/rehabilitation intervention is to try to support the birth of a new and better relationship and to set the cognition in motion.

Traditionally, a TR session is divided into grooming phase, horseback riding phase or phase with the horse, and in the last part of final restitution. The general environment in the TR session can be empathic or unpleasant, but certainly not apathetic, because in this case nothing circulates, nothing is exchanged, and nothing happens.

The horse is proposed to the patient for what it is and relates to him without superstructures or mediations, which are not included in its usual behavioral codes. The horse is at the same time subject of a defined situation but "watches" the setting also from outside, from its point of view, which is opposite to the human one. The psychotic patients, for their part, often confuse dreamlike language and reality: they follow the time and rhythm of their ego in conflict with the reality principle (experienced as disturbing), threatening their defensive structure (Vygotskij, 1980).

In this way, the patient creates a defensive and waterproof space to external relationships. The aim of the therapeutic riding intervention is trying to make a breach in the closed space and set in motion the relational circles. This approach reflects a deep understanding of how therapeutic environments can foster significant changes in the psychosocial dynamics of individuals with severe mental health conditions (Amiot & Bastian, 2015).

Grooming

Grooming operations are the first approach to the work session. The following list defines the subsequent phases:

- Length: about 10–15 minutes.
- Setting type: group setting is standard, located in the stable, whose members are patients, therapists, and horses.
- Tools used: stable equipment and the harnesses.
- Purpose of activity: based on relational and metacognitive aspects.
- Communication codes: mostly used by horses—tactile, visual and olfactive—are used, allowing a first acquaintance with man, in order to establish a simple, linear, clear, and reassuring communication. It is the first direct approach with the animal, the confrontation with its imposing body presence, the first possibility to establish a "dialogue" where words are not necessary. It is one approach to another, which has no stigma and changes its attitude with any one in front of. It is through metacognition that the psychotic is able to act in this phase.

Horseback Riding and Horse-Assisted Activity

Effective equine-assisted therapy does not necessarily require riding a horse. A therapeutic relationship can be established through handling, rope leading, or simply observing the horse. Therapists choose the most suitable approach based on the specific goals of the intervention. For individuals with schizophrenic psychosis, horseback riding is often considered most appropriate due to its unique benefits in fostering a relationship between the human and the horse.

When riding, communication with the horse is primarily based on "corporeality"—the rider's body movements convey information to the horse. Using the reins through the hands and upper limbs establishes the necessary "contact" to guide the horse. This interaction requires the rider to plan actions within a defined timeframe, adapting to stimuli and cues from the horse and the environment. Horseback riding also helps improve spatio-temporal orientation, symmetry, rhythm, and self-confidence. Self-confidence, often compromised in individuals with schizophrenia, can be significantly bolstered through horseback riding. As Searles (1974) notes, chronic schizophrenics frequently feel immobilized by profound disappointment. However, when a patient learns to independently handle a strong and imposing animal like a horse, they begin to regain confidence in their abilities, moving away from feelings of disappointment and frustration. This newfound confidence reflects in improved social functioning and allows patients to develop more critical thinking skills, enhancing their ability to relate to the outside world. Addressing the stigma associated with mental illness is another critical aspect of rehabilitation. Engaging in therapeutic activities that resemble competitive sports places patients on the same level as other participants, thereby reducing stigmatization.

Lastly, therapeutic riding contributes to overall wellness. Although the primary goal is not recreational riding, the physical activity involved is a form of "sport technique." Regular participation helps reduce body mass index (BMI) and counteract weight gain, which is often a side effect of neuroleptic therapies. This holistic approach to therapy supports both the mental and physical health of participants, offering a comprehensive benefit to those with schizophrenia.

Final Restitution Phase

The last phase of rehabilitation sessions, known as restitution, is a crucial time for evaluation and reflection on the activities conducted. During this phase, the operators can enhance their level of communication with the patients. This final restitution is tied to the last grooming phase, like the initial grooming, and unfolds in a semistructured manner. While it does not constitute a form of psychotherapy, it serves to collect, reorganize, and assign meaning to the experiences during the TR session.

Significant psychodynamic elements often surface during these final restitution moments. However, these elements are not typically addressed within the TR setting itself. Instead, it is advisable to relay this information to the psychiatric professionals overseeing the patient's psychotherapy. This ensures that these insights are analyzed in a more suitable clinical context. In light of this, maintaining a stable exchange with therapists who manage the patient's care in other settings is highly beneficial. Such collaboration helps in sharing assessments and establishing common therapeutic goals (Table 1).

Table 1 The main stages of the TR session

Grooming phase	First and last part of working session 10–15 minutes Group activity	Relational and metacognitive purposes
Horse riding phase	30–40 minutes Group activity	Relational, metacognitive, stigma, self-esteem purposes
Final restitution phase	10–15 minutes Group activity Semistructured speech	Final reflection on awareness, self-esteem, insight

The administration of possible evaluation tests of the ongoing rehabilitation program should not interfere with the structure of the rehabilitation session itself. So the possible test administration should be planned in different times and far from the moments when doing work with the horse.

Future Directions

The field of animal and horse-assisted interventions is rapidly advancing, driven by a focus on establishing interventions based on solid scientific principles and expanding research studies (Ministero della Salute, 2015). However, several challenges remain that future researchers must address to provide better, reliable, and accurate findings.

Firstly, it is necessary to increase the sample sizes in studies to achieve statistical significance. The significance level, determined at the study's design stage, is a critical threshold for validating results. Unfortunately, many TR studies do not meet this criterion. Including a statistician within the research team could help address this issue.

Secondly, it is important to distinguish between outcomes specifically related to clinical improvements and those related to quality of life, the latter being more achievable with animal interventions. Therefore, goals should not only focus on symptom mitigation and psychopathological improvements but also on enhancing social functioning, employment inclusion, and economic self-management.

In psychiatry, several standardized tests validated across different countries allow for quantitative evaluations of study results and are well-regarded within the international scientific community. Utilizing scientifically validated tests to evaluate the effectiveness of interventions is the most robust method to gain recognition. In contrast, qualitative data are considered less robust, which is why obtaining quantitative data is essential in TR studies (Cirulli et al., 2011).

Looking to the future, the goals for research in this field are not yet clearly defined. However, recent years have seen the development of non-profit organizations across various countries that aim to identify, improve, and propose best practices or guidelines for equine-assisted activities. These organizations, comprising experts from diverse disciplines (medicine, psychology, veterinary, social sciences, education, etc.), strive to enhance knowledge and disseminate best practices in TR.

Among these organizations are the Horses Education and Therapy International (HETI) in the UK, and the European Equine Facilitated Therapy Network (EEFTN), which focuses on standardizing terminology and sharing educational models and best practices across Europe. In the United States, Horse for Mental Health raises awareness and funds for programs using horses for mental health and personal growth. Additionally, the American Psychological Association includes a section dedicated to human–horse interaction and equine-assisted psychotherapy, signifying its potential future growth in traditional therapeutic settings.

Ekholm (2021) introduced a conceptual approach to horse-mediated psychotherapy, suggesting that interaction with horses enhances existing treatment approaches rather than acting as a standalone intervention.

The International Association of Human Animal Interaction Organizations (IAHAIO) serves as a global association promoting animal-assisted activities and therapy. It published a white paper in 2018 on "Definitions for Animal Assisted Intervention and Guidelines for Wellness of Animals Involved" (2014) and recently established international research teams to define IAHAIO standards for education and training in animal-assisted interventions.

Italy has taken institutional steps by issuing guidelines in 2013 through the Ministry of Health, describing various animal-assisted activities, the species involved, operator training programs, and criteria for animal health and wellness.

This evolving path will increasingly require the participation of specialists and institutions dedicated to clinical research. Ultimately, we can hope that soon, horse-assisted activities in mental health will transition from being viewed as "alternative" or "non-conventional" therapies to being recognized as valid treatments with clear and established results.

References

AAI. (2014). *IAHAIO definitions for animal assisted intervention and guidelines for wellness of animals involved* (IAHAIO White Paper). AAI.

Alvarez, W. C. (1964). Frank H. Krusen, MD: Pioneer in physical medicine. *Archives of Internal Medicine, 114*(1), 1. https://hekint.org/2017/01/28/frank-h-krusen-the-father-of-physical-medicine-and-rehabilitation/

Amati, A. (2012). *Contatto e relazione con il paziente psicotico, II Convegno "Riabilitazione Equestre in Psichiatria"*. FISE.

American Psychiatric Association. (2017). *Manuale diagnostico e statistico dei disturbi mentali*. R. Cortina.

Amiot, C. E., & Bastian, B. (2015). Toward a psychology of human-animalrelations. *Psychological Bulletin, 141*(1), 6–47.

Bánszky, N., Kardos, E., Rózsa, L., & Gerevich, J. (2012). Az állatok által asszisztált terápiák pszichiátriai vonatkozásai [The psychiatric aspects of animal assisted therapy]. *Psychiatria Hungarica, 27*(3), 180–190.

Bateson, G. (1977). *Verso un'ecologia della mente*. Adelphi.

Benvenuti, G. (1760). *Riflessioni sopra gli effetti del moto a cavallo*. Giunti.

Berry, A., Borgi, M., Francia, N., Alleva, E., & Cirulli, F. (2013). Use of assistanceand therapy dogs for children with autistic spectrum disorders: A critical review of the current evidences. *Journal of Alternative and Complementary Medicine, 2*, 73–80.

Bizub, A. L., Joy, A., & Davidson, L. (2003). "It's like being in another world": Demonstrating the benefits of therapeutic horseback riding for individuals with psychiatric disability. *Psychiatric Rehabilitation Journal, 26*(4), 377–384.

Cappelen, H., Ivarsson, A., & Jormfeldt, H. (2023). The effects of an equine-assisted therapeutic intervention on well-being in persons diagnosed with schizophrenia. A pilot study. *Issues in Mental Health Nursing, 44*(2), 104–111.

Carter, C. S. (1998). Neuroendocrine perspectives on social attachment and love. *Psychoneuroendocrinology, 23*(8), 779–818.

Cerino, S. (2015). *La Riabilitazione Equestre con Pazienti Psicotici*. Aracne.
Cerino, S. (2022). Interventi Assistiti con il cavallo e salute Mentale. In F. I. Brescianini (Ed.), *Interventi Assistiti con Animali. Manuale per operatori*. Maggioli Ed.
Cerino, S., Cirulli, F., Chiarotti, F., & Seripa, S. (2011). Non conventional psychiatric rehabilitation in schizophrenia using therapeutic riding: The FISE multicentre Pindar project. *Annali dell'Istituto Superiore di Sanità, 47*(4), 409–414.
Chu, C. I., Liu, C. Y., Sun, C. T., & Lin, J. (2009). The effect of animal-assisted activity on inpatients with schizophrenia. *Journal of Psychosocial Nursing and Mental Health Services, 47*(12), 42–48.
Cirulli, F., Borgi, M., Berry, A., Francia, N., & Alleva, E. (2011). Animal-assisted interventions as innovative tools for mental health. *Annali dell'Istituto Superiore di Sanità, 47*(4), 341–348.
Coen, A. (2017). *Addressing comorbidity between mental disorders and major noncommunicable diseases* (WHO Regional Publication, European Series). WHO.
Colton, C. W., & Manderscheid, R. W. (2006). Congruencies in increased mortality rates, years of potential life lost, and causes of death among public mental health clients in eight states. *Preventing Chronic Disease, 3*(2), A42.
Corring, D., Lundberg, E., & Rudnick, A. (2013). Therapeutic horseback riding for ACT patients with schizophrenia. *Community Mental Health Journal, 49*(1), 121–126.
De Lubersac R., & Lallery H. (1962). reeducation parl L'Equitation, Crepin-Leblond Editions.
Druschky, E. (1961). Gymnastik zu Pferde—ein Weg zur Heilung. *Reiter Revue International, 4*, 246–247.
Ekholm, N. (2021). Conceptualization of psychotherapy incorporating equine interactions in the United States. *Human-Animal Interaction Bulletin, 9*(3), 94–114.
Freud, S. (1977). *Opere* (Vol. 7). Boringhieri.
Galli, M. L. (2002). *Il cavallo e l'uomo. Psicologia, simbolo, mito*. Equitare.
Geldmacher, J. (1968). Möglichkeiten des Therapeutischen Reitens bei Sportverletzungenaus der Sicht des Unfallchirurgen. *Reiter Revue International, 9*, 186–187.
Hengst, C. (1968). *Das therapeutische Reiten—eine Betrachtung der bedingungen, Möglichkeiten und Aufgaben* (Semesterarb., Pädagog. Hochschule). Sommersemester.
Hoffmann, F. (1719). *Gründliche Anweisung wie ein Mensch durch vernünftigen Gebrauch der Leibes-Bewegungen seine gesundheit erhalten kann, 5. teil* (pp. 310–312). Rengerische Bucchandulung.
Jaspers, K. (1965). *Psicopatologia generale*. Il Pensiero Scientifico.
Jormfeldt, H., & Carlsson, I.-M. (2018). Equine-assisted therapeutic interventions among individuals diagnosed with schizophrenia. A systematic review. *Issues in Mental Health Nursing, 39*(8), 647–656.
Kraepelin, E. (1904). *Psychiatrie: eine Lehrbuch für Studierende und Aertze* (7 Aufl). JA Barth. Tr-it Trattato di psichiatria. 7a ed. G. Guidi e A. Tamburini, Ed. Vallardi Milano 1907.
Ledermann, J. (1968). Therapeutisches Reiten als Rehabilitations – mabnahme bei Körperbehinderten Kindern. *Rehabilitation, 7*, 120–122.
Lieberman, R. B. (1997). *La riabilitazione Psichiatrica*. Cortina.
Loch, A. A., Wang, Y. P., Guarniero, F. B., Lawson, F. L., Hengartner, M. P., Rosserl, W., & Gattaz, W. F. (2014). Patterns of stigma toward schizophrenia among the general population. A latent profile analysis. *The International Journal of Social Psychiatry, 60*(6), 595–605.
Mercuriale, G. (2008). *De arte Gymnastica*. Olschki.
Ministero della Salute. (2015). *Linee Guida in Materia di Interventi Assistiti con animali*.
Nedelmann, H. (1967). Therapeutisches Reiten mit spastisch gelähmten Kindern. *Das behinderte Kind, 3*, 14–17.
Nurenberg, J. R., Schleifer, S. J., Shaffer, T. M., Yellin, M., Desai, P. J., Amin, R., Bouchard, A., & Montalvo, C. (2015). Animal-assisted therapy with chronic psychiatric inpatients: Equine-assisted psychotherapy and aggressive behavior. *Psychiatric Services, 66*(1), 80–86.
Ovsiew, F. (2000). An end to Kraepelinian nosology? *The Journal of Neuropsychiatry and Clinical Neurosciences, 12*(3), 297–299.

Payne, J. S. (1900). *Thomas Sydenham*. T.F. Unwin.

Pickenbach, R. (1909). Der Einflub des Reitsports auf den menschlichen Organismus. *Medizinische Klinik, 5*, 315–318.

Reichenbach, M. (1965). *Reiten allein tu es nicht?* Lapp.

Resnik, S., Antonetti, A., & Ficacci, M. A. (1982). *Semeiologia dell'incontro. Studi di psicopatologia clinica*. Il Pensiero Scientifico.

Rossom, R., et al. (2022). Cardiovascular risks for patients with and without schizophrenia, schizoaffective disorder, or bipolar disorder. *JAMA, 11*(6), e021444.

Scheidhacker, M. (1998). Das Pferd – reales Beziehungsobjekt und archetypisches Symbol. *Therapeutisches Reiten, 25*(H. 1), 11–15.

Scheidhacker, M., & Kupsch, M. (2010). Die Wirksamkeit von Psychotherapeutischem Reiten als stationäre Kurzzeit-gruppenpsychotherapie. In *Schizophrenie Beiträge zu Forschung, Therapie und psychosozialem Management; Mitteilungsorgan der gfts* [*Gesellschaft zur Förderung empirisch begründeter Therapiekonzepte bei schizophrenen Menschen*] (Jahrgang 26, pp. 54–69). https://www.deutsche-digitale-bibliothek.de/organization/gnd/2113329-3

Searles, F. H. (1974). *Scritti sulla Schizofrenia*. Boringhieri.

Senator, M. (1930). *Der gesundheitliche Wert des Reitens*. Verlag von Schickhardt & Ebner [Konrad Wittwer].

Stahl, G. E. (1733). Del movimento artificiale del corpo umano. *Archiwum Historii Medycyny, 44*(2), 163–187.

Tandon, B., & Maj, M. (2008). Nosological status and definition of schizophrenia: Some considerations for DSM-V and ICD-11. *Asian Journal of Psychiatry, 1*(2), 22–27.

UNICEF. (2021). www.data.unicef.org

UNICEF Office of Research. (2021). *Life in lockdown*. https://files.eric.ed.gov/

Vygotskij, L. S. (1980). *Il processo cognitivo*. Boringhieri.

Watzlawick, P., Beavin, J. H., & Jackson, D. D. (1967). *Pragmatica della comunicazione umana*. Astrolabio.

Winnicott, D. (1975). *Dalla pediatria alla Psicoanalisi*. Martinelli.

World Health Organization. (2014). *Mental health: A state of well-being*. Available from www.who.int/health-topics/mentalhealth

World Health Organization. (2022, June). *World mental health*. https://www.who.int/publications/i/item/9789240049338

World Health Organization. (2014). *Mental disorders*. Available from http://www.who.int/health-topics/mental-health

World Health Organization. (2013). *Mental disorders*. Available from http://www.who.int/news-room/facts-sheets/detail/mental-disorders

How Hippotherapy Can Tackle Posttraumatic Stress Disorders in Traumatic or Vascular Conditions of the Central Nervous System

Hélène Viruega and Manuel Gaviria

Introduction

Posttraumatic stress disorder (PTSD) has been considered a psychic disorder that occurs after a major traumatic event. It is characterized by four groups of symptoms: intrusion and reliving, avoidance and numbing, negative mood and altered cognition, and hyperarousal. The first group includes unwanted intrusive memories, ranging from mild recollections to complete dissociative flashbacks during which the individual momentarily believes he or she is reliving the traumatic experience. This group of symptoms also embraces sometimes overwhelming nightmares of the traumatic event. The second includes avoidance of any cues, context, or person related to the trauma. At that point, the individual becomes more isolated, often not leaving home. Indeed, as time goes, the outside world becomes a source of events that trigger such avoidance. The third comprises a wide range of symptoms, including trauma-related depressive symptoms, anhedonia, emotional numbness, and difficulties to concentrate. The fourth includes sleep disturbances, increased startle response, hypervigilance, and irritability, as well as aggressive and arousal-related self-destructive behavior (Bisson et al., 2013; Monsour et al., 2022; Ressler et al., 2022).

There is no single standard treatment for PTSD. Four main therapeutic techniques have been used, namely cognitive behavioral therapy, exposure therapy, eye movement desensitization and reprocessing (EMDR), and pharmacotherapy. However, and particularly in the case of pharmacotherapy, a wide percentage of patients who receive treatment fail to respond (Hong & Park, 2022).

H. Viruega (✉) · M. Gaviria
Institute Equiphoria, La Canourgue, France

Clinical Neurosciences, Alliance Equiphoria, La Canourgue, France
e-mail: helene.viruega@equiphoria.com; manuel.gaviria@equiphoria.com

Y. Neria et al. (eds.), *Guide to Equine Assisted Therapy*,
https://doi.org/10.1007/978-3-031-74426-6_10

In this chapter, we will review how PTSD can represent an issue for rehabilitation in neurological deficits resulting from traumatic brain injury (TBI), spinal cord injury (SCI), and stroke (intracerebral infarction and hemorrhage). We will also review how hippotherapy can tackle this condition based on a decade of practice at the Institute Equiphoria. Case presentations will follow to provide examples of how specific techniques in hippotherapy are used at the institute to address the rehabilitation needs of patients shuddering with PTSD and neurotrauma.

Chronic Disability After TBI, SCI, and Stroke: State of the Art

Traumatic brain injury, spinal cord injury, and brain stroke affect several million people worldwide and are among the leading causes of disability (Feigin et al., 2020; World Health Organization, 2006). TBI, SCI, and stroke are associated with significant morbidity and add medical expenses and loss of productivity on top of the hardships shouldered by both the patients and their caregivers.

Neurorehabilitation programs vary, ranging from specialized interdisciplinary institutional programs (involving different configurations of teams and techniques), to ambulatory specific types of therapies (Rice et al., 2016). In such rehab delivery configuration, quality issues arise. Ideally, patients should receive a comprehensive continuum program of care to address their individual needs (Wissel et al., 2013). A fluid interaction is deeply needed. Also, a comprehensive understanding of the linkage between the nervous system, the body, the environment, and the many issues shaping neurological functions is instrumental in providing appropriate rehabilitation solutions to disabled individuals (Corbett et al., 2015; Khan et al., 2017; Malá & Rasmussen, 2017; Rice et al., 2016; Wissel et al., 2013). Outside of therapy sessions, patients with moderate to severe disabilities, according to the modified Rankin Scale (Bonita & Beaglehole, 1988), spend much of their time isolated and inactive since inclusive activities of daily living are generally not available even in the most developed societies (Emerson et al., 2021; Macdonald et al., 2018).

Stroke

According to the Global Burden of Diseases, Injuries, and Risk Factors Study (GBD) and the World Stroke Organization (WSO), over 12.2 million people suffer a stroke each year worldwide (1.1 million in Europe and 0.79 million in the United States), and there are over 101 million people currently living who have experienced stroke (Feigin et al., 2020; Johnson et al., 2019). Mortality is about 50% by 5 years. A third of survivors experience significant disability 5 years after stroke due to physical, cognitive, and/or emotional deficits (Hankey, 2017; Luengo-Fernandez et al., 2013). Much of the scientific efforts focus on medical programs involving acute care and inpatient rehabilitation. However, long-term disability often occurs, and patients may continue to experience serious daily difficulties.

New approaches to post-stroke care are highly needed. Indeed, the late rehabilitative phase is essential to both patients and their caregivers (Pindus et al., 2018; Tyagi et al., 2021). Patients must be able to comprehend the objectives of each phase of their rehabilitation, and the challenges they face at each stage, to gain autonomy and project themselves into the future.

The notion of reaching a plateau in stroke recovery is questioned by a growing number of studies (Demain et al., 2006). Accordingly, there is a need to design and assess therapeutic interventions in neurorehabilitation that promote sustained recovery from stroke over time. Indeed, it has been observed that significant functional improvement can occur years after stroke when rehabilitation training is applied (Ballester et al., 2019; Bernhardt et al., 2017a, b; Sun et al., 2015). Multidisciplinary programs may be developed to cover the complex stroke continuum with the ultimate goal of reducing its large burden (Bernhardt et al., 2017b). There is growing evidence that a multidisciplinary and cross-sectoral approach is pivotal to allow optimal post-stroke functional recovery (Corbett et al., 2015; Malá & Rasmussen, 2017).

Traumatic Brain Injury

Traumatic brain injury (TBI) is a major source of mortality, morbidity, and disability worldwide. The annual incidence of TBI is estimated to be between 27 million people (1.26 million in Europe and 1.11 million in the United States) with a prevalence of 55.5 million people (James et al., 2019). Many survivors live with substantial permanent disabilities. This results in a major socio-economic burden. In 2010, the economic impact of TBI in the United States, for example, was estimated at $76.5 billion in direct and indirect costs (Dewan et al., 2018; GBD 2016 Traumatic Brain Injury and Spinal Cord Injury Collaborators, 2019).

There are two main categories of brain injury following a TBI: focal and diffuse. Focal lesions include cortical or subcortical contusions and lacerations, as well as intracranial bleeding. Diffuse lesions are caused by stretching and tearing of brain tissue. The main form of diffuse injury is diffuse axonal injury (DAI), which is caused by acceleration/deceleration forces shearing axons (Blennow et al., 2012). After TBI, regardless of severity, a significant number of patients suffer cognitive and emotional difficulties that, even in the absence of motor or sensory deficits, may prevent a normal life with a return to work and other social activities. TBI is increasingly recognized as a global health priority due to the need for complex and expensive medical care. According to the National Academies of Sciences, Engineering, and Medicine, although many patients with moderate or severe TBI can benefit from interdisciplinary inpatient rehabilitation, most are discharged home or to care facilities that do not always offer comprehensive or specialized therapy, or functional reassessment protocols. Lack of access to brain-injury-sensitive outpatient physical and mental health services and lack of awareness or resources to meet the needs of people returning to work or school after TBI can seriously hamper their future (National Academies of Sciences et al., 2022).

Spinal Cord Injury

The spinal cord is not just a tissue providing a structural and functional linkage between the brain and the periphery. It relies on complex circuits capable of learning and adapting, with peripheral feedback (proprioceptive, exteroceptive, interoceptive) allowing adjustments in motor control to bring about changes in the body's relationship with its environment (Fouad et al., 2021). Spinal cord injury (SCI) is a devastating, multifaceted disorder resulting in behavioral and physiological problems, primarily involving motor and sensory dysfunction below the level of injury, manifesting as chronic paralysis, sensory alterations, pain syndromes, loss of independence, and decreased quality of life. SCI is thus a major cause of disability that generally strikes young and healthy people (55% occurring in <25-year-old individuals). The worldwide incidence of SCI is estimated to be 0.9 million people (0.11 million in Europe and 0.09 million in the United States) with a prevalence of 27 million people (James et al., 2019). Currently, at least half of all people with SCI are tetraplegic due to cervical spinal cord injury, and about 45% of them have an incomplete injury. The majority of tetraplegic patients have a neurological impairment level of C4 or C5 (Hutson & Di Giovanni, 2019; Siddiqui et al., 2015; Torregrossa et al., 2020).

Over the past few decades, patients have benefited greatly from improved initial management. In fact, improved treatment of spinal cord patients has reduced both morbidity and mortality, primarily by preventing secondary complications (Torregrossa et al., 2020). Combining biological strategies (cell therapy, gene therapy) based on the pathophysiology of the injury, targeted technological interventions made to increase neuroplasticity, followed by rehabilitation to direct circuit reorganization, may facilitate clinically meaningful recovery from SCI. However, current results remain marginal (Hutson & Di Giovanni, 2019).

PTSD: A Major Issue After Neurotrauma?

Neurological Perspective

Recent studies have revealed the extreme complexity and the extent of brain disruption as a result of PTSD from chemical and functional points of view. Indeed, it has been established that PTSD, a common pathophysiological condition, perpetuates brain damage secondary to neurotrauma through extensive neuroinflammation, oxidative stress, excitotoxicity, and structural changes (Mahan & Ressler, 2012; Monsour et al., 2022). Neuroinflammation can be one of the adverse consequences of PTSD. While acute inflammation can be neuroprotective, promoting neurogenesis, spatial learning abilities, and reducing the risk of infection, it can also evolve into chronic neuroinflammation. In PTSD, acute neuroinflammation leads to microglia proliferation and chronic activation of this cell population for at least 20 years after neurotrauma, significantly impairing neuronal function and structure (Monsour et al., 2022). Chronic microglial activation can generate severe oxidative stress via reactive species that lead to increased brain–blood barrier (BBB) permeability, impaired neuronal plasticity and neurotransmission, and altered neuronal morphology. Neuroinflammation and oxidative stress combined can trigger a disastrous cycle of neuronal damage through the phenomenon of excitotoxicity (Kaplan et al., 2018). Glutamate is then released by necrotic cells, overactivating N-methyl-D-aspartate (NMDA) and α-amino-3-hydroxy-5-methyl-4-isoxazolepropionic acid (AMPA) receptors. This glutamate supersaturation occurs in cortical and hippocampal regions and has also been observed in the amygdala. Excessive activation of AMPA and NMDA receptors ultimately impacts cognition, in particular concentration, memory, attention, and executive functions. PTSD also leads to significant changes in brain morphology. More specifically, white matter disruptions are apparent in brain regions that have an impact on cognition and executive functions. PTSD exhibits disrupted neuronal plasticity and dendritic remodeling, contributing to morphological changes and symptomatology (Kaplan et al., 2018). Altered gray and white matter morphology can be observed in the prefrontal cortex, hippocampus, and amygdala, contributing to the emotional, behavioral, and somatic symptoms of PTSD (memory, attention, fear processing, executive functions, reasoning) (Monsour et al., 2022).

Psychiatric Perspective

The functional and structural changes described above create a very complex clinical picture and affect the psyche considerably. In this context, the notion of discontinuity, of dissociation of states of consciousness is at stake (Bækkelund et al., 2018; Bromberg, 2000). As stated by Bromberg in his work, to maintain a relative behavioral continuity, the traumatic experiences and the associated states of consciousness become sequestered "islets." These are separated and invisible from the other states accessible to consciousness at a given moment (Bromberg, 2000). During the time lapse between the accident and the return to active life, or even beyond if not addressed, the individual, in an instinct for survival, will put aside or transform the memory of the event that she/he unconsciously considers to be endangering or weakening her/him. Therefore, the patient feeling vulnerable will be unable to optimally take advantage of the neurorehabilitation offered to him/her. This invisible resistance impacts the functional outcome and quality of life of the patient (Haagsma et al., 2015; Sherin & Nemeroff, 2011). To alleviate the resistance, an in-dept approach to PTSD requires a safe and containing environment, considering that each person has its own timing and rhythm to address it.

How Hippotherapy Addresses PTSD

Hippotherapy: A Powerful Holistic Approach

Hippotherapy is an emerging specialized rehabilitation and neurorehabilitation approach, performed on a specially trained horse via its movement at a walk, by a team of accredited health professionals (e.g., physicians, psychologists, physical therapists, occupational therapists, and psychomotor therapists among others) and equine specialists to lead the horse (Oh et al., 2018; Mutoh et al., 2019; Guindos-Sanchez et al., 2020; Marquez et al., 2020; Moraes et al., 2020; Wood & Fields, 2021; Maresca et al., 2022; Potvin-Bélanger et al., 2022; Viruega et al., 2022). Hippotherapy provides a safe and containing environment for the patient in several ways. First, there is the powerful symbolism of the horse carrying and moving forward; then, there is the fundamental notion of the patient setting into motion on a powerful animal (Hallberg, 2008; Irwin & Weber, 2001; Roberts, 2001). Hippotherapy allows for this setting into motion, which is first of all physiological because it is biomechanically similar to human movement during walking (Uchiyama et al., 2011). It is also global because it simultaneously engages the physical, cognitive, emotional, and social spheres (Romaniuk et al., 2018; Mutoh et al., 2019; Viruega et al., 2019, 2020, 2022; Moraes et al., 2020; Santos de Assis et al., 2022). Finally, it offers the person a nonrestrictive elsewhere far from the clinical environment (the patient progressively moves from the context of grief to the discovery of a large palette of personal potentials).

Hippotherapy can tackle the neurorehabilitation challenges by providing a self-committed, efficient, nonintrusive, custom-made framework of the patient's physical, mental, emotional, and spiritual spheres (Romaniuk et al., 2018; Mutoh et al., 2019; Viruega et al., 2019, 2020, 2022; Moraes et al., 2020; Santos de Assis et al., 2022). Equiphoria has developed a hippotherapy program that enables patients to push back the limits of disability and synergizes the results of conventional approaches to optimize functional outcomes (Buetow et al., 2019; Kapur, 2020; Viruega & Gaviria, 2022).

The hippotherapy program targets various entangled health functioning processes: reinforcement of global postural balance and fine-tuning of postural responses; strengthening of different muscle groups; work on upper limbs' fine motor skills and coordination; work on the smoothness of movement and psycho-corporal relaxation; reinforcement of the body schema and body image; breathing techniques and visualizations; attention to body/emotional feelings; support for attention, concentration, working memory, and executive functions; reinforcement of the notions of success, pleasure, and disinhibition; social and cognitive flexibility; reinforcement of communication skills; stimulation of proactive postures, involvement and motivation; self-esteem and self-transcendence; work on values, meaning, appropriation of symbols; posttraumatic stress disorder work, grieving process, creation of a new life course meaning; linguistic activity of creating meaning (describing, explaining, reappropriating, reinventing, and projecting herself) (see Table 1). The intensity of the exercises is fully tailored and depends on the patient's clinical heterogeneity, fatigability, and confounding factors (Viruega et al., 2023).

Table 1 Functional items measured and their link to the exercises addressed by the hippotherapy protocol targeting various interrelated health functioning processes

	Contribution through hippotherapy
Functional items	
Physical functioning	Reinforcement of global postural balance and fine-tuning of postural responses Strengthening of different muscle groups Work on upper limbs' fine motor skills and coordination Work on smoothness of movement and psycho-corporal relaxation Reinforcement of the body schema and body image Breathing techniques and visualizations
Role functioning	Social and cognitive flexibility Reinforcement of communication skills Stimulation of proactive postures, involvement and motivation Self-esteem and self-transcendence
Emotional functioning	Attention to body/emotional feelings Reinforcement of the notions of success, pleasure, and disinhibition Self-esteem and self-transcendence Reinforcement of communication skills Linguistic activity of creating meaning (describing, explaining, reappropriating, reinventing, and projecting oneself)
Cognitive functioning	Support for attention, concentration, working memory, and executive functions Reinforcement of communication skills Linguistic activity of creating meaning (describing, explaining, reappropriating, reinventing, and projecting oneself)
Social functioning	Reinforcement of the notions of success, pleasure, and disinhibition Social and cognitive flexibility Reinforcement of communication skills Stimulation of proactive postures, involvement and motivation work on values, meaning, appropriation of symbols
Symptoms	
Fatigue	Work on smoothness of movement and psycho-corporal relaxation Breathing techniques and visualizations Attention to body/emotional feelings Reinforcement of the notions of success, pleasure, and disinhibition Post-traumatic stress disorder work, grieving process, creation of a new life course meaning

(continued)

Table 1 (continued)

	Contribution through hippotherapy
Mental fatigue	Stimulation of proactive postures, involvement, and motivation Self-esteem and self-transcendence Work on values, meaning, appropriation of symbols Post-traumatic stress disorder work, grieving process, creation of a new life course meaning
Physical fatigue	Reinforcement of global postural balance and fine-tuning of postural responses (eyes open and closed) Strengthening of different muscle groups Work on upper limbs' fine motor skills and coordination Work on smoothness of movement and psycho-corporal relaxation
Motivational fatigue	Reinforcement of the notions of success, pleasure, and disinhibition Stimulation of proactive postures, involvement and motivation
Activity reduction	Reinforcement of the notions of success, pleasure, and disinhibition Stimulation of proactive postures, involvement and motivation
Pain	Reinforcement of global postural balance and fine-tuning of postural responses Work on smoothness of movement and psycho-corporal relaxation Reinforcement of the body schema and body image Breathing techniques and visualizations Attention to body/emotional feelings Post-traumatic stress disorder work, grieving process, creation of a new life course meaning
Respiratory discomfort	Work on smoothness of movement and psycho-corporal relaxation Reinforcement of the body schema and body image Breathing techniques and visualizations Attention to body/emotional feelings Post-traumatic stress disorder work, grieving process, creation of a new life course meaning
Insomnia	Work on smoothness of movement and psycho-corporal relaxation Breathing techniques and visualizations Post-traumatic stress disorder work, grieving process, creation of a new life course meaning
Appetite loss	Regulation through movement of bidirectional signaling between ENS and CNS neuromodulatory substances
Cognitive performance	
Cognitive abilities	Support for attention, concentration, working memory, and executive functions Reinforcement of the notions of success, pleasure, and disinhibition Social and cognitive flexibility Self-esteem and self-transcendence Linguistic activity of creating meaning (describing, explaining, reappropriating, reinventing, and projecting oneself)
Comments from other people on the patient's cognitive impairment	Social and cognitive flexibility Reinforcement of communication skills Self-esteem and self-transcendence

Table 1 (continued)

	Contribution through hippotherapy
Psychological functioning	
Body image	Work on smoothness of movement and psycho-corporal relaxation Reinforcement of the body schema and body image Attention to body/emotional feelings Reinforcement of the notions of success, pleasure, and disinhibition Self-esteem and self-transcendence Linguistic activity of creating meaning (describing, explaining, reappropriating, reinventing, and projecting oneself)
Anxiety	Work on smoothness of movement and psycho-corporal relaxation Breathing techniques and visualizations Reinforcement of the body schema and body image Self-esteem and self-transcendence Post-traumatic stress disorder work, grieving process, creation of a new life course meaning Linguistic activity of creating meaning (describing, explaining, reappropriating, reinventing, and projecting oneself)
Depression	Attention to body/emotional feelings Reinforcement of the notions of success, pleasure, and disinhibition Stimulation of proactive postures, involvement and motivation Post-traumatic stress disorder work, grieving process, creation of a new life course meaning Linguistic activity of creating meaning (describing, explaining, reappropriating, reinventing, and projecting oneself)
Future perspectives	Work on values, meaning, appropriation of symbols Post-traumatic stress disorder work, grieving process, creation of a new life course meaning Linguistic activity of creating meaning (describing, explaining, reappropriating, reinventing, and projecting oneself)

Neurorehabilitation, Neural Plasticity, and Hippotherapy

Functional recovery is a complex process as the patient's needs change over time and depend on the severity and type of injury, pre-accident functional status, and levels of medical, psychological, and social support. Neurorehabilitation is a multilayered intervention in which the active constituents are not always accurately identifiable with respect to needs (Greenlee et al., 2017; Lyman et al., 2018). Patients with neurological deficits resulting from TBI, SCI, and stroke exhibit clinical heterogeneity (degree and type of deficit, degree of disability) and confounding factors (comorbidities, different rehabilitation methods and approaches, unequal access to rehabilitation services, dissimilar quality of rehabilitation structures) (Pollock et al., 2014; Slade et al., 2002). Also, the floor/ceiling effects of certain clinical evaluations such as the functional independence measure can limit sensitivity to treatment effects, and even standardized measures may behave differently in different cultures and contexts (Khan et al., 2017). Since the clinical decision-making process can be subjective and biased (Elstein & Schwartz, 2002), clinicians may have real difficulty incorporating the patient/caregiver perspective into decision-making, and many issues essential to the patient may be disregarded (e.g., communication skills, environmental constraints, lifestyle habits) (Khan et al., 2007, 2010).

The minimum effective quantity of the required neurorehabilitation is hard to define. So far, the effectiveness of many rehabilitation methods has not been systematically demonstrated. According to a seminal paper (Pollock et al., 2014), scientific evidence is lacking and studies have biases of several kinds such as high heterogeneity (e.g., type of rehabilitation, included patients, quality of structures, and type of evaluation) and low methodological quality. The argued rehabilitation effectiveness has been validated from older studies generally mainly showing reductions in mortality, dependency rates, and risk of institutionalization. In this rather empirical context, daily sessions of at least 45 minutes by type of rehabilitation have been commonly acknowledged at least 5 days a week. Rehabilitation is supposed to be conducted for at least 8 weeks. During the first 2 weeks, frequent, short sessions of progressive intensity are preferred. However, the intensity with which rehabilitation is conducted varies depending on dispensing structures. Rehabilitation in a specialized service with full hospitalization or day hospitalization offers possibilities to perform intensive multiple protocols. This care is harder to guarantee in private practice outside the hospital (Pollock et al., 2014).

On the other hand, a hippotherapy session lasts 1 hour per day (effective time on the horse: 30–45 minutes) during which between 3000 and 4500 contractions of each postural muscle are sequentially realized in a background mode (horse at a walk) in addition to the therapist's exercises. The intensity of each session mobilizes the individual in his/her entirety (i.e., somatic, sensory, cognitive, emotional, and motivational, and psychic spheres). The duration of the patient's processing of physical/mental skills and the ensuing fatigue are properly integrated. Also, thanks to the enriched environment brought by hippotherapy, continuous functional improvements has been noticed, even beyond the theoretical period of consolidation of the neurological outcome after injury (Frasca et al., 2013; Khan et al., 2017). The degree of change associated with neuroplasticity through hippotherapy is most likely linked to both the relevance of the activity and the intensity and frequency of the elements that constitute it (Diaz Heijtz et al., 2003; Horn, 2004; Kolb & Muhammad, 2014).

Improvement has been postulated to occur secondary to synaptic changes/remodeling in response to the various stimuli (Kolb & Muhammad, 2014). The horse movement at a walk is biomechanically similar to the human movement when walking and yields to comparable micro-adjustments of the patient's postural balance, gross and fine motor activity, and reinforcement of sensorimotor control (Uchiyama et al., 2011). Furthermore, through multimodal inputs (sensory, exteroceptive, proprioceptive, and interoceptive), hippotherapy has a direct action on the individual's cognitive abilities and emotional regulation by the interactions of several neural networks (Fisher et al., 2021; Gabriels et al., 2015; Lee et al., 2017; Maresca et al., 2022; Menor-Rodríguez et al., 2021; Moraes et al., 2021; Viruega et al., 2019, 2020). During hippotherapy, the execution and repetition of a task are key elements of learning, strengthening, and promoting a function and a robust rehabilitation process (Fisher et al., 2021; Lee et al., 2017; Maresca et al., 2022; Menor-Rodríguez et al., 2021; Moraes et al., 2021; Silkwood-Sherer & McGibbon, 2022; Viruega et al., 2020). One of the fundamental properties of the central nervous system is the ability to adapt to a wide range of complex external changes but also internal ones generated by injury. This inherent neural plasticity promotes efficient functional outputs in healthy individuals or, at least, some degree of functional outcome in disease (Buch et al., 2017; Fornito et al., 2015; Hartwigsen et al., 2012, 2013, 2017; Kolb & Muhammad, 2014; Sale et al., 2014). In the latter, spontaneous mechanisms of repair are rarely sufficient to support significant long-term recovery (Viruega & Gaviria, 2021, 2022). Under physiological conditions, emotional and motivational processing shapes brain responses by increasing functional connections across dissimilar brain hubs and regions (Pessoa, 2017; Pessoa & McMenamin, 2017). It has been proposed that such interactions lead to improved behavioral performance on complex tasks, and that networks would be dynamic processes whose evolution is closely linked to the underlying mechanisms supporting behavior (Gaviria et al., 2020). The spectrum of neurological injury, remodeling, and recovery must be seen not as individual actions (motion, cognition, emotion) but rather as integrated elements of a rehabilitative ecosystem.

Hippotherapy and PTSD: Why Does It Work?

Hippotherapy represents a powerful approach since it utilizes the movement of the body to physiologically stimulate the pathways that subserve the patient's needs for neurological recovery. Putting the patient back into motion in the nonrestrictive hippotherapy context acts directly on the body and contextualizes it. It strongly stimulates both reward and motivation. Hippotherapy may enhance the remodeling of brain activity (Wirtshafter & Wilson, 2021). The septo-hippocampal system (which includes the hippocampus, lateral septum, and medial septum, and communicates with the amygdala and hypothalamus) has been involved in a number of key functions, such as movement and context coding, as well as in emotional and motivational behaviors (Wirtshafter & Wilson, 2019, 2020, 2021). The colocalization of such functions and their modulation in these structures have fundamental behavioral implications here. The alterations in emotional regulation (fear, hypervigilance, irritability, anxiety, depression, demotivation, anhedonia, isolation), present in PTSD patients, are likely to disrupt many everyday situations requiring a context–action association (Wirtshafter & Wilson, 2021). Instead, the lateral septum can transmit a reward signal proportional to movement through changes in the level of activation of place (context), movement, and reward-related circuits.

Through contextualized and meaningful multimodal inputs (sensory, exteroceptive, proprioceptive, interoceptive), hippotherapy has a robust action on the motor abilities of the person (Maravita et al., 2003; Viruega et al., 2019, 2020, 2022). In parallel to setting into motion, the work of understanding the instantaneous needs of the patients is fundamental. This is conducted within a framework of decontextualization in relation to the patients' pathology (a world away from the hospital), which reduces the stigma and, consequently, the level of anxiety of these neurological patients. This framework included two levels: (i) the patient's listening to their own body and its possibilities, without any necessary cognitive elaboration on their part through the horse's pace and its presence and (ii) the therapist listening, which allows one to constantly adapt the exercises. Here again, the hippocampus will play a major integrating role by participating in the processing of sensory inputs, according to the context (Crochet et al., 2019). Indeed, to adapt their behavior in their daily lives, individuals must first detect and respond to changes in external and internal environments. Sensory and motor systems exhibit amazing responsiveness and plasticity in their structures and functions to adapt to constantly changing environmental conditions (Buch et al., 2017; Manière & Coureaud, 2019). Sensorimotor processing is strongly influenced by learning, perception, motivation, context, and the state of the brain (in healthy or pathological conditions) (Crochet et al., 2019). The hippocampus responds to somatosensory (Le Merre et al., 2018), visual (Muller & Kubie, 1987), auditory (Aronov et al., 2017), and olfactory (Li et al., 2017) stimuli. It has been considered as a top-level sensory area (Kassab & Alexandre, 2015). It anticipates and synthesizes representations of the world far beyond the real-time inputs of the sensorium (Maguire & Mullally, 2013). Hippotherapy, by stimulating the hippocampus, might be the basis for the remarkable and early reinforcement of role functioning and social functioning, enhanced integration of body image, and an improved representation of future perspectives in these neurological patients. The positive effects on physical aspects would also be supported by the integration of multimodal inputs at the level of the hippocampus–lateral septum–amygdala–hypothalamus–ventral tegmental area–prefrontal cortex system. This integration has a direct relieving impact on fatigue (Viruega et al., 2023) and pain, as well as a reversal effect on usually observed activity reduction of PTSD patients.

Self-induced movement has key effects in the synthesis and release of hormones and peptides strongly involved in brain modulation (Consorti et al., 2021; Di Liegro et al., 2019; Fernandes et al., 2017). Hippotherapy initiates a physiologic passive movement that rapidly becomes self-induced. This close-to-human gait movement is strongly imprinted in the patient's body (Uchiyama et al., 2011). Within this movement framework, the patient doesn't feel that he/she is putting him/herself in danger and gets the space to welcome reward (experiencing pleasure, relaxation, and feeling ready to let go). Through the pelvic and enteric stimulation, hippotherapy therefore conceivably has a physiological effect on the regulation of bidirectional signaling between the enteric nervous system (ENS) and central nervous system (CNS) involving the endogenous pharmacotherapy path (Sale et al., 2014). Vagus nerve stimulation exerts a significant effect on arousal and brain activation state through a direct action on the concentration of key neuromodulatory substances (serotonin, dopamine, melatonin, norepinephrine, acetylcholine, gamma-aminobutyric acid (GABA)) at the brain level (Collins et al., 2021; Rodenkirch et al., 2022; Thomas et al., 2017). Improved regulation of mood, motivation, and reward due to the direct effect of hippotherapy on the ENS (and CNS) may be the basis for rapid improvement in functions such as emotional regulation, stamina, appetite, and physical and mental efficiency (concentration, mental acuity, verbal fluency, executive functions, decision-making). Also, self-perceptions such as emotional, cognitive, and social functioning, notion of pleasure, or relief of fatigue might be positively impacted. In addition, other neuromodulatory substances probably play a major role in the restoration of a homeostasis beyond the survival mode of the PTSD patients. Indeed, the dialogue between the ENS and the CNS through the stimulation provided in the context of hippotherapy is likely to promote the up-/down-regulation of the synthesis and release of other neuroactive substances: brain-derived neurotrophic factor (BDNF) involved in the consolidation phenomena of structural plasticity and behavioral adaptation (Koroleva et al., 2020; Lee et al., 2017; Qin et al., 2014); neuropeptide Y (NPY), in the control of inflammatory processes, pain, emotions, mood, cognition, stress resistance, and energy homeostasis (Holzer et al., 2012; Holzer & Farzi, 2014); vasoactive intestinal peptide (VIP) in the regulation of hippocampal memory processes, central biological clock, sleep, and inflammation (Cunha-Reis & Caulino-Rocha, 2020; Shen et al., 2022; Welsh et al., 1995); and plausibly, endogenous opioids and endocannabinoids in the control of pain, inflammation, and stress (Hackler et al., 1997; Siebers et al., 2021; Zadina et al., 1997). Finally, the decrease of some key hormones related to stress and immune response has been suggested after hippotherapy (Tabares et al., 2012). Thus, this modulation at the molecular level might be the chemical substrate for the relief of symptoms such as pain, insomnia, anxiety, depression, and other, as well as for the sustainable improvement noticed in PTSD patients.

Examples of Clinical Cases

Case 1: John

John is a 35-year-old man who suffered a traumatic brain injury at the age of 18, after a domestic fall from his own height. He presented a large brain hemorrhage. He had surgery 7 hours after the trauma and was in a coma for 10 days. He walked up with a double severe spastic hemiplegia prevailing at right and severe impairment of swallowing and phonation without alterations in the cognitive sphere. After a period of acute treatment and inpatient rehabilitation, he returned home and continued an outpatient rehabilitation program with very little progress. All pharmacological treatments directed to spasticity and pain were discontinued after 6 years of the injury. Together with the help of his parents very present for him, he decided to seek other options of non-conventional treatment all over the world: myotenofasciotomy and intensive neurorehabilitation in Barcelona, Spain; biofeedback in Miami, United States; Kozyavkin method in Lviv Oblast, Ukraine; Padovan method in Brazil; robotic rehabilitation through Lokomat and Armeo, as well as chiropractic in France. These therapies started to have a positive effect on John's physical and psychological spheres. However, after 5 years of exploration of those techniques, he reached a plateau. He continued to search for innovative approaches and found Equiphoria 10 years after the accident.

John was a very strong and dedicated man who didn't give up on the hope of walking and talking again. The first evaluation at Equiphoria showed a very severe disability panorama: a non-walking patient moving in an electric wheelchair, which he controlled with his left hand; a double hemiplegia of right predominance; a severe spasticity of several axial and peripheral muscle groups with severe spasms of the pectoral muscles, which propelled him uncontrollably forward; altered seated posture with body deviation to the left of the midline; impaired sitting balance and spatial awareness; impaired fine motor skills, especially of the right upper limb. He was completely self-reliant for diet, appearance care, sphincter control, wheelchair locomotion on adapted surfaces, communication, and world awareness. He had a modified independence for oral expression for which he used a keyboard in support. He needed assistance for grooming, dressing or toileting, and transfers.

The program targeted the following: improvement of posture and balance, attenuation of global spasticity, reinforcement of motor and phonic endurance, stimulation of motor and walking patterns, working on fine motor skills, work on breath control, and on praxis at the orofacial level (see Table 1 for functional areas targeted with hippotherapy).

What caught the staff's eyes was the huge physical disability that didn't match his obvious potential and capabilities. The first plan was to work on global dynamic postural control with the repetitive movement of the horse simulator (Viruega et al., 2019) to improve the gross motor control and muscle hypertonia. When the postural reactions were safe enough, he was put on the horse. The chosen horse for this first stage elicits verticality, opening of the chest with a forward driven energy. The initial techniques used were breathing and visualization on the horse at a walk with a regular pace. Mechanically, John worked hard on the therapeutic aims that we had identified. Very quickly, the team observed encouraging results: better transfers with one person's support; self-control of spastic reactions of the axial and peripheral muscle groups; improved seated posture without head forward tilt; improved spatial awareness; enhanced fine motor skills through a systematic symmetrical solicitation and pelvic girdle release coupled with slight shoulder and trunk release. However, after 60 hours of hippotherapy (three 2-week sessions per year for 2 years), we also reached a plateau. The body control (postural control and gross and fine motricity) was much better, but the forward tilt because of spastic reactions of the upper body muscles continued to stop John is his track.

It was time to tackle the invisible: the uncontrollable fear of falling, the uncontrollable fear of falling again. John met a new horse that will support him for the journey within. This horse has a hypnotic deep regular movement that stimulates intensively the pelvis and the enteric nervous system (the second brain). Its energy created the appropriate environment and conditions to reach John's mysterious and intimate world and made them accessible to consciousness. He was ready to tackle PTSD.

After some spectacular sessions of release and restructuring, John no longer struggled with spasms and the fear of falling. He started to adjust his actions and movements with confidence and worked on "new rhythm," allowing him to enhance transfers, motor skills, and postural balance through new sensorimotor schemes and reshaping of the existing ones for better autonomy. He is currently building his own house for a new start in life.

Case 2: Mary

Mary is a 66-year-old woman who suffered a hemorrhagic right brain stroke at 63 years old. She presented a left hemiplegia with a massive flaccid paralysis of the upper limb (maintained by an arm sling), and the possibility of standing and walking with the help of some orthopedic devices (foot orthosis, orthopedic shoe, tripod cane). After the initial inpatient neurorehabilitation period in a specialized rehabilitation center, Mary entered a retirement home where she gradually declined despite a basic physiotherapy program (three sessions a week) and some cognitive and occupational activities (reading, crosswords, board games).

Her son scheduled a program at Equiphoria for her, being concerned of her disengagement in all spheres. We found at her arrival, a very negative woman expressing through her speech a lot of rage and frustration. She complained about everything including her son who shared with the staff that he was lost and desperate. She also stated repeatedly being painful with no evident trigger patterns.

The program targeted the following: strengthening of the dynamic postural balance; work on verticalization; improvement of pelvic and scapular girdle dissociation; body symmetry reinforcement; work on anxiety and psychic appeasement; work on body relaxation and the notion of pleasure; pain management; identification and adaptation of her potentials to promote autonomy (see Table 1 for functional areas targeted with hippotherapy).

With a lot of resistance from her part, she was put on the simulator. The tension and her negative feedback made that first session extremely difficult. The therapists were unable to interact with her. First thing first, she was put in movement on the simulator with very little verbal interaction, just enough to allow her to feel the movement. Very quickly, she started to relax and smiled for the first time. The session was stopped at that point to create the "wanting more" for the next day. The non-verbal communication felt essential for this program to elicit introspection and stop the outer allowed her to be carried in a safe and solid framework with a strong moving forward pattern. She immediately changed the attitude and energy and remained positive and appreciative throughout the program. Amazing changes were observed throughout that first program that lasted a week (five 1-hour sessions in total). Mary was smiling and voiced her well-being and pleasure in the sessions. Her body movement was progressively more supple; she also improved her balance and gained better dynamic stability and adjustment. Mary also shared that she had many apprehensions that limited her autonomy and her projects, and that she could thus work on distinguishing between pain during physical effort and pain triggered by apprehension.

On the second program, Mary arrived enthusiastic to be back and showed real intrinsic motivation to transcend herself. The horse was changed to convey a new message, introducing her to a new horse with a smoother pace. It was time for her to softly accept herself and her disability to reinvent herself and peacefully improve her autonomy and quality of life. The movement of that horse was coupled with breathing techniques and positive reinforcement as well as visualizations.

During that second program, Mary strengthened the integration of the left side of her body (amplitude and duration of the movement of the arm when grooming the horse with her left hand assisted by her right one) and improved the transfers and upright position (duration of the transfers). She also strengthened her self-confidence and self-transcendence and was able to take initiative and become more autonomous (stood up from her wheelchair to groom). Mary improved her sitting and standing balance, her postural endurance, and her axial alignment (measurement of the center of pressure on the simulator (Viruega et al., 2019)).

Making peace with oneself is also an important step for people who suffered stroke to deal with PTSD and move forward.

Case 3: Jimmy

Jimmy is a 19-year-old man who suffered a traumatic cervical dislocation at the level of C5–C6 vertebral column after a trampoline accident, an activity that he practiced as a semiprofessional athlete. He presented an almost complete tetraplegia below the C6 level with a non-impairing spasticity of the leg muscles. He was treated urgently for the surgical reduction of the cervical dislocation, anterior stabilization, and fusion of the vertebral column at C5–C6, followed by 10 days in the intensive care unit and 8 months of inpatient rehabilitation. From the functional point of view, when he went back home Jimmy used a manual wheelchair for mobility and performed self-catheterization several times a day. His plane-to-plane transfers were non-functional. He also complained of neuropathic pain below the level of the lesion. He was referred by his health insurer for a neurorehabilitation through hippotherapy program at Equiphoria.

The staff found at his arrival a young man not very talkative and rather somber, looking to his father for the answers to our questions. He was on the internet a lot where he posted videos to share his everyday life struggles as a newly disabled person with a sense of humor. On the physical front, there was room for improvement. It soon became clear that his sense of humor on the internet covered a great deal of insecurity and moral suffering. His father voiced doubts about his ability to sit on a horse without back support.

The program targeted the following: stimulation of the sub-injured spinal cord; improvement of postural balance, axial straightening, and body symmetry; dissociation of the scapular and pelvic girdles; harmonization of muscle tone; work around the perception of physical sensations; work on verticalization; work on self-confidence and motivation; work on transcending oneself (see Table 1 for functional areas targeted with hippotherapy).

The simulator was first started to quickly wipe out the doubt he had to maintain sitting postural balance. Within 15 minutes with a lot of concentration, Jimmy relaxed and was able to follow the movement and adjust himself only with a slight external aid (a contact reference on hands). Considering Jimmy's abilities and state of mind as an athlete, his therapy was customized with immediate challenges for him to tackle in order to awaken his competitive nature, which in turn would help him deal with PTSD; that meant long hippotherapy sessions on a very dynamic horse with complex patterns requiring stamina. The strong demanding physical effort stimulated the enteric nervous system (Collins et al., 2021; Rodenkirch et al., 2022) by producing hormones such as dopamine, serotonin, endomorphins 1 and 2, alpha-melanocyte hormone (α-MSH), which regulate motivation, reward, mood, pleasure, energy metabolism, pain and stress pathways among others.

As of the second day of therapy, Jimmy was more expressive, talking to the staff, smiling, and engaging in the exercises. He said he began to feel positive body sensations (e.g., tingling in his legs, shivers, cold and hot sensations in his upper and lower back) and he started to discretely move his toes while on the horse and when laying down in bed. The third day was powerful enough to give him a reason to raise himself (standing position with a solid support), hands on the horse after the mount. In the second program, none of the effort accomplished in the first program was lost. Jimmy had worked hard at home, and he was ready to visit again the day of his accident, the reason of his accident, the root of his pain. He is now on his way to build a new life for himself at his own pace.

Conclusion

Some basic ideas are conveyed in the hippotherapy approach of PTSD at Equiphoria. As a first step, the patient is invited to take the time during the program to identify the symptoms that have arisen after the accident and that are hindering his/her rehabilitation process.

When the patient is ready to work on PTSD (circumstances and consequences of TBI, SCI, and stroke), the time has come to look at the accident and its consequences in a temporal context (current physical and emotional difficulties, questions and upheavals, and their place in the patient's daily life). By activating neural mechanisms in response to context and specific actions, hippotherapy promotes the integration of strong emotions that the patient has suppressed to know how to protect him/herself. He/she is gradually led to revisit the time of the accident accompanied by the presence of the horse. The framework allows him/her to take the time to voice tensions and sensations, and to let go by releasing emotions and thoughts that have become almost overwhelming. Through the presence of the horse and its movement at a walk, and with the support of the therapists, the patient is led toward a form of self-understanding and self-improvement, quickly gaining confidence, and easily sharing feelings.

The work of simultaneously integrating and harmonizing the various spheres (emotional, cognitive, physical) through specific exercises enables the patient to identify, elaborate, and release the blockages and to feel liberated and lighter. It is important for the patient to have a clearer picture of how the event unfolded and thus to better understand the consequences that he/she observes in his/her body and mind. The patient feels then able to talk about the accident with greater precision and calm and to resume the course of his/her life to move forward and reinvent him/herself, with a new perspective of a more integrated identity. This will be an opportunity for the patient to set new short-term goals while lucidly identifying his/her difficulties and strengths.

Other key notions reinforce this hippotherapy approach. The notion of systemics and synergy of the different members of the team in real time is instrumental to allow a permanent adjustment to the patient's outputs. The notion of sustainability of the changes occurring after the patient is set into motion and goes with the flow allows him/her greater availability, capacity of listening and self-adjustment; the patient often reports seeing a new perspective on the future. The notion of the ripple effect and its impact when actions are initiated will provoke changes beyond the immediately noticeable or conceivable. The notion of prioritization of the patient's self-needs is based on his/her own rhythm and choices. Each individual has his/her own rhythm and therefore the appropriate time to address PTSD, which cannot be imposed by standardized health protocols (Viruega & Gaviria, 2022). The horse allows an easier identification of the better gateway to address PTSD no matter how old the trauma is, in a very smooth and natural way. Therefore, hippotherapy empowers the person thanks to the strengthening of his/her own vital force.

References

Aronov, D., Nevers, R., & Tank, D. W. (2017). Mapping of a non-spatial dimension by the hippocampal-entorhinal circuit. *Nature, 543*(7647), 719–722. https://doi.org/10.1038/nature21692

Bækkelund, H., Frewen, P., Lanius, R., Ottesen Berg, A., & Arnevik, E. A. (2018). Trauma-related altered states of consciousness in post-traumatic stress disorder patients with or without comorbid dissociative disorders. *European Journal of Psychotraumatology, 9*(1), 1544025. https://doi.org/10.1080/20008198.2018.1544025

Ballester, B. R., Maier, M., Duff, A., Cameirão, M., Bermúdez, S., Duarte, E., Cuxart, A., Rodríguez, S., San Segundo Mozo, R. M., & Verschure, P. F. M. J. (2019). A critical time window for recovery extends beyond one-year post-stroke. *Journal of Neurophysiology, 122*(1), 350–357. https://doi.org/10.1152/jn.00762.2018

Bernhardt, J., Borschmann, K., Boyd, L., Carmichael, S. T., Corbett, D., Cramer, S. C., Hoffmann, T., Kwakkel, G., Savitz, S., Saposnik, G., Walker, M., & Ward, N. (2017a). Moving rehabilitation research forward: Developing consensus statements for rehabilitation and recovery research. *Neurorehabilitation and Neural Repair, 31*(8), 694–698. https://doi.org/10.1177/1545968317724290

Bernhardt, J., Hayward, K. S., Kwakkel, G., Ward, N. S., Wolf, S. L., Borschmann, K., Krakauer, J. W., Boyd, L. A., Carmichael, S. T., Corbett, D., & Cramer, S. C. (2017b). Agreed definitions and a shared vision for new standards in stroke recovery research: The Stroke Recovery and Rehabilitation Roundtable taskforce. *International Journal of Stroke: Official Journal of the International Stroke Society, 12*(5), 444–450. https://doi.org/10.1177/1747493017711816

Bisson, J. I., Roberts, N. P., Andrew, M., Cooper, R., & Lewis, C. (2013). Psychological therapies for chronic post-traumatic stress disorder (PTSD) in adults. *The Cochrane Database of Systematic Reviews, 2013*(12), CD003388. https://doi.org/10.1002/14651858.CD003388.pub4

Blennow, K., Hardy, J., & Zetterberg, H. (2012). The neuropathology and neurobiology of traumatic brain injury. *Neuron, 76*(5), 886–899. https://doi.org/10.1016/j.neuron.2012.11.021

Bonita, R., & Beaglehole, R. (1988). Recovery of motor function after stroke. *Stroke, 19*(12), 1497–1500. https://doi.org/10.1161/01.str.19.12.1497

Bromberg, P. (2000). Standing in the spaces: Essays on clinical process, trauma, and dissociation. *Psychoanalytic Psychology, 17*. https://doi.org/10.1037//0736-9735.17.2.432

Buch, E. R., Liew, S.-L., & Cohen, L. G. (2017). Plasticity of sensorimotor networks: Multiple overlapping mechanisms. *The Neuroscientist: A Review Journal Bringing Neurobiology, Neurology and Psychiatry, 23*(2), 185–196. https://doi.org/10.1177/1073858416638641

Buetow, S. A., Martínez-Martín, P., & McCormack, B. (2019). Ultrabilitation: Beyond recovery-oriented rehabilitation. *Disability and Rehabilitation, 41*(6), 740–745. https://doi.org/10.1080/09638288.2017.1406997

Collins, L., Boddington, L., Steffan, P. J., & McCormick, D. (2021). Vagus nerve stimulation induces widespread cortical and behavioral activation. *Current Biology: CB, 31*(10), 2088–2098.e3. https://doi.org/10.1016/j.cub.2021.02.049

Consorti, A., Di Marco, I., & Sansevero, G. (2021). Physical exercise modulates brain physiology through a network of long- and short-range cellular interactions. *Frontiers in Molecular Neuroscience, 14*, 710303. https://doi.org/10.3389/fnmol.2021.710303

Corbett, D., Jeffers, M., Nguemeni, C., Gomez-Smith, M., & Livingston-Thomas, J. (2015). Chapter 19 – Lost in translation: Rethinking approaches to stroke recovery. In N. Dancause, S. Nadeau, & S. Rossignol (Eds.), *Progress in brain research* (Vol. 218, pp. 413–434). Elsevier. https://doi.org/10.1016/bs.pbr.2014.12.002

Crochet, S., Lee, S.-H., & Petersen, C. C. H. (2019). Neural circuits for goal-directed sensorimotor transformations. *Trends in Neurosciences, 42*(1), 66–77. https://doi.org/10.1016/j.tins.2018.08.011

Cunha-Reis, D., & Caulino-Rocha, A. (2020). VIP modulation of hippocampal synaptic plasticity: A role for VIP receptors as therapeutic targets in cognitive decline and mesial temporal lobe epilepsy. *Frontiers in Cellular Neuroscience, 14*. https://www.frontiersin.org/articles/10.3389/fncel.2020.00153

Demain, S., Wiles, R., Roberts, L., & McPherson, K. (2006). Recovery plateau following stroke: Fact or fiction? *Disability and Rehabilitation, 28*(13–14), 815–821. https://doi.org/10.1080/09638280500534796

Dewan, M. C., Rattani, A., Gupta, S., Baticulon, R. E., Hung, Y.-C., Punchak, M., Agrawal, A., Adeleye, A. O., Shrime, M. G., Rubiano, A. M., Rosenfeld, J. V., & Park, K. B. (2018). Estimating the global incidence of traumatic brain injury. *Journal of Neurosurgery*, 1–18. https://doi.org/10.3171/2017.10.JNS17352

Di Liegro, C. M., Schiera, G., Proia, P., & Di Liegro, I. (2019). Physical activity and brain health. *Genes, 10*(9), E720. https://doi.org/10.3390/genes10090720

Diaz Heijtz, R., Kolb, B., & Forssberg, H. (2003). Can a therapeutic dose of amphetamine during pre-adolescence modify the pattern of synaptic organization in the brain? *The European Journal of Neuroscience, 18*(12), 3394–3399. https://doi.org/10.1046/j.0953-816x.2003.03067.x

Elstein, A. S., & Schwartz, A. (2002). Clinical problem solving and diagnostic decision making: Selective review of the cognitive literature. *BMJ (Clinical Research Ed.), 324*(7339), 729–732. https://doi.org/10.1136/bmj.324.7339.729

Emerson, E., Fortune, N., Llewellyn, G., & Stancliffe, R. (2021). Loneliness, social support, social isolation and wellbeing among working age adults with and without disability: Cross-sectional study. *Disability and Health Journal, 14*(1), 100965. https://doi.org/10.1016/j.dhjo.2020.100965

Feigin, V. L., Vos, T., Nichols, E., Owolabi, M. O., Carroll, W. M., Dichgans, M., Deuschl, G., Parmar, P., Brainin, M., & Murray, C. (2020). The global burden of neurological disorders: Translating evidence into policy. *The Lancet Neurology, 19*(3), 255–265. https://doi.org/10.1016/S1474-4422(19)30411-9

Fernandes, J., Arida, R. M., & Gomez-Pinilla, F. (2017). Physical exercise as an epigenetic modulator of brain plasticity and cognition. *Neuroscience and Biobehavioral Reviews, 80*, 443–456. https://doi.org/10.1016/j.neubiorev.2017.06.012

Fisher, P. W., Lazarov, A., Lowell, A., Arnon, S., Turner, J. B., Bergman, M., Ryba, M., Such, S., Marohasy, C., Zhu, X., Suarez-Jimenez, B., Markowitz, J. C., & Neria, Y. (2021). Equine-assisted therapy for posttraumatic stress disorder among military veterans: An open trial. *The Journal of Clinical Psychiatry, 82*(5), 21m14005. https://doi.org/10.4088/JCP.21m14005

Fornito, A., Zalesky, A., & Breakspear, M. (2015). The connectomics of brain disorders. *Nature Reviews. Neuroscience, 16*(3), 159–172. https://doi.org/10.1038/nrn3901

Fouad, K., Popovich, P. G., Kopp, M. A., & Schwab, J. M. (2021). The neuroanatomical–functional paradox in spinal cord injury. *Nature Reviews. Neurology, 17*(1), 53–62. https://doi.org/10.1038/s41582-020-00436-x

Frasca, D., Tomaszczyk, J., McFadyen, B. J., & Green, R. E. (2013). Traumatic brain injury and post-acute decline: What role does environmental enrichment play? A scoping review. *Frontiers in Human Neuroscience, 7*, 31. https://doi.org/10.3389/fnhum.2013.00031

Gabriels, R. L., Pan, Z., Dechant, B., Agnew, J. A., Brim, N., & Mesibov, G. (2015). Randomized controlled trial of therapeutic horseback riding in children and adolescents with autism spectrum disorder. *Journal of the American Academy of Child and Adolescent Psychiatry, 54*(7), 541–549. https://doi.org/10.1016/j.jaac.2015.04.007

Gaviria, M., Celeghin, A., Michael-Titus, A. T., & Pallier, P. N. (2020). Editorial: Brain plasticity and contribution of the emotional brain to neural remodelling after injury. *Frontiers in Neurology, 11*. https://www.frontiersin.org/articles/10.3389/fneur.2020.606271

GBD 2016 Traumatic Brain Injury and Spinal Cord Injury Collaborators. (2019). Global, regional, and national burden of traumatic brain injury and spinal cord injury, 1990–2016: A systematic analysis for the Global Burden of Disease Study 2016. *The Lancet. Neurology, 18*(1), 56–87. https://doi.org/10.1016/S1474-4422(18)30415-0

Greenlee, H., DuPont-Reyes, M. J., Balneaves, L. G., Carlson, L. E., Cohen, M. R., Deng, G., Johnson, J. A., Mumber, M., Seely, D., Zick, S. M., Boyce, L. M., & Tripathy, D. (2017). Clinical practice guidelines on the evidence-based use of integrative therapies during and after breast cancer treatment. *CA: A Cancer Journal for Clinicians, 67*(3), 194–232. https://doi.org/10.3322/caac.21397

Guindos-Sanchez, L. D., Lucena-Anton, D., Moral-Munoz, J. A., Salazar, A., & Carmona-Barrientos, I. (2020). The effectiveness of hippotherapy to recover gross motor function in children with cerebral palsy: A systematic review and meta-analysis. *Children (Basel, Switzerland), 7*(9), E106. https://doi.org/10.3390/children7090106

Haagsma, J. A., Scholten, A. C., Andriessen, T. M. J. C., Vos, P. E., Van Beeck, E. F., & Polinder, S. (2015). Impact of depression and post-traumatic stress disorder on functional outcome and health-related quality of life of patients with mild traumatic brain injury. *Journal of Neurotrauma, 32*(11), 853–862. https://doi.org/10.1089/neu.2013.3283

Hackler, L., Zadina, J. E., Ge, L. J., & Kastin, A. J. (1997). Isolation of relatively large amounts of endomorphin-1 and endomorphin-2 from human brain cortex. *Peptides, 18*(10), 1635–1639. https://doi.org/10.1016/s0196-9781(97)00259-3

Hallberg, L. (2008). *Walking the way of the horse: Exploring the power of the horse-human relationship*. iUniverse.

Hankey, G. J. (2017). Stroke. *Lancet (London, England), 389*(10069), 641–654. https://doi.org/10.1016/S0140-6736(16)30962-X

Hartwigsen, G., Bestmann, S., Ward, N. S., Woerbel, S., Mastroeni, C., Granert, O., & Siebner, H. R. (2012). Left dorsal premotor cortex and supramarginal gyrus complement each other during rapid action reprogramming. *The Journal of Neuroscience: The Official Journal of the Society for Neuroscience, 32*(46), 16162–16171a. https://doi.org/10.1523/JNEUROSCI.1010-12.2012

Hartwigsen, G., Saur, D., Price, C. J., Ulmer, S., Baumgaertner, A., & Siebner, H. R. (2013). Perturbation of the left inferior frontal gyrus triggers adaptive plasticity in the right homologous area during speech production. *Proceedings of the National Academy of Sciences of the United States of America, 110*(41), 16402–16407. https://doi.org/10.1073/pnas.1310190110

Hartwigsen, G., Bzdok, D., Klein, M., Wawrzyniak, M., Stockert, A., Wrede, K., Classen, J., & Saur, D. (2017). Rapid short-term reorganization in the language network. *eLife, 6*, e25964. https://doi.org/10.7554/eLife.25964

Holzer, P., & Farzi, A. (2014). Neuropeptides and the microbiota-gut-brain axis. *Advances in Experimental Medicine and Biology, 817*, 195–219. https://doi.org/10.1007/978-1-4939-0897-4_9

Holzer, P., Reichmann, F., & Farzi, A. (2012). Neuropeptide Y, peptide YY and pancreatic polypeptide in the gut–brain axis. *Neuropeptides, 46*(6), 261–274. https://doi.org/10.1016/j.npep.2012.08.005

Hong, J., & Park, J.-H. (2022). Efficacy of neuro-feedback training for PTSD symptoms: A systematic review and meta-analysis. *International Journal of Environmental Research and Public Health, 19*(20), 13096. https://doi.org/10.3390/ijerph192013096

Horn, G. (2004). Pathways of the past: The imprint of memory. *Nature Reviews. Neuroscience, 5*(2), 108–120. https://doi.org/10.1038/nrn1324

Hutson, T. H., & Di Giovanni, S. (2019). The translational landscape in spinal cord injury: Focus on neuroplasticity and regeneration. *Nature Reviews. Neurology, 15*(12), 732–745. https://doi.org/10.1038/s41582-019-0280-3

Irwin, C., & Weber, B. (2001). *Horses don't lie: What horses teach us about our natural capacity for awareness, confidence, courage, and trust*. Da Capo Press.

James, S. L., Theadom, A., Ellenbogen, R. G., Bannick, M. S., Montjoy-Venning, W., Lucchesi, L. R., Abbasi, N., Abdulkader, R., Abraha, H. N., Adsuar, J. C., Afarideh, M., Agrawal, S., Ahmadi, A., Ahmed, M. B., Aichour, A. N., Aichour, I., Aichour, M. T. E., Akinyemi, R. O., Akseer, N., et al. (2019). Global, regional, and national burden of traumatic brain injury and spinal cord injury, 1990–2016: A systematic analysis for the Global Burden of Disease Study 2016. *The Lancet Neurology, 18*(1), 56–87. https://doi.org/10.1016/S1474-4422(18)30415-0

Johnson, C. O., Nguyen, M., Roth, G. A., Nichols, E., Alam, T., Abate, D., Abd-Allah, F., Abdelalim, A., Abraha, H. N., Abu-Rmeileh, N. M., Adebayo, O. M., Adeoye, A. M., Agarwal, G., Agrawal, S., Aichour, A. N., Aichour, I., Aichour, M. T. E., Alahdab, F., Ali, R., et al. (2019). Global, regional, and national burden of stroke, 1990–2016: A systematic analysis for the Global Burden of Disease Study 2016. *The Lancet Neurology, 18*(5), 439–458. https://doi.org/10.1016/S1474-4422(19)30034-1

Kaplan, G. B., Leite-Morris, K. A., Wang, L., Rumbika, K. K., Heinrichs, S. C., Zeng, X., Wu, L., Arena, D. T., & Teng, Y. D. (2018). Pathophysiological bases of comorbidity: Traumatic brain injury and post-traumatic stress disorder. *Journal of Neurotrauma, 35*(2), 210–225. https://doi.org/10.1089/neu.2016.4953

Kapur, N. (2020). Paradoxes in rehabilitation. *Disability and Rehabilitation, 42*(11), 1495–1502. https://doi.org/10.1080/09638288.2019.1572795

Kassab, R., & Alexandre, F. (2015). Integration of exteroceptive and interoceptive information within the hippocampus: A computational study. *Frontiers in Systems Neuroscience, 9*, 87. https://doi.org/10.3389/fnsys.2015.00087

Khan, F., Turner-Stokes, L., Ng, L., & Kilpatrick, T. (2007). Multidisciplinary rehabilitation for adults with multiple sclerosis. *The Cochrane Database of Systematic Reviews, 2007*(2), CD006036. https://doi.org/10.1002/14651858.CD006036.pub2

Khan, F., Amatya, B., & Ng, L. (2010). Use of the International Classification of Functioning, Disability and Health to describe patient-reported disability: A comparison of Guillain Barré syndrome with multiple sclerosis in a community cohort. *Journal of Rehabilitation Medicine, 42*(8), 708–714. https://doi.org/10.2340/16501977-0592

Khan, F., Amatya, B., Galea, M. P., Gonzenbach, R., & Kesselring, J. (2017). Neurorehabilitation: Applied neuroplasticity. *Journal of Neurology, 264*(3), 603–615. https://doi.org/10.1007/s00415-016-8307-9

Kolb, B., & Muhammad, A. (2014). Harnessing the power of neuroplasticity for intervention. *Frontiers in Human Neuroscience, 8*, 377. https://doi.org/10.3389/fnhum.2014.00377

Koroleva, E. S., Tolmachev, I. V., Alifirova, V. M., Boiko, A. S., Levchuk, L. A., Loonen, A. J. M., & Ivanova, S. A. (2020). Serum BDNF's role as a biomarker for motor training in the context of AR-based rehabilitation after ischemic stroke. *Brain Sciences, 10*(9), Article 9. https://doi.org/10.3390/brainsci10090623

Le Merre, P., Esmaeili, V., Charrière, E., Galan, K., Salin, P.-A., Petersen, C. C. H., & Crochet, S. (2018). Reward-based learning drives rapid sensory signals in medial prefrontal cortex and dorsal hippocampus necessary for goal-directed behavior. *Neuron, 97*(1), 83–91.e5. https://doi.org/10.1016/j.neuron.2017.11.031

Lee, N., Park, S., & Kim, J. (2017). Hippotherapy and neurofeedback training effect on the brain function and serum brain-derived neurotrophic factor level changes in children with attention-deficit or/and hyperactivity disorder. *Journal of Exercise Nutrition & Biochemistry, 21*(3), 35–42. https://doi.org/10.20463/jenb.2017.0018

Li, Y., Xu, J., Liu, Y., Zhu, J., Liu, N., Zeng, W., Huang, N., Rasch, M. J., Jiang, H., Gu, X., Li, X., Luo, M., Li, C., Teng, J., Chen, J., Zeng, S., Lin, L., & Zhang, X. (2017). A distinct entorhinal cortex to hippocampal CA1 direct circuit for olfactory associative learning. *Nature Neuroscience, 20*(4), 559–570. https://doi.org/10.1038/nn.4517

Luengo-Fernandez, R., Paul, N. L. M., Gray, A. M., Pendlebury, S. T., Bull, L. M., Welch, S. J. V., Cuthbertson, F. C., Rothwell, P. M., & Oxford Vascular Study. (2013). Population-based study of disability and institutionalization after transient ischemic attack and stroke: 10-year results of the Oxford Vascular Study. *Stroke, 44*(10), 2854–2861. https://doi.org/10.1161/STROKEAHA.113.001584

Lyman, G. H., Greenlee, H., Bohlke, K., Bao, T., DeMichele, A. M., Deng, G. E., Fouladbakhsh, J. M., Gil, B., Hershman, D. L., Mansfield, S., Mussallem, D. M., Mustian, K. M., Price, E., Rafte, S., & Cohen, L. (2018). Integrative therapies during and after breast cancer treatment: ASCO Endorsement of the SIO Clinical Practice Guideline. *Journal of Clinical Oncology: Official Journal of the American Society of Clinical Oncology, 36*(25), 2647–2655. https://doi.org/10.1200/JCO.2018.79.2721

Macdonald, S. J., Deacon, L., Nixon, J., Akintola, A., Gillingham, A., Kent, J., Ellis, G., Mathews, D., Ismail, A., Sullivan, S., Dore, S., & Highmore, L. (2018). 'The invisible enemy': Disability, loneliness and isolation. *Disability & Society, 33*(7), 1138–1159. https://doi.org/10.1080/09687599.2018.1476224

Maguire, E. A., & Mullally, S. L. (2013). The hippocampus: A manifesto for change. *Journal of Experimental Psychology. General, 142*(4), 1180–1189. https://doi.org/10.1037/a0033650

Mahan, A. L., & Ressler, K. J. (2012). Fear conditioning, synaptic plasticity and the amygdala: Implications for posttraumatic stress disorder. *Trends in Neurosciences, 35*(1), 24–35. https://doi.org/10.1016/j.tins.2011.06.007

Malá, H., & Rasmussen, C. P. (2017). The effect of combined therapies on recovery after acquired brain injury: Systematic review of preclinical studies combining enriched environment, exercise, or task-specific training with other therapies. *Restorative Neurology and Neuroscience, 35*(1), 25–64. https://doi.org/10.3233/RNN-160682

Manière, G., & Coureaud, G. (2019). Editorial: From stimulus to behavioral decision-making. *Frontiers in Behavioral Neuroscience, 13*, 274. https://doi.org/10.3389/fnbeh.2019.00274

Maravita, A., Spence, C., & Driver, J. (2003). Multisensory integration and the body schema: Close to hand and within reach. *Current Biology: CB, 13*(13), R531–R539. https://doi.org/10.1016/s0960-9822(03)00449-4

Maresca, G., Portaro, S., Naro, A., Crisafulli, R., Raffa, A., Scarcella, I., Aliberti, B., Gemelli, G., & Calabrò, R. S. (2022). Hippotherapy in neurodevelopmental disorders: A narrative review focusing on cognitive and behavioral outcomes. *Applied Neuropsychology. Child, 11*(3), 553–560. https://doi.org/10.1080/21622965.2020.1852084

Marquez, J., Weerasekara, I., & Chambers, L. (2020). Hippotherapy in adults with acquired brain injury: A systematic review. *Physiotherapy Theory and Practice, 36*(7), 779–790. https://doi.org/10.1080/09593985.2018.1494233

Menor-Rodríguez, M. J., Sevilla Martín, M., Sánchez-García, J. C., Montiel-Troya, M., Cortés-Martín, J., & Rodríguez-Blanque, R. (2021). Role and effects of hippotherapy in the treatment of children with cerebral palsy: A systematic review of the literature. *Journal of Clinical Medicine, 10*(12), 2589. https://doi.org/10.3390/jcm10122589

Monsour, M., Ebedes, D., & Borlongan, C. V. (2022). A review of the pathology and treatment of TBI and PTSD. *Experimental Neurology, 351*, 114009. https://doi.org/10.1016/j.expneurol.2022.114009

Moraes, A. G., Copetti, F., Ângelo, V. R., Chiavoloni, L., & de David, A. C. (2020). Hippotherapy on postural balance in the sitting position of children with cerebral palsy – Longitudinal study. *Physiotherapy Theory and Practice, 36*(2), 259–266. https://doi.org/10.1080/09593985.2018.1484534

Moraes, A. G., Neri, S. G. R., Motl, R. W., Tauil, C. B., von Glehn, F., Corrêa, É. C., & de David, A. C. (2021). Effects of hippotherapy on postural balance, functional mobility, self-perceived fatigue, and quality of life in people with relapsing-remitting multiple sclerosis: Secondary results of an exploratory clinical trial. *Multiple Sclerosis and Related Disorders, 52*, 102948. https://doi.org/10.1016/j.msard.2021.102948

Muller, R. U., & Kubie, J. L. (1987). The effects of changes in the environment on the spatial firing of hippocampal complex-spike cells. *The Journal of Neuroscience: The Official Journal of the Society for Neuroscience, 7*(7), 1951–1968.

Mutoh, T., Mutoh, T., Tsubone, H., Takada, M., Doumura, M., Ihara, M., Shimomura, H., Taki, Y., & Ihara, M. (2019). Impact of long-term hippotherapy on the walking ability of children with cerebral palsy and quality of life of their caregivers. *Frontiers in Neurology, 10*, 834. https://doi.org/10.3389/fneur.2019.00834

National Academies of Sciences, E, Division, H. and M, Services, B. on H. C, Policy, B. on H. S, Care, C. on A. P. in T. B. I. R, Matney, C., Bowman, K., & Berwick, D. (2022). Rehabilitation and long-term care needs after traumatic brain injury. In *Traumatic brain injury: A roadmap for accelerating progress*. National Academies Press (US). https://www.ncbi.nlm.nih.gov/books/NBK580075/

Oh, Y., Joung, Y.-S., Jang, B., Yoo, J. H., Song, J., Kim, J., Kim, K., Kim, S., Lee, J., Shin, H.-Y., Kwon, J.-Y., Kim, Y.-H., & Jeong, B. (2018). Efficacy of hippotherapy versus pharmacotherapy in attention-deficit/hyperactivity disorder: A randomized clinical trial. *Journal of Alternative and Complementary Medicine (New York, N.Y.), 24*(5), 463–471. https://doi.org/10.1089/acm.2017.0358

Pessoa, L. (2017). A network model of the emotional brain. *Trends in Cognitive Sciences, 21*(5), 357–371. https://doi.org/10.1016/j.tics.2017.03.002

Pessoa, L., & McMenamin, B. (2017). Dynamic networks in the emotional brain. *The Neuroscientist: A Review Journal Bringing Neurobiology, Neurology and Psychiatry, 23*(4), 383–396. https://doi.org/10.1177/1073858416671936

Pindus, D. M., Mullis, R., Lim, L., Wellwood, I., Rundell, A. V., Abd Aziz, N. A., & Mant, J. (2018). Stroke survivors' and informal caregivers' experiences of primary care and community healthcare services—A systematic review and meta-ethnography. *PLoS One, 13*(2), e0192533. https://doi.org/10.1371/journal.pone.0192533

Pollock, A., Baer, G., Campbell, P., Choo, P. L., Forster, A., Morris, J., Pomeroy, V. M., & Langhorne, P. (2014). Physical rehabilitation approaches for the recovery of function and mobility following stroke. *The Cochrane Database of Systematic Reviews, 2014*(4), CD001920. https://doi.org/10.1002/14651858.CD001920.pub3

Potvin-Bélanger, A., Vincent, C., Freeman, A., & Flamand, V. H. (2022). Impact of hippotherapy on the life habits of children with disabilities: A systematic review. *Disability and Rehabilitation*, 1–15. https://doi.org/10.1080/09638288.2021.2012847

Qin, L., Jing, D., Parauda, S., Carmel, J., Ratan, R. R., Lee, F. S., & Cho, S. (2014). An adaptive role for BDNF Val66Met polymorphism in motor recovery in chronic stroke. *Journal of Neuroscience, 34*(7), 2493–2502. https://doi.org/10.1523/JNEUROSCI.4140-13.2014

Ressler, K. J., Berretta, S., Bolshakov, V. Y., Rosso, I. M., Meloni, E. G., Rauch, S. L., & Carlezon, W. A. (2022). Post-traumatic stress disorder: Clinical and translational neuroscience from cells to circuits. *Nature Reviews. Neurology, 18*(5), 273–288. https://doi.org/10.1038/s41582-022-00635-8

Rice, D., Janzen, S., McIntyre, A., Vermeer, J., Britt, E., & Teasell, R. (2016). Comprehensive outpatient rehabilitation program: Hospital-based stroke outpatient rehabilitation. *Journal of Stroke and Cerebrovascular Diseases, 25*(5), 1158–1164. https://doi.org/10.1016/j.jstrokecerebrovasdis.2016.02.007

Roberts, M. (2001). *Horse sense for people* (Reprint édition). HarperCollins.

Rodenkirch, C., Carmel, J. B., & Wang, Q. (2022). Rapid effects of vagus nerve stimulation on sensory processing through activation of neuromodulatory systems. *Frontiers in Neuroscience, 16*, 922424. https://doi.org/10.3389/fnins.2022.922424

Romaniuk, M., Evans, J., & Kidd, C. (2018). Evaluation of an equine-assisted therapy program for veterans who identify as "wounded, injured or ill" and their partners. *PLoS One, 13*(9), e0203943. https://doi.org/10.1371/journal.pone.0203943

Sale, A., Berardi, N., & Maffei, L. (2014). Environment and brain plasticity: Towards an endogenous pharmacotherapy. *Physiological Reviews, 94*(1), 189–234. https://doi.org/10.1152/physrev.00036.2012

Santos de Assis, G., Schlichting, T., Rodrigues Mateus, B., Gomes Lemos, A., & Dos Santos, A. N. (2022). Physical therapy with hippotherapy compared to physical therapy alone in children with cerebral palsy: Systematic review and meta-analysis. *Developmental Medicine and Child Neurology, 64*(2), 156–161. https://doi.org/10.1111/dmcn.15042

Shen, Y.-C., Sun, X., Li, L., Zhang, H.-Y., Huang, Z.-L., & Wang, Y.-Q. (2022). Roles of neuropeptides in sleep–wake regulation. *International Journal of Molecular Sciences, 23*(9), 4599. https://doi.org/10.3390/ijms23094599

Sherin, J. E., & Nemeroff, C. B. (2011). Post-traumatic stress disorder: The neurobiological impact of psychological trauma. *Dialogues in Clinical Neuroscience, 13*(3), 263–278.

Siddiqui, A. M., Khazaei, M., & Fehlings, M. G. (2015). Translating mechanisms of neuroprotection, regeneration, and repair to treatment of spinal cord injury. *Progress in Brain Research, 218*, 15–54. https://doi.org/10.1016/bs.pbr.2014.12.007

Siebers, M., Biedermann, S. V., Bindila, L., Lutz, B., & Fuss, J. (2021). Exercise-induced euphoria and anxiolysis do not depend on endogenous opioids in humans. *Psychoneuroendocrinology, 126*, 105173. https://doi.org/10.1016/j.psyneuen.2021.105173

Silkwood-Sherer, D. J., & McGibbon, N. H. (2022). Can hippotherapy make a difference in the quality of life of children with cerebral palsy? A pragmatic study. *Physiotherapy Theory and Practice, 38*(3), 390–400. https://doi.org/10.1080/09593985.2020.1759167

Slade, A., Tennant, A., & Chamberlain, M. A. (2002). A randomised controlled trial to determine the effect of intensity of therapy upon length of stay in a neurological rehabilitation setting. *Journal of Rehabilitation Medicine, 34*(6), 260–266. https://doi.org/10.1080/165019702760390347

Sun, Y., Boots, J., & Zehr, E. P. (2015). The lingering effects of a busted myth—False time limits in stroke rehabilitation. *Applied Physiology, Nutrition, and Metabolism = Physiologie Appliquee, Nutrition Et Metabolisme, 40*(8), 858–861. https://doi.org/10.1139/apnm-2014-0523

Tabares, C., Vicente, F., Sánchez, S., Aparicio, A., Alejo, S., & Cubero, J. (2012). Quantification of hormonal changes by effects of hippotherapy in the autistic population. *Neurochemical Journal, 6*(4), 311–316. https://doi.org/10.1134/S1819712412040125

Thomas, R. J., Kenfield, S. A., & Jimenez, A. (2017). Exercise-induced biochemical changes and their potential influence on cancer: A scientific review. *British Journal of Sports Medicine, 51*(8), 640–644. https://doi.org/10.1136/bjsports-2016-096343

Torregrossa, F., Sallì, M., & Grasso, G. (2020). Emerging therapeutic strategies for traumatic spinal cord injury. *World Neurosurgery, 140*, 591–601. https://doi.org/10.1016/j.wneu.2020.03.199

Tyagi, S., Koh, G. C.-H., Luo, N., Tan, K. B., Hoenig, H., Matchar, D. B., Yoong, J., Chan, A., Lee, K. E., Venketasubramanian, N., Menon, E., Chan, K. M., De Silva, D. A., Yap, P., Tan, B. Y., Chew, E., Young, S. H., Ng, Y. S., Tu, T. M., et al. (2021). Role of caregiver factors in outpatient medical follow-up post-stroke: Observational study in Singapore. *BMC Family Practice, 22*(1), 74. https://doi.org/10.1186/s12875-021-01405-z

Uchiyama, H., Ohtani, N., & Ohta, M. (2011). Three-dimensional analysis of horse and human gaits in therapeutic riding. *Applied Animal Behaviour Science, 135*(4), 271–276. https://doi.org/10.1016/j.applanim.2011.10.024

Viruega, H., & Gaviria, M. (2021). Functional weight of somatic and cognitive networks and asymmetry of compensatory mechanisms: Collaboration or divergency among hemispheres after cerebrovascular accident? *Life (Basel, Switzerland), 11*(6), 495. https://doi.org/10.3390/life11060495

Viruega, H., & Gaviria, M. (2022). After 55 years of neurorehabilitation, what is the plan? *Brain Sciences, 12*(8), 982. https://doi.org/10.3390/brainsci12080982

Viruega, H., Gaillard, I., Carr, J., Greenwood, B., & Gaviria, M. (2019). Short- and mid-term improvement of postural balance after a neurorehabilitation program via hippotherapy in patients with sensorimotor impairment after cerebral palsy: A preliminary kinetic approach. *Brain Sciences, 9*(10), E261. https://doi.org/10.3390/brainsci9100261

Viruega, H., Gaillard, I., Briatte, L., & Gaviria, M. (2020). Inter-day reliability and changes of surface electromyography on two postural muscles throughout 12 weeks of hippotherapy on patients with cerebral palsy: A pilot study. *Brain Sciences, 10*(5), 281. https://doi.org/10.3390/brainsci10050281

Viruega, H., Imbernon, C., Chausson, N., Altarcha, T., Aghasaryan, M., Soumah, D., Lescieux, E., Flamand-Roze, C., Simon, O., Bedin, A., Smadja, D., & Gaviria, M. (2022). Neurorehabilitation through hippotherapy on neurofunctional sequels of stroke: Effect on patients' functional independence, sensorimotor/cognitive capacities and quality of life, and the quality of life of their caregivers—A study protocol. *Brain Sciences, 12*(5), Article 5. https://doi.org/10.3390/brainsci12050619

Viruega, H., Galy, C., Loriette, C., Jacquot, S., Houpeau, J. L., & Gaviria, M. (2023). Breast cancer: How hippotherapy bridges the gap between healing and recovery-A randomized controlled clinical trial. *Cancers, 15*(4), 1317. https://doi.org/10.3390/cancers15041317

Welsh, D. K., Logothetis, D. E., Meister, M., & Reppert, S. M. (1995). Individual neurons dissociated from rat suprachiasmatic nucleus express independently phased circadian firing rhythms. *Neuron, 14*(4), 697–706. https://doi.org/10.1016/0896-6273(95)90214-7

Wirtshafter, H. S., & Wilson, M. A. (2019). Locomotor and hippocampal processing converge in the lateral septum. *Current Biology: CB, 29*(19), 3177–3192.e3. https://doi.org/10.1016/j.cub.2019.07.089

Wirtshafter, H. S., & Wilson, M. A. (2020). Differences in reward biased spatial representations in the lateral septum and hippocampus. *eLife, 9*, e55252. https://doi.org/10.7554/eLife.55252

Wirtshafter, H. S., & Wilson, M. A. (2021). Lateral septum as a nexus for mood, motivation, and movement. *Neuroscience and Biobehavioral Reviews, 126*, 544–559. https://doi.org/10.1016/j.neubiorev.2021.03.029

Wissel, J., Olver, J., & Sunnerhagen, K. S. (2013). Navigating the poststroke continuum of care. *Journal of Stroke and Cerebrovascular Diseases, 22*(1), 1–8. https://doi.org/10.1016/j.jstrokecerebrovasdis.2011.05.021

Wood, W. H., & Fields, B. E. (2021). Hippotherapy: A systematic mapping review of peer-reviewed research, 1980 to 2018. *Disability and Rehabilitation, 43*(10), 1463–1487. https://doi.org/10.1080/09638288.2019.1653997

World Health Organization. (2006). *Neurological disorders: Public health challenges* (p. 218). World Health Organization.

Zadina, J. E., Hackler, L., Ge, L. J., & Kastin, A. J. (1997). A potent and selective endogenous agonist for the mu-opiate receptor. *Nature, 386*(6624), 499–502. https://doi.org/10.1038/386499a0

Equine-Assisted Therapy for Substance Use and Mental Health Disorders

Espen Ajo Arnevik and Christina Thorpe

Introduction

The therapeutic use of horses, often referred to as equine therapy, has a long history that dates back centuries. The healing properties of horses have been recognized in various cultures and civilizations throughout time. In ancient Greek and Roman civilizations, riding was often prescribed as a form of exercise for physical and mental well-being. Similarly, in ancient China, horse riding was considered a way to promote physical and mental balance. The use of horses for therapy gained significant attention in the twentieth century, and there have been numerous early pioneers, but specific records of the first published study on equine therapy might be challenging to pinpoint due to a more gradual and organic development of the field over time. Since its inception, equine-assisted therapy (EAT) has grown in the scope of clinical applications and is now offered in more than 50 countries around the world (HETI, 2022). In this chapter, we will review the development and application of EAT to support individuals with substance abuse, summarize the current clinical research results, and present the structure of an EAT treatment facility.

E. A. Arnevik (✉)
Oslo University Hospital, Department of Mental Health and Addiction Treatment, Oslo, Norway

University of Oslo, Institute of Psychology, Oslo, Norway
e-mail: esarne@ous-hf.no

C. Thorpe
Oslo University Hospital, Department of Mental Health and Addiction Treatment, Oslo, Norway
e-mail: chra@ous-hf.no

Y. Neria et al. (eds.), *Guide to Equine Assisted Therapy*,
https://doi.org/10.1007/978-3-031-74426-6_11

Substance Use Disorders

In 2021, about 46.3 million people in the United States had a substance use disorder (SUD). Among them, 29.5 million had issues with alcohol, 24.0 million with drugs, and 7.3 million struggled with both alcohol and drugs. Only 4.1 million people received treatment in specialized facilities (SAMHSA, 2022).

Each person has a unique story and pathway leading to SUD, as well as distinct ways of dealing with psychological, social, and addictive problems. On the other side, various forms of addiction also have common traits, such as using addictive substances or behaviors to cope with negative emotions, experiencing interpersonal problems related to addiction, lacking motivation for change, and facing challenges in both family and work life (Kim & Hodgins, 2018). Moreover, years of SUDs might lead to feelings of inferiority and low self-esteem, especially if maladaptive self-perceptions were not present initially. The social stigma associated with addiction further compounds these challenges.

EAT for Patients with Substance Use Disorders

EAT is an opportunity to work with SUD within a three-way client-horse-therapist treatment relationship (Hallberg & Irwin, 2008; Karol, 2007; Shambo et al., 2013). The interaction with horses brings new dimensions to the therapy. Being with an animal brings smell, touch and sheer size and power of the horse, and its capacity to carry you can bring emotions that might be surprising in one way or another (Yorke et al., 2008). Other benefits might be a result of the inherent characteristics of the horse, such as learning from its herd-based and co-operative behavior, initiating an experience, affect, or new forms of behavior (Burgon, 2011; Kohanov, 2007). The horse can also be used as a metaphor; it is nonjudgmental and can be motivational in itself. The social interaction with the horse can also initiate reflections on the patient's own relational patterns and the meaning of how we relate to each other, and by doing that, it gives possibilities for behavior change (Hamilton, 2011; Kohanov, 2007). Hallberg and Irwin (2008) refer to horses' communication as "completely congruent, honest, sensitive, and non-manipulative." This congruence can be a useful mirror and a positive way for us to see or become more aware of our own behavior and lack of congruence.

Among those who engage in SUD treatment sessions, the dropout rates across in-person psychosocial treatments average 50% (Brorson et al., 2013). Many influential supporters of EAT argue that working with horses is beneficial for patients struggling with addiction and substance abuse (Fry, 2021; Hallberg & Irwin, 2008; Kohanov, 2007; Notgrass & Pettinelli, 2015). The integration of equines into the treatment of psychological disorders has been extensively documented. Following EAT, participants have reported significant reductions in symptoms of psychological distress (Bivens et al., 2007), hyperactive behaviors (Tsantefski et al., 2017), violent behaviors (Nurenberg et al., 2015), posttraumatic stress disorder (PTSD) (Burton et al., 2019; Earles et al., 2015), and anxiety (Alfonso et al., 2015; Earles et al., 2015).

Although individuals have reported the positive impact of EAT on SUD, there is limited empirical evidence to substantiate its effectiveness, with only a handful of studies offering experimental or nonanecdotal support. A scoping review from 2022 assessed 188 titles reporting on studies where patients with SUD had received EAT (Diaz et al., 2022).

They found that there might be a potential positive effect of EAT on SUD treatment retention and completion, as well as on the participants' mental health. However, the studies are limited by small sample sizes, and demonstrating the effectiveness of EAT in the treatment of individuals with SUD remains elusive.

The Clinical Benefits of EAT for Patients with Substance Use Disorders

Because quantitative studies lack sufficient definitive evidence, we have to rely on qualitative studies to guide the development of EAT concerning important clinical topics. Here, we present a summary of the recurring themes found in qualitative studies (Diaz et al., 2022; Kern, 2017).

A Mutual Relationship with the Horse

Patients report that bonding with the horses helps them develop trust (Dell et al., 2011). These bonds are likely formed because participants perceive the horses as nonjudgmental (Leif Hallberg, 2018). Patients can say, "the horse accepts you, like, for who you are" (Kern-Godal et al., 2016b).

The "Nature of the Relationship"

The relationship with the horse can be described as "special and mutual" where the patients perceive the horse as communicative, nonjudgmental, and accepting them for who they are. "I feel that he recognizes me, and that we are good together, and we trust each other, both of us" (Kern-Godal et al., 2016b). The horse is also perceived as having the capacity to understand: "Like, if you let people know you've had a pretty bad day, I feel that's easier for the horse to handle, than for a person" (Kern-Godal et al., 2016b).

Self-Efficacy and Empowerment

EAT is said to empower patients (Kern-Godal et al., 2016b), and many patients report increased self-efficacy through working with the horses (Kern-Godal et al., 2016a). Mastery is a frequently mentioned therapeutic value arising from the relationship with the horse, but the meaning of the word varies. Some describe a rewarding experience of managing an animal of such size, synonymous with "control." Others emphasize succeeding in tasks through perceived cooperation with the horses, thus indicating a meaning of "achievement." Patients who describe feeling nervous or afraid when being with the horses conveyed a third meaning, namely, coping with their own nervousness and "overcoming fear." All three meanings capture a sense of self-efficacy, success, and empowerment—with the horse, with a task, and with the self. Self-efficacy measures like GSES-5 are used in different studies and have been found to be potential mediators of emotion regulation (Dampsey, 2017). It has also been found to be a positive factor that potentially is a buffer against negative psychological influences (Mikkelsen et al., 2020). According to Bandura, self-efficacy may be an important determinant of changing behavior, because it may influence a person's persistence, intention, and effort when facing challenges (Leganger et al., 2000).

Positive Emotional Affect

Being with the horses is expressed in very positive and personal terms. It is described as feeling good: "I just like to be with the horses. Because it is really fun. It is kind of playful. And you can think of other things," and as feeling tranquil: "It's because of [horse] that I get rid of my anxiety. My anxiety and uneasiness and depression." Moreover, feeling self-aware: "If I'm calm then the horse is calm…. Horse therapy means a lot to me in a way, because I have to be present and consistent" (Kern-Godal et al., 2016a). Emotions are often described in relation to each other, with some patients emphasizing that they have to turn their focus away from themselves and onto the horse. The effect may be similar, but in a positive way, to the effect of drugs: "…it kind of makes me forget everything. Actually, it's crazy—because you can compare it to drugs…."

Patients also express happiness as well as a sense of calmness when engaging in EAT (Atherton et al., 2020), and several patients report that EAT has an effect on their mental health, particularly depression. One patient stated that upon leaving EAT; "I come out happy and not so depressed" (Kern-Godal et al., 2016b).

A Break from Traditional Treatment

Another qualitative theme seen across studies is the feeling that EAT represents a break from usual/traditional treatment for participants. Stiltner (Stiltner, 2013) reported that participants felt EAT made their residential facility seem less like an institution and credited the horses with making things feel "homey." In parallel, patients at the Gaustad Stable describe EAT as a "pleasant variation" from usual treatment (Kern-Godal et al., 2016a). Participants especially enjoyed the hands-on aspect of EAT versus traditional talk therapy (Adams et al., 2015; Kern-Godal et al., 2016a). EAT also provides an opportunity to participate in a new activity with the possibility to enhance activity and social relations outside of treatment (Dell et al., 2011).

Treatment Motivation

Patients often bring forward the motivational impact of EAT in their treatment. They describe EAT as being a motivational factor for participants to come to treatment in the first place (Kern-Godal et al., 2016a), as well as describing the horses as a motivation for continuing treatment (Stiltner, 2013).

Negative/Indifferent Experiences

There are some reports of negative or indifferent patient experiences of EAT. Some patients might feel that EAT has little to do with their motivation to succeed in treatment, and some do not look forward to their EAT sessions due to a fear of horses and displeasure with being outdoors (Kern-Godal et al., 2016a; Stiltner, 2013). Haig and Skinner (2022) have reported findings of increased maladjustment in some of the participants in a study of youths participating in EAT compared to the control group. There have also been some reports of patients complaining that the equine facility is "cold" and "stinky like a farm" (Dell et al., 2011).

Attachment

Some of the relevance of EAT to SUD treatment also lies in the consistency with attachment theory. There are similarities between the basic concepts of attachment theory (Ainsworth & Bowlby, 1991; Shaver & Mikulincer, 2009) and central features of equine-assisted psychotherapy, such as security, affect mirroring, mentalization or reflective functioning, nonverbal communication, and body experience (Bachi, 2013). When patients experience these contacts as unconditional and non-judgemental, it may give associations to developing safe attachment at a pre-verbal level (Vincent & Farkas, 2017).

Specific examples of attachment-related processes involving the horse are evident. For example, growing "attachment" might be indicated in the patient's accounts of feeling "understood," "secure," "calm," and their perceptions of the horse's affirmation of the individual. "Mentalization" (reflective functioning) can be seen in the patient's understanding and processing of how recognition of the horse's reactions to them could influence their own behavior (mirroring).

Alliance

Therapeutic alliance is one of the strongest predictors of positive psychological treatment (Horvath & Luborsky, 1993). It is often considered to be a common factor in positive treatment, predicting engagement and retention. Early therapeutic alliance predicts engagement and retention (Meier et al., 2006). In SUD, impaired attachment can add additional challenges to productive patient-therapist alliance due to trust and abandonment issues (Shorey & Snyder, 2006). Flores (2006) points to the benefits to be derived from addiction treatment approaches which increase affective bonds and repair associated disruptions arising from poor attachment.

In EAT, the therapeutic alliance is usually described in terms of a tripartite relationship (Carlsson et al., 2015), in which the horses increase rapport between client and therapist (Carlsson et al., 2014; Hallberg & Irwin, 2008). In one study, the reported alliance became more secure and trusting, and possibly observed the mutual respect and cooperation between the horse and therapist (Carlsson et al., 2015). Combined with the positive contextual influence of the stable's social and emotional environment, EAT might facilitate recognition and projection of the patient's "true" identity. It is likely that EAT enables therapists to see and interact with their patients somewhat differently than therapists in traditional therapy settings (Carlsson et al., 2014).

How We Use a Horse for Therapy

There are many ways of working with the horse: observing the herd, stable work, horse care, groundwork, mounted work, and driving. The different modes of work can address different parts of the patient's problems and can be used for tailoring the treatment for each patient's individual needs.

Observing the herd is a useful tool for initiating discussion, building an alliance with the patient, discussing goals and ways to work, and monitoring affect arousal. It is also a good opportunity to talk about topics like bonding between foal and mother and their interaction with the rest of the herd. We can observe attachment behavior in the horses, "bullying" their "window of tolerance," and how they use their senses to regulate themselves like humans do. During the estrus, many mares have a clearly inviting behavior; they "offer themselves," and this can often create good conversations about difficult things such as shame, falling in love, daring to make yourself vulnerable to others, coping with rejection, and similar topics.

In the stable, there are routines that must be established, and individual responsibility can be negotiated. A feeling of recognition and acceptance might arise in the patient, laying a foundation of attachment and security for psychological growth. While carrying out the caring routines for the horses, these themes of routine work, relationship, trust, and self-esteem issues might become more accessible for the patient. Some patients also describe that the stable work is a break from in-patient treatment. A place where they have a feeling of being needed and becoming more of the person they were before starting to use drugs (Kern-Godal et al., 2016a).

The physical and emotional safety can be even more established and strengthened through groundwork with the horse, where the patient might experience joy and increased social interactions. Groundwork also requires impulse control, understanding one's own limitations as well as the horse's limitations, and developing the capacity to take others perspective and see oneself from the outside. This will be mentalization training in action (Fonagy et al., 2002) and can be further extended with exercises focusing on boundary settings and contact, aggression, anxiety, trust, and communication. When mastering groundwork tasks, the low self-esteem is coming into play and becoming accessible for slowly altering.

Mounted work (riding) is a more body-oriented mode of treatment. Many patients with SUD have low body awareness connected to experienced violence or sexual traumas or due to the excessive use of drugs. Mounted work can promote increased awareness through connected emotional experiences. Thus, mounted work can be challenging for some. On the other side, mounted work can also increase coordination and balance, help getting a better posture, and be beneficial for deepening the attachment by being carried by a caring horse. The increased ability of riding will also help developing self-esteem and a sense of mastering.

Driving is a more group-oriented mode of EAT. Sitting in a carriage while driving develops forward thinking and focus. Giving the commands is empowering (or frightening for some), and working with the acceptance of care and responsibility for the group sitting in the carriage extends the focus from self to others.

When using the different treatment modes, rather than targeting a specific addictive behavior, which is the traditional treatment approach, it may be possible to simultaneously influence a variety of current and emerging addictive behaviors and psychiatric comorbidities by targeting common underlying mechanisms and vulnerabilities.

Textbox 1

What can be learned from the different forms of using the horse in therapy?

Observing the herd is a useful tool for:

- Initiating discussion
- Mentalization
- Feelings/arousal monitoring

Stable work can be useful for establishing:

- Routine
- Responsibility
- Resilience
- Recognition and acceptance

Horse care is useful for addressing:

- Routine, relationship, trust, and self-esteem issues

Groundwork with the horse can be used to address issues relating to:

- Physical and emotional safety
- Play—having fun leads to joy and social interaction
- Impulse control/understanding limitations
- Boundary setting and contact
- Aggression
- Anxiety/trust
- Communication
- Mastering

Mounted work (riding) can help promote:

- Attachment ("being carried by a caring horse")
- Body awareness
- Balance/centering
- Co-ordination
- Posture
- Rhythm/regulation
- Mastering

Driving can be beneficial for:

- Early outings/discussion
- Forward thinking and focus
- Extending outlook (from self)
- Empowerment and giving commands
- Acceptance of care and responsibility (for group)

An EAT Model for Patients with Comorbidities: The "Gaustad Model"

EAT has been provided as a complementary, but integral, part of the specialist health treatment program for patients with SUDs at Oslo University Hospital in Norway since 2004 (Kern, 2017). It has been developed over time, going from activity, stable work, and training horses toward a more body-oriented psychotherapy (Lysell, 2011). Today, the focus is on attachment and relations, building on the EAGALA, PEATT, and HEAL models, primarily through groundwork (see Textbox 2).

Textbox 2
EAT models

EAGALA: Equine-Assisted Growth and Learning Association is an experiential approach where the participants learn about themselves and others. This is a method that is based on groundwork, involving a team of a licenced mental health professional, an equine specialist and loose horses working with the client(s). It is solution-oriented and has high ethical standards for practicing the method (EAGALA, 2019).

PEATT: Psychodynamic Equine-Assisted Trauma Therapy is a methodological treatment that is based on primarily psychodynamic concepts and where the principles of EAGALA are integrated into the psychodynamic treatment approach (Parent, 2016).

HEAL: Human-Equine Alliance for Learning uses a set of interrelated principles for understanding and managing emotion that they call "Six Keys to Relationship". The model focuses on the limbic/emotional communication between horse and human (https://humanequinealliance.com/the-heal-model/).

The Horses

At the Gaustad Stable, there is a team taking care of the horses on a daily basis. Horse welfare is in focus, and a lot of work is put into ensuring that the therapy horses have a good life outside of therapy with their basic needs met. The band of horses used in EAT is Norwegian endangered cold-blooded breeds, such as Fjords, Dølahorse, and Lyngs/Nordlands-horse. These breeds were originally used as working horses in agricultural work and are bred to be calm, good-natured, co-operative, and versatile. They are well adapted to a Norwegian climate with large variations in temperature and weather. They are kept in a herd of seven horses, who live together outdoors all year round. They are not trained for therapy but are chosen due to some specific criteria; it is preferred that the horses communicate well with humans, that they are friendly and calm, and that they have not been exposed to trauma earlier in life. The Gaustad Stable wants to have a herd with both mares and geldings of different ages and with individuals who are born into the herd. The horses are trained in riding, driving, and various forms of groundwork by the staff. The purpose of the training is to provide the horses with solid foundational fitness and enriching experiences beyond their usual day-to-day living environment.

The Patients

All patients are referred by their treating clinician, and the decision on suitability and the treatment objectives of the individual's EAT participation is agreed on at a preparatory meeting between the EAT therapist, the patient, and the patients' clinician. The EAT therapists become part of the patient's clinical team, with full access to the patient's clinical record. Treatment objectives should be specific and dependent on the goal of the treatment. The patients are placed in one of six modules together with other patients with similar goals. The modules help setting the tasks for each session, and four to five patients within the same module create a group. In this way, it is possible to a certain extent to ensure that patients receive help at the level they are at, regardless of diagnosis. The patients are helped by being motivated and focusing on their goal of change, and they are required to be active in their own treatment.

Textbox 3
The modules in the "Gaustad model"
The treatment goals are based on the following six modules:

1. Stabilization, presence, and body orientation
2. Emotions and emotion regulation
3. Inner critic and self-care
4. Relationships and attachment: good boundaries and positive assertiveness
5. Exploration, interest, mastery, and resources
6. Existence, identity, and sense of purpose

The Sessions

The course of therapy usually lasts 12 weeks, with one group session a week. Each session lasts usually 1 hour and is planned and provided by two or three qualified therapists. The program design is structured for small groups but includes provision for individual work on specific needs if required. The sessions take place at different locations on the property. There are several enclosures, some with trees and grass, one small enclosure where the horses usually are groomed, one large arena with a small house with a lot of props for building different scenarios, or they can stay at the pasture where the horses usually live. Usually, the horses are together in the herd—sometimes all seven or sometimes just a few of them.

The EAT therapists describe the therapy as a three-way interactive (positive triangulated) process in which the patient works in physical and emotional safety with the horse on activities selected with his/her therapist to address the goals agreed upon. The first part of each session starts with a "check-in" where the patients are asked what they bring into the session today or if something from the last session is important to address. Based on the feelings or thoughts they brought up in the check-in and their individual treatment plan (module), all group members get "today's task." The therapists invite the patients to seek out the horses with this task (for examples of tasks, see Textbox 4). After the session, there is a "check-out" where the group gathers together with the therapists to reflect and work through the experiences with the horses. The goal is to share and raise awareness of the feelings and thoughts evoked when being with the horses. Based on the reactions and sharing, the therapists use their clinical experience to address the different topics emerging using therapeutic tools such as psychoeducation, confirmations, containing, and mirroring, depending on the patients' needs and therapeutic process. When the session is over, the therapists will evaluate the session, asking each other how it worked, how the co-treatment worked, and which of the themes should be explored in more detail next session.

Textbox 4
The tasks in the "Gaustad model"

Check-in (5–10 minutes):

- What has been brought into today's session?
- Is there something from last session that needs to be addressed?

Setting the task for today (Examples include):

- Seek out the horses and try to notice what comes up in you, of feelings and thoughts, when meeting the horses
- Seek out the horses and try to notice how they communicate with you or each other
- Seek out the horses and notice your own senses, try to find something about the horses that you can see, hear, smell, feel (tactile)

Horse time (30 minutes):

- Being with a horse or the herd
- Therapists observe the horses and the interaction with the patients. They do observations according to the EAGALA/PEATT observation categories

Check-out (20 minutes):

- Open questions: What happened, how was that?
- The group members share what they experienced
- Was there anything about the horses that stood out to you?
- If patients have not discussed specific horse-related experiences, the treatment team may initiate by sharing their own observations regarding the horses
- Reflections in the group

Case Example

During the group session, the prevalent theme of rejection persisted, echoing throughout the hours. As patients interacted with the horses, the animals often distanced themselves, reflecting the patients' fear of rejection in their own lives. This fear hindered them from expressing their true selves openly. To address this, the treatment team decided to conduct a horse education session, emphasizing the concept of "congruence"—the alignment between inner emotions and outward expressions.

The group was encouraged to approach the horses authentically, allowing their inner thoughts and feelings to surface without restraint. During the session, therapists observed significant shifts in horse behavior, from standing still to actively seeking human interaction. Multiple instances of mutual grooming were noted, with horses approaching individuals and reciprocating the physical contact. A particularly unique moment occurred when a horse laid down beside a person, who then sat down, finding solace in the gentle presence of the horse's head in their lap.

These observations were categorized into shifts, patterns, and unique interactions. The team noted a common belief that equine behavior mirrors human emotions, creating an opportunity for patients to experience emotional shifts paralleling the horses' actions. This linkage offered patients a chance for corrective emotional experiences, making horse observations a vital aspect of the therapy.

In the check-out session, participants reported that they initially felt uneasy expressing themselves to the horses. However, as the horses responded with profound connection, the patients gradually shed their inhibitions. The abundant contact with the horses allowed them to immerse themselves fully in the present moment, transcending their fear of rejection. By the end, they described feeling like being part of the herd, highlighting a transformative experience. They marveled at the horses' distinct responses when they were authentic, emphasizing the pivotal role congruence played in their interactions.

Future Directions

Standardizing Equine Interventions Terminology

In the realm of equine-assisted therapies (EAT), a significant challenge persists in the absence of standardized terminology. Both popular media and academic literature have succumbed to the use of ambiguous terms, hindering replicable research (Wood et al., 2021). This lack of standardization not only obstructs the evaluation of EAT interventions but also impedes scientific advancements (Marchand et al., 2021). Hallberg (2018) underscores the criticality of a standardized language, asserting that understanding the clinical impact of interventions necessitates clear terminology (Hallberg, 2018). Thus, there is a need for a unified vocabulary in

EAT. Researchers must also provide detailed protocols, ensuring replicability regardless of nomenclature conventions (Staudt & Cherry, 2017).

Social Well-Being and Equine Interaction

Social well-being is an underlying theme in EAT as well as in ordinary recreational horse activities. In recent years, general horse discourse has addressed bio-social aspects of human-horse interaction and the accrued well-being of humans resulting from that interaction (Birke & Hockenhull, 2015; Davis & Maurstad, 2016). Explorations into the human-horse bond and the patient-horse-therapist triad increasingly emphasize relational factors (Burgon, 2014). Bachi's (2013) application of attachment theory to equine-facilitated psychotherapy is a valuable contribution, especially in the context of EAT and SUD treatment, warranting further exploration.

Addressing Comorbidities: Understanding the Core Components

Depression, anxiety, aggression, poor motivation, and low self-esteem are also common elements of addiction comorbidity and demand comprehensive attention (Mueser et al., 2002). Addressing the underlying core components of different psychiatric diseases might prove meaningful and enlighten the mechanisms of EAT. As many as two-thirds of the patients who receive substance abuse treatment might need parallel treatment for mental illness, with comorbid conditions acting as a predictor of relapse (Landheim et al., 2002, p. 315, 2006). Managing comorbidities poses significant challenges, and integrated treatment as advocated by Mueser et al. (2006, p. 35) emerges as the most sensible approach for this patient group.

Recognizing the Need for Recognition

An often overlooked aspect is the vital human need for recognition. This has not been among the focus of studies but might be important for further discussions. It seems plausible that the participant's description of the recognition of their "real-self," which they can experience in the stable, meets a basic need. Being recognized as an important individual might enhance the patients' self-image. Skatvedt and Schou (2010) found that the SUD residents in their study identified "…themselves as something more than drug abusers in specific interaction situations, in contrast to who they were in most situations." This, they concluded, motivated the patients to move forward (Skatvedt & Schou, 2010).

By addressing these key aspects—terminological clarity, social well-being, understanding comorbidity, and the need for recognition—EAT can progress toward more profound therapeutic impacts and comprehensive scientific evaluations.

In Memory of Ann Kern Godal 1943–2017

References

Adams, C., Arratoon, C., Boucher, J., Cartier, G., Chalmers, D., Anne Dell, C., et al. (2015). The helping horse: How equine assisted learning contributes to the wellbeing of First Nations youth in treatment for volatile substance misuse. *Human-Animal Interaction Bulletin, 1*(1), 52–75.

Ainsworth, M. S., & Bowlby, J. (1991). An ethological approach to personality development. *American Psychologist, 46*(4), 333.

Alfonso, S. V., Alfonso, L. A., Llabre, M. M., & Fernandez, M. I. (2015). Project stride: An equine-assisted intervention to reduce symptoms of social anxiety in young women. *Explore, 11*(6), 461–467.

Atherton, W. L., Meola, C. C., & Pritchard, K. S. (2020). Innovative equine facilitated psychotherapy intervention for adolescent addiction treatment: A pilot study. *International Journal of High Risk Behaviors and Addiction, 9*(3), e103877.

Bachi, K. (2013). Application of attachment theory to equine-facilitated psychotherapy. *Journal of Contemporary Psychotherapy, 43*(3), 187–196. https://doi.org/10.1007/s10879-013-9232-1

Birke, L., & Hockenhull, J. (2015). Journeys together: Horses and humans in partnership. *Society & Animals, 23*(1), 81–100.

Bivens, A., Leinart, D., Klontz, B., & Klontz, T. (2007). The effectiveness of equine-assisted experiential therapy: Results of an open clinical trial. *Society & Animals, 15*(3), 257–267.

Brorson, H. H., Ajo Arnevik, E., Rand-Hendriksen, K., & Duckert, F. (2013). Drop-out from addiction treatment: A systematic review of risk factors. *Clinical Psychology Review, 33*(8), 1010–1024. https://doi.org/10.1016/j.cpr.2013.07.007

Burgon, H. L. (2011). "Queen of the world": Experiences of "at-risk" young people participating in equine-assisted learning/therapy. *Journal of Social Work Practice, 25*(2), 165–183. https://doi.org/10.1080/02650533.2011.561304

Burgon, H. L. (2014). *Equine-assisted therapy and learning with at-risk young people*. Springer.

Burton, L. E., Qeadan, F., & Burge, M. R. (2019). Efficacy of equine-assisted psychotherapy in veterans with posttraumatic stress disorder. *Journal of Integrative Medicine, 17*(1), 14–19.

Carlsson, C., Nilsson Ranta, D., & Traeen, B. (2014). Equine assisted social work as a mean for authentic relations between clients and staff. *Human-Animal Interaction Bulletin, 2*(1), 19–38.

Carlsson, C., Nilsson Ranta, D., & Traeen, B. (2015). Mentalizing and emotional labor facilitate equine-assisted social work with self-harming adolescents. *Child and Adolescent Social Work Journal, 32*, 329–339.

Dampsey, E. (2017). *The effects of equine-assisted psychotherapy on emotion regulation: Self-efficacy and self-awareness as potential mediators*. Fielding Graduate University.

Davis, D. L., & Maurstad, A. (2016). Meaning of horses. In *The meaning of horses* (pp. 1–19). Routledge.

Dell, C. A., Chalmers, D., Bresette, N., Swain, S., Rankin, D., & Hopkins, C. (2011). *A healing space: The experiences of first nations and Inuit youth with equine-assisted learning (EAL)*. Paper presented at the Child & Youth Care Forum.

Diaz, L., Gormley, M. A., Coleman, A., Sepanski, A., Corley, H., Perez, A., & Litwin, A. H. (2022). Equine-assisted services for individuals with substance use disorders: A scoping review. *Substance Abuse Treatment, Prevention, and Policy, 17*(1), 81. https://doi.org/10.1186/s13011-022-00506-x

EAGALA. (2019). *Fundamentals of EAGALA model practice: Equine Assisted Psychotherapy certification program* (9th ed.). EAGALA.

Earles, J. L., Vernon, L. L., & Yetz, J. P. (2015). Equine-assisted therapy for anxiety and posttraumatic stress symptoms. *Journal of Traumatic Stress, 28*(2), 149–152. https://doi.org/10.1002/jts.21990

Federation of Horses in Therapy and Education International (HETI). (2022). Retrieved from https://hetifederation.org/

Flores, P. J. (2006). Conflict and repair in addiction treatment: An attachment disorder perspective. *Journal of Groups in Addiction & Recovery, 1*(1), 5–26.

Fonagy, P., Target, M., Gergely, G., & Jurist, E. J. (2002). *Affect regulation, mentalization and the development of the self.* Other Press.

Fry, N. E. (2021). Conceptualization of psychotherapy incorporating equine interactions in the United States. *Human-Animal Interaction Bulletin, 9*(3), 94–114. https://doi.org/10.1079/hai.2021.0036

Haig, L., & Skinner, K. (2022). Use of equine-assisted services to improve outcomes among at-risk and indigenous youth: A scoping review. *Frontiers in Public Health, 10*, 730644. https://doi.org/10.3389/fpubh.2022.730644

Hallberg, L. (2018). *The clinical practice of equine-assisted therapy: Including horses in human healthcare* (1st ed.). Routledge.

Hallberg, L., & Irwin, C. (2008). *Walking the way of the horse: Exploring the power of the horse-human relationship*. iUniverse.

Hamilton, A. J. (2011). *Zen mind, Zen horse: The science and spirituality of working with horses*. Storey Publishing.

Horvath, A. O., & Luborsky, L. (1993). The role of the therapeutic alliance in psychotherapy. *Journal of Consulting and Clinical Psychology, 61*(4), 561.

Karol, J. (2007). Applying a traditional individual psychotherapy model to equine-facilitated psychotherapy (EFP): Theory and method. *Clinical Child Psychology and Psychiatry, 12*(1), 77–90. https://doi.org/10.1177/1359104507071057

Kern, A. (2017). *The relevance of horse assisted therapy to young adults' substance use disorder treatment* [PhD dissertation]. University of Oslo, Oslo, Norway.

Kern-Godal, A., Brenna, I. H., Arnevik, E. A., & Ravndal, E. (2016a). More than just a break from treatment: How substance use disorder patients experience the stable environment in horse-assisted therapy. *Substance Abuse, 10*, 99–108. https://doi.org/10.4137/sart.S40475

Kern-Godal, A., Brenna, I. H., Kogstad, N., Arnevik, E. A., & Ravndal, E. (2016b). Contribution of the patient-horse relationship to substance use disorder treatment: Patients' experiences. *International Journal of Qualitative Studies on Health and Well-being, 11*, 31636. https://doi.org/10.3402/qhw.v11.31636

Kim, H. S., & Hodgins, D. C. (2018). Component model of addiction treatment: A pragmatic Transdiagnostic treatment model of behavioral and substance addictions. *Frontiers in Psychiatry, 9*, 406. https://doi.org/10.3389/fpsyt.2018.00406

Kohanov, L. (2007). *The tao of equus: A woman's journey of healing and transformation through the way of the horse*. New World Library.

Landheim, A. S., Bakken, K., & Vaglum, P. (2002). Sammensatte problemer og separate systemer: Psykiske lidelser blant rusmisbrukere til behandling i russektoren. *Norsk Epidemiologi, 12*(3), 309–318. https://doi.org/10.5324/nje.v12i3.383

Landheim, A. S., Bakken, K., & Vaglum, P. (2006). Impact of comorbid psychiatric disorders on the outcome of substance abusers: A six year prospective follow-up in two Norwegian counties. *BMC Psychiatry, 6*(1), 44–44. https://doi.org/10.1186/1471-244X-6-44

Leganger, A., Kraft, P., & Røysamb, E. (2000). Perceived self-efficacy in health behaviour research: Conceptualisation, measurement and correlates. *Psychology & Health, 15*(1), 51–69. https://doi.org/10.1080/08870440008400288

Lysell, J. (2011). Bruk av hest i terapi. In M. Toril (Ed.), *Psykisk helsearbeid – mer enn medisiner og samtaleterapi* (pp. 162–179). Fagbokforlaget.

Marchand, W. R., Andersen, S. J., Smith, J. E., Hoopes, K. H., & Carlson, J. K. (2021). Equine-assisted activities and therapies for veterans with posttraumatic stress disorder: Current state, challenges and future directions. *Chronic Stress, 5*, 2470547021991556.

Meier, P. S., Donmall, M. C., McElduff, P., Barrowclough, C., & Heller, R. F. (2006). The role of the early therapeutic alliance in predicting drug treatment dropout. *Drug and Alcohol Dependence, 83*(1), 57–64.

Mikkelsen, H. T., Haraldstad, K., Helseth, S., Skarstein, S., Småstuen, M. C., & Rohde, G. (2020). Health-related quality of life is strongly associated with self-efficacy, self-esteem, loneliness, and stress in 14-15-year-old adolescents: A cross-sectional study. *Health and Quality of Life Outcomes, 18*(1), 352–352. https://doi.org/10.1186/s12955-020-01585-9

Mueser, K. T., Rosenberg, S. D., Goodman, L. A., & Trumbetta, S. L. (2002). Trauma, PTSD, and the course of severe mental illness: An interactive model. *Schizophrenia Research, 53*(1–2), 123–143. https://doi.org/10.1016/s0920-9964(01)00173-6

Mueser, K. T., Noordsy, D. L., Drake, R. E., Fox, L., & Linderoth, L. (2006). *Integrert behandling: av rusproblemer og psyksike [psykiske] lidelser* (T. M. Andersen, Trans.). Universitetsforl.

Notgrass, C. G., & Pettinelli, J. D. (2015). Equine assisted psychotherapy: The Equine Assisted Growth and Learning Association's model overview of equine-based modalities. *The Journal of Experiential Education, 38*(2), 162–174. https://doi.org/10.1177/1053825914528472

Nurenberg, J. R., Schleifer, S. J., Shaffer, T. M., Yellin, M., Desai, P. J., Amin, R., et al. (2015). Animal-assisted therapy with chronic psychiatric inpatients: Equine-assisted psychotherapy and aggressive behavior. *Psychiatric Services, 66*(1), 80–86.

Parent, I. B. (2016). *Fundamentals of equine assisted trauma therapy: With practical examples from working with members of the armed*. Minds-n-Motion.

SAMHSA. (2022). *Key substance use and mental health indicators in the United States: Results from the 2021 National Survey on Drug Use and Health* (HHS Publication No. PEP22-07-01-005, NSDUH Series H-57). Retrieved from https://www.samhsa.gov/data/report/2021-nsduh-annual-national-report

Shambo, L., Young, D., & Madera, C. (2013). *The listening heart: The limbic path beyond office therapy*. Human-Equine Alliances for Learning Heal.

Shaver, P. R., & Mikulincer, M. (2009). An overview of adult attachment theory. In *Attachment theory and research in clinical work with adults* (pp. 17–45). The Guilford Press.

Shorey, H. S., & Snyder, C. (2006). The role of adult attachment styles in psychopathology and psychotherapy outcomes. *Review of General Psychology, 10*(1), 1–20.

Skatvedt, A., & Schou, K. C. (2010). The potential of the commonplace: A sociological study of emotions, identity and therapeutic change. *Scandinavian Journal of Public Health, 38*(5_suppl), 81–87.

Staudt, M., & Cherry, D. (2017). Equine-facilitated therapy and trauma: Current knowledge, future needs. *Advances in Social Work, 18*(1), 403–414.

Stiltner, C. (2013). *Equine-assisted psychotherapy in a residential substance abuse treatment program for male adolescents*. Capella University.

Tsantefski, M., Briggs, L., Griffiths, J., & Tidyman, A. (2017). An open trial of equine-assisted therapy for children exposed to problematic parental substance use. *Health & Social Care in the Community, 25*(3), 1247–1256.

Vincent, A., & Farkas, K. J. (2017). Application of attachment theory to equine-facilitated therapy. *Society Register, 1*(1), 7–22. https://doi.org/10.14746/sr.2017.1.1.02

Wood, W., Alm, K., Benjamin, J., Thomas, L., Anderson, D., Pohl, L., & Kane, M. (2021). Optimal terminology for services in the United States that incorporate horses to benefit people: A consensus document. *The Journal of Alternative and Complementary Medicine, 27*(1), 88–95.

Yorke, J., Adams, C., & Coady, N. (2008). Therapeutic value of equine-human bonding in recovery from trauma. *Anthrozoös, 21*(1), 17–30. https://doi.org/10.2752/089279308X274038

Part III
Equine Assisted Therapy for Children and Youth

Equine-Assisted Interventions for Youth with Anxiety

Mary C. Acri, Aviva Vincent, Meghan A. Morrissey, Lauren Seibel, and Kimberly Eaton Hoagwood

Anxiety Among Children and Adolescents

Anxiety is the most common mental health problem among youth (Acri et al., 2021; Hoagwood et al., 2022; Seibel et al., 2021). Across the United States, 5.8 million children and adolescents between 3 and 17 years of age have a diagnosable anxiety disorder (CDC, 2022), such as generalized anxiety disorder, panic disorder, social anxiety disorder, and separation anxiety disorder (nih.gov). Further, the number of youths with anxiety has increased markedly due to the COVID-19 pandemic (Hawes et al., 2022), although even prior to the pandemic, the percentage of youth who screened positive for anxiety increased from 34.1% in 2012 to 44% in 2018 (Hoagwood et al., 2022). Anxiety can negatively impact multiple life domains. For example, excessive worry can interfere with a child's ability to focus at school, or avoidance of social situations can prevent a child from forming new peer relationships (Hoagwood et al., 2022; Seibel et al., 2021).

If unaddressed, anxiety can recur or become more detrimental to the child's overall mental health and well-being as it is associated with depressive disorders and substance use in adulthood (Hoagwood et al., 2021, 2022). There is a societal and monetary cost to anxiety also; roughly 43–47 billion US dollars are spent annually on mental health treatment, unneeded medical services, lower work productivity, and losses in earnings due to premature mortality (Hoagwood et al., 2022).

M. C. Acri · M. A. Morrissey · K. E. Hoagwood (✉)
New York University Langone Health, New York, NY, USA
e-mail: kimberly.hoagwood@nyulangone.org

A. Vincent
School of Social Work, College of Health, Cleveland State University, Cleveland, OH, USA

L. Seibel
Department of Psychology, George Mason University, Fairfax, VA, USA

Y. Neria et al. (eds.), *Guide to Equine Assisted Therapy*,
https://doi.org/10.1007/978-3-031-74426-6_12

The purpose of this chapter is to provide an overview of animal-assisted services (AAS), and specifically, an innovative adaptive horseback riding program that incorporates cognitive-behavioral therapy, for children and adolescents with anxiety.

Cognitive-Behavioral Therapy

Cognitive-behavioral therapy (CBT) is considered the gold standard of treatment for youth with mild and moderate anxiety (Hoagwood et al., 2021, 2022). CBT is a short-term treatment that is based on the theory that thoughts, behaviors, and feelings are connected and influence each other (Beck, 2011). CBT focuses on first the identification of unhelpful or harmful thoughts, then disrupting the thought pattern by implementing specific techniques, practicing relaxation strategies, and engaging in graduated exposure. From this process, youth learn to problem solve and cope effectively when faced with an anxiety-provoking situation (American Psychological Association [APA], n.d.).

CBT is one of the most well-studied and effective treatments for anxiety. Between 60% and 80% of children and adolescents with anxiety demonstrated significant clinical improvement, and between 50% and 70% achieved remission following CBT in several studies (Warwick et al., 2017). Further, a meta-analysis of 19 studies found similar results; between 47.6% and 66.4% of youth achieved full recovery from anxiety when they received CBT compared to 20.6% and 21.3% assigned to an alternate therapy or waitlist control (Warwick et al., 2017). CBT has also shown long-term, post-treatment therapeutic gains of up to 16 years (Wei & Kendall, 2014).

Barriers to Mental Health Treatment

Over half of all youth with mental health symptoms serious enough to necessitate treatment do not receive mental health services, however (Acri et al., 2021; Seibel et al., 2021). In a review of the existing literature and theoretical models of help seeking, Staudt (2007) identified five areas associated with a child's receipt of treatment: (1) caregiver's perception of the relevance of treatment and perceived acceptability of services, (2) perceptions and beliefs about treatment, (3) family stressors, which may distract caregivers from engaging in treatment, (4) logistical or external obstacles, and (5) caregiver's therapeutic alliance with their child's provider. Ingoldsby (2010) and Acri et al. (2021) emphasize the impact of external barriers (i.e., provider and organizational-level factors), which include agency waiting lists, workforce shortages and turnover, lack of geographically accessible services, and language barriers. Additionally, Kazdin (2019) adds the dominant mode of treatment (in-person, one-on-one sessions, licensed master's-level therapist, and clinic setting) is itself a barrier because it lacks ecological validity.

The US Surgeon General recently called for the delivery of effective services in a range of natural settings in order to reach more children (Murthy, 2022). Further, most youth who would benefit from mental health services do not receive evidence-based practices (EBP) such as CBT because trained providers are largely unavailable or inaccessible to most youth (Bruns et al., 2016). State mental health authorities report that only 3% of their delivered services for youth are evidence based. As such, making effective services available to youth and families is a paramount public health goal (Acri et al., 2021).

Animal-Assisted Services (AAS)

In response to the fragmented child mental health service system and inequities in access, coupled with increased mental health services need due to the COVID-19 pandemic, Hoagwood and Kelleher (2020) published a Marshall Plan to build the mental health service system back better after the pandemic. As part of their plan, they recommended delivering services in community-based settings such as schools, community centers, and homeless shelters to meet families where they are at and expand access to mental health services. Further, they suggested that providing additional services such as housing and economic supports can stabilize the family unit, and training non-licensed service providers including community health workers, parent support specialists, and paraprofessionals to deliver services including screening and diagnostic assessments, psychoeducation, and support groups can expand the workforce.

Animal-Assisted Services (AAS; Binder et al., 2024) are a promising approach that embodies multiple recommendations put forth by Hoagwood and Kelleher (2020), including broadening the mental health workforce through training non-licensed service providers and providing evidence-based treatment in community settings. AAS is defined as a service that is "facilitated, guided, or mediated by a health or human service provider or educator, who works with and maintains the welfare of a … qualifying animal to provide therapeutic, educational, supportive and/or ameliorative processes aimed at enhancing the well-being of humans." AAS can include mental health treatment, education, or socio-emotional support (Binder et al., 2024). Treatment-focused sessions are sometimes delivered by human-service professionals with specialized expertise (Balluerka et al., 2014; Bass et al., 2009; Dietz et al., 2012; Kamioka et al., 2014) and are often a complement or adjunct to other therapies. Animals are chosen because they are perceived as having a therapeutic benefit to the client (Balluerka et al., 2014), enabling a safe and trusting relationship to be created between the child and the animal (Hoagwood et al., 2016; Vincent & Farkas, 2017).

Adaptive Horseback Riding

Adaptive horseback riding, which has historically been referred to as therapeutic riding, is a type of AAS and includes equine-assisted learning or equine-assisted psychotherapy. Horses can be useful in therapeutic contexts in part because they act as a biofeedback mechanism or mirror. Horses are innately highly attuned to the mood or behavior of humans and non-human animals. Horses offer immediate feedback about the youth's emotional state similar to the benefits achieved via group work (Almeras & Bresciani, 2024; Lac, 2023; Naber et al., 2023).

In equine-assisted learning or psychotherapy, the horse becomes an assistive aid in the therapeutic process. This can be especially important when teaching emotional regulation to youth with anxiety (Wilson et al., 2016). For example, if the rider is anxious, the horse may react to their anxiety, highlighting to the child how their affect is perceived and experienced by others in their environment. Peters et al. (2022) found that self-regulation, and specifically changes in irritability and hyperactivity, mediated the relationship between group assignment, social communication, and social cognition. The authors suggested that horseback riding led to a self-regulation and calming effect, which then allowed children to better develop social skills and express themselves socially.

Some psychophysiological data on adaptive horseback riding has emerged as well. A randomized controlled trial of equine-assisted learning in personal development showed decreased cortisol levels in the intervention group of adolescents at post-test, also suggesting that equine interactions may be beneficial in decreasing youth stress or anxiety (Pendry et al., 2014).

Existing Evidence

In 2014, Anestis and colleagues reviewed the methodology of studies published on psychotherapy incorporating horses and adaptive horseback riding aimed at improving mental health. The authors found that all the studies in their review had several threats to the validity of the results; some of these threats came from design issues, namely, a lack of randomization, manualized treatments, or fidelity checks. These issues are beginning to be addressed in studies incorporating mental health interventions in adaptive horseback riding, including stronger designs, randomization, the inclusion of fidelity checks and standardized protocols, and the use of an active control group (e.g., Gabriels et al., 2012). Examples of studies using more rigorous designs can be found in Aviv et al. (2021) and Wharton et al. (2019), which also incorporated horses for veterans with post-traumatic stress disorder.

Recent studies have explored trauma-focused CBT (TF-CBT) applied to therapeutic riding (Roberts & Honzel, 2020). A recent review and meta-analysis of 16 studies of equine-assisted services (EAS) for youth mental health showed statistically significant medium effect sizes for studies examining improved youth psychosocial outcomes (Fuller-Lovins et al., 2023). More specifically, they found a medium effect on externalizing symptoms and a small to medium effect on internalizing symptoms and adaptive skills. While these results are promising, more rigorous studies of the use of horses in psychotherapy and adaptive horseback riding are still needed to further strengthen the evidence base and examine the mechanisms of action (see Hoagwood et al., 2021, 2022; Vincent & Peth-Pierce, 2023).

Reining in Anxiety

Reining in Anxiety (RiA) is a novel, manualized adaptive horseback riding intervention with evidence-based cognitive-behavioral elements for youth with mild to moderate anxiety, delivered by Certified Therapeutic Riding Instructors (CTRIs), who are credentialed professionals through the Professional Association of Therapeutic Horsemanship International (PATH Intl.). CTRIs provide adaptive/therapeutic horseback riding lessons, both mounted and unmounted (Hoagwood et al., 2021). CTRIs are trained to teach people with disabilities horsemanship skills but are not trained as mental health professionals—an important distinction given the known challenges of the target population. Some CTRIs may hold a master's degree or license in a mental health field, but the trainings are independent of each other.

Development of the intervention, and subsequent manual, was based on information drawn from PracticeWise®, a website that contains synthesized research findings from randomized controlled studies of effective psychosocial therapies for children and adolescents with mental health conditions. In a search of the PracticeWise® database for the "best-supported research" protocols to treat youth with anxiety disorders, the top five most effective treatment elements were: in vivo exposure (92%), cognitive restructuring (66%), client psychoeducation (56%), relaxation (44%), and caregiver psychoeducation (40%; practicewise.com). These elements were incorporated into the intervention protocol.

RiA consists of ten weekly group sessions, each lasting 1 hour, with up to four youths per group. One CTRI facilitates the session with varying levels of volunteer support, including a lead walker and/or side walkers (individuals that walk alongside the horse near the youth to ensure their safety), as deemed necessary by the CTRI.

Session Structure

Each session starts with a review of the homework journal and allows the youth an opportunity for the journal to be filled out with the CTRI if not completed since the previous session. The riding instructor also allows space for riders to share their "crises of the week" (COW) or questions since the last session. This allows the

CTRI to gauge any acute anxiety, set the foundation for practicing skills, and provide a space for the youth to discuss their current cognitive state prior to starting the session. The six components of each session are as follows:

1. *Groom and Connect*: This initial groundwork and grooming connects the rider to the horse and provides the riding instructor an opportunity to advise riders on what to expect in a session and teach grooming and horse care.
2. *Warm-up*: The warm-up consists of warming up the horse with movement, which serves to physically warm up the rider's muscles as well as allows the riding instructor to assess the rider's current mental status with predictable directives.
3. *Session activity*: The session activity focuses on a mental health element, while using horse interaction and play to engage the rider in learning. Session one, for example, teaches riders about thoughts, feelings, and behaviors; riders sort index cards with words that convey a thought, feeling, or behavior into designated buckets that are placed throughout the arena. This activity teaches identification and differentiation of thoughts, feelings, and behaviors, while simultaneously building horsemanship skills as the rider directs the horse to walk, steer, and stop around the arena. The horse interaction allows ample opportunity for riding instructors to provide horsemanship skill feedback.
4. *Cool down*: This cool down period consists of a mindfulness practice or relaxation exercise as well as horse cool-out activities. A grounding exercise such as a sense scan can be done by prompting riders to pay attention to what they see, hear, smell, feel, or taste.
5. *Parent/caregiver psychoeducation*: At the end of each session, the riding instructor and youth debrief with the parent/caregiver, and the riding instructor coaches the rider to advise the parent of skills learned or practiced, including how to apply the session's skill to everyday anxiety-provoking scenarios their child faces. Brief adjunctive caregiver education programs have been shown to improve outcomes for children with mood disorders (Fristad et al., 2009). The American Academy of Child and Adolescent Psychiatry anxiety treatment guidelines delineate the importance of caregiver psychoeducation and participation in their child's therapy for improving their symptoms of anxiety (Walter et al., 2020).
6. *Homework/journal*: Homework, assigned weekly, reinforces the skills learned in the session. Assignments begin with self-monitoring and identifying anxiety-provoking situations that occur outside of the sessions and build to include thought records to identify cognitive distortions and aim to practice thought changing. The curriculum is designed to flex from basic to advanced equine skill levels and allows for more instructor creativity in later sessions when mental health skill building becomes more repetitive (Acri et al., 2021).

Training and Supervision

In RiA, a licensed clinical mental health professional trains and supervises CTRIs throughout the intervention. The intervention is designed to be delivered in a horseback riding arena. Training is conducted over 3 days and consists of an overview of the therapeutic stance, practice of the CBT skills, small group discussion, and content evaluation to ensure material retention.

To accompany the training, instructors are provided session props, checklists, and implementation supports such as a belt bag with rubber bands, markers, index cards, and other session-specific supplies. Once study sessions commence, CTRIs receive supervision from the same licensed clinical mental health professional via weekly hour-long consultations, augmented by additional phone consultations as needed. If the intervention has a research component, random in-person fidelity checks are also conducted.

Establishing an Evidence Base

A pilot study of RiA was conducted from 2018 to 2020 to determine the feasibility, preliminary effectiveness, and fidelity of the intervention to ensure that the core components of the model were delivered as intended. The developers partnered with a local not-for-profit, PATH Intl. accredited stable, GallopNYC, which provides an array of individual and group therapeutic and recreational programs with horses at four stables in New York City. Working collaboratively with GallopNYC's CTRIs, the research team refined the manual to maximize its fit with the existing lesson structure, schedule, and need. For example, the protocol was originally eight sessions long, but two additional sessions were included to match GallopNYC's 10-week standard session schedule. An "in review" session was added as the fourth session to reinforce content from sessions one through three, and an additional session on problem-solving was added since that was the next most common discrete practice element (found in 27% of protocols) identified in Practice-Wise®.

The final sample size consisted of 41 youth/caregiver dyads who were randomly assigned to RiA ($n = 22$) versus services as usual (SAU; $n = 19$). Participants in the SAU group received 10 weekly GallopNYC standard adaptive horseback riding lessons, which consisted of teaching horsemanship skills and horseback riding to the children in a manner adapted to their skill level, in accordance with PATH standards for adaptive riding. PATH-certified instructors employed at GallopNYC delivered the intervention and SAU (Hoagwood et al., 2021).

Youth were assessed via caregiver report at baseline and after the last session of the 10-week semester on symptoms of anxiety and self-efficacy and by instructors on general functioning. Caregivers also provided sociodemographic data at baseline. Baseline measures were administered in person, with caregivers answering either paper surveys or online on an iPad provided. Post-survey measures were sent to caregivers via email and completed online at home. Youth who received RiA showed significant improvements in emotional self-efficacy and a significant decrease in the severity of anxiety symptoms as compared to the comparison group, which received standard adaptive horseback riding (Hoagwood et al., 2021).

Additionally, fidelity checks were conducted on 100% of the 25 completed sessions in the first semester of the trial and 22.8% of subsequent sessions, resulting in a total of 46 sessions that were assessed. In order to conduct the fidelity checks, a standard checklist of key elements was developed for each session. Research staff then observed and rated whether the elements were present in the session; if it was not, the rater did not endorse the element on the checklist. Between 93.3% and 100% of elements were present across sessions ($M = 98.7\%$), which indicates excellent fidelity to the intervention. These findings strongly suggest that CTRIs can be trained to deliver RiA with fidelity.

Finally, for 22% of the 46 sessions for which fidelity was assessed, a second research team member observed and rated the sessions. Inter-rater reliability was excellent ($k = 0.92$). Our initial fidelity data confirms that the intervention was delivered as intended and that delivery of the intervention attained a high level of fidelity (98.7%), well beyond the threshold for high fidelity (e.g., >80%) established in the literature (Garbacz et al., 2014; Seibel et al., 2021).

A second study of RiA was conducted at a different equine facility, in a different state, with a new sample of youths and caregivers, and a different group of riding instructors who were trained to deliver the intervention. The sample, similar to GallopNYC, consisted of 39 riders at Fieldstone Farm Therapeutic Riding Center (FSF), a premiere PATH-accredited facility in Ohio. However, this study differed by adding psychophysiological measures such as cortisol, alpha-amylase, and oxytocin for riders, horses, and volunteers. Researchers collected data at weeks 1 (baseline), 4, 7, and 10 (post-test) for the youth, volunteers, and horses both before and after the session. The researchers were interested in examining the overall impact of RiA on all beings in the arena—not just the youth. This addition also directly addressed calls for increased attention to equine welfare in AAS (Hoagwood et al., 2022).

This second study addressed four goals. First was examining whether changes in anxiety symptoms, emotional regulation, and emotional self-efficacy found in the first trial could be replicated. Second was whether fidelity to the program was reliable. The third goal was to assess the feasibility of collecting saliva samples from horses and children to measure stress (cortisol and alpha-amylase) and relaxation (oxytocin). The fourth goal was to determine the feasibility of collecting salivary assays of cortisol as a physiological measure of stress/anxiety, alpha-amylase as a surrogate indicator of stress, and oxytocin as a measure of relaxation/bonding, and to determine whether there were changes during each lesson and over the course of the 10 weeks for horses, youth, and volunteers (Hoagwood et al., 2022).

For the collection of physiological data, youth used a sterile vial and straw to collect pooled saliva. Due to the COVID-19 pandemic, caregivers were encouraged to collect their rider's saliva, while wearing sterile gloves. If youth were unable to generate 1 mL of saliva or were unable to collect pooled saliva due to their disability, researchers allowed the use of a cotton swab to be placed under the rider's tongue ($n = 2$). While not the same as collecting pooled saliva, the cotton swab absorbed as much pooled saliva as possible from the rider. To collect horses' saliva, each horse had an individual bitless bridle with a modified bit attached (Vincent et al., 2021). The modified bit was created based on Contreras-Aguilar et al.' (2019) design; the tubing, made of pliable rubber, had slits cut to allow for the collection of pooled saliva. Health data regarding the horses' health, age, and typical workload were also tracked to holistically understand the physiological data.

Eight CTRIs were trained in the delivery of the RiA protocol, and fidelity data were recorded per session. Consistent with the first study, anxiety, as measured by caregiver self-report, significantly decreased from pre- to post-test, while emotional regulation scores significantly increased. No significant changes in self-efficacy from pre- to post-test were observed. Further, saliva samples obtained from participants before and after riding sessions showed a consistent decrease in cortisol and a significant increase in oxytocin at two of the four timepoints (Week 1 and Week 7), but no overall pre- to post-changes. There were no significant changes in oxytocin or cortisol upon analysis of the horses' saliva, suggesting that the horses did not have an increase in stress created by the intervention. Finally, fidelity scores per individual session (i.e., per week) ranged from 88.4% to 100%. Average fidelity scores by instructor ranged from 92.5% to 100%. The average fidelity percentage across all sessions was 97.14%.

A separate analysis of data collected on the volunteers was also conducted. Volunteers directly impact the rider-horse bond by increasing accessibility to riding for children/riders and by fostering a meaningful bond between the rider and horse. Forty-one volunteers participated in the RiA study at Fieldstone Farm. Volunteer saliva assays showed a non-significant, positive trend in oxytocin and alpha-amylase, while cortisol remained level. The responses in the survey suggested that volunteers perceived their role positively, with nuanced experiences of a sense of responsibility to ensure safety and enjoyment in assisting the riders. While their sense of responsibility is evidenced by an increase in stress (e.g., cortisol remaining level and an increase in alpha-amylase), it is not necessarily negative stress, as there was simultaneously affiliative bonding expressed (oxytocin). The complex emotions and experiences of volunteers are important to understand to create meaningful, sustainable volunteer engagement. This is particularly important in the equine-assisted service industry, which is reliant on volunteerism.

Future Directions

AAS with horses demonstrates promise as a therapeutic approach for children and adolescents with anxiety. AAS with horses may address key barriers by enhancing the acceptability of treatment and decreasing stigma. By using the manualized protocol of RiA, youth can access cognitive-behavioral therapy techniques commonly included in rigorous research protocols for youth anxiety within an adaptive horseback riding program delivered by CTRIs, rather than having to seek separate mental health services through clinics. Fidelity data suggest that this intervention can be delivered effectively by CTRIs with training and supervision by a licensed clinical mental health provider. Considering that there are at least 860 PATH Intl. centers, this intervention can be an additional resource for increasing access to community-based mental health services that target anxiety, the most common mental health condition affecting youth. One implication of this intervention is its potential to expand access to services and expand the mental health workforce (Jones et al., 2019; London et al., 2020; Trujillo et al., 2020; Wilson et al., 2016).

Opportunities and Future Research

Randomized clinical trials—the gold standard for scientific evidence—are greatly needed to strengthen knowledge about the effectiveness of AAS with horses, as well as address the core question: for whom is this intervention effective, and under what conditions? Because AAS with horses is still underdeveloped scientifically, it is difficult to tease out the active mechanisms of change. Thus, research is needed that includes the collection of physiological indicators such as cortisol, oxytocin, and heart rate (Pendry et al., 2018), as well as neuroimaging studies to assess the impact of rhythmic riding on neural pathways in youth (Arnold et al., 1985; Arnold, 2015; Acri et al., 2021).

Adaptations of interventions including but not limited to RiA may also benefit the community at large. Not all who enjoy horses choose to ride, and not all therapeutic environments with horses are PATH International centers. Thus, considering how RiA can be adapted for ground-based programming (partnering with horses from the ground, not riding) will be advantageous to serving a larger population. As riding a horse for the first time can be an anxiety-provoking experience, many youths with anxiety may refuse to participate in the mounted version of RiA groups. Additionally, some disabilities and medical conditions are potential contraindications for therapeutic horseback riding according to the PATH Intl., and all PATH centers have weight limits. The unmounted adaptation of the RiA protocol could decrease disparities in access for youth who might benefit from it. Many equine-assisted learning and psychotherapy programs are delivered in an unmounted format. Thus, expanding the protocol to unmounted settings could allow the RiA program to be disseminated more broadly to EAS practitioners and improve the reach of services to more youth.

Finally, the need to expand research on alternative forms of therapeutic support for children and youth has never been more important. The crisis affecting children's mental health in this country continues to deepen. Identifying nontraditional provider-delivered interventions to expand the reach of mental health support is essential (Dodge et al., 2024). There will never be a sufficient number of licensed psychologists, psychiatrists, social workers, or counselors to meet the mental health needs of children and youth. Thus, identifying alternative settings, alternative providers, and training opportunities for enhancing the mental health workforce to deliver evidence-based services will help ameliorate the current mental health crisis.

References

Acri, M., Morrissey, M., Peth-Pierce, R., Seibel, L., Seag, D., Hamovitch, E. K., et al. (2021). An equine-assisted therapy for youth with mild to moderate anxiety: Manual development and fidelity. *Journal of Child and Family Studies, 30*(10), 2461–2467.

Almeras, H. S., & Bresciani, S. (2024). Experiential learning with horses for leadership and communication skills development: Toward a model. *International Journal of Learning and Change, 16*(1), 86–111. https://doi.org/10.1504/IJLC.2024.135624

Anestis, M. D., Anestis, J. C., Zawilinski, L. L., Hopkins, T. A., & Lilienfeld, S. O. (2014). Equine-related treatments for mental disorders lack empirical support: A systematic review of empirical investigations. *Journal of Clinical Psychology, 70*(12), 1115–1132.

APA. (n.d.). *What is cognitive behavioral therapy?* https://www.apa.org. Retrieved April 5, 2024, from https://www.apa.org/ptsd-guideline/patients-and-families/cognitive-behavioral

Arnold, L. E. (2015). The alone rangers and silver. *Journal of the American Academy of Child & Adolescent Psychiatry, 54*(7), 535–536. https://doi.org/10.1016/j.jaac.2015.04.010

Arnold, L. E., Clark, D. L., Sachs, L. A., Jakim, S., & Smithies, C. (1985). Vestibular and visual rotational stimulation as treatment for attention deficit and hyperactivity. *American Journal of Occupational Therapy, 39*(2), 84–91. https://doi.org/10.5014/ajot.39.2.84

Aviv, T.-L. M., Katz, Y. J., & Berant, E. (2021). The contribution of therapeutic horseback riding to the improvement of executive functions and self-esteem among children with ADHD. *Journal of Attention Disorders, 25*(12), 1743–1753. https://doi.org/10.1177/1087054720925898

Balluerka, N., Muela, A., Amiano, N., & Caldentey, M. A. (2014). Influence of animal-assisted therapy (AAT) on the attachment representations of youth in residential care. *Children and Youth Services Review, 42*, 103–109. https://doi.org/10.1016/j.childyouth.2014.04.007

Bass, M. M., Duchowny, C. A., & Llabre, M. M. (2009). The effect of therapeutic horseback riding on social functioning in children with autism. *Journal of Autism and Developmental Disorders, 39*, 1261–1267.

Beck, J. S. (2011). *Cognitive behavior therapy: Basics and beyond* (2nd ed., pp. xix, 391). Guilford Press.

Binder, A. J., Parish-Plass, N., Kirby, M., Winkle, M., Skwerer, D. P., Ackerman, L., Brosig, C., Coombe, W., Delisle, E., Enders-Slegers, M.-J., Fowler, J.-A., Hey, L., Howell, T., Kaufmann, M., Kienast, M., Kinoshita, M., Ngai, D., & Wijnen, B. (2024). Recommendations for uniform terminology in animal-assisted services (AAS). *Human-Animal Interactions, 12*(1), 1–10. https://doi.org/10.1079/hai.2024.0003

Bruns, E. J., Kerns, S. E. U., Pullmann, M. D., Hensley, S. W., Lutterman, T., & Hoagwood, K. (2016). Research, data, and evidence-based treatment use in state behavioral health systems, 2001–2012. *Psychiatric Services (Washington, D.C.), 67*(5), 496–503. https://doi.org/10.1176/appi.ps.201500014

CDC. (2022, June 3). *Data and statistics on children's mental health.* Centers for Disease Control and Prevention. https://www.cdc.gov/childrensmentalhealth/data.html

Contreras-Aguilar, M. D., Henry, S., Coste, C., Tecles, F., Escribano, D., Cerón, J. J., & Hausberger, M. (2019). Changes in saliva analytes correlate with horses' behavioural reactions to an acute stressor: A pilot study. *Animals, 9*, 993. [CrossRef] [PubMed].

Dietz, T. J., Davis, D., & Pennings, J. (2012). Evaluating animal-assisted therapy in group treatment for child sexual abuse. *Journal of Child Sexual Abuse, 21*(6), 665–683.

Dodge, K. A., Prinstein, M. J., Evans, A. C., Ahuvia, I. L., Alvarez, K., Beidas, R. S., ... & Shaw, D. S. (2024). Population mental health science: Guiding principles and initial agenda. American Psychologist, 79(6), 805–823. https://doi.org/10.1037/amp0001334

Fristad, M. A., Verducci, J. S., Walters, K., & Young, M. E. (2009). Impact of multifamily psychoeducational psychotherapy in treating children aged 8 to 12 years with mood disorders. *Archives of General Psychiatry, 66*(9), 1013–1021.

Fuller-Lovins, S., Kanamori, Y., Myers, C., & Cornelius-White, J. (2023). The effectiveness of equine-assisted mental health interventions for youth: A meta-analysis of controlled studies. *Adolescent Research Review, 8*, 1–12. https://doi.org/10.1007/s40894-023-00209-9

Gabriels, R. L., Agnew, J. A., Holt, K. D., Shoffner, A., Zhaoxing, P., Ruzzano, S., & Mesibov, G. (2012). Pilot study measuring the effects of therapeutic horseback riding on school-age children and adolescents with autism spectrum disorders. *Research in Autism Spectrum Disorders, 6*(2), 578–588.

Garbacz, L. L., Brown, D. M., Spee, G. A., Polo, A. J., & Budd, K. S. (2014). Establishing treatment fidelity in evidence-based parent training programs for externalizing disorders in children and adolescents. *Clinical Child and Family Psychology Review, 17*(3), 230–247. https://doi.org/10.1007/s10567-014-0166-2

Hawes, M. T., Szenczy, A. K., Klein, D. N., Hajcak, G., & Nelson, B. D. (2022). Increases in depression and anxiety symptoms in adolescents and young adults during the COVID-19 pandemic. *Psychological Medicine, 52*(14), 3222–3230.

Hoagwood, K. E., & Kelleher, K. J. (2020). A Marshall Plan for children's mental health after COVID-19. *Psychiatric Services, 71*(12), 1216–1217. https://doi.org/10.1176/appi.ps.202000258

Hoagwood, K. E., Acri, M., Morrissey, M., & Peth-Pierce, R. (2016). Animal-assisted therapies for youth with or at risk for mental health problems: A systematic review. *Applied Developmental Science, 21*(1), 1–13.

Hoagwood, K. E., Acri, M., Morrissey, M., Peth-Pierce, R., Seibel, L., Seag, D. E., et al. (2021). Adaptive riding incorporating cognitive-behavioral elements for youth with anxiety: An exploratory randomized controlled study. *Human-Animal Interaction Bulletin, 9*(3), 60–78.

Hoagwood, K., Vincent, A., Acri, M., Morrissey, M., Seibel, L., Guo, F., et al. (2022). Reducing anxiety and stress among youth in a CBT-based equine-assisted adaptive riding program. *Animals, 12*(19), 2491.

Ingoldsby, E. M. (2010). Review of interventions to improve family engagement and retention in parent and child mental health programs. *Journal of Child and Family Studies, 19*(5), 629–645. https://doi.org/10.1007/s10826-009-9350-2

Jones, M. G., Rice, S. M., & Cotton, S. M. (2019). Incorporating animal-assisted therapy in mental health treatments for adolescents: A systematic review of canine assisted psychotherapy. *PLoS One, 14*(1), e0210761.

Kamioka, H., Okada, S., Tsutani, K., Park, H., Okuizumi, H., Handa, S., et al. (2014). Effectiveness of animal-assisted therapy: A systematic review of randomized controlled trials. *Complementary Therapies in Medicine, 22*(2), 371–390.

Kazdin, A. E. (2019). Annual Research Review: Expanding mental health services through novel models of intervention delivery. *Journal of Child Psychology and Psychiatry, and Allied Disciplines, 60*(4), 455–472. https://doi.org/10.1111/jcpp.12937

Lac, V. (2023). Chapter 6: Breathing into relationships: The HERD Institute approach to equine-facilitated psychotherapy. In C. Meola (Ed.), *Integrating horses into healing* (pp. 81–93). Academic Press. https://doi.org/10.1016/B978-0-443-19195-4.00017-0

London, M. D., Mackenzie, L., Lovarini, M., Dickson, C., & Alvarez-Campos, A. (2020). Animal assisted therapy for children and adolescents with autism spectrum disorder: Parent perspectives. *Journal of Autism and Developmental Disorders, 50*(12), 4492–4503. https://doi.org/10.1007/s10803-020-04512-5

Murthy, V. H. (2022). The mental health of minority and marginalized young people: An opportunity for action. *Public Health Reports, 137*(4), 613–616. https://doi.org/10.1177/00333549221102390

Naber, A., Völk, M., Hediger, K., & Zink, R. (2023). Can equine communication via audible exhales improve the welfare of therapy horses? – A pilot practice project. *Human-Animal Interactions, 11*, 0039. https://doi.org/10.1079/hai.2023.0039

Pendry, P., Smith, A. N., & Roeter, S. M. (2014). Randomized trial examines effects of equine facilitated learning on adolescents' basal cortisol levels. *Human-Animal Interaction Bulletin*, 2014. https://doi.org/10.1079/hai.2014.0003

Pendry, P., Carr, A. M., & Vandagriff, J. L. (2018). Adolescents' affective and physiological regulation shape negative behavior during challenging equine assisted learning activities. *Frontiers in Veterinary Science, 5*, 300. https://doi.org/10.3389/fvets.2018.00300

Peters, B. C., Pan, Z., Christensen, H., & Gabriels, R. L. (2022). Self-regulation mediates therapeutic horseback riding social functioning outcomes in youth with autism spectrum disorder. *Frontiers in Pediatrics, 10*, 884054. https://doi.org/10.3389/fped.2022.884054

Practicewise. (2024, May 22). *What works in children's mental health.* https://practicewise.com

Roberts, H., & Honzel, N. (2020). The effectiveness of equine-facilitated psychotherapy in adolescents with serious emotional disturbances. *Anthrozoös, 33*(1), 133–144. https://doi.org/10.1080/08927936.2020.1694317

Seibel, L., Seag, D. E. M., Guo, F., Morrissey, M., Peth-Pierce, R., Acri, M., Hamovitch, E. K., Horwitz, S., & Hoagwood, K. E. (2021). Adaptive riding incorporating cognitive behavioral elements for youth with anxiety: Fidelity outcomes. *Human-Animal Interaction Bulletin, 9*(3), 45–59.

Staudt, M. (2007). Treatment engagement with caregivers of at-risk children: Gaps in research and conceptualization. *Journal of Child and Family Studies, 16*(2), 183–196. https://doi.org/10.1007/s10826-006-9077-2

Trujillo, K. C., Kuo, G. T., Hull, M. L., Ingram, A. E., & Thurstone, C. C. (2020). Engaging adolescents: Animal assisted therapy for adolescents with psychiatric and substance use disorders. *Journal of Child and Family Studies, 29*(2), 307–314.

Vincent, A., & Farkas, K. J. (2017). Application of attachement theory to equine-facilitated therapy. *Society Register, 1*(1), 7–22. https://doi.org/10.14746/sr.2017.1.1.02

Vincent, A., Peth-Pierce, R. M., Morrissey, M. A., Acri, M. C., Guo, F., Seibel, L., & Hoagwood, K. E. (2021). Evaluation of a modified bit device to obtain saliva samples from horses. *Veterinary Sciences, 8*(10), 232. https://doi.org/10.3390/vetsci8100232

Vincent, A., & Peth-Pierce, R. (2023). Around the arena: Equine-assisted services' foundation in understanding human-horse interactions. In *The Routledge international handbook of human-animal interactions and anthrozoology*. Routledge. https://doi.org/10.4324/9781032153346

Walter, H. J., Bukstein, O. G., Abright, A. R., Keable, H., Ramtekkar, U., Ripperger-Suhler, J., & Rockhill, C. (2020). Clinical practice guideline for the assessment and treatment of children and adolescents with anxiety disorders. *Journal of the American Academy of Child & Adolescent Psychiatry, 59*(10), 1107–1124.

Warwick, H., Reardon, T., Cooper, P., Murayama, K., Reynolds, S., Wilson, C., & Creswell, C. (2017). Complete recovery from anxiety disorders following Cognitive Behavior Therapy in children and adolescents: A meta-analysis. *Clinical Psychology Review, 52*, 77–91. https://doi.org/10.1016/j.cpr.2016.12.002

Wei, C., & Kendall, P. C. (2014). Parental involvement: Contribution to childhood anxiety and its treatment. *Clinical Child and Family Psychology Review, 17*(4), 319–339. https://doi.org/10.1007/s10567-014-0170-6

Wharton, T., Whitworth, J., Macauley, E., & Malone, M. (2019). Pilot testing a manualized equine-facilitated cognitive processing therapy (EF-CPT) intervention for PTSD in veterans. *Psychiatric Rehabilitation Journal, 42*(3), 268–276. https://doi.org/10.1037/prj0000359

Wilson, K., Buultjens, M., Monfries, M., & Karimi, L. (2016). Equine-assisted psychotherapy for adolescents experiencing depression and/or anxiety: A therapist's perspective. *Clinical Child Psychology and Psychiatry, 22*(1), 16–33.

From Disability to Advantage: Equine-Assisted Therapy (EAT) in Children with Attention-Deficit/ Hyperactivity Disorder

Tal-li Matild Aviv

Introduction

Attention-deficit/hyperactivity disorder (ADHD) is a developmental disorder that manifests in childhood, characterized by inattention, easy distractibility, hyperactivity, and enhanced impulsivity. This chapter will focus on two specific areas of neurological dysfunction: difficulties in executive function and cognitive sensory processing, as well as challenges in regulating behavior according to environmental and sensory information. The rationale for therapeutic riding for children with ADHD is based on the accumulated knowledge of impairments in executive functions and sensory processing. Horseback riding engages both executive functions and the sensory system, offering therapeutic benefits. This chapter will present studies supporting the effectiveness of therapeutic riding, discussing its clinical advantages for children with ADHD, and providing recommendations for future treatments.

ADHD Behavioral Components and Diagnosis

ADHD is a common neurodevelopmental disorder among children and adolescents, disturbing their functioning and development, and may continue into their adult life. This disorder occurs in 5% of the Western population, though only 2.5% of adults suffer from it (American Psychiatric Association, 2013). The disorder can present with the following key characteristics:

T.-l. M. Aviv (✉)
Jerusalem College in the Department of Education, Bayit VeGan, Jerusalem, Israel

Y. Neria et al. (eds.), *Guide to Equine Assisted Therapy*,
https://doi.org/10.1007/978-3-031-74426-6_13

1. Inattentiveness—which can be expressed by inattention to detail, an inability to maintain attention, difficulty completing tasks, the challenges which accompany planning and organization, difficulty returning equipment and even losing it, etc.
2. Hyperactive-impulsiveness—which can be expressed by motoric restlessness, difficulty in quietly going about leisure activities, excessive speech, impatience when waiting in line, self-restraint, etc.

The child needs to have exhibited symptoms prior to the age of 12, both at home and at school, to receive a diagnosis of ADHD. ADHD is twice as common among boys as girls, and in adults, it occurs at a ratio of approximately 1.6:1 (APA, 2013). The basis of the disorder is neurological, but there are also genetic and environmental factors (Mohammadi et al., 2012). In brain imaging studies (fMRI) of those suffering from ADHD, an abnormal structure of the brain was observed in the frontal areas (Bush, 2011; Krain & Castellanos, 2006), and hyperactivity was found in the areas activated by the executive functions (Cortese, 2012), which often indicates low functions in tests of different aspects of the executive functions (Tarver et al., 2014). This is connected to abnormal development, impairment of maturity of the brain, and hypoactivity in prefrontal areas, related to cognitive, emotional, judgmental, and attentional functions (Acosta et al., 2009; APA, 2013; Cortese, 2012). In these studies, it seems that the developmental delay in the maturation of the brain was 2–3 years and was reflected in the thickness of the cerebral cortex. The difference was especially noticeable in the frontal cortex, which is related to executive functions in general and attention functions in particular.

Self-Worth

The experience of self-worth is subjective and develops because of a combination of innate ability and the environment in which the child lives. A child's subjective experience is a central axis in the development of their self-worth. Circular interaction patterns are formed between the reactions of the environment (parents, teachers, friends) and the difficulties that the child has. For example, a child who has trouble tidying his room may receive a negative reaction to his conduct from the parent, thus creating a negative connection to the event. As a result, the child is considered incompetent, and their self-esteem will be damaged. This, in turn, will cause a negative cycle to develop. The atmosphere which develops in the family is saturated with stress and criticism, which do not contribute to the building of positive self-worth. An encouraging response from the parent and assistance in arranging the room may encourage a positive cycle (Palombo, 2001).

Family Impact

Many parents of children with ADHD seek help due to feeling helpless in managing their child's challenges. Motor restlessness, organizational difficulties, and issues with planning and self-restraint can create substantial friction between parents and their children. Often, these parents adopt an authoritarian parenting style, marked by high demands and low responsiveness to their child's needs (Belsky et al., 1996). This style emphasizes discipline without openness to negotiation (Baumrind, 1991) and often results in impatience with the child's behavioral challenges. Consequently, such parents are less emotionally supportive and may resort to physical punishment to manage their child's behavior (Alizaden et al., 2007).

The child's difficulties also strain relationships with siblings, leading to conflicts when the child with ADHD inadvertently oversteps boundaries due to impulse control issues. Siblings may not understand why their ADHD sibling receives different treatment and may sometimes reject them (Barkley, 1997a, b). Furthermore, extended family gatherings can become sources of tension, as relatives often criticize parenting methods and offer unsolicited advice, prompting parents to limit their participation in such events.

Within the immediate family, disagreements on parenting strategies can cause friction between parents, leading to increased stress and potential breakdowns in their relationship. Over time, this stress can escalate, resulting in significant marital dissatisfaction.

Academic Performance

The educational system and the extended family may criticize the parents' education methods and their child's behavior. The school reports to them regarding poor academic achievements and when their child has trouble functioning as a student, as well as when their child has disagreements with other children or when their child bothers their friends. The process of identifying the child's problem can sometimes be delayed due to a misdiagnosis of learning disabilities or other learning-related issues, even though the behaviors described reflect the prominent ADHD symptom of hyperactive-impulsiveness.

Executive Functions and ADHD

Up until now, we have examined the symptoms and external manifestations of ADHD, but what is at the core of the problem? Research indicates that one of the primary difficulties among individuals with ADHD lies in executive functioning (Barkley, 2014). Executive functions encompass a broad range of cognitive processes, including planning, working memory, attention, inhibition, self-monitoring, self-regulation, and initiative. These functions are essential for adaptive behavior in society, allowing individuals to set and achieve goals. They represent the summative and integrative activities in the frontal areas of the brain. Diamond (2012) identified three core components of executive functioning: inhibition, working memory, and cognitive flexibility.

Executive functions are crucial for self-regulation in cognitive, emotional, and behavioral areas. They enable a person to plan and organize information using working memory, develop activities based on that information, and evaluate those activities. The ability to be attentive is a fundamental executive function essential for goal-oriented behavior, which requires recognition, understanding, planning, and action. In other words, success in both social and academic contexts depends on performing executive functions as expected by the child's environment.

Damage to executive functions can appear in a wide range of neurodevelopmental disorders, including ADHD (Barkley, 2014). Studies have documented high levels of impaired executive functions (between 89% and 98%) among children with ADHD (Barkley & Murphy, 2011). A comprehensive meta-analysis of 83 studies found that individuals with ADHD showed impairment in a broad range of executive function components to at least a moderate degree (Willcutt et al., 2005). Barkley (1997a, b) argues that difficulty in self-regulation is the core issue, focusing on behavioral response inhibition. Response inhibitions manifest as three different internal interaction processes when an event occurs:

1. The person's automatic initial response is inhibition to allow an internal cognitive process to occur.
2. This process assists in deciding on a desired response to the event.
3. To think about the desired response without acting impulsively, the person needs to be attentive and not distracted.

Impaired behavioral response inhibition disrupts the integration of other executive functions: self-regulation, self-monitoring, and working memory. Higher self-awareness of one's emotions and behaviors enhances the ability to foresee future events, analyze situations in retrospect, and make decisions. Problems with behavioral response inhibition can lead to outbursts, inappropriate speech, or uncalculated behaviors. A child with this impairment might frequently hear, "Think before you act… What were you thinking?"

Difficulty in regulating emotions often accompanies inhibition problems, leading to uncontrollable emotional outbursts, such as laughter ending in tears or anger escalating to violence. Issues with working memory can impede a child's ability to remember a sequence of tasks, while problems with planning and organizing make task completion difficult. These challenges explain why children with ADHD may struggle to complete tasks, forget parts of their assignments, and have trouble organizing their surroundings. Affected working memory can make it difficult for the child to keep the sequence of events in mind, leading to perceptions of irresponsibility or insincerity. This often results in the child being asked, "But what did I do?" causing frustration in those around them. Deficits in the executive function of initiating can make these children seem passive and unable to solve problems they encounter.

Sensory Processing and Modulation and ADHD

Attention is defined as the process of focusing concentration on relevant stimuli while blocking out irrelevant stimuli. Sensory processing is the neurological organization of sensory stimuli to sort said stimuli based on their relevance (Eggen & Kauchak, 2004). Sensory processing is a person's ability to receive information via the senses, to integrate it, and to respond to the information received from the environment via the sensory system by acclimating to it both motorically and behaviorally (Ayres, 1972). Any deficiency in the sensory processing refers to the inability of the nervous system and the brain to organize and process in an integrative manner the information flow received from the various sensory systems (touch, movement, smell, taste, sight, and hearing) and to the system's inability to provide a person with clear and precise information about themselves and about the world around them, which are all necessary to a person's ability to form appropriate responses. A mistaken interpretation of stimuli from one's body and environment can lead to an inability to adapt and difficulty in handling external demands. Such a person would also have trouble being flexible enough to handle the sensory challenges they would meet daily (Hern & Hynd, 1992; Mangeot et al., 2001; Swaab-Barneveld et al., 2000). A connection was also found between ADHD and problems with muscle tone, coordination and gross and fine motor skills, weaknesses with vestibular processing, and in most areas of praxis or motor planning (APA, 2013; Cortese, 2012; Hern & Hynd, 1992; Mulligan, 1996).

Difficulty with sensory modulation and processing can provide an additional point of view, one which can explain the behavioral problems of a child with ADHD. Sensory modulation is part of sensory processing (Ayres, 1972; Lane et al., 2000), and it is a basic human ability which allows people to create meaningful interactions with their environment. It is manifested in the person's ability to control the quality and intensity of his or her reactions to external and internal stimuli such that an optimal range of implementation and socially acceptable compatibility with challenges can be achieved through an ability to maintain both an internal and an interpersonal dialogue (Bronson, 2000; Lane et al., 2000). Kids who have sensory modulation problems will have trouble following directions or initiating or ceasing a behavior, depending on the circumstances. They may have trouble regulating the intensity, frequency, and duration of their behavior, as well as delaying gratification and implementing socially appropriate or acceptable behavior with the help of external monitoring (Bronson, 2000). They may have trouble adjusting their emotional reactions, planning based on an understanding of cause and effect, and solving problems on their own.

Williamson and Anzalone (2001) suggested a model which assumes that one's natural ability for sensory processing and modulation of reactions is based on four basic observable functions. This model can also support and explain the connection between ADHD and difficulty in sensory modulation and processing.

The basic functions are as follows:

1. Awareness—The child's ability to maintain optimal awareness and to be able to transition between a state of sleep and wakefulness.
2. Attention—The ability to selectively focus on a stimulus or a desired assignment while filtering out any unwanted stimuli which are irrelevant to the situation, and the ability to transfer attention from one stimulus to another in as flexible a manner as possible.
3. Affect—Usually a sensation creates emotional reactions which teach us, to a certain degree, how a child experiences a specific sensory experience and how the child subjectively deals with it.
4. Action—An action which is planned out and goal-oriented. Such an action involves the organization of thought processes to operate purposefully.

These four functions contribute to a young child's behavioral organization and, together, create the core of the child's self-regulation. A child who has a sensory processing deficiency may find it difficult to muster optimal excitation and therefore may have trouble focusing on a goal and acting accordingly. In addition, when a child has trouble reacting to sensory stimulation in an adaptive manner, he or she may display emotional responses which are either overblown or superficial.

Treatments for ADHD

Interventions at an early age can be of great significance in lessening the risk of a wider range of challenges at a later age, which can affect quality of life.

Medical treatment constitutes an important part of the strategy for comprehensive treatment in children with ADHD. The medications used are stimulants (methylphenidate, dexmethylphenidate, and others) and non-stimulant drugs (such as atomoxetine) (Acosta et al., 2009; Cortese, 2012). The role of stimulants is to block the reuptake of dopamine and norepinephrine into the presynaptic neuron (Biederman & Spencer, 1999). This leads to a decrease in the intensity of the symptoms (including hyperactivity, inattentiveness, and impulsiveness), increases cognitive processing, and improves academic achievements. It has been found that the lessening of symptoms improves the ability of the parents and the family in general to cope with the child (Tancred & Greeff, 2015). Alongside reports of the improvement in the child's situation due to medical treatment, there have been studies that report that 20–30% of children do not report any significant change, and 4–10% of children were reported as suffering from side effects which make it difficult to continue taking the medication (trouble sleeping, changes in appetite, stomachaches, headaches, and agitation) (Santosh & Taylor, 2000). Medical treatment is an important platform for treatment but does not provide an all-encompassing answer to this complicated problem.

Supplementary treatments to the medication have been developed using different forms of intervention, which can be split into three main groups: parental guidance, behavioral intervention in the classroom, and behavioral work within a group of peers.

The goal of this comprehensive work is to create a structure and routine for the child, to prepare him or her for changes, to create opportunities for him or her to succeed, to give immediate rewards, and to identify future stumbling blocks. All of these allow for an environment which encourages adaptive behavior. The work is most efficient when all three fronts work in parallel—parents, teachers, and children—along with professionals from different areas of expertise.

Even though there is a broad base of knowledge about the effects of medication and comprehensive intervention, it has been found that they are limited in their long-term effects (Climie & Mastoras, 2015), and, though it is possible to improve the symptoms, it is difficult to maintain the improvement in the long term (Jensen et al., 2007). Additionally, the different interventions, including medications, do not necessarily treat problems with executive functions (such as problems with planning and organization) or sensory processing.

Executive Function-Focused Interventions

In the past decade, a focused intervention for the treatment of executive functions has been developed based on the understanding that the core of ADHD is how the deficits of the executive functions affect the child's ability to manage his or her emotional, academic, and social life (Halperin & Schulz, 2006; Halperin & Healey, 2011). A treatment that focuses on executive functions has the potential to lessen the intensity of ADHD symptoms, to positively influence the functional aspect of development, and as a result to lessen the parents' stress (Graziano et al., 2011). Focused treatment is not a modification of the child's behavior but rather a focused change in executive functions while receiving feedback from one's surroundings which allows for the continuation of that change (Tamm et al., 2014). Despite the effectiveness of executive function-focused interventions, they do not provide a sufficient solution for motor skills and the processing of sensory regulations which are linked to ADHD.

Equine-assisted therapy (EAT) is executive function-focused work which involves motor and sensory skills (Aviv et al., 2021). During the equine-assisted therapy session, the rider receives feedback from the horse regarding his or her behavior toward it, which allows the rider to improve his or her progress as well as improve upon executive functions. The horse's feedback is mediated through a counselor, thereby eliminating criticism of the rider. The result is that success is experienced by the rider in a manner that is different from what he or she has experienced in previous settings.

The Clinical Advantages of Equine-Assisted Therapy in Children with ADHD

Levinson (1969) was the first therapist to use animals as a treatment method, asserting the healing power of animals and claiming that they provide a natural object onto which one can project, which is better than projecting onto inanimate objects. Animals are available, mobile, active, and can express affection (Karen, 1994). Making a connection with a living creature allows for a wide behavioral range as well as creating patterns for mutual relationships. On the one hand, the patient projects his or her emotions and feelings onto the animal, while on the other hand, the animal provides the patient with his or her need for physical contact, friendship, and unconditional acceptance. For a child with ADHD, working with animals constitutes a space with no criticism, which strengthens the child's sense of self-worth.

Equine-assisted therapy is a by-product of animal therapy. It is a psychotherapeutic process which is assisted by the incorporation of horses as a treatment method, and it combines work using different aspects: physical, emotional, and interpersonal relationships. The therapeutic process includes activities that are connected to horses: riding, taking care of the horse, working in the stable, and training the horse (as per the definition provided by the North American Association of Riding for the Handicapped—NARH).

Why Equine Therapy?

People commonly see a horse as an animal with grace that is vulnerable, strong, patient, noble, and compassionate. It is a symbol which evokes strong emotional intensity. The horse's qualities are all utilized for the therapeutic process. A horse is naturally a type of prey, and living in a herd provides it with a sense of protection and safety. Living in a herd with a hierarchy means that the horse adapts itself to suit its place in the herd, and it communicates with the other horses using its body (Smith-Osborne & Selby, 2010). Despite its need to be close to the herd, the horse is sensitive to its own personal space and communicates with others in order to maintain a comfortable distance between them. The horse's sensitivity to others is utilized when communicating with the patient. As a survival instinct, the horse reacts to the rider in an immediate and constant manner. As a result, the rider needs to learn to be sensitive to the horse and to communicate with it in an exact fashion while being aware of the messages that the horse is transmitting.

A child with ADHD who comes to a horse farm will be inundated with powerful physical stimuli (smell, touch, and unfamiliar noises). All of the work that needs to be done on a farm and specifically with a horse will require the child to pay attention and integrate executive functions. The child will receive a lot of information through his or her senses, but due to the difficulty in sensory processing, he or she may have trouble adapting their reactions to their surroundings and to the horse.

Equine-assisted therapy for children with ADHD focuses on improving executive functions while paying attention to sensory aspects.

Equine-Assisted Therapy's Contribution to Improving Executive Functions

During equine-assisted therapy, similar to focused interventions for treating executive functions, the child is tasked with activities that engage various executive functions. To avoid confusing the horse, it is crucial for the child to learn several skills: planning actions, organizing before execution, paying attention to the surroundings, preparing based on the environment, initiating movement, planning and organizing motor behavior, remembering necessary actions and how to perform them, emotional self-regulation and inhibition, and monitoring actions for correction.

The challenges faced by the child are specifically tailored to their individual abilities, ensuring that tasks are not compared to those of others. Exercises are built incrementally, with difficulty increasing gradually to provide a continuous challenge and build trust. These guidelines are essential for successful focused interventions in treating executive functions.

Inhibition, which is a core component according to Barkley (2000), is a central player in the riding process. The self-awareness that develops while riding is a very important part of the inhibition process and provides the ability to foresee and analyze, retrospectively, the decision-making process. Since a horse cannot understand double meanings but does understand the rider's body language, horseback riding requires that the child find a way to be as precise as possible in his or her communications with the horse. This raises the child's awareness of his or her processes—either via the horse's reaction or through the counselor's mediation. In the unique circumstance of equine-assisted therapy, the rider receives immediate feedback from the horse, and through the counselor's mediation, the rider practices correcting his or her performance of the exercise. Over time, there will be a generalization that will be expressed by the ability to monitor oneself and the application of the same principles when performing similar tasks. The counselor is there to help the rider with complicated tasks. Correcting one's performance of a task strengthens one's feeling of success, raises the rider's self-efficacy and allows one to raise the level of difficulty. In order to improve one's interaction with the horse, we will choose a horse that can adapt to being around a lot of people, that is calm and has a stable temperament. In this way, the control over the reactions to external stimuli is transferred to internal factors which have internal expressions. It can be assumed that when internal factors develop which can inhibit a person's reactions, that person's executive functioning will be durable.

In addition, working with the horse makes the child more flexible in his or her ability to transition. Because the horse is sensitive to its surroundings, it is likely to react to what is happening nearby which does not necessarily have any connection to the rider. The horse's reactions will place the rider in new and varied situations which he or she will have to deal with by being flexible and by shifting from one situation to another as fluidly as possible. This will reinforce the child's awareness when making a plan and when strategizing the management of that plan.

As a result of working on executive functions, the child's functional toolbox becomes more stabilized, along with reinforcing the motivation which allows continued development in both the present and the future (Maeir et al., 2014).

In addition to working on practical executive function-focused interventions, the child also works on meta-cognition strategies. The counselor teaches the child to think about his or her actions and about the horse's reactions and, based on that, how to control his or her work. Adapting the work to the child's abilities helps to minimize feelings of frustration, adds to the enjoyment of the activity, and increases motivation.

Equine-Assisted Therapy and Improving Sensory Regulation and Processing

To describe equine-assisted therapy's contribution to sensory regulation and processing, we will use two categories which refer to the expressions of difficulty in sensory processing which affect children with ADHD (Miller et al., 2007).

Sensory Regulation Deficiency

Sensory Hyper-Reactivity

People who suffer from hyper-reactivity react with more-than-usual intensity and longer duration to various stimuli. This prevents the person from reacting effectively to the situation, and it stands out when the person is in a new situation or making a transition. A person's reaction is involuntary, physiological, and subconscious. The feeling of not being able to control a stimulus increases the intensity of the reaction. The range of behavior can span oppositional behavior, aggressiveness, impulsiveness, passiveness, and abstention.

People who suffer from hyper-reactivity need to feel in control in order to lessen the intensity of their sensory reaction (Miller-Kuhaneck et al., 2007). Horseback riding increases the feeling of control, and the rider usually learns to control his or her reactions to many different stimuli through his or her connection with the horse and the environment. As a result of this sense of control, the rider seemingly learns to generalize his or her reactions to sensory stimuli. In addition, the rider's intense reaction to stimuli will garner feedback from the horse, who will "teach" the child how to touch it appropriately. When the child does so successfully, he or she will experience greater self-control and greater control over the intensity of stimuli.

Sensory Sub-Reactivity

People who suffer from sub-reactivity do not react to sensory stimuli and have trouble identifying new sensory information. Their lack of awareness of stimuli can lead to apathy. They seem not to be motivated to initiate anything or to investigate the world. Their difficulty is not a lack of motivation but a failure to precisely perceive the sensory stimulus to which they were exposed. At times, in order to respond to a stimulus, they will have to feel it in an extreme manner. Their behavior is characterized by a hesitation to be involved, a lack of attention or concentration, and they are lost in their own inner world. Often their observers will treat them as lazy and lacking motivation. Since they require a heightened awareness, with which their observers have a hard time providing them, they display difficulty in tactile diagnosis and struggle with body image and clumsiness. These difficulties often lead to organizational challenges.

The interaction with the horse and its surroundings exposes the rider to the intense stimuli that he or she needs. The pungent odor, the contact with the horse's body, and the movement of the horse provide intense stimuli. The exposure to these intense stimuli allows the rider to be in a higher state of awareness than he or she is used to, thereby creating a base for learning functions such as sensory regulation, curiosity, initiation, etc. The interaction with various sensory stimuli allows the rider to develop a higher awareness of his or her body and to feel control over his or her body and the surrounding environment, all of which will affect his or her planning and organization.

Sensory Search

The child displays an unquenchable desire to have a sensory experience and is therefore constantly busy with activities that will expose him or her to strong sensory experiences (such as spicy food and loud noise). Due to his or her need for an intense sensory experience, the child may have trouble maintaining distance from others and may behave in an intrusive manner. This can lead to rejection and difficulty in social situations. The child's behavior may not be cautious but rather impulsive, and he or she will sometimes be seen as demanding and attention-seeking. Their behavior, which leads them to take things to the extreme, can negatively affect their attentiveness. They are often seen as children with disciplinary problems. Precise sensory stimuli, which are focused on the child's needs, can have an organizing and regulating effect on him or her. The horse naturally allows the child to use relatively strong physical contact, due to its large body and thick skin, but it is important to the horse to maintain its personal space, and it will react clearly and obviously to any overt intrusion of that space. The connection with the horse can provide the child with the strong physical contact that he or she needs, but at the same time can teach the child boundaries and the necessary space he or she should maintain when near others. With the counselor's mediation of its reactions, the horse will teach the rider what distance it needs to feel relaxed and to cooperate with the rider. The child needs to plan his or her actions better, and the child's body awareness will assist him or her in maintaining the horse's personal space without making the horse uncomfortable.

A precise and specific sensory stimulus can have an organizing and regulating effect. Equine-assisted therapy can affect the ability to process information via the senses (sight, hearing, taste, and smell). In order for the child to succeed at horseback riding, he or she will learn to observe their body's precise proprioceptive sensations in order to direct their reactions in an exact manner as well as to regulate those reactions. Part of the learning process is that the counselor exposes the rider to specific stimuli in a gradual manner. For example: making physical contact with different parts of the horse's body while the horse is walking or running, the intensity with which the rider holds the reins, vision, and planning. It can be assumed that the child's focus on a particular stimulus will increase his or her ability to organize sensory information and to react in an appropriate manner such that he or she will experience success upon completing the tasks at hand.

Motor-Based Sensory Disorder

This issue is divided into two sub-categories:

Balance

A difficulty producing willful movements and balance. People with this disorder suffer from an imbalance between flexibility and inflexibility in their body parts, trouble with their posture, and with correcting their movements in order to regain balance. This challenge is expressed in having trouble sitting down or standing up in a stable manner. They will have difficulty managing their movements as necessary. As a result, these people will avoid such movements altogether.

Studies have shown a connection between ADHD and problems with muscle tone, coordination, gross motor skills, and fine motor skills (APA, 2013). There are testimonies to the close connection between problems with gross and fine motor skills and attention-deficit disorders. Trouble with fine motor skills can be attributed to trouble with sensory processing and its sub-category of attention. In order to carry out fine motor actions, one needs to have an abundance of attention. The ability to maintain balance and stability is essential in order to succeed in functioning on a daily basis, and it requires an intact ability to pay attention.

Horseback riding is a motor activity requiring the rider to work with his or her own body, to have good posture, and to use their own pelvic motion in tandem with the horse's movements. In this way, riding provides the ability to trust and to improve one's posture while in motion or at rest. Most people who have trouble with their posture prefer to carry out their actions from a sitting position. Sitting on a horse is not passive; rather, it requires active movement, and therefore it constitutes an effective stimulus which promotes body awareness. This requires the rider to maintain good posture and balance in order not to fall off the horse. The rider also needs to process the physical stimuli from the horse's movements and learn to regulate his or her reaction to stimuli.

Diffraction

This is a difficulty in planning and managing new actions. It is difficult to assess the strength that has to be applied by a child who has trouble with diffraction, and as a result they are likely to start to break things. They may have trouble judging the amount of time they will need to complete a task; it will be challenging for them to come up with new ideas, and they will therefore respond with inflexibility. They will prefer to continue with familiar activities and not try new ones. Their working memory and sensory regulation may hurt their motor planning ability and may make it challenging for them to complete the required tasks.

While horseback riding in the arena, the rider is asked to plan out his or her actions. He or she learns to carry out motor tasks in a specific order and, in doing so, is able to get from one point to the next. Among other things, the rider learns to hold the reins in an efficient manner which will allow for precise communication with the horse, as well as how to regulate moving his or her legs while holding the reins, such that the horse will understand what is being asked of it. The rider also learns the importance of the order of his or her actions when caring for the horse, which allows the rider and the horse to form a partnership. The rider learns rules which he or she can put into practice while engaging in various activities with the horse. It can be assumed that these experiments will improve his or her ability to plan in other areas of his or her life as well.

The Contribution of the Emotional Aspect of Horseback Riding

The fact that the horse is a large animal raises different powerful emotions in the child, such as excitement, fear, and even frustration when he or she experiences difficulty in dealing with the horse. Working with the horse, with an emphasis on making a connection with it and maintaining effective communication with it, can make the child feel proud and can strengthen his or her self-confidence.

Brooks (2006) introduced the three-way model as a basis for equine-assisted therapy by which one can aspire to make a change. The three-way model considers interactions among the three participants, including messages from the horse to the rider or the counselor in reaction to these interactions. The horse is sensitive to human energy as expressed in a person's movements. This energy can be expressed in words or behavior and can take place between any two of the three participants.

Sudden movements can make the horse shy away due to the element of surprise as well as the horse's need to maintain a personal distance. The horse is a curious animal; therefore, a person who stays calm and is not aggressive will cause the horse to draw closer. The horse is also affected by the disparity between a person's words and their behavior, and it will usually react to the person's behavior. The horse's reactions are immediate, honest, and clear, and they hold no judgment. The horse feels comfortable when the person's emotions are authentic and their behavior is expressed in appropriate body language. The patient's relationship with the horse is not a one-sided affair; rather, it requires the creation of a sense of mutual security and mutual interaction. The counselor's role is to assist them in achieving this relationship. The horse has the natural ability to pick up on the rider's non-verbal communications as expressed through body language and mannerisms, and it can reflect the message that it has received—a kind of biofeedback—but without the counselor's help, the information that the horse reflects back cannot be utilized through the horse's behavior alone. The counselor observes the horse and the patient and uses his or her knowledge about horse behavior to understand the rider's behavior. The horse acts as a "mirror," bringing to the forefront a particular behavior on the part of the patient. As a result, the counselor will reflect to the patient his or her understandings of the horse. This will help the patient learn to behave toward the horse in a more precise manner using body language, which is the horse's language, and this will teach the patient to regulate his or her behavior and emotions and to respect the horse's boundaries. The rider experiences successes and receives immediate feedback from the horse. This style of work increases motivation.

Three-way work affects the rider's emotional world. The child makes a connection with the horse much in the same way as he or she makes a connection with the people around him or her. If the child feels insecure or lacks trust, this will be reflected in his or her relationship with the horse, and one of the goals of working with the horse will be dealing with that. Since the horse is not critical but reflects the rider's progress, the rider will feel more comfortable trying to change his or her patterns of behavior. The horse's authentic and immediate response gives one a feeling of validity that allows the patient to look at himself or herself and to try to reveal his or her inner world. The immediate and consistent responses of the horse are part of what allows the rider to build up trust and a sense of security in the horse and the process itself. Seeing the horse subjectively, as having feelings and needs of its own, teaches the rider to see others from their point of view and allows him or her to behave authentically and to develop the ability to be empathetic, which can be applied to other relationships as well.

The resilience paradigm emphasizes that each individual can develop an emotional resilience that can determine how a person will handle negative situations (Burt et al., 2008). This resilience is developed by giving the person positive feedback. A sense of belonging, self-worth, and independence can grow through the child's connection to his or her own strengths. Working with the horse strengthens the rider's resilience by assigning challenging tasks where the main focus is an optimal opportunity for success and encouragement of the rider's sense of capability. The rider feels that he or she is "helping" and caring for the horse. Horseback riding helps create a sense of autonomy and temper coping mechanisms, which in turn increases resilience and the ability to deal with "failures." Success and contact with the horse constitute a propulsion factor and increase the pleasure from the process itself.

In addition to the roles of the horse and the counselor in treating a child who suffers from ADHD, it is important to consider the contribution of the space in which the equine-assisted therapy occurs.

The Outdoor Space

The work is done in an open space, in nature or in a barn, in the horse's natural environment. This may be a contributing factor to the rider's sense of calm alongside the internal awareness which arises from contact with the horse. Since the horse is authentic and not judgmental, and since the work is done in an open space, in which there is less sense of formality, the therapeutic atmosphere of the experience is softened. Working in the horse's natural environment exposes the rider to the horse's various needs and draws the rider into caring for the horse over time and consistently, while at the same time delaying gratification. The consideration of the horse's needs requires the rider to inhibit his impulses and desires, and this contributes to the strengthening of inhibition. The rider learns to feel successful when making concessions and commitments to the horse. The permanent work environment is subject to natural changes, such as weather, shifts in the horse's mood, and other changes which are brought on by exposure to external stimuli. All of these changes provide a significant challenge for the counselor, who needs to maintain a feeling of stability and security for the patient, just as is needed in a traditional therapy environment. The open environment encourages flexibility and openness, but the counselor must create virtual borders in order to provide a sense of security. One way of creating such borders is with a set treatment plan and schedule and by providing clear guidelines for the other staff members to ensure the patient's privacy. Carlsson et al. (2014) discovered that the patient trusted the counselor because of working with the horse and agreed to bare their feelings in the barn as opposed to in an institution. They described the development of an authentic relationship between the patient and the therapeutic team. The therapeutic space is different from the environment in which a child with ADHD grows up, wherein he suffers from constant criticism and people are not satisfied with anything he does.

In summary, when a child experiences success, his or her executive functions improve, and his or her sensory processing and behavior improve as well, and then he or she receives positive feedback from the environment. The parents' distress then lessens, allowing them to develop a positive connection with their child.

Session Highlights

Safety During the first stage, the patient learns how to read the horse's body language for signs of displeasure and learns to maintain a safe distance between themselves and the horse. This requires planning, organization, working memory, and inhibition, combined with awareness and monitoring of the horse's body language.

Gripping the reins The reins are connected to a bit in the horse's mouth, which is a delicate and sensitive organ. To avoid hurting the horse and to ensure precise communication with the horse, it is essential to learn the proper grip on and use of the reins. While riding there can be several challenges:

A. Holding the reins too tightly, which will cause the horse to resist.
B. Holding the reins too loosely, to which the horse will not react.
C. Trouble holding the reins properly for an extended period of time as a result of difficulties in planning and organization.

Posture in the saddle There are stirrups attached to the saddle where the rider needs to place his or her feet. The better the rider's posture is and the more fluid it is, the better he or she will communicate with the horse using his or her body in the best way possible. The rider learns how to be aware of his or her posture and how to monitor it throughout the session in relation to what the horse wants to do.

Handling the horse Horseback riding combines work with the reins, the rider's legs, and the movement of the rider's pelvis. It is crucial to combine all of these movements in order to direct the horse to where the rider wants to go. During the session, a path is chosen, and, to succeed in planning and then executing the task, the patient will need to get organized on the horse, use his or her working memory in order to remember the instructions, inhibit his or her reactions, and regulate his or her emotions. After completing the task, the rider will need to review his or her actions and draw conclusions about the remainder of the work to be done. The counselor will be physically present near the rider and will interpret the horse's body language for him or her.

Caring for the horse
A. Brushing the horse with various types of brushes, as needed
B. Cleaning the hooves while raising the horse's leg
C. Filling bags of hay
D. Feeding the horse
E. Mucking out the stalls

These tasks require the patient to use executive functions, and the work done integrates the sensory domain as needed (hyper-reactivity and sub-reactivity).

Equine-assisted therapy contributes to children with ADHD in the following aspects: executive functions, sensory processing, creating successful experiences, and improving relationships.

Past Research

When equine-assisted therapy was first introduced, it focused mainly on children with physical disabilities such as cerebral palsy, but over time it has been extended to apply to children with emotional needs as well. Over the last 20 years, studies have been done judging the effect that equine-assisted therapy has on a variety of populations and specifically its effect on children with ADHD. In a systematic review (White et al., 2020), ten studies were found that met the researchers' requirements. The reported effect of equine-assisted therapy on physical, psychological, and behavioral symptoms in children with ADHD was investigated. The chosen studies indicate an improved sense of independence and self-esteem and the development of problem-solving skills and communication. Increased body awareness helped these children with sensory processing and improved their behavior.

In another systematic review (Helmer et al., 2021), 12 studies were found that met the researchers' requirements. Eight of these studies did not have a control group, and four of them had a randomized control group. Most of the studies investigated the effect that equine-assisted therapy has on the motoric, emotional, and psychological domains. The studies indicated that there was an improvement in physical functions, specifically executive functions, and an improvement in self-esteem. These improvements went beyond their work with the horses.

A comprehensive study found that after 20 riding sessions, there was an improvement in executive functions and sensory processing, self-esteem was elevated, and the mothers' stress level had lessened (Aviv, 2017; Aviv et al., 2021).

Conclusion

Though evidence exists regarding the positive effect that equine-assisted therapy may have among children with ADHD, there is a need for thorough research based on sound methodology, including control interventions, large enough samples, and standardized measurements. Furthermore, it is essential to set up treatment protocols for working with children with ADHD that specifically address the underlying basis of executive functions and difficulties with sensory processing and regulation.

References

Acosta, M. T., Arcos-Burgos, M., & Mueke, M. (2009). Attention deficit/hyperactivity disorder. In G. G. Berntson & J. T. Cacioppo (Eds.), *Handbook of neuroscience for the behavioral science* (pp. 1020–1042). Wiley.

Alizaden, H., Applequist, K. F., & Coolidge, F. L. (2007). Parental self-confidence, parenting styles, and corporal punishment in families of ADHD children in Iran. *Child Abuse and Neglect, 31*, 567–572. https://doi.org/10.1016/j.chiabu.2006.12.005

American Psychiatric Association [APA]. (2013). *Diagnostic and statistical manual of mental disorders: DSM-5* (5th ed.). Author.

Aviv, T. M. (2017). *The contribution of therapeutic riding and maternal attachment pattern to the improvement of executive function, sensory processing, the experience of self-esteem, the child's attachment pattern and the maternal distress level among children with ADHD* [Unpublished doctoral dissertation]. Bar-Ilan University.

Aviv, T. M., Katz, Y. J., & Berant, E. (2021). The contribution of therapeutic horseback riding to the improvement of executive functions and self-esteem among children with ADHD. *Journal of Attention Disorders, 25*(12), 1743–1753. https://doi.org/10.1177/1087054720925898

Ayres, A. J. (1972). *Sensory integration and learning disorders*. Western Psychological Services.

Barkley, R. A. (1997a). Behavioral inhibition, sustained attention, and executive functions: Constructing a unifying theory of ADHD. *Psychological Bulletin, 121*, 65–94. https://doi.org/10.1037/0033-2909.121.1.65

Barkley, R. A. (1997b). *Taking charge of ADHD: The complete, authoritative guide for parents*. Guilford.

Barkley, R. A. (2000). Genetics of childhood disorders: XVII. ADHD, Part 1: The executive functions and ADHD. *Journal of the American Academy of Child and Adolescent Psychiatry, 39*, 1064–1068. https://doi.org/10.1097/00004583-200008000-00025

Barkley, R. A. (2014). *Attention-deficit hyperactivity disorder: A handbook for diagnosis and treatment* (4th ed.). Guilford.

Barkley, R. A., & Murphy, K. R. (2011). The nature of executive function (EF) deficits in daily life activities in adults with ADHD and their relationship to performance on EF tests. *Journal of Psychopathology and Behavioral Assessment, 33*, 137–135. https://doi.org/10.1007/s10862-011-9217-x

Baumrind, D. (1991). The influence of parenting style on adolescent competence and substance use. *Journal of Early Adolescence, 11*, 56–95. https://doi.org/10.1177/0272431691111004

Belsky, J., Woodworth, S., & Crnic, K. (1996). Trouble in the second year: Three questions about family interaction. *Child Development, 67*, 556–578. https://doi.org/10.1111/j.1467-8624.1996.tb01751.x

Biederman, J., & Spencer, T. (1999). Attention-deficit/hyperactivity disorder (ADHD) as a noradrenergic disorder. *Biological Psychiatry, 46*, 1234–1242. https://doi.org/10.1016/S0006-3223(99)00192-4

Biederman, J., Monuteaux, M. C., Spencer, T., Wilens, T. E., & Faraone, S. V. (2009). Do stimulants protect against psychiatric disorders in youth with ADHD? A 10-year follow-up study. *Pediatrics, 124*, 71–78.

Bronson, M. B. (2000). *Self-regulation in early childhood: Nature and nurture*. Guilford Press.

Brooks, S. M. (2006). Animal-assisted psychotherapy and equine-facilitated psychotherapy. In N. B. Webb (Ed.), *Working with traumatized youth in child welfare*. Guilford.

Burt, K. B., Obradovic, J., Long, J. D., & Masten, A. S. (2008). The interplay of social competence and psychopathology over 20 years: Testing transactional and cascade models. *Child Development, 79*, 359–374. https://doi.org/10.1111/j.1467-8624.2007.01130.x

Bush, G. (2011). Cingulate, frontal and parietal cortical dysfunction in attention deficit hyperactivity disorder. *Biological Psychiatry, 69*, 1160–1167. https://doi.org/10.1016/j.biopsych.2011.01.022

Canning, G. (1973). *The occasional horseman*. Chaucer.

Carlsson, C., Nilsson-Ranta, D., & Træen, B. (2014). Equine-assisted social work as a mean for authentic relations between clients and staff human-animal interaction. *Human-Animal Interaction Bulletin, 2*(1), 19–38.

Climie, E. A., & Mastoras, S. M. (2015). ADHD in schools: Adopting a strengths-based perspective. *Canadian Psychology, 56*, 295–300. https://doi.org/10.1037/cap0000030

Cortese, S. (2012). The neurobiology and genetic of attention deficit/hyperactivity disorder (ADHD): What clinician should know. *European Journal of Paediatric Neurology, 16*, 422–433. https://doi.org/10.1016/j.ejpn.2012.01.009

Diamond, A. (2012). Activities and programs that improve children's executive function. *Current Directions in Psychological Science, 21*, 335–341. https://doi.org/10.1177/0963721412453722

Eggen, P., & Kauchak, D. (2004). *Educational psychology: Windows on classrooms*. Prentice Hall.

Graziano, P. A., McNamara, J. P., Geffken, G. R., & Reid, A. (2011). Severity of children's ADHD symptoms and parenting stress: A multiple mediation model of self regulation. *Journal of Abnormal Child Psychology, 39*, 1073–1083. https://doi.org/10.1007/s10802-011-9528-0

Halperin, J. M., & Healey, D. M. (2011). The influences of environmental enrichment, cognitive enhancement, and physical exercise on brain development: Can we alter the developmental trajectory of ADHD? *Neuroscience and Biobehavioral Reviews, 35*, 621–634. https://doi.org/10.1016/j.neubiorev.2010.07.006

Halperin, J. M., & Schulz, K. P. (2006). Revisiting the role of the prefrontal cortex in the pathophysiology of attention deficit/hyperactivity disorder. *Psychological Bulletin, 132*, 560–581. https://doi.org/10.1037/0033-2909.132.4.560

Helmer, A., Wechsler, T., & Gilboa, Y. (2021). Equine-assisted services for children with attention deficit/hyperactivity disorder: A systematic review. *Journal of Alternative and Complementary Medicine, 27*, 477–488. https://doi.org/10.1089/acm.2020.0482

Hern, K. L., & Hynd, G. W. (1992). Clinical differentiation of the attention deficit disorder subtypes: Do sensorimotor deficits characterize children with ADD/WO? *Archives of Clinical Neuropsychology, 7*, 77–83. https://doi.org/10.1016/0887-6177(92)90020-N

Jensen, P. S., Arnold, L. E., Swanson, J. M., Vitiello, B., Abikoff, H. B., Greenhil, L. L., et al. (2007). 3-year follow-up of the NIMH MTA study. *Journal of the American Academy of Child and Adolescent Psychiatry, 46*, 989–1002. https://doi.org/10.1097/CHI.0b013e3180686d48

Karen, R. (1994). Becoming attached: First relationships and how they shape our capacity to love. Oxford: Oxford University Press.

Krain, A. L., & Castellanos, F. X. (2006). Brain development and ADHD. *Clinical Psychology Review, 26*, 433–444. https://doi.org/10.1016/j.cpr.2006.01.005

Lane, S. J., Miller, L. J., & Hanft, B. (2000). Towards a consensus in terminology in sensory integration theory and practice: Part 2: Sensory integration: Patterns of function and dysfunction. *Sensory Integration Special Interest Section Quarterly, 23*(2), 1–3.

Lee, D., Riccio, C. A., & Hynd, G. W. (2004). The role of executive function in attention deficit hyperactivity disorder: Testing predictions from two model. *Canadian Journal of School Psychology, 19*, 167–189. https://doi.org/10.1177/082957350401900109

Levinson, B. M. (1969). *Pet-oriented child psychotherapy*. Thomas.

Maeir, A., Fisher, O., Traub Bar-Ilan, R., Boas, N., Berger, I., & Landau, Y. E. (2014). Effectiveness of Cognitive-Functional (Cog-Fun) occupational therapy intervention for young children with attention deficit hyperactivity disorder: A controlled study. *American Journal of Occupational Therapy, 68*, 260–267. https://doi.org/10.5014/ajot.2014.011700

Mangeot, S. D., Miller, L. J., McIntosh, D. N., McGrath-Clarke, J., Simon, J., Hagerman, R. J., & Goldson, E. (2001). Sensory modulation dysfunction in children with attention-deficit-hyperactivity disorder. *Developmental Medicine and Child Neurology, 43*, 399–406. https://doi.org/10.1111/j.1469-8749.2001.tb00228.x

Miller, L. J., Anzalone, M. E., Lane, S. J., Cermak, S. A., & Osten, E. T. (2007). Concept evolution in sensory integration: A proposed nosology for diagnosis. *The American Journal of Occupational Therapy, 61*, 135–140. https://doi.org/10.5014/ajot.61.2.135

Miller-Kuhaneck, H., Henry, D. A., Glennon, T. J., & Mu, K. (2007). Development of the Sensory Processing Measure-School: Initial studies of reliability and validity. American Journal of Occupational Therapy, *61*, 170–175. https://doi.org/10.5014/ajot.61.2.170

Mohammadi, M. R., Farokhzadi, F., Alipour, A., Rostami, R., Dehestani, M., & Salmanian, M. S. (2012). Marital satisfaction amongst parents of children with attention deficit hyperactivity disorder and normal children. *Iranian Journal of Psychiatry, 7*, 120–125.

Mulligan, S. (1996). An analysis of score patterns of children on sensory integration and praxis test. *American Journal of Occupational Therapy, 50*, 647–654. https://doi.org/10.5014/ajot.50.8.647

Palombo, J. (2001). *Learning disorders and disorders of the self in children and adolescents*. Norton.

Pan, C.-Y., Tsai, C.-L., Chu, C.-H., Sung, M.-C., Huang, C.-Y., & Ma, W.-Y. (2019). Effects of physical exercise intervention on motor skills and executive function in children with ADHD: A pilot study. *Journal of Attention Disorders, 23*(4), 384–397. https://doi.org/10.1177/1087054715569282

Pfeiffer, B., Henry, A., Miller, S., & Witherell, S. (2008). Effectiveness of Disc "O" Sit cushions on attention to task in second grade students with attention difficulties. *American Journal of Occupational Therapy, 62*, 274–281. https://doi.org/10.5014/ajot.62.3.274

Santosh, P. J., & Taylor, E. (2000). Stimulant drugs. *European Child & Adolescent Psychiatry, 9*, 27–43.

Smith-Osborne, A., & Selby, A. (2010). Implications of literature on equine-assisted activities for use as complementary intervention in social work practice with children and adolescents. *Child and Adolescent Social Work Journal, 27*, 291–307. https://doi.org/10.1007/s10560-010-0201-1

Swaab-Barneveld, H., de Sonneville, L., Cohen-Kettenis, P., Gielen, A., Buitelaar, J., & van Engeland, H. (2000). Visual sustained attention in a child psychiatric population. *Journal of the American Academy of Child and Adolescent Psychiatry, 39*, 651–659. https://doi.org/10.1097/00004583-200005000-00020

Tamm, L., Nakonezny, P. A., & Hughes, C. W. (2014). An open trial of metacognitive executive function training for young children with ADHD. *Journal of Attention Disorders, 18*, 551–559. https://doi.org/10.1177/1087054712445782

Tancred, E. M., & Greeff, A. (2015). Mothers' parenting styles and the association with family coping strategies and family adaptation in families of children with ADHD. *Clinical Social Work Journal, 43*, 442–451. https://doi.org/10.1007/s10615-015-0524-7

Tarver, J., Daley, D., & Sayal, K. (2014). Attention-deficit hyperactivity disorder (ADHD): An updated review of the essential facts. *Child: Care, Health and Development, 40*, 762–774. https://doi.org/10.1111/cch.12139

Vuijk, P. J., Hartman, E., Mombarg, R., Scherder, E., & Visscher, C. (2011). Associations between the academic and motor performance in a heterogeneous sample of children with learning disabilities. *Journal of Learning Disabilities, 44*, 276–282. https://doi.org/10.1177/0022219410378446

White, E., Zippel, J., & Kumar, S. (2020). The effect of equine assisted therapies on behavioral, psychological and physical symptoms of children with attention deficit/hyperactivity disorder: A systematic review. *Complementary Therapies in Clinical Practice, 39*, 101101. https://doi.org/10.1016/j.ctcp.2020.101101

Willcutt, E. G., Doyle, A. E., Nigg, J. T., Faraone, S. V., & Pennington, B. F. (2005). Validity of the executive function theory of attention-deficit/hyperactivity disorder: A meta-analytic review. *Biological Psychiatry, 57*, 1336–1346. https://doi.org/10.1016/j.biopsych.2005.02.006

Williamson, G. G., & Anzalone, M. E. (2001). *Sensory integration and self-regulation in infants and toddlers: Helping very young children interact with their environment*. Zero to Three.

Introducing ASTride: An Equine-Assisted Occupational Therapy Intervention for Children with ADHD

Anne Helmer and Orit Bart

Introduction

Attention-deficit hyperactivity disorder (ADHD) is a prevalent pediatric neurodevelopmental disorder. In 2022, around 6.4 million children aged 3–17 in the United States were diagnosed with ADHD, with boys having nearly twice the prevalence as girls (The National Survey of Children's Health, 2023). ADHD is characterized by inattention, hyperactivity, and impulsivity, and (American Psychiatric Association, 2013) involves an ongoing impairment of executive functions (EFs), which are high-level cognitive self-management processes often associated with the frontal lobes of the brain. The EF enables a person to adapt to novel situations and perform goal-oriented behavior. They are high-level cognitive self-management processes (Friedman & Miyake, 2017). EFs enable individuals to regulate their behavior, thoughts, and emotions and thereby enable self-control, goal-directed behavior, response inhibition, interference control, working memory, and set shifting.

ADHD is often associated with impairment of psychosocial functioning (Wehmeier et al., 2010), including emotional impulsiveness, deficient emotional self-regulation, anxiety, depression, and aggressive behavior. Low self-esteem has also been reported among the ADHD population compared to the neuro-typical population (Molavi et al., 2020). Deficit in these psychological functions can lead to significant difficulties in academic achievements and in social and personal relationships (Wehmeier et al., 2010). Children with ADHD also may present sensory-motor impairments, as researchers found that children with ADHD had more sensory processing problems than those without ADHD, thus influencing their quality of life (QoL) (Engel-Yeger & Ziv-On, 2011; Yoldaş et al., 2020).

A. Helmer (✉) · O. Bart
Department of Occupational Therapy, School of Health Professions, Faculty of Medicine and Health Sciences, Tel Aviv University, Tel Aviv, Israel
e-mail: henanneh@mail.tau.ac.il; oritbert@tauex.tau.ac.il

Y. Neria et al. (eds.), *Guide to Equine Assisted Therapy*,
https://doi.org/10.1007/978-3-031-74426-6_14

Taking together, all these difficulties, the ability to perform a wide variety of daily tasks might be affected, and reduced participation in everyday activities at the home and school environment may be present (Yoldaş et al., 2020). Participation is an important part of human development and is defined as involvement in life situations (World Health Organization, 2001). Through participation, people acquire skills and competencies, connect with others in their communities, and find purpose and meaning in life. The level of participation in daily activities is often used as an outcome measure in occupational therapy (OT) practice by using standardized questionnaires such as the children participation questionnaire (CPQ) (Law, 2002; Bart et al., 2010). To enable a child with ADHD to participate satisfactorily in everyday occupations and activities, treatment must address factors that hinder performance, including sensory-motor difficulties, EFs deficits, and psychological challenges.

The current recommendation for the most effective intervention for children with ADHD is a combination of administration-approved pharmacological drug medication and/or evidence-based psychological and behavioral therapy interventions. The most common pharmacological treatment is stimulant medication (methylphenidate and amphetamine), which has been shown to reduce symptoms (Wolraich et al., 2019). Other non-pharmacological interventions focus on cognitive training of single or multiple domains of EFs, such as working memory, inhibition, or cognitive flexibility. These approaches are led by neuroplasticity principles and are based on intensive repetitive training and immediate feedback (Dovis et al., 2015). While these approaches address core symptoms such as hyperactivity and inhibition, they do not address everyday performance; they therefore cannot be applied to functional tasks (Hahn-Markowitz et al., 2020).

Effective OT interventions for children with ADHD are client-centered and occupation-based, emphasizing personal functional goals and strategy acquisition (Hahn-Markowitz et al., 2017). While conventional OT approaches have shown significant efficacy in enhancing EFs and functional or academic skills, they often overlook psychological difficulties. On the other hand, psychological interventions like behavioral programs, psychoeducation for parents, and expressive therapies focus on emotional and psychological aspects but are not occupation-based and do not facilitate strategy acquisition (Pelham Jr & Fabiano, 2008). Existing interventions typically target either core symptoms, EFs, everyday functions, or emotional symptoms, rarely addressing the multifaceted nature of ADHD (Hahn-Markowitz et al., 2020). Thus, there is a crucial need for interventions that address core symptoms, EFs, sensory-motor functions, and emotional deficits using an inclusive therapeutic approach.

Equine-Assisted Services (EAS) and Occupational Therapy (OT)

Integrating animals into interventions aimed at enhancing human health, quality of life, and participation is becoming increasingly popular. This approach is referred to as animal-assisted intervention (AAI), where animals act as intermediaries to facilitate improvements in an individual's physical, mental, and social attributes (Bass et al., 2009).

Equine-assisted services (EAS), formerly known as equine-assisted activities and therapies (EAAT), encompass a range of intricate and multimodal activities and therapies aimed at achieving therapeutic objectives through interactions between clients and horses. These interventions vary in their therapeutic aims and the providers who administer them, with each intervention customized to suit individual needs (Wood et al., 2021). EAS are classified into three broad divisions of professional work: equine-assisted learning (EAL), equine-assisted therapy (EAT), and the horsemanship division.

The therapy division encompasses a wide range of therapeutic practices in which licensed professionals incorporate horses as active participants in five distinct therapies: occupational therapy, counseling, physical therapy, psychotherapy, and speech-language pathology. These professionals work within the scope of their specific discipline, integrating equine activities and/or the equine environment into their therapeutic approach (Wood et al., 2021). Equine-assisted occupational therapy (EAOT) integrates the horse as a therapeutic partner along with the surrounding equine environment, employing occupational therapy (OT) approaches. The equine partner and the environment play a crucial role in therapy, as interacting with horses impacts the rider cognitively, emotionally, and physiologically.

Riding involves transference, an immersive experience where immediate feedback from the horse's movements helps in physical and mental self-regulation (So et al., 2017), along with requiring full attention and engagement in order to succeed in riding (Gilboa & Helmer, 2020). Succeeding would be assessed through the ability to ride the horse in different places and steer it while keeping the rider's posture. Additionally, riding requires the use of strategies such as planning when steering, monitoring one's actions, and problem-solving while on the horse, in order to succeed in riding it (Gilboa & Helmer, 2020). For example, when beginning a walk with a horse, the rider must maintain a specific posture and carefully regulate the amount of strength used. If too much force is applied, the horse may start running. Conversely, if too little force is used, the horse may not begin walking, necessitating constant monitoring. This force regulation can then be transferred to activities such as playing other sports, when hugging a person, and maintaining personal space. Another example is steering. If a rider wants to steer toward a certain point, they need to look in that direction and adjust their posture accordingly. If the rider is unclear in signaling with their body, the horse may not reach the desired endpoint. Instead, the horse might remain stationary or move where it chooses. These develop awareness of body position, body sensations, and regulation. These enable the development of body scheme and are the basis for planning any motor activity, such as riding a bicycle or writing with a pencil. Later on in therapy, these could be related to emotions that accompany these physical feelings and to coping strategies that may be used, such as planning an alternative way of action in different environments such as the home environment or the school environment (Gilboa & Helmer, 2020; Bachi et al., 2012; Martin et al., 2018). For instance, when a child becomes angry and has an outburst, the initial goal should be to help the child pause and recognize their bodily sensations, identify the emotion that follows anger, and then employ a strategy to regulate this emotion instead of resorting to hitting.

The interaction with the horse has also been found to reduce anxiety, enhance self-perception, and promote positive emotions and secure attachment (Anderson & Meints, 2016). The tactile and physical contact with the horse releases endorphins in the nervous system, alleviating anxiety and fostering feelings of love and confidence (Fine, 2019). Non-verbal communication with animals facilitates attachment without the need for words, providing a safe, non-judgmental social connection (Anderson & Meints, 2016; Borgi et al., 2016; Holm et al., 2014) that enhances self-esteem (Beetz et al., 2012). Moreover, horses and their surroundings reduce negative emotions and foster psychological growth (Weldon, 2017). As the rider and horse work as a team to achieve a mutual goal, it was found to increase motivation for action (Bracher, 2000).

Furthermore, EAOT incorporates a variety of sensory-motor stimuli, including the movement, touch, and scent of the horse in order to enhance sensory-motor regulation. Engel (1984) noted the positive impact of vestibular stimulation on sensory integrative function, as it is proposed that sensory stimulation during both ground-level and mounted activities can regulate physiological arousal levels due to the rhythmic and continuous movement the horse provides (Bracher, 2000; Weldon, 2017).

These benefits are evident in therapeutic horseback riding, but the application of OT interventions and therapeutic approaches can further enhance bodily functions and skill acquisition. This, in turn, promotes increased participation in daily activities, fosters social interaction, and facilitates the transfer of acquired skills to everyday life and functioning (Gilboa & Helmer, 2020).

Practical and Theoretical Approaches Incorporated in the Intervention Protocol

ADHD skills therapy (ASTride) intervention is based on the multi-context approach (Toglia & Katz, 2011), the cognitive orientation to daily occupation performance approach (CO-OP) (Polatajko et al., 2001), and sensory integration (SI) theory and approach (Ayres, 1972a) (see Table 1). These OT approaches are commonly used in promoting children with ADHD along with other neurodevelopmental disorders

Table 1 Occupational therapy (OT) approaches incorporated in ASTride

Approach	Principles	Goals	Examples
Cognitive orientation to occupational performance (CO-OP)	Focuses on teaching cognitive strategies to improve occupational performance	Improve cognitive and functional skills	Teaching problem-solving strategies, promoting self-regulation, enhancing goal setting
Sensory integration (SI)	Uses sensory-based activities to improve sensory processing and integration	Enhance sensory-motor functions	Activities like swinging, balancing, and deep pressure touch to improve sensory modulation
Multi-context approach	Encourages transfer of skills across different contexts and tasks	Generalize learned skills to various settings	Practicing skills in different environments to promote adaptability and flexibility
Parental training	Educates parents on effective strategies to support their children's needs	Improve parental coping and child outcomes	Workshops, coaching, and resources for parents on managing ADHD behaviors and enhancing EFs

such as developmental coordination disorder (DCD), sensory modulation disorder (SMD), and mental health diagnoses such as schizophrenia.

The multi-context approach to cognitive rehabilitation refers to strategy acquisition that can be applied across a wide range of meaningful activities to foster generalization and improve functional performance. This approach highlights the importance of directly and explicitly training for the transfer of skills. Key elements include (a) focusing on strategy development, self-generation, and training. Self-generating strategy refers to the child initiating the idea for a strategy. For example, when riding a horse, one must sit with their shoulders aligned straight with their pelvis and heels. Instead of asking a rider to straighten their back, the therapist might suggest thinking of a favorite hero or movie star. Whenever the name of the hero is mentioned, it would mean the rider should straighten their back. In this way, the therapist guides the child toward a certain strategy for body awareness, but the child self-generates the specific method of implementation; (b) practicing across various contexts while gradually reducing physical similarity along a continuum. For example, using a list of required steps when tacking up a horse when the end goal might be using a list of required steps when getting ready in the morning; (c) emphasizing metacognitive training. For example, practicing inhibition with the horse at various paces, such as walking and trotting, helps the child recognize how much effort is needed for each pace. Later, inhibition can be practiced in the home environment when the child is asked to stop playing a board game or video game and get in the shower, focusing on the effort required. During therapy sessions, inhibition as an executive function will be discussed and explored in different contexts; and (d) using everyday activities tailored to an individual's optimal challenge level that would be set according to the therapist's assessment at the beginning of riding. Treatment activities are structured to progressively challenge the application of strategies in different situations, taking into account the person, activity, and environment to enhance performance (Toglia & Katz, 2011). For example, the ability to ride a horse and concentrate on a specific task, such as an obstacle course, can be developed incrementally. The therapist would consider the rider's ADHD and select an appropriate environment, starting in a small round pen with no other horses. As the rider's abilities improve (both concentration levels and EFs), sessions can progress to a larger arena with other horses and riders. The therapist might begin with a course that includes only two or three obstacles, gradually increasing the number of obstacles to match the rider's growing ability.

The CO-OP method is a client-centered, performance-driven approach focused on problem-solving, facilitating skill acquisition through strategic use and guided discovery, with an emphasis on applying skills broadly. It teaches the overarching strategy Goal-Plan-Do-Check (Polatajko et al., 2001), which is applied to basic riding skills such as walking, halting, and steering. For example, when teaching how to walk, the Therapist and rider would set a Goal of walking. Then Plan how to perform the goal (body position and signing: the rider will look forward, click with their tongue, press gently with their feet, and release when the horse starts walking). The Do part will include executing the Plan phase and finally Checking whether the rider managed to reach the goal and walk with the horse. If the rider did not achieve it, then he will check whether the planning phase was not good enough or whether he did not execute it well and repeat it as needed. Both the multi-context and CO-OP approaches employ enabling principles and strategy acquisition techniques, including extrinsic reinforcement, direct instruction methods, visual aids for task comprehension, decision-making through modeling, physical cue prompts, skill chaining for sequence learning, and gradual independence through fading (Halayko et al., 2016). These strategies are integrated into EAOT interventions to teach fundamental riding skills tailored to each rider's abilities. The acquired strategies are then transferred to daily activities, considering how they can be applied according to each rider's specific goals and needs. For example, a rider who is struggling to do his homework might use the Goal-Plan-Do-Check strategy after he has used it in riding. The Goal would be to do all his homework. The Plan phase might include coming home from school and doing homework straight away before going to watch TV, for if he starts with TV first, he does not remember to do his homework afterward. The Do phase will include practicing it a few times during the week, before the next riding session. The Check phase will include checking to see whether this plan worked and if not, what can be changed. Perhaps he needs an adult to sit with him in addition, and so on.

The third theoretical model refers to sensory-based principles, particularly the sensory integration (SI) model developed by Ayres (1972a). SI theory represents a neurophysiological approach linking sensory processing with behavior. Sensory processing refers to the central nervous system's ability to regulate and organize an individual's responses to sensory input in a graded and adaptive manner (James et al., 2011). The sensory systems encompass somatosensory, visual, auditory, olfactory, gustatory, vestibular, proprioceptive (James et al., 2011), and interoceptive systems (Mahler, 2015). Impaired sensory processing can lead to various learning, developmental, emotional, or other disabilities (Ayres, 1972b). Sensory-based principles emphasize sensory input and its continuous interaction with movement.

Horses and their environment offer a wide range of simultaneous sensory stimuli, aiding in the integration of various sensory systems and enhancing overall functionality (Ayres, 1972b; Fisher & Bundy, 1992). For instance, grooming the horse provides tactile feedback through direct contact and exposure to environmental scents and necessitates precise movement planning. The act of riding delivers significant vestibular stimulation, which has been shown to improve balance, reduce anxiety, and boost self-esteem (Bart et al., 2009). Additionally, auditory stimuli arise from the horse's neighs and the need to discern directional commands. Selecting the appropriate equipment among diverse visual stimuli further engages the senses. Both horse care and riding deliver substantial proprioceptive input due to the movement and stimulation of receptors in the tendons, muscles, and joints. These elements are crucial for developing proper body schema and advanced motor planning. When combined with the cognitive aspects of horse care and riding, this approach provides a comprehensive and inclusive therapeutic experience. Therefore, sensory integration is crucial in EAOT, where riding offers diverse sensory inputs, tactile stimulation, continuous motion, and subsequent vestibular stimulation (Bracher, 2000).

Research on Equine-Assisted Services (EAS) and ADHD varies significantly in terms of sample size, variables studied, measurement methods, session duration, and procedural approaches. Some studies incorporate groundwork alongside horseback riding, while others focus exclusively on riding.

To date, there are no established evidence-based protocols for Equine-Assisted Services (EAS) tailored specifically for children with ADHD, although these children are often referred for such services. Similarly, there is a lack of established protocols for Equine-assisted occupational therapy (EAOT) designed for children with ADHD, despite initial indications of its feasibility; therefore, there is a need to develop and validate suited protocols.

Empirical evidence and research in evidence-based methodologies are essential for validating clinical practices and promoting the adoption of intervention protocols and manuals (Carroll & Nuro, 2002). While intervention protocols may be criticized for potentially restricting therapist flexibility, they are crucial for the systematic evaluation of therapeutic interventions (Pyatak et al., 2015). To be integrated into clinical practice, an intervention protocol must be clearly articulated, valid, and reliable. To develop a protocol that can be validated and implemented by professionals, several stages must be followed. These stages include initial idea development, conducting a thorough theoretical and literature review, piloting the protocol, and validating its effectiveness (Carroll & Nuro, 2002). This chapter describes the process of developing an equine-assisted occupational therapy (EAOT) intervention protocol for children aged 6–12 with attention deficit hyperactivity disorder (ADHD), including the theoretical framework and initial validation, along with future implications (see Fig. 1).

Despite this diversity, existing research suggests that participating in 8–12 sessions of EAS may lead to reductions in ADHD symptoms such as hyperactivity and impulsivity. Clinical characteristics of ADHD include persistent patterns of inattention and/or hyperactivity-impulsivity. These were assessed in different studies using

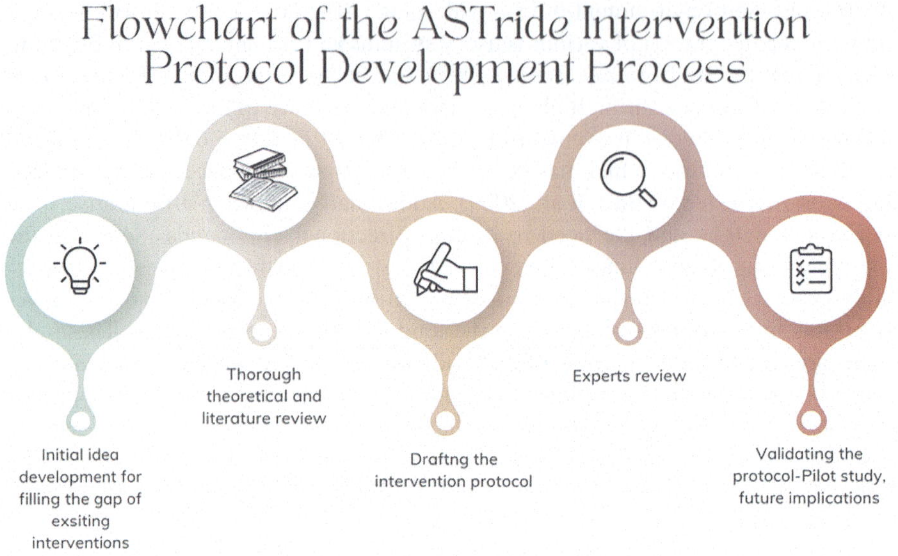

Fig. 1 Flowchart pf the ASTride intervention protocol development process

the Strengths and Difficulties Questionnaire (SDQ), which found improvements in ADHD symptomatology. Differences in these clinical variables were measured with the Korean version of the Attention-Deficit/Hyperactivity Disorder Scale (K-ARS), while clinical and adaptive variables were measured using the Korean Child Behavior Checklist, which showed significant differences in the "social problems" subscale. The Attention-Deficit Hyperactivity Disorder Rating Scale (ARS) and the Behavior Rating Inventory of Executive Function (BRIEF) questionnaire were also used to assess executive functions (EFs) and core symptoms of impulsivity (Gilboa & Helmer, 2020; Pérez-Gómez et al., 2020; Helmer et al., 2021).

Additionally, EAS shows promise in enhancing therapeutic relationships and improving physical, cognitive, social, and emotional functions (Pérez-Gómez et al., 2020). Studies have shown improvements in depression, somatization, anxiety, and depression. While the effects on depression and attention were moderate, the impact on anxiety and self-esteem was smaller (White et al., 2020; Pérez-Gómez et al., 2020).

Positive effects have also been observed across domains including body structures and functions, activity levels, participation in daily life, and overall quality of life (Helmer et al., 2021). Physical elements that have been studied focused on gait balance, muscular strength, cardiorespiratory fitness, body composition, and motor performance. These studies generally found improvements in all these physical measures, indicating positive outcomes using the Developmental Coordination Disorder Questionnaire (DCD-Q) (White et al., 2020).

Evidence supporting equine-assisted occupational therapy (EAOT) interventions for ADHD populations is limited, and there is currently no established intervention protocol specifically designed for this group. Therefore, this chapter outlines the ASTride protocol for children aged 6–12 with ADHD, its initial validity, and future implications as we aim to fill in the gap and provide more evidence-based research.

ASTride Protocol Development

Manual Development—Content Validity

Twelve Guideline Principles for Intervention

Prior to conducting a pilot study, a comprehensive literature review was conducted regarding EAS, ADHD, and OT approaches. Initial guidelines were drafted based on this review and clinical expertise (Helmer et al., 2024) (see Table 2).

Subsequently to developing the guidelines, the protocol underwent review by a focus group comprising experts from the EAS and OT fields. To ensure thorough reporting and transparency, the SPIRIT checklist (2013) was adhered. This

Table 2 Twelve guideline principles for ASTride therapy intervention

Guideline principle description		
1	Develop awareness	Help the child recognize difficulties while riding or working with the horse using guided discovery.
2	Teach executive strategies	Teach and acquire executive strategies with parental guidance, transferring learned strategies from the stable to relevant surroundings.
3	Problem identification and solving	Identify a problem and practice problem-solving skills.
4	Reflect on mutual interaction	Reflect on interactions with the horse, understanding that actions affect the horse and vice versa, and transfer that knowledge to interpersonal relationships.
5	Emotional discourse	Engage in emotional discourse to identify and understand emotions.
6	Foster responsibility	Promote responsibility and care for the horse, such as proper grooming and feeding, to improve responsibility.
7	Learn from success	Analyze the steps that led to success to reinforce learning.
8	Sensory stimulation	Provide vestibular, somatosensory, and proprioceptive stimulation while riding the horse.
9	Praxis and movement planning	Practice praxis and movement planning, such as using hand and counter leg simultaneously.
10	Physical activity	Engage in physical activity to release endorphins and promote physical well-being.
11	Promote independence	Encourage independence while riding and gradually reduce verbal instructions.
12	Diverse environment exposure	Expose the child to diverse environments, promoting adaptation to various smells, textures of different horses, and materials like hay and grain.

checklist based on the SPIRIT checklist offers evidence-based guidelines for the essential elements needed when developing and presenting a clinical trial protocol (Chan et al., 2013). The protocol review involved responding to 20 Likert scale questions ranging from 1 (strongly disagree) to 10 (strongly agree), along with open-ended questions for suggestions and comments. Upon receiving feedback, an analysis was conducted using the intraclass correlation coefficient (ICC) test ($\alpha = 0.776$). Experts provided comments on the protocol, and revisions were made accordingly. Following these updates, experts reviewed the changes and completed the feedback form once more, after which the ICC test was conducted again. The high Alpha Cronbach value for agreement among experts ($\alpha = 0.851$) indicated a strong consensus on the protocol revisions.

Protocol Description

The ASTride intervention consists of 12 weekly sessions, each lasting 45 minutes and led by a certified professional. Each session follows a structured format, beginning with setting riding goals, familiarizing with the horse, preparing for mounting, warming up, and then focusing on skill acquisition and strategy practice. A session summary concludes the session, including a "planning phase" where the functional goal is discussed along with its application in different environments such as home, school, and after-school activities. This planning phase involves both parents and the child, making decisions on how and where the goal will be practiced. For instance, if the strategy involves using a checklist for horse preparation, the home assignment might involve creating and using a checklist for morning routines. Parents receive guidance on supporting these assignments, such as using visual reminders or specific strategies. Consistency is emphasized, requiring either one or both parents to attend all sessions to aid in learning and skill transfer. At the end of each session, the EAOT professional documents the session and completes clinical notes. In addition, three questions are presented to the participant:

1. From 1 to 10, how much did you anticipate coming to the session today (1-did not anticipate at all, 10-highly anticipated).
2. From 1 to 10, how much progress do you feel you have made (1-no progress at all, 10-the most progress).
3. From 1 to 10, to what extent did you enjoy the lesson today? (1-did not enjoy, 10-highly enjoyed).

During the intervention, sessions focus on developing and practicing functional goals related to occupational performance using specific strategies. Participants initially learn a global problem-solving strategy inspired by the CO-OP approach, aimed at acquiring strategies and skills. This global strategy is intended for application outside of therapy sessions (e.g., at home), facilitating improvements in occupational performance. The intervention is personalized for individual instruction and allows for adaptability to meet the unique needs of each participant, with the goal of gradually reducing direct instruction and fostering independence over time. It is anticipated that as participants gain independence, they will apply learned strategies and transfer their skills to various environments (Helmer et al., 2024).

Piloting the Protocol: Predictive Validity

Following the development of the final protocol, a pilot study was conducted, aiming to evaluate the efficacy of the ASTride intervention. A convenience sample of five participants (mean age = 10.40 years, SD 2.96), diagnosed with ADHD by a pediatric neurologist, participated in the study. The children were referred to EAS at Yehuda Mountain Stable, Israel, and underwent 12 weeks of intervention, following the ASTride protocol. Inclusion criteria required participants to be between 6 and 12 years old, have a medical diagnosis of ADHD based on DSM-5 criteria, and have a general doctor's approval for EAS participation. Exclusion criteria included moderate to severe cognitive impairment, neurological disorders, additional developmental disorders, recent changes in medication, and severe sensory loss (Helmer et al., 2024).

Procedure and Ethical Considerations

After obtaining ethical approval from Tel-Aviv University's institutional review board (IRB) ethical committee (number 0003949-3), relevant participants were invited to join the study. Upon obtaining signed consent from both the child and their parents, participants completed a baseline assessment consisting of standardized tests to be filled out by both parents and children: the Tower of Hanoi Test (TOH) (Lezak et al., 2004) and the Behavior Rating Inventory of Executive Function (BRIEF) (Gioia et al., 2000) for measuring EFs; the Hebrew adaptation of The Children's Hope Scale (Lezak et al., 2004; Snyder et al., 1997) for measuring hope perception among the children; the Child Performance Skill Questionnaire (PSQ) (Bart et al., 2010); and the Canadian Occupational Performance Measure (COPM) (Law et al., 2014) for assessing everyday performance. After the 12-week EAOT intervention, a post-intervention assessment using the same measures was conducted. Assessments were administered by a research assistant blinded to the participants' stages in the intervention (Helmer et al., 2024).

Measures

The study utilized several standardized tools to assess different aspects of the participants' performance and functions. To evaluate the change in EFs, we chose to use a task assessment and a parents fill questionnaire. The TOH test was used for the participants and the BRIEF questionnaire for the parents. The TOH test requires that differently sized disks be moved across three pegs according to a picture depicting the goal layout with all disks at the right peg as quickly and with as few moves as possible. The number of moves and time taken to complete the task are measured. The tower of hanoi (THO) measures EFs with non-verbal content and requires spatial perception of position. It requires executing the sequence of moves while inhibiting the incorrect once (Ahonniska et al., 2000). The BRIEF, an 86-item rating scale filled out by parents, provided insights into eight EF's components, including inhibition, shifting, emotional control, initiating, working memory, organization of materials, planning, and monitoring. These scales are composed of two scales, including a behavioral regulation index (BRI) and a metacognitive index (MI), along with a total score of the global executive composite (GEC). The parents are asked to refer to different sentences regarding their children's EFs and rate how often each item occurs if relevant.

The PSQ was used to assess different everyday skills according to the parent's report. These skills included gross and fine motor skills such as walking and keeping one's balance; communication skills such as the ability to express oneself, negotiate, and speak loud and clear; and organizational skills such as being persistent while doing a specific task, organizing materials, following specific steps, etc.

The Children's Hope Scale, filled out by the participants, where they had to rate different items that measured hope perception, focusing on agency and pathway thinking.

The COPM, a client-centered tool, was used to set and evaluate occupational performance goals pre- and post-intervention, referring to everyday activities such as doing homework, organizing one's room or closet, and performing daily tasks such as bathing, brushing teeth, and getting organized in the morning or before bedtime.

Results

Findings suggest statistically significant improvements in EFs were observed in the TOH test, specifically in the number of moves required for the solution, though time measures did not show significant changes ($z = 2.02$; $p < 0.04$). Most BRIEF scales showed improvement post-intervention, with significant changes noted in the behavior rating index (BRI) ($z = 2.02$; $p < 0.04$), which includes the subscales of inhibition ($z = 1.6$; $p < 0.1$), shifting ($z = 1.13$; $p < 0.25$), and emotional regulation ($z = 1.6$; $p < 0.1$). However, the Metacognitive Index (MI)and its components did not exhibit significant improvements ($z = 1.21$; $p < 0.22$). The GEC scale, which includes both the BRI and the MI, improved as well, with a $z = 1.62$ and $p < 0.1$ post-intervention (Helmer et al., 2024). Performance skills, assessed by the PSQ, showed no significant changes, though some improvement in organizational skills was noted with a median score of 3.38 pre-intervention and a median score of 3.75 post-intervention. The Children's Hope Scale showed a statistically significant improvement in hope scores post-intervention (Helmer et al., 2024).

Using the COPM, treatment goals were set with input from both children and parents, focusing on areas of everyday living such as school performance, self-care, and leisure activities. Post-intervention results indicated improvements in occupational performance and satisfaction, as rated by both children and parents with more than two points change in satisfaction, performance, and importance rating (Helmer et al., 2024). For example, J', one of the parents who participated in the research stated: "I didn't have any expectations from the therapy, but I was very impressed when I found out how it's working, and all the steps involved. It was child centered and age appropriate for my child, and really answered his need regarding what he needed to work on as opposed to general therapy... and I think it was a good reminder for us as parents to work with him at home weekly. That we should maybe pick a small goal each week, not just during the 12 sessions but also after they are done as we would do our own program with him."

Discussion

This chapter has presented the ASTride protocol, an EAOT intervention for children 6–12 diagnosed with ADHD, along with the results of the pilot study evaluating the protocol as an evidence-based intervention (Helmer et al., 2024). The study showed promising improvements in EFs, behavioral regulation, occupational performance, and parental satisfaction, along with hope perception among participants, highlighting the potential of EAOT as a multifaceted intervention for ADHD.

Given that EAS encompasses a wide range of interventions from various disciplines and targets diverse populations, it is essential to develop and implement standardized protocols and interventions. This will facilitate a clearer understanding of which therapy involving equines is most effective for a specific population. Developing ASTride along with other equine interventions and guidelines not only facilitates the systematic evaluation of therapeutic interventions but also ensures that these interventions can be reliably replicated by different practitioners. This standardization is essential for validating the effectiveness of EAOT and promoting its adoption in clinical practice.

Integration of Therapy Methods

Although defined under the Therapy division as a part of EAS, other than being performed by a licensed therapist (Wood et al., 2021), as of today there are no specific guidelines for occupational therapists regarding the incorporation of equines within their practice. ASTride refers specifically to children with ADHD, thus serving as preliminary guidelines for practice for occupational therapists in the equine field. The integration of various therapeutic approaches within EAOT, such as the multi-context approach, the CO-OP method, and the SI theory, is particularly beneficial for addressing the multifaceted nature of ADHD. These approaches complement each other, providing a holistic treatment that addresses not only the core symptoms of ADHD but also the associated emotional, cognitive, and sensory-motor challenges. By combining these methods, EAOT can offer a more comprehensive and effective intervention, targeting the diverse needs of children with ADHD.

Understanding the Potential of EAOT for ADHD and Mechanism of Change

Along with developing working guidelines and integrating therapy methods, this intervention enables us to better understand how incorporating equines as therapy partners can influence children with ADHD. EAOT, through its unique integration of occupational therapy with equines, may offer a novel approach that combines physical, cognitive, and emotional elements. Along with preliminary results, it is important to understand the underlying mechanism that enables the treatment changes while taking into consideration the small sample size of the current study and the need to replicate the results in future studies. Regarding EFs, it is hypothesized that the strategies discussed and practiced during the sessions, along with their application in daily tasks, likely contributed to improvements in EFs. For instance, participants learned to tack a horse using a pictorial list, checking off each item, which facilitated inhibition and working memory. These skills were then transferred to everyday activities, such as organizing morning or bedtime routines with similar pictorial lists. Another example refers to steering the horse through an obstacle course. Participants had to plan how they would steer the horse and then ride the course. They then had to check whether they succeeded. If they did, a discussion regarding what facilitated success was held. If they didn't, they were asked to check whether the problem was with their plan or performance. Later, a home assignment could involve planning a school assignment and checking as they finished whether they went through all the instructions and answered everything. The improved inhibition observed in the TOH test was consistent with the enhanced inhibition indicated by the BRIEF questionnaire, along with improvement in shifting and emotional control subscales. While the improvement noted in the PSQ questionnaire regarding organizational skills was not substantial, a larger sample size could potentially facilitate a more comprehensive study of this aspect. The improvement in inhibition as indicated by the BRIEF and TOH likely led to better emotional regulation, enabling participants to inhibit inappropriate responses and select effective coping strategies as riding a horse requires constant inhibition and control of muscle movements, planning, and selecting appropriate strategies for various riding activities. Additionally, riding requires planning, steering, and awareness of other horses, which demand both physical and cognitive skills. As ADHD is characterized by impulsivity and inhibition deficits, these offer an opportunity to acquire and practice skills that can facilitate the core impairments of these children. Immediate feedback from the horse's movements further necessitates regulation and inhibition, supporting the development of these EFs (Bass et al., 2009; Borgi et al., 2016; So et al., 2017).

The BRIEF results were supported by the Hope questionnaire, which showed increased levels of hope among participants after the intervention. Children with ADHD typically have lower levels of hope due to developmental challenges and daily life deficits (Einav & Margalit, 2022). Hope is essential for setting meaningful goals, identifying ways to achieve them, and planning strategies to overcome obstacles. Furthermore, enhanced hope may improve cognitive functions like planning, shifting, inhibiting, and regulating. Both parents' and children's hopeful beliefs serve as protective factors that help in coping with deficits and achieving life goals (Shiri et al., 2014). Additionally, the challenges presented by riding foster a sense of capability, mastery, and success, further enhancing hopefulness (Martin et al., 2018).

Along with cognitive and emotional outcomes, the COPM have demonstrated improvement in occupational performance. As ASTride essentially aims to help children with ADHD acquire the skills to cope with their difficulties, it is essential that the skills learned during therapy sessions will later be transferred to other environments where the difficulties are manifested, including the home and school environment. Involving the parents who are present during the session may have an important role as they become partners and part of the therapy sessions and can later be mediators and help the children implement their acquired skills in different tasks and environments. Moreover, research has found that equipping parents of children with ADHD with knowledge and strategies tailored to their child's EFs deficits improved parental coping skills and subsequently enhanced the child's daily functioning and behavior (Frisch et al., 2019). As there are no guidelines in EAS regarding parental role in therapy, it is important to further understand their part in it.

Where Do We Go on from Here—The Need for Further Research

Despite promising preliminary findings, there is an urgent need for further research to establish the effectiveness of EAOT for children with ADHD. The pilot study has its limitations including a small sample size and lack of a control condition and randomization. In addition, existing body of research on EAS and ADHD is scarce and diverse regarding intervention length, providers, session structure and sample size, making it difficult to draw definitive conclusions. Comprehensive studies with larger sample sizes, standardized measurement methods, and consistent procedural approaches are essential to validate the benefits of EAOT. Future research should also explore the long-term effects of EAOT and its impact on various domains of functioning, including academic performance, social relationships, and overall quality of life. It should also seek to understand the effect on core symptoms including inattention and hyperactivity while better understanding the underlying mechanism that leads to the above improvements.

In conclusion, the development of standardized protocols for EAOT is essential for its validation and integration into clinical practice. The holistic approach of EAOT, integrating multiple therapeutic methods, shows the potential in addressing the complex needs of children with ADHD. However, further research is necessary to establish its efficacy and ensure that EAOT can be effectively utilized to improve the lives of children with ADHD.

Author Disclosure Statement No competing financial or conflict of interests exist.

References

Ahonniska, J., Ahonen, T., Aro, T., Tolvanen, A., & Lyytinen, H. (2000). Repeated assessment of the Tower of Hanoi test: Reliability and age effects. *Assessment, 7*(3), 297–310. https://doi.org/10.1177/107319110000700308

American Psychiatric Association. (2013). *Diagnostic and statistical manual of mental disorders* (p. 216). Text revision. American Psychiatric Association.

Anderson, S., & Meints, K. (2016). Brief report: The effects of equine-assisted activities on the social functioning in children and adolescents with autism spectrum disorder. *Journal of Autism and Developmental Disorders, 46*(10), 3344–3352. https://doi.org/10.1007/S10803-016-2869-3/TABLES/1

Ayres, A. J. (1972a). Types of sensory integrative dysfunction among disabled learners. *American Journal of Occupational Therapy, 26*(1), 13–18.

Ayres, J. (1972b). Sensory integration and learning disorders. *American Journal of Occupational Therapy*. https://cir.nii.ac.jp/crid/1130282273180619136

Bachi, K., Terkel, J., & Teichman, M. (2012). Equine-facilitated psychotherapy for at-risk adolescents: The influence on self-image, self-control and trust. *Clinical Child Psychology and Psychiatry, 17*(2), 298–312. https://doi.org/10.1177/1359104511404177

Bart, O., Bar-Haim, Y., Weizman, E., Levin, M., Sadeh, A., & Mintz, M. (2009). Balance treatment ameliorates anxiety and increases self-esteem in children with comorbid anxiety and balance disorder. *Research in Developmental Disabilities, 30*(3), 486–495.

Bart, O., Rosenberg, L., Ratzon, N., & Jarus, T. (2010). Development and initial validation of the Performance Skills Questionnaire (PSQ). *Research in Developmental Disabilities, 31*(1), 46–56.

Bass, M. M., Duchowny, C. A., & Llabre, M. M. (2009). The effect of therapeutic horseback riding on social functioning in children with autism. *Journal of Autism and Developmental Disorders, 39*(9), 1261–1267. https://doi.org/10.1007/S10803-009-0734-3

Beetz, A., Uvnäs-Moberg, K., Julius, H., & Kotrschal, K. (2012). Psychosocial and psychophysiological effects of human-animal interactions: The possible role of oxytocin. *Frontiers in Psychology*. https://doi.org/10.3389/fpsyg.2012.00234

Borgi, M., Loliva, D., Cerino, S., Chiarotti, F., Venerosi, A., Bramini, M., Nonnis, E., Marcelli, M., Vinti, C., De Santis, C., Bisacco, F., Fagerlie, M., Frascarelli, M., & Cirulli, F. (2016). Effectiveness of a standardized equine-assisted therapy program for children with autism spectrum disorder. *Journal of Autism and Developmental Disorders, 46*(1), 1–9. https://doi.org/10.1007/S10803-015-2530-6

Bracher, M. (2000). Therapeutic horse riding: What has this to do with occupational therapists? *British Journal of Occupational Therapy, 63*(6), 277–282. https://doi.org/10.1177/030802260006300606

Carroll, K., & Nuro, K. F. (2002). One size cannot fit all: A stage model for psychotherapy manual development. *Clinical Psychology: Science and Practice, 9*(4), 396–406. https://doi.org/10.1093/clipsy.9.4.396

Chan, A. W., Tetzlaff, J. M., Altman, D. G., Laupacis, A., Gøtzsche, P. C., Krleža-Jerić, K., Hróbjartsson, A., Mann, H., Dickersin, K., Berlin, J. A., Doré, C. J., Parulekar, W. R., Summerskill, W. S. M., Groves, T., Schulz, K. F., Sox, H. C., Rockhold, F. W., Rennie, D., & Moher, D. (2013). SPIRIT 2013 statement: Defining standard protocol items for clinical trials. *Annals of Internal Medicine, 158*(3), 200–207. https://doi.org/10.7326/0003-4819-158-3-201302050-00583

Dovis, S., Van Der Oord, S., Wiers, R. W., & Prins, P. J. M. (2015). Improving executive functioning in children with ADHD: Training multiple executive functions within the context of a computer game. A randomized double-blind placebo controlled trial. *PloS One*. https://doi.org/10.1371/journal.pone.0121651

Engel, B. T. (1984). The horse as a modality for occupational therapy. *Occupational Therapy in Health Care, 1*(1), 41–47.

Engel-Yeger, B., & Ziv-On, D. (2011). The relationship between sensory processing difficulties and leisure activity preference of children with different types of ADHD. *Research in Developmental Disabilities, 32*(3), 1154–1162.

Einav, M., & Margalit, M. (2022). The Hope theory and specific learning disorders and/or attention deficit disorders (SLD/ADHD): Developmental perspectives. *Current Opinion in Psychology*. https://www.sciencedirect.com/science/article/pii/S2352250X22001920

Fine, A. (2019). *Handbook on animal-assisted therapy: Foundations and guidelines for animal-assisted interventions*. Academic Press.

Fisher, A. G., & Bundy, A. C. (1992). Sensory integration theory. In *Movement disorders in children* (Vol. 36, pp. 16–20). Karger Publishers.

Friedman, N., & Miyake, A. (2017). *Unity and diversity of executive functions: Individual differences as a window on cognitive structure*. Elsevier.

Frisch, C., Tirosh, E., & Rosenblum, S. (2019). Parental occupation executive training (POET): An efficient innovative intervention for young children with attention deficit hyperactive disorder. *Physical & Occupational Therapy in Pediatrics, 40*(1), 47–61. https://doi.org/10.1080/01942638.2019.1640336

Gilboa, Y., & Helmer, A. (2020). Self-management intervention for attention and executive functions using equine-assisted occupational therapy among children aged 6–14 diagnosed with attention deficit/hyperactivity disorder. *The Journal of Alternative and Complementary Medicine, 26*(3), 239–246. https://doi.org/10.1089/acm.2019.0374

Gioia, G. A., Isquith, P. K., Guy, S. C., & Kenworthy, L. (2000). Test review behavior rating inventory of executive function. *Child Neuropsychology, 6*(3), 235–238. https://doi.org/10.1076/chin.6.3.235.3152

Hahn-Markowitz, J., Berger, I., Manor, I., & Maeir, A. (2017). Impact of the cognitive–functional (Cog–Fun) intervention on executive functions and participation among children with attention deficit hyperactivity disorder: An RCT. *American Journal of Occupational Therapy*. https://doi.org/10.5014/ajot.2017.022053

Hahn-Markowitz, J., Berger, I., & Manor, I. (2020). Efficacy of cognitive-functional (Cog-Fun) occupational therapy intervention among children with ADHD: An RCT. *Journal of Attention Disorders, 24*(5), 655–666. https://doi.org/10.1177/1087054716666955

Halayko, J., Magill-Evans, J., Smith, V., & Polatajko, H. (2016). Enabling 2-wheeled cycling for youth with Down syndrome. *Pediatric Physical Therapy, 28*(2), 224–230. https://doi.org/10.1097/PEP.0000000000000240

Helmer, A., Wechsler, T., & Gilboa, Y. (2021). Equine-assisted services for children with attention-deficit/hyperactivity disorder: A systematic review. *Journal of Alternative and Complementary Medicine, 27*(6), 477–488. https://doi.org/10.1089/ACM.2020.0482/ASSET/IMAGES/LARGE/ACM.2020.0482_FIGURE2.JPEG

Helmer, A., Delore, E., & Bart, O. (2024). Equine assisted occupational therapy for children with ADHD (ASTride): Protocol development and preliminary study. *Clinical Neuropsychiatry, 21*(1), 88. https://doi.org/10.36131/CNFIORITIEDITORE20240106

Holm, M. B., Baird, J. M., Kim, Y. J., Rajora, K. B., D'Silva, D., Podolinsky, L., Mazefsky, C., & Minshew, N. (2014). Therapeutic horseback riding outcomes of parent-identified goals for children with autism spectrum disorder: An ABA′ multiple case design examining dosing and generalization to the home and community. *Journal of Autism and Developmental Disorders, 44*(4), 937–947. https://doi.org/10.1007/S10803-013-1949-X

James, K., Miller, L. J., Schaaf, R., Nielsen, D. M., & Schoen, S. A. (2011). Phenotypes within sensory modulation dysfunction. *Comprehensive Psychiatry, 52*(6), 715–724. https://doi.org/10.1016/j.comppsych.2010.11.010

Law, M. (2002). Participation in the occupations of everyday life. *The American Journal of Occupational Therapy, 56*, 640–649. https://research.aota.org/ajot/article-abstract/56/6/640/4673

Law, M., Baptiste, S., Carswell, A., McColl, M., Polatajko, H., & Pollock, N. (2014). *COPM Canadian Occupational Performance Measure 2005*. www.caot.ca/copm/

Lezak, M., Howieson, D., Loring, D., & Fischer, J. (2004). *Neuropsychological assessment*. Oxford University Press.

Mahler, K. (2015). *Interoception: The eighth sensory system*. AAPC.

Martin, R. A., Graham, F. P., Taylor, W. J., & Levack, W. M. M. (2018). Mechanisms of change for children participating in therapeutic horse riding: A grounded theory. *Physical and Occupational Therapy in Pediatrics, 38*(5), 510–526. https://doi.org/10.1080/01942638.2017.1400492

Molavi, P., Nadermohammadi, M., Vicario, C. M., Nitsche, M. A., & Salehinejad, M. A. (2020). *Cognitive correlates of ADHD subtypes and its association with self-esteem: A quantitative difference*. https://doi.org/10.21203/rs.3.rs-21331/v1

Pelham, W. E., Jr., & Fabiano, G. A. (2008). Evidence-based psychosocial treatments for attention-deficit/hyperactivity disorder. *Journal of Clinical Child & Adolescent Psychology, 37*(1), 184–214. https://doi.org/10.1080/15374410701818681

Pérez-Gómez, J., Amigo-Gamero, H., Collado-Mateo, D., Barrios-Fernandez, S., Muñoz-Bermejo, L., Garcia-Gordillo, M. A., Carlos-Vivas, J., & Adsuar, J. C. (2020). Equine-assisted activities and therapies in children with attention-deficit/hyperactivity disorder: A systematic review. *Journal of Psychiatric and Mental Health Nursing, 00*(6), 1–13. https://doi.org/10.1111/jpm.12710

Polatajko, H. J., Mandich, A. D., Missiuna, C., Miller, L. T., Macnab, J. J., Malloy-Miller, T., & Kinsella, E. A. (2001). Cognitive orientation to daily occupational performance(CO-OP). *Physical & Occupational Therapy in Pediatrics, 20*(42038), 107–123. https://doi.org/10.1080/J006V20N02_07

Pyatak, E. A., Carandang, K., & Davis, S. (2015). Developing a manualized occupational therapy diabetes management intervention: Resilient, empowered, active living with diabetes. *OTJR Occupation, Participation and Health, 35*(3), 187–194. https://doi.org/10.1177/1539449215584310/ASSET/IMAGES/LARGE/10.1177_1539449215584310-FIG2.JPEG

Shiri, S., Tenenbaum, A., Sapir-Budnero, O., & Wexler, I. D. (2014). Elevating hope among children with Attention deficit and hyperactivity disorder through virtual reality. *Frontiers in Human Neuroscience, 8*(198). https://doi.org/10.3389/fnhum.2014.00198

Snyder, C. R., Hoza, B., Pelham, W. E., Rapoff, M., Ware, L., Danovsky, M., Highberger, L., Rubinstein, H., & Stahl, K. J. (1997). The development and validation of the Children's Hope Scale 1. *Journal of Pediatric Psychology, 22*(3), 399–421. https://academic.oup.com/jpepsy/article/22/3/399/917485

So, W. Y., Lee, S. Y., Park, Y., & Seo, D. I. (2017). Effects of 4 weeks of horseback riding on anxiety, depression, and self esteem in children with attention deficit hyperactivity disorder. *Journal of Men's Health, 13*(2), e1–e7. https://doi.org/10.22374/1875-6859.13.2.2/1-7.PDF

Child and Adolescent Health Measurement Initiative. (2024). *Fast facts: 2023 National Survey of Children's Health.* Data Resource Center for Child and Adolescent Health, supported by the U.S. Department of Health and Human Services, Health Resources and Services Administration (HRSA), Maternal and Child Health Bureau (MCHB). Retrieved [2023, November 22], from https://www.childhealthdata.org/docs/default-source/nsch-docs/2023-nsch-fast-facts_cahmi_drc.pdf

Toglia, J., & Katz, N. (2011). The dynamic interactional model of cognition in cognitive rehabilitation. In N. Katz (Ed.), *Cognition, occupation, and participation across the life span: Neuroscience, neurorehabilitation, and models of intervention in occupational therapy* (pp. 161–201). American Occupational Therapy Association. https://psycnet.apa.org/record/2012-33545-009

Wehmeier, P. M., Schacht, A., & Barkley, R. A. (2010). Social and emotional impairment in children and adolescents with ADHD and the impact on quality of life. *Journal of Adolescent Health, 46*(3), 209–217. https://doi.org/10.1016/J.JADOHEALTH.2009.09.009

Weldon, T. (2017). *An evaluation of human-horse interactions, children's attachment, and trust.* https://search.proquest.com/openview/1148dde9e391dd5e5be0235db61baf80/1?pq-origsite=gscholar&cbl=18750

White, E., Zippel, J., & Kumar, S. (2020). The effect of equine-assisted therapies on behavioral, psychological and physical symptoms for children with attention deficit/hyperactivity disorder: A systematic review. *Complementary Therapies in Clinical Practice, 39*, 101101.

Wolraich, M., Hagan, J., Allan, C., & Chan, E. (2019). Clinical practice guideline for the diagnosis, evaluation, and treatment of attention-deficit/hyperactivity disorder in children and adolescents. *Pediatrics.* https://publications.aap.org/pediatrics/article-abstract/144/4/e20192528/81590

Wood, W., Alm, K., Benjamin, J., Thomas, L., Anderson, D., Pohl, L., & Kane, M. (2021). Optimal terminology for services in the United States that incorporate horses to benefit people: A consensus document. *The Journal of Alternative and Complementary Medicine, 27*(1), 88–95. https://doi.org/10.1089/acm.2020.0415

World Health Organization. (2001). *ICF: International Classification of Functioning, Disability and Health.* https://pesquisa.bvsalud.org/portal/resource/pt/mis-33532

Yoldaş, T. Ç., Huri, M., Kayıhan, H., Karakaya, J., & Özmert, E. N. (2020). Sensory profile, ferritin and zinc levels in preschool-aged children with symptoms of attention deficit hyperactivity disorder. *The Turkish Journal of Pediatrics, 62*(6), 970–978. https://doi.org/10.24953/turkjped.2020.06.008

Efficacy of EAIs on Relieving Adolescent Stress and Improving Social Competence: Theoretical Models and Empirical Evidence

Patricia Pendry

Introduction

This chapter focuses on equine-assisted interventions (EAIs) that promote adolescents' social competence and ability to regulate stress, two interdependent aspects of functioning which are significantly associated with the development of mental, emotional, and behavioral adjustment problems. The rationale for focusing on this population and these interrelated competencies is informed by the recognition that adolescence is a developmental period associated with psychosocial and physiological factors of vulnerability, as well as by growing evidence that the promotion of these competencies during this period is an effective strategy to prevent mental, emotional, and behavioral disorders in adulthood (O'Connell et al., 2009). We begin the chapter by defining the nature of these two interdependent aspects of functioning and their implications for mental, emotional, and behavioral development. We next share the rationale for employing EAIs to enhance adolescents' social competence and ability to cope with stress by discussing theoretical perspectives that guide their implementation and efficacy. In addition to discussing the role of equine characteristics, the EAI environment, and the nature of relevant human-equine interactions, we give special attention to the workings of the human-animal interaction (HAI)–hypothalamic pituitary adrenal (HPA) Transactional model (Pendry & Vandagriff, 2020), a framework for understanding the mechanisms that underlie effects of the EAI effect on cortisol—a marker of HPA axis activity—and correlates. Next, we present the findings of the PATH to Success Study (PTS), an example of empirical work that examined the efficacy of an equine-assisted learning (EAL) program in shaping adolescent social competence and physiological markers of stress using an experimental design with an adequately powered sample size.

P. Pendry (✉)
Washington State University, Pullman, WA, USA
e-mail: ppendry@wsu.edu

Y. Neria et al. (eds.), *Guide to Equine Assisted Therapy*,
https://doi.org/10.1007/978-3-031-74426-6_15

Last, we discuss the strengths and limitations of the findings and interpret their significance for theory, practice, and future research.

While we originally set out to focus on *therapeutic* approaches such as equine-assisted therapy and psychotherapy (EAT/P), our own review of the literature revealed that the target population and outcomes of interest are most served using equine-assisted learning (EAL) approaches. EAL is an experiential learning approach that combines experiential learning, interaction with equines, and life skills education to increase participants' affective, physiological, and behavioral regulation. While EAL resembles therapeutic approaches, it does not require facilitation by licensed therapy professionals in counseling, psychotherapy, or occupational, speech-language, and physical therapy.

EALs are designed with the identified goals or desires of the participant(s) in mind and—similar to EAT—follow a process of assessment, planning, and documentation. The EAL approach is most used to promote the adaptive functioning of *typically* developing participants to *prevent* the onset of symptoms and/or the development of psychiatric disorders. As such, EAL tends to be offered to participants who are (1) *at risk* of developing a disorder due to the presence of known risk factors associated with the emergence of physical and/or mental health issues (e.g., exposure to acute or chronic stress) or (2) to those whose symptoms have recently emerged or feature levels below a clinical threshold of disorder. In contrast, EAT is more likely to target populations with special needs and/or clinical or developmental disorders. Programs that incorporate EAL have become extremely popular because they are perceived as being well-suited as community or school-based prevention programs, require less staff training and less clinical expertise in comparison to EAT/P, and enjoy positive public perception.

Adolescents' Social Competence and Coping with Stress

Social competence refers to the ability of a child or adolescent to successfully interact with others in a way that demonstrates an awareness of and ability to manage emotions in an age—and contextually appropriate manner (Rubin et al., 2006). Often erroneously summarized as "having good social skills," social competence encompasses several social, emotional, and cognitive skills and behaviors (e.g., social awareness, self-awareness, goal-directed behavior, optimistic thinking, personal responsibility, self-management, relationship skills, emotion regulation) that, combined, inform social adaptation.

Deficits in adolescents' social competence can affect several domains of functioning. Poor social competence manifests as difficulty in maintaining positive relationships and experiencing frequent conflict with peers, teachers, and parents, both of which are associated with a variety of other negative outcomes, including feelings of loneliness and isolation, anxiety, depression, and social withdrawal. These outcomes are problematic as they are associated with engagement in bullying or victimization by their peers which may lead to reduced engagement in classroom activities, decreased participation in group projects, and limited opportunities for academic support which can ultimately affect academic performance.

Unsurprisingly, deficits in social competence and their impacts on social relationships, mental health, and academic achievement can lead adolescents with poor social competence to experience tremendous stress. Not only do they encounter more stressful situations due to their inability to navigate social dynamics effectively, but also the stress they experience in turn impacts their ability to regulate their emotions during interpersonal interactions, resulting in a dynamic, bi-directional "feedback" loop. Given that these adolescents are less likely to have the social skills needed to seek support during stress exposure, they are also more likely to use avoidant or maladaptive coping mechanisms, which can exacerbate stress and risky behaviors, including substance use, early sexual activity, and delinquency.

Physiological Correlations of Poor Social Competence and Stress

Along with the *behavioral* implications of poor social competence and associated stress, there are *physiological* correlates of stress known to play a role in the development of physical and mental health issues. One example is dysregulation of cortisol production, which marks activity of the hypothalamic pituitary adrenal (HPA) axis, one of the body's stress-sensitive systems that plays a role in responding to acute and chronic social, emotional, and psychological stressors. Overall, decades of research have shown that exposure to chronic and/or severe acute stress during adolescence is associated with dysregulation of HPA axis activity and emerging psychopathology (Lupien et al., 2009). However, cortisol production is informed not only by the frequency or intensity of the exposure to stress but also by appraisal processes (Herman & Cullinan, 1997), which include the individual's interpretation of stressors, and their assessment of the availability and adequacy of their coping resources, which are likely affected by poor social competence. Since heightened HPA axis activity also occurs in response to normal puberty-associated neurobiological changes (Stroud et al., 2009), the combination of developmental and psychosocial vulnerabilities observed during adolescence presents a period of urgency and opportunity to improve social competence and stress management through intervention.

Theoretical Rationale: EAI and Social Competence

There is not one specific theory that proposes how EAIs may enhance adolescents' social competence; however, Social Cognitive Theory (Bandura, 1986) and Social Role—Activity Theory (Brickel, 1982) may provide useful frameworks.

Social Cognitive Theory

According to Bandura's social cognitive theory, individuals acquire new skills, behaviors, and beliefs through observation, cognitive processes (attention, memory, and self-regulation), and continuous interactions with the social environment (Bandura, 1986). In other words, individuals are not merely passive responders to external stimuli; they actively shape their environment, can influence the behavior of others through their actions, as well as learn new behaviors by *observing and imitating* the actions of others. Social cognitive theory emphasizes the importance of *self-efficacy*, which refers to an individual's belief in their ability to perform specific tasks or achieve certain goals. Higher levels of self-efficacy are associated with increased efforts, perseverance, and positive outcomes in various domains. Social cognitive theory also considers *outcome expectations*, which are an individual's beliefs about the consequences of their actions. If an individual expects positive outcomes from a behavior, they may be more motivated to engage in that behavior. Conversely, if they anticipate negative consequences, they might avoid the behavior. These factors are not static or independent; rather, they are *reciprocal and dynamic*; each behavior witnessed or experienced can change a person's way of thinking (cognition) and vice versa.

EAI and the Social Cognitive Framework

Participation in EAIs provides adolescent participants with many opportunities to experience the complex interplays outlined in this framework. First, equines possess several intrinsic and physical attributes that strongly influence the cognitions, behavior, and environments of those interacting with them (McGreevy & McLean, 2007, 2010). Equines are *prey animals*, characterized by a highly attuned awareness of their physical surroundings and a strong, instinctual inclination for a fight-or-flight response. This is evidenced by equines' extreme sensitivity to subtle behavioral cues from other equines and humans. This characteristic necessitates that those who want to interact with them are aware of their own behavior, thoughts, and emotional intent. These interactions also require humans to develop excellent verbal and non-verbal communication skills to ensure their personal safety, as well as to enhance their ability to communicate effectively with the equine. Reflecting on the meaning and impact of their behavioral cues—intended or not—participants experience opportunities to fine-tune and control their behavior. They also learn to regulate their emotional and arousal states since equines are sensitive to threat cues, which may lead them to otherwise disengage or move away from humans (Kohanov, 2013).

Another equine characteristic is that they communicate through consistent body language. This includes movement and position of ears, lips, face, and tail; verbalizations such as breathing and snorting; body positioning; distance and proximity;

and mirroring of another animal's body language. Since equines provide consistent, immediate, meaningful feedback—pinning ears, swishing tail, licking lips, blinking—participants in EAI simultaneously gain experience in observing and interpreting non-verbal cues. During EAI, through interacting with equines in the context of horsemanship activities, adolescents learn to provide clear non-verbal communication cues to their equine partner (e.g., pressure, release, posture, intent) with the purpose of eliciting specific behavioral responses from the equine (e.g., moving over, stepping forward, backward). As participants—with the help from program facilitators—attempt to manage and direct their own behavior and arousal to evoke desirable responses from the horse (e.g., licking lips, blinking, resting foot), rather than less desirable responses (e.g., swishing tail, pinning ears, tuning out), reciprocal interactions between horse and adolescent—and facilitator—play a central role in shaping participants thoughts and behavior. This also includes opportunities to practice appropriate social and horsemanship behavior through *imitation*—modeling—of equine handlers and fellow participants. Moreover, using human-equine interactions as an analogy, program facilitators encourage participants to reflect on their behavior, thoughts, feelings, and communication skills and apply their knowledge to communication with a *human* partner. Practicing pro-social behaviors, reflecting on thoughts, feelings, and feedback from the equine and facilitator may improve self and social awareness, personal responsibility, goal-directed behavior, and communication skills. Experiencing positive interactions and overcoming challenges with the horse in the context of EAI improve participants' self-efficacy and positive outcome expectations about social interactions with equines and humans.

Social Role-Activity Theory

Another relevant theoretical model is the social role-activity theory (Brickel, 1982), which proposes that when individuals assume a new positive role (e.g., team leader) and experience success, a positive behavioral change may result. This framework provides several avenues for human-equine interaction to shape positive change. First, since equines are herd animals, they tend to oscillate between seeking and/or assuming leadership or accepting it from others. This tendency provides a unique opportunity for humans to assert leadership using progressive shaping techniques (McGreevy & McLean, 2007, p. 114), negative reinforcement to direct the equine's movement, as well as rewarding compliant responses from the horse (e.g., release of pressure). During these interactions, EAI facilitators explicitly emphasize the importance of self-management and goal-directed behavior (i.e., giving clear non-verbal and well-measured cues to the equine), relationship skills (i.e., fostering a give-and-take relationship with their horse through release of pressure when the equine responds), quick decision-making (i.e., responding in a timely fashion), and optimistic thinking (i.e., communicating confidence and leadership). EAI participants thus learn to assume a leadership role—in the small equine herd or dyad—which they may infrequently experience in their daily lives. Combined, these experiences lead to improvements in social competence, self-efficacy, positive outcome expectations, and effective use of social supports of peers, facilitators, and the equine.

EAI and Stress Management: Theoretical Rationale

The mechanisms underlying the effects of EAIs in preventing, alleviating, or remediating *physiological dysregulation* are captured in the HAI-HPA Transactional model (Pendry & VandaGriff, 2020). Before delving into the specific workings of the model, it is important to first understand that in practice, *physiological dysregulation* is not commonly a state that is assessed as a risk factor or outcome of interest using biological measures; rather, the presence of potential dysregulation of cortisol production is implied—based on reports of high levels of stress exposure and/or the presence of stress-related symptoms such as behavioral, cognitive or mood problems, or physical health symptoms. Similarly, it is uncommon to determine the therapeutic success of EAIs in reducing stress or modifying physiological dysregulation of the HPA axis through assessment of physiological measures unless conducted within a research project, where relevant cortisol parameters and other stress-sensitive markers can be examined to enable comparisons by treatment condition.

Second, the hypothesized physiological effects of participation in EAI are thought to operate by "tapping" into the biological stress-system's tendency toward homeostasis, a biological process in which an organism maintains a stable internal environment despite external changes or fluctuations (Silverthorn, 1983). When the human body perceives a stressor, it activates the hypothalamus, which releases corticotropin-releasing hormone (CRH) which travels to the pituitary gland, which in turn responds by releasing adrenocorticotropic hormone (ACTH). Its production signals the adrenal glands to release cortisol, which then helps regulate various physiological processes (e.g., glucose production, blood pressure, and immune functioning) to allow the body to respond to the perceived stressor while regulating essential biological processes. This so-called cortisol cascade results in rising cortisol levels which in turn signal the hypothalamus and pituitary to decrease the release of CRH and ACTH, respectively, which is referred to as a negative feedback loop. This negative feedback loop thus helps maintain cortisol levels within an optimal range, ensuring the stress response is appropriately activated and terminated. Ideally, once the stressor has been resolved—through coping or removal—the HPA axis returns to its baseline activity. Dysregulation of the HPA axis can occur when chronic, intense, or repeated exposure to stressors disrupts this negative feedback loop, resulting in an overactive or underactive stress response as indicated by high or low basal or average levels, blunted or heightened momentary responses, or non-adaptive circadian rhythms. While the prior description may admittedly oversimplify this complex process, it helps us to describe the construct of dysregulation of HPA axis activity in response to acute or chronic stress as well as *how* EAI may support and enhance the body's tendency toward homeostasis through the dynamic interplay with the HPA axis feedback loop described.

The HAI-HPA Transactional Model

Adapted from prior stress and coping models (Cohen & Wills, 1985; Lazarus & Folkman, 1984, 1987) and conceived to capture effects of human-animal interactions (HAI), the HAI-HPA transactional model (Pendry & Vandagriff, 2020) captures how EAI may provide opportunities to *promote* optimal management of homeostasis of the cortisol cascade. According to the model (see Fig. 1), EAI provides (1) experiences that induce perceived stress, (2) experiences that foster improved coping with these stressors through enhanced cognitive appraisal and reappraisal, and (3) experiences that induce physiological relaxation. The model captures short-term regulatory responses during EAI activities and long-term processes that occur over time through homeostatic adaptation when engagement in equine activities and interactions are repeated frequently and regularly.

Engagement in EAI may strengthen adaptive HPA axis activity by *promoting optimal stress and appraisal experiences.* In the equine context, this includes both negative events (e.g., fear of the horse and anxiety about performing a task in front of a group of peers) and positive events (e.g., grooming a horse, enjoying social

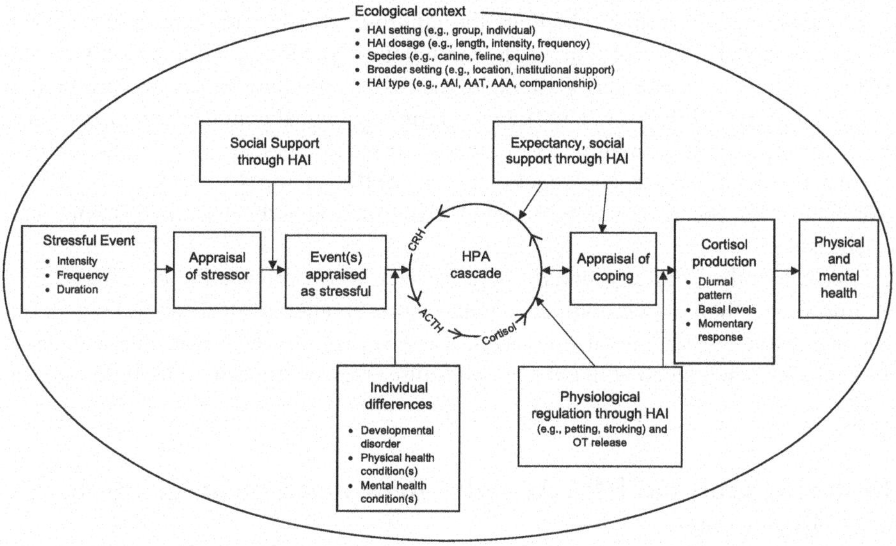

Fig. 1 HAI – HPA Transactional Model. HAI = Human-animal interaction; HPA = Hypothalamic-pituitary-adrenal; CRH = corticotropin releasing hormone; ACTH = adrenocorticotropin hormone. Adapted from and expanding upon model proposed in "Stress, Social Support, and the Buffering Hypothesis," by S. Cohen and T. A. Wills, 1985, *Psychological Bulletin, 98*(2), p. 310–357.

support, and experiencing moments of self-efficacy), as well as experience events that are novel (e.g., riding, doing groundwork with the equine). Of course, individual differences in how these stressors and events are perceived exist and change over the course of EAI engagement, as do participants' responses to these perceived stressors.

Once a stressor is perceived, the participant engages in cognitive appraisal of that stressor, which is likely influenced by the perceived level of social support (e.g., encouragement from staff and peers, trust in the equine responding to cues) as well as the participants' own outcome expectations (e.g., optimistic thinking and emotion regulation). Over time, appraisal and reappraisal of perceived stressors may result in the perception of the same stressor as less overwhelming than originally perceived, through increased self-efficacy and positive outcome expectancy generated through continuous positive experiences with EAI. This process of stress perception, appraisal, and reappraisal, increased self-efficacy and expectancy is thought to be dynamic and bi-directional and a central component of an enhanced ability to manage the stress that informs activation and cessation of the HPA cascade during equine activities as well as in participants' daily lives.

According to the model, another central component underlying the effect of EAI on participants' HPA axis activity is through *explicit momentary downregulation* of physiological arousal in response to equine events and activities. This process is achieved through providing engagement in relaxation activities that facilitate relaxed emotion states and physiological downregulation, as well as increased self-awareness and recognition of these physical states and processes. This is achieved by co-occurring physiological responses through physical contact with the equine (e.g., grooming and riding) which are thought to lead to the production of oxytocin (OT) (Beetz, 2012) and subsequent downregulation of cortisol (Chiodera & Geenen, 1988) which may momentarily attenuate the cascade by interrupting the production of CRH and ACTH (Legros, 1988). In addition to physical contact, being in proximity of the equine, (e.g., making eye contact and standing close) may evoke feelings of trust, connection, love, and attachment toward the equine (Uvnäs-Moberg, 2003), which have also been shown to activate OT production and subsequent suppression of cortisol.

Taken together, participants are hypothesized to experience the benefits of EAI by improving their social competence and stress management through behavioral, cognitive, and physiological processes, as such *preventing* dysregulation of HPA axis activity when faced with current and future stressors present in their daily lives.

Restoring Optimal HPA Activity: Repeated Downregulation and Homeostasis

In addition to strengthening adaptive stress perception, coping, and relaxation, engagement in EAI may *restore* participants' optimal HPA axis activity through the following processes. Given that dysregulation has likely occurred through frequent and/or prolonged *activation* of the cortisol cascade and disruption of the negative feedback loop, reversing dysregulation is hypothesized to necessitate *frequent or prolonged downregulation* of stress system activity. Thus, repeated exposure to equine activities that momentarily downregulate cortisol production is central to effective EAIs. According to the model, these relaxed physiological states can be achieved by emphasizing rhythmic physical contact with the equine (e.g., grooming and bareback riding) which facilitates OT production and subsequent downregulation of cortisol production.

Over time, the participants' stress-system functioning gradually changes through the body's tendency toward homeostasis, resulting in more adaptive HPA axis activity as marked by observation of what are considered healthy patterns and levels of cortisol production throughout the day, as well as measured responses and recovery to stress exposures. As participants become more aware of feelings, thoughts, and behaviors that facilitate physiological relaxation, participants will likely increase their awareness of bodily sensations that accompany relaxed physiological states, which may over time facilitate increased regulation of arousal. Over time, this may allow exposure to potentially more challenging equine activities (e.g., horsemanship activities and riding) which can gradually reshape their interpretation and perception of stress, cognitive appraisal, emotion regulation, and increased self-efficacy as described. While comprehensive testing of the proposed causal pathways is ongoing, there is empirical evidence to suggest that the processes described are operant, as evidenced by the research described in the following section.

Empirical Evidence of EAI Effects on Adolescents' Social Competence and Stress

Since the beginning of EAI implementation, there has been a call to conduct scientific research on its effects on participants' physical and mental health, well-being, and development. Studies that feature experimental designs characterized by randomly assigning participants to theoretically sound comparison conditions have become especially popular for their high internal validity, allowing us to make causal inferences. Similarly, researchers recognize the importance of conducting experimental trials with adequately sized and powered samples so significant and meaningful effects can be detected while considering the role of confounding, mediating, and moderating variables, which may shed light on underlying mechanisms.

In the next section, we share the findings of the PATH to Success Study (PTS), which was a randomized controlled trial funded by a grant to the first author of this chapter (NIH: 5R03 HD066590-02) examining the efficacy of an 11-week EAL on social competence and stress on typically developing 10–14-year-old adolescents. Designed according to the theoretical perspectives outlined above, the PTS program featured once-weekly, 90-minute themed lessons focused on individual, team, and group-centered equine activities based on principles of equitation science and natural horsemanship (McGreevy & McLean, 2007, 2010). The lessons combined mounted and unmounted human-equine interactions, observation of equine behavior, engagement in equine management (e.g., grooming and haltering), in-hand horsemanship (e.g., natural horsemanship games), some riding, and personal and group reflection. Participants were taught a series of in-hand horsemanship activities, which were based on themed natural horsemanship approaches during which participants applied gradually increasing levels of direct and indirect pressure on the horse as a way of directing movement of the horse's front and hind quarters. An important component of these interactions was to teach participants subtle equine behavioral cues associated with compliance, along with the timely release of pressure as a reward for even the slightest try on behalf of the horse. In a directed effort to strengthen social competence, participants were encouraged to reflect on their cognitions, behavior, and emotional intent and their potential effect on the quality of human-equine interaction during these activities. Program facilitators also helped children recognize analogies between horse and human interactions to those between humans in various social contexts (e.g., school and family). For example, since participants were taught to use gradually increasing amounts of finger pressure on the horse—hair, skin, muscle, bone—as a way of moving the equine hind quarters, facilitators facilitated reflection on how participants could use analogous behaviors—ask, move, shove, or push—to make requests of peers in social settings with peers. To facilitate adaptive stress and coping, regular inquiries were made by facilitators to engage participants in appraising perceived challenges and successes, as well as providing them with instrumental tools to downregulate physiological arousal. Examples of relaxation activities included silent grooming, rhythmic stroking of the horse, encouraging slow breathing, muscle relaxation, and rhythmicity during mounted activity, as well as encouraging optimistic thinking, reflecting on emotions experienced during the lesson, and utilizing cognitive, behavioral, and physiological coping strategies toward adaptive self-management. Throughout, facilitators modeled social competence while facilitating optimal communication between participants and program staff in dyadic and group contexts during reflection. Facilitators received extensive training before each session which emphasized the theoretical connections between activities and intended outcomes as well as fostered the use of explicit language to emphasize core constructs relevant to social competence and stress.

One hundred thirty-one typically developing adolescents were recruited through school-based recruitment and referrals with the aim of recruiting a sample with approximately 30% of adolescents experiencing high levels of stress or the presence of stress-related internalizing and/or externalizing behavioral symptoms. After the screening (e.g., history of animal abuse and the ability of parents to complete the assessment in English), participants ($N = 113$; 64% female; M age = 11.35 yrs) were randomly assigned to either an experimental ($n = 53$) or waitlisted control condition ($n = 60$). Outcomes in both groups were assessed before and after program completion, including parent reports on social competence (Devereux Student Strengths Assessment (DESSA); LeBuffe et al., 2009) and various developmentally appropriate self-report measures of depression, anxiety, worry, stress, coping, and psychosomatic health. Participants' behavior was assessed weekly by three independent observers

(Psychosocial Session Form, SF; Chandler, 2012). Adolescents completed thirty short reports on positive and negative emotional states at various time points during sessions and in response to relevant equine activities such as riding (before mounting, after dismounting) and grooming, using an 11-item checklist based on the Experienced Sampling Method (ESM; Csikszentmihalyi & Larson, 1987).

Before random assignment took place, participants collected six salivary cortisol samples (wake up, 4 pm, bedtime) over two consecutive days, from which indices of diurnal cortisol activity were derived. Six additional in-home cortisol samples were collected post-intervention. Each week, participants also provided three to five additional samples of salivary cortisol, reflecting their basal cortisol level at the end of their school day, their cortisol levels linked to the beginning and end of equine activities and their emotion states, and the end of the equine lessons.

Results

Results indicated that program participation caused a moderate effect ($d = 0.55$; $p = 0.02$) on participants' overall social competence (Pendry et al., 2014a), which was independent of pretest levels of social competence, age, gender, and referral status. Examinations of participants' weekly psychosocial behavioral trajectories showed significant improvements, evidenced in increased positive and decreased negative behavior, which was significantly associated with attendance when participant characteristics were controlled. Results also showed lower average cortisol concentrations per waking hours (Area Under the Curve (AUC)) ($d = 0.48$) and lower afternoon cortisol levels ($d = 0.48$) for participants in the experimental condition (Pendry et al., 2014b) compared with those waitlisted. Program effects on the afternoon and average cortisol per waking hour were independent of baseline (pretest) levels of cortisol, child gender, age, and referral status.

In addition to observed causal effects in response to program participation, we also examined adolescents' momentary reactivity levels marked by salivary cortisol and associations with their affective and behavioral responses to their first, mounted equine-assisted learning (EAL) activity. The goal was to better understand the role of participants' physiological regulation in shaping their program experiences and behavior. During the fifth week of the program, when the first mounted activity occurred, adolescents with higher cortisol levels immediately before mounting reported higher levels of negative emotion and lower levels of positive emotion, while basal levels and potential markers associated with dysregulation of cortisol diurnal patterns were statistically controlled (Pendry et al., 2018). Greater *cortisol reactivity* in response to 10 minutes of riding was linked to higher negative and lower positive emotions experienced *after* dismounting. Higher levels of pre-ride negative emotion and lower levels of post-ride positive emotion, and an increase in cortisol reactivity in response to riding also predicted higher levels of negative behavior during the 90-minute session that day. Statistically significant causal effects on participants' overall levels of depression, anxiety, worry, or psychosomatic health were not observed. Given the experiential design with random assignment to conditions, its large sample size, and comprehensive measurement of behavioral and physiological outcomes, the PTS study provides strong scientific evidence demonstrating that EAL can be an effective approach to improve typically developing adolescents' social competence and ability to regulate stress.

Interpretation, Strengths, and Limitations

While the effect on social competence was moderate, it had meaningful implications. In particular, the social competence measure used was originally designed as a tool for parents and teachers to identify adolescents in *need of improvement* in their social competence based on normed comparisons to their peers, resulting in group-level identifiers. Based on these criteria, EAL participation not only led to differences in total social competence scores by treatment condition, but closer examination also revealed that adolescents in the experimental condition were more likely to be lifted out of the *needs improvement* group to now feature *typical* levels, which reflects a meaningful clinical effect of participation in EAI.

The cortisol findings are particularly meaningful as they reflect the first evidence demonstrating significant impacts of an equine-assisted intervention on indicators of HPA axis activity. The effect of reducing the average amount of cortisol per waking hour—especially in the afternoon—in the featured sample can be interpreted as optimizing adaptive diurnal functioning of HPA axis activity based on extensive literature suggesting that increased average levels as well as higher afternoon levels tend to be indicative of dysregulated diurnal cortisol activity. While it would be an oversimplification to merely suggest that lower levels of (afternoon) cortisol are always a sign of adaptive functioning, the effects of modulating adolescents' cortisol levels in response to an 11-week program are a promising and meaningful finding.

In addition, the embedded correlational study examining the momentary reactivity of cortisol in response to riding highlights the role of participants' physiological and affective experiences in shaping behavioral responses to common EAL activities. The dynamics between markers of momentary HPA axis activation, stress perception, and appraisal as hypothesized in the HAI-HPA transactional model clearly led to participants' individual differences in positive and negative emotion, subsequent arousal, and behavior during equine activities (Pendry et al., 2018). As such, the participants' own affective and psychological profiles we aim to target may in fact limit the development of self-efficacy or positive outcome expectations thought to underlie intervention success. Revealing physiological correlates underlying these bi-directional processes demonstrates the dynamic relationship between participants' emotions, cortisol levels, and behavior and how, combined, they shape the pathways by which EAL can get "under the skin" to influence program success toward adaptive HPA regulation. This is an important finding as it demonstrates that facilitators should not only consider participants' behavior but also their momentary emotional and physiological state which are likely to contribute to undesired behavior (e.g., expressions of anger, fear, impatience, not listening, and not following directions). As such, helping participants recognize and regulate physiological arousal during EAI through relaxation using EAI activities (e.g., grooming and stroking) may be of central importance to activity success rather than trying to address behavioral challenges through reward, encouragement, reinforcement, or punishment. Overall, the findings not only provide support for the efficacy of EAL in the downregulation of cortisol levels over time but also provide support for the reciprocal, bi-directional pathways highlighted in the HAI-HPA transactional model.

Caveats and Implications for Practice

The PTS study is not without limitations. Since adolescents and parents had a choice to enroll in the program, we don't know whether the program would be effective for those less willing to interact with horses. While this limitation is often presented as somehow unique to EAI, given that adolescents are minors, this is operant for most therapeutic interventions. It does speak to the role of expectancy, which is the participant's belief in the efficacy of the intervention, or the role of the equine therein, which is likely to shape program experiences through outcome expectations. This belief could also influence reports of parents who tend to intimately *know* the child but are not blind to their treatment status, which may have presented bias as they completed the social competence measure at the posttest. While limitations are present, the quality of implementation, rigor of measurement, and novelty of findings render the PTS study a meaningful contribution to theory and research.

Despite our promising results, it is important not to overstate the practical implications of this research. Until replication has occurred, we should consider that the program effects are specific to this program as it was implemented—under optimal and highly controlled conditions (e.g., highly trained staff, strong control of curriculum, and data collection procedures) created to conduct an efficacy trial. Also, it would be unwise to promote the results as warranting scaling up of equine-assisted learning programs *in general,* as we cannot assume similar treatment effects for populations with different characteristics (e.g., adolescents who have experienced trauma) or different, related outcomes (e.g., self-esteem, academic achievement, and substance use).

Conclusion and Recommendations

There are several gaps in our knowledge that our field should further explore. For example, we know little about the differential importance or role of core components embedded in the EAIs under study (e.g., riding, natural horsemanship, grooming and mindfulness-based exercises, and peer-partnered activities). What are the elements essential in accomplishing these observed effects? We also have a limited understanding of what dosage levels (e.g., program length and session length) are needed to achieve desired outcomes. What is the ideal program or session length needed to change participants' outcomes in meaningful, lasting ways? Does it depend on the outcomes we aim to target? In addition to a lack of knowledge about essential program characteristics and activities, we don't know much about the extent to which—or way in which—participant characteristics (e.g., age and gender) and risk and protective factors (e.g., presence of mood-related symptomatology and history of trauma) may shape participants' program experiences and moderate their intended effects. Are the effects of EAIs equally achieved by individuals with varying levels of risk? Which participant characteristics enhance or undermine expected treatment effects? As we engage in research, we must investigate whether EAIs confer benefits *beyond* evidence-based programs that do not include equine participants. If so, how do we balance the needs of our equine partners with those of the client we serve?

While the focus of research questions matters, the importance of research design and methods cannot be overstated. If we want to learn whether, for whom, how, and under what conditions EAI provides causal benefits to humans, we should consider evidence based on randomized controlled trials with adequate sample sizes and meaningful comparison conditions. To be clear, this does not imply that correlational, descriptive, and case studies do not play a valuable and important role in our field; however, they should not be used to make causal arguments about program efficacy. Last, the sequencing toward implementation of interventions (e.g., testing efficacy under tightly controlled conditions and examining effectiveness in real-life settings) and ongoing evaluation of efficacy and fidelity of implementation are rarely adhered to. Addressing these critiques is important so therapeutic horsemanship professionals have access to reliable, scientific resources to help guide the implementation of evidence-based EAI programs. Ultimately, demonstrating engagement in evidence-based practice will foster greater respect for EAIs as a professional discipline and recognition that it provides a viable treatment modality that warrants reimbursement by health care insurers.

Acknowledgments The scientific review of empirical literature was conducted by Taylor Diane Pearson and Richelle Keikilaninopihahauoli Gouveia, undergraduate students in Psychology and Human Development. The PATH to Success program was designed and implemented in collaboration with Sue Jacobson, WSU's former Director of the Palouse Area Therapeutic Horsemanship (PATH) program, and Professor Phyllis Erdman, counseling psychologist at WSU's College of Education.

References

Bandura, A. (1986). *Social foundations of thought and action: A social cognitive theory*. Prentice Hall.

Beetz, A., Uvnäs-Moberg, K., Julius, H., & Kotrschal, K. (2012). Psychosocial and psychophysiological effects of human- animal interactions: The possible role of oxytocin. *Frontiers in Psychology, 3*, 1–15. https://doi.org/10.3389/fpsyg.2012.00234

Brickel, C. M. (1982). Pet-facilitated psychotherapy: A theoretical explanation via attention shifts. *Psychological Reports, 50*, 71–74. https://doi.org/10.2466/pr0.1982.50.1.71
Chiodera, P., & Geenen, V. (1988). Inhibitory action of exogenous oxytocin on plasma cortisol in normal human subjects: Evidence of action at the adrenal gland. *Neuroendocrinology, 48*, 204–206.
Cohen, S., & Wills, T. A. (1985). Stress, social support, and the buffering hypothesis. *Psychological Bulletin, 98*(2), 310–357. https://doi.org/10.1037/0033-2909.98.2.310
Csikszentmihalyi, M., & Larson, R. (1987). Validity and reliability of the experience-sampling method. In M. Csikszentmihalyi (Ed.), *Flow and the foundations of positive sychology: The collected works of Mihaly Csikszentmihalyi* (pp. 35–54). Springer Netherlands. https://doi.org/10.1007/978-94-017-9088-8_3
Herman, J. P., & Cullinan, W. E. (1997). Neurocircuitry of stress: Central control of the hypothalamo- pituitary-adrenocortical axis. *Trends in Neurosciences, 20*(2), 78–84. https://doi.org/10.1016/S0166-2236(96)10069-2
Lazarus, R. S., & Folkman, S. (1984). *Stress, appraisal and coping*. Springer, Inc.
Lazarus, R., & Folkman, S. (1987). Transactional theory and research on emotion and coping. *European Journal of Personality, 1*, 141–169. https://doi.org/10.1002/per.2410010304
LeBuffe, P. A., Shapiro, V. B., & Naglieri, J. A. (2009). *The Devereux student strengths assessment (DESSA)*. Kaplan Press.
Legros, J. J., Chiodera, P., & Geenen, V. (1988). Inhibitory action of exogenous oxytocin on plasma cortisol in normal human subjects: Evidence of action at the adrenal gland. *Neuroendocrinology, 48*, 204–206.
Lupien, S. J., McEwen, B. S., Gunnar, M. G., & Heim, C. (2009). Effects of stress throughout the lifespan on the brain, behaviour and cognition. *Nature Reviews Neuroscience, 10*, 434–445. https://doi.org/10.1038/nrn2639
McGreevy, P. D., & McLean, A. N. (2007). Roles of learning theory and ethology in equitation. *Journal of Veterinary Behavior: Clinical Applications and Research, 2*, 108–118. https://doi.org/10.1016/j.jveb.2007.05.003
McGreevy, P. D., & McLean, A. N. (2010). *Equestrian science*. Blackwell Publishing.
O'Connell, M. E., Boat, T., & Warner, K. E. (2009). *Preventing mental, emotional, and behavioral disorders among young people: Progress and possibilities*. The National Academic Press.
Pendry, P., & Vandagriff, J. L. (2020). Salivary studies of the social neuroscience of human–Animal interaction. In M. K. Taylor & D. A. Granger (Eds.), *Salivary bioscience* (pp. 555–581). Springer International Publishing. https://doi.org/10.1007/978-3-030-35784-9_23
Pendry, P., Carr, A. M., Smith, A. N., & Roeter, S. M. (2014a). Improving adolescent social competence and behavior: A randomized trial of an 11-week equine facilitated learning prevention program. *Journal of Primary Prevention, 35*(4), 281–293. https://doi.org/10.1007/s10935-014-0350-7
Pendry, P., Smith, A. N., & Roeter, S. M. (2014b). Randomized trial examines effects of equine facilitated learning on adolescents' basal cortisol levels. *Human Animal Interaction Bulletin, 2*(1), 80–95.
Pendry, P., Carr, A. M., & Vandagriff, J. L. (2018). Adolescents' affective and physiological regulation shape negative behavior during challenging equine assisted learning activities. *Frontiers in Veterinary Science, 5*(300). https://doi.org/10.3389/fvets.2018.00300
Rubin, K. H., Bukowski, W., & Parker, J. G. (2006). Peer interactions, relationships, and groups. In N. Eisenberg (Ed.), *Handbook of child psychology: Social, emotional, and personality development* (Vol. 3, pp. 571–645). Wiley.
Stroud, L. R., Foster, E., Papandonatos, G. D., Handwerger, K., Granger, D. A., Kivlighan, K. T., & Niaura, R. (2009). Stress response and the adolescent transition: Performance versus peer rejection stressors. *Development and Psychopathology, 21*, 47–68. https://doi.org/10.1017/S0954579409000042
Uvnäs-Moberg, K. (2003). *The oxytocin factor: Tapping the hormone of calm, love, and healing*. Da Capo Press.

Part IV
Cherishing Equines: A Journey of Remembrance and Care

Horses in Service: A Historical Military Context

Matthew Ryba

Introduction

Whenever discussion arises about the work being done in the equine therapy field with veterans, one aspect that seems to be overlooked is the use of horses by military men and women in a historical context. This historical relationship is something that is rarely talked about among this cohort when discussing the use of horses in post traumatic stress disorder (PTSD) therapy, yet it seems deeply connected to the idea that for nearly all of history, humans have depended on horses for their many roles in warfare. Perhaps there is a deeper classical mechanism in understanding the relationship of therapy horses helping heal the trauma of military personnel. Quite often veterans who have interacted with horses in the context of therapy talk about feelings of a natural bond with the animal, even if they have no previous experience with equines. Very quickly, it seems even if there is initial hesitation in approaching these large and intimidating animals for the first time, veterans become very comfortable around the horses and report feeling natural working with them. At the same time, these veterans often have trouble describing why they feel so connected to the animals. Likely, this is in part because of a familiar, subconscious connection to horses, used in a historical military sense in warfare.

When we think of therapy animals, there are two that often come to mind immediately: dogs and horses. It is no coincidence that both animals, the two that have been domesticated to not only live but work among humans, are also the two animals most widely used in military applications. Canines are often used for therapy, emotional support, or even as guide dogs for wounded military veterans. Dogs are also familiar to military personnel in their roles with military police, in application

M. Ryba (✉)
Columbia University Department of Psychiatry, Anxiety Disorders Clinic PTSD Research and Treatment Team, New York State Psychiatric Institute, New York, NY, USA
e-mail: Matthew.ryba@nyspi.columbia.edu

Y. Neria et al. (eds.), *Guide to Equine Assisted Therapy*,
https://doi.org/10.1007/978-3-031-74426-6_16

as bomb detection dogs to help explosive ordinance disposal technicians sniff out improvised explosive devices (IEDs), and even as service mascots. The Marine Corps has adopted the bulldog as its mascot since 1922, when the Germans gave the Marines fighting in the First World War the nickname "teufel hunden," affectionately still exchanged as a nickname among Marines to this day, as "Devil Dogs."

Although dogs have accompanied militaries in battle for most of recent history, horses have a much longer chronicle of military application. Militaries around the world have been reliant on equine partners on the battlefield in some way or another for nearly all recorded history. Apart from maybe the last 50–100 years, horses were not only present on the battlefield but primary to mission accomplishment, used in multiple capacities that were instrumental to military success. As a result of this, there has been a centuries-long natural evolution of the relationship between equines and fighting men and women.

Since these links between horses and humans have existed for thousands of years, it is important to understand the context of horses in their military capacity to better inform us of their relationship with military service members. This chapter will explore the historical military timeline of equine use in campaigns and combat, as well as some historical examples of specific horse/human relationships to lay a foundational understanding of how equine/veteran relationships are unique, how horses used in combat contribute to human resilience, and how horses may help to heal mental health problems common to service members following their time in the military.

A Brief Historical Timeline of Military Equine Use

Horses have been used in military applications since the first horse was broken to be ridden by a human. Evidence of horses used in warfare dates back as far as 4000 BCE and the ancient Sumerians (Bennett et al., 2022). Throughout all recorded history, there has been a relationship between military fighting forces and equines. The Greeks wrote the guide to chariot training in warfare in 1350 BCE. The surviving Kikkuli Text, written by Kikkuli, a Hurrian who served in the Hittite court, has detailed instruction of the seven-month process of breaking a horse for combat, covering everything from dietary needs, grooming routines, night maneuvers, swimming, interval training to increase heart strength, and chariot maneuvers (Raulwing, n.d.).

The campaigns of the Roman Empire spanned over 1000 years, using horses as military transport, cavalry in battle, to pull chariots, and in parades. The Mongol armies led by the Khans were some of the greatest horseback archers ever known. Up to 40% of the Khan's armies were cavalry on horseback. The use of saddles and stirrups allowed archers to move swiftly, to be able to fire up to 12 arrows per minute at ranges of 350 yards while moving ("Devil's Horsemen": Why Mongol Horse Archers Were History's Most Feared, 2023). Horses are believed to have begun becoming domesticated around 1400 BCE by the Mongols and are extremely culturally significant in Mongolia to this day, not just for work and in previous warfare, but to produce mares' milk, the staple of sustenance in the Step.

By 400–1350 CE, horse warfare had reached the Golden Age of heavy cavalry. Light horses, also known as prickers, were fast-moving and used primarily for reconnaissance. Larger draught horses were utilized to pull carts, cannons, wagons, and carry supplies. Medium-weight horses, called destriers, carried mounted infantry and cavalry into battle (Military Technology – The Age of Cavalry, C. 400 Ce–1350 | Britannica, 2020).

The uses of these equines in warfare continued through the Napoleonic wars in the 1700s and into the Americas. Paul Revere's famed midnight ride to warn Boston that the British were coming began at about eleven o'clock at night when Revere set off on horseback. After narrowly avoiding capture just outside of Charlestown, Revere rode through Medford, where he alarmed Isaac Hall, the captain of the local militia, informing him of the British movements. He then alarmed almost all the houses from Medford through Menotomy (today known as Arlington). Revere carefully avoided the Royall Mansion owned by Isaac Royall, a well-known British loyalist, and arrived in Lexington sometime after midnight (The Paul Revere House, 2016). Horses were used throughout the American Revolution, the American Indian wars, the Civil War, and the settlement of the West.

In more recent history, through the 1900s, horses saw battle in both Great Wars. Military equines were heavily relied on in the First World War and the Second World War. Over eight million horses and other equines died in services in the First World War (The Real War Horses – Faithful unto Death, 2019). Technological advances in the Second World War saw less use of horses, but it's estimated that between two and five million died in combat (War Horse Facts | Brooke, 2019). In the Vietnam War, the spirit of the horse remained when the US Army introduced the Air Cavalry—the insignia of a yellow shield with a diagonal black line and horse bust, trading rides on horseback for rides in helicopters to insert troops quickly in hard-to-reach places. Most recently, the first battle of US troops in Afghanistan, the story of 12 strong, Task Force Dagger, was fought on horseback alongside the Northern Alliance against Al Qaeda in 2001. The men who fought in Task Force Dagger are memorialized in the famed horse soldier statue at the World Trade Center in New York City.

Military Personnel and Their Beloved War Horses

There are many instances of the relationship between a specific horse and soldier in wartime that stand out as exceptional, beyond the call of duty. Part of the reason that horses are valuable in a therapeutic sense is because they provide a nonjudgmental and accepting environment. This allows veterans to form a bond with the animal and connect in a healing and comforting way. Certainly, these same therapeutic benefits contribute to these kinds of relationships between horse and soldier on the front, as well as in a therapeutic setting after combat. There are key components of the horse-human relationship cited in equine therapy that become very apparent when put in the context of horse and soldier relationships in battle.

Sergeant Reckless

Horses have been known to be of such value to troops on the warfront that in some instances they even attain a recognized military rank, as in the case of Sergeant Reckless. Reckless was the first animal to achieve the rank of Sergeant in the United States Marine Corps. In 1952 during the Korean War, Lt. Eric Pedersen of the Recoilless Rifle Platoon, Anti-Tank Company, 5th Marine Regiment, 1st Marine Division, went searching to purchase a horse to help his men haul the six-foot recoilless rifle and 75mm shells his unit were responsible for employing. Reckless, originally known as Ah-Chim Hai or "Morning Flame" in Korean, was bred to be a racehorse, but her stable hand sold the horse to the Marines to pay for a prostatic leg for his sister (Franco, 2023).

Reckless went through Marine Corps Equine boot camp, known as "hoof camp," and was trained for the realities of war. In addition to carrying supplies, Reckless became so acquainted with the members of the platoon. She soon learned and understood various hand signals, including how to take cover when she heard cries of "Incoming!" and even how to find her way back to the platoon when she got lost. She became a part of the platoon and followed them everywhere. She would sleep with the Marines in their tents, and she ate the same diet as the Marines, enjoying breakfasts of bacon, eggs, and coffee and the occasional candy bar or Coca-Cola to raise morale. The Marines treated her as one of their own (Franco, 2023).

In the 5-day Battle for Outpost Vegas, one of the bloodiest battles of the Korean War that saw over 1000 US casualties and twice as many Chinese casualties, Reckless remained faithful to her men. She made 51 trips across rice paddies and mountainous terrain, bringing more than 9000 pounds of ammunition and equipment to the front lines while also hauling back injured Marines. She was wounded twice, hit above the eye and in her left side, but continued to make the treks despite her wounds because her men needed her. As a result of her bravery, Reckless was awarded two purple hearts, in addition to her rank of Sergeant, and several other high military honors. Following the armistice, Sergeant Reckless is said to have celebrated with her Marines, indulging in drinks with the men and later seen staggering around camp. Sergeant Reckless returned to the United States following the war and was retired at Camp Pendleton, where she received the rank of Staff Sergeant and a 19-cannon salute at her retirement ceremony. Her awards included two Purple Hearts, the Marine Corps Good Conduct Medal, the Navy Presidential Unit Citation with bronze star, the National Defense Service Medal, the Korean Service Medal, the United Nations Korea Medal, the Navy Unit Commendation, and the Republic of Korea Presidential Unit Citation, worn on her horse blanket. When Reckless passed away in 1968, she was buried with full military honors (Franco, 2023).

The relationship between Sergeant Reckless and her men highlights some of the key aspects of human-equine relations that contribute to the therapy environment of equines and veterans: Non-verbal communication, trust and partnership, emotional connection, and mutual benefit. Not surprisingly, these are all aspects of the human-equine relationship observed in equine-assisted therapy.

Human-equine relations rely heavily on non-verbal communication. Horses are highly perceptive and respond to subtle cues, including body language and facial expressions. Horses often mirror the emotions of their handler and pick up on these subtle non-verbal cues. What has been observed in equine-assisted therapy with veterans is that the veterans realize the horses act a certain way in response to their own feelings and emotions in real time, helping to inform the veteran of their own emotional state.

Building trust is also essential to human-equine relations. Horses are prey animals and naturally cautious. This requires their handlers to earn the trust of the horse for the horse to follow commands. Developing this kind of partnership involves respect, understanding, and clear communication. In equine-assisted therapy, the veterans build this trust through a series of tasks that challenge both the horse and human's boundaries so both understand each other and how to communicate.

Humans often build strong emotional connections with horses, and because of the horses known ability to sense and respond to human emotions, horses can be therapeutic in a comforting sense, helping individuals process and heal from emotional trauma. This is why equine-assisted therapy focuses on emotions in the present, with grounding exercises and being wholly in the moment during the sessions, rather than discussing and reliving past traumatic experiences. This focus on emotions in the present is extremely attractive to veterans, especially those who experience the horrors of trauma in combat. Unlike some other therapy modalities that require veterans to repeat exposures to those traumas, equine-assisted therapy focuses on learning how to regulate emotions in the present moment. The horses, who are always living in the moment, help guide the veterans to be present as well.

Finally, human-equine relations are unique in that they often involve mutual benefit. Horses are social animals and enjoy human companionship, while humans benefit from the physical, emotional, and mental well-being that interacting with horses can bring. Whether it's through recreational riding, therapy, or simply working through a task together, both humans and horses can experience positive outcomes from their relationship. There was a very clear and obvious mutual benefit between Sergeant Reckless and the troops she served with; companionship on a level higher than most human-animal relationships, where she not only fought with them on the front lines but shared meals with them, slept in their tents, and was assimilated as one of their own in the platoon. Sergeant Reckless and the men of the Fifth Marine Regiment are just one of many examples of this unique relationship between horses and military service members.

Ulysses Grant and His Horses

The human-equine relationship in the military is a testament to the profound connection that can be forged between the two species. Horses have been steadfast companions to soldiers, contributing to their success and survival in countless military campaigns throughout history.

This enduring partnership highlights the remarkable capabilities of both horses and humans and serves as a reminder of the unique bond that can develop between these animals and those who rely on them.

Ulysses S. Grant has been heralded by many historians as perhaps having the most exemplary horsemanship skills in American history. Known for his stoic and determined nature, Grant developed a strong bond with his faithful equine companions. His horses were not just means of transportation; they were trusted allies that accompanied him through the trials and triumphs of war. The general's connection with his horses went beyond practicality, as he found solace and comfort in their presence amid the chaos of battle. Grant's relationship with his horses exemplified the profound partnership that can exist between humans and these noble creatures.

Born Hiram Grant, the two-term President, and commanding general of the Union Army in the American Civil War, grew up the son of a hide tanner. From a young age, working alongside his father and on the family property, Grant showed remarkable horsemanship skills.

His father, Jesse Root Grant, realizing his son's affinity for the animals, would give Grant chores around the horses, including plowing, hauling wood, and driving teams of horses' long distances. In his free time, he would ride bareback and perform stunts on horses from as young as the age of five. Grant's neighbors would enlist him to train their stubborn horses. At the age of 17, Grant was sent to West Point, and realizing there was no one with the name Hiram Grant listed as a new cadet, changed his name on the spot to Ulysses (Biography: Ulysses S. Grant | American Experience | PBS, n.d.).

Grant's performance at the academy was very average, graduating 21st out of a class of 39, but his best performances were in mathematics and horsemanship. Just before the West Point graduation ceremony, Grant saw an opportunity to show off his horsemanship skills to the Corps of Cadets and graduation spectators and mounted a notoriously difficult horse, York. As the spectators watched, the riding master, Sergeant Herschberger, lifted the jumping bar higher than his own head, fixed it in place, and called out to Cadet Grant. One account of a newly joined cadet student at the Academy, James Fry, described the event; "a slender little cadet dashed from the ranks on a big sorrel, wheeling and galloping down toward the far end of the hall, turned [the horse] York, and then the two of them came thundering down toward the bar, faster, faster—then into the air and over." In Fry's words, "it seemed as if man and beast had been welded together." After the crowd saw this feat of horsemanship, all Sergeant Herschberger could say was "well done Sir, class dismissed." Ulysses S. Grant began his career as an officer in the US Army on that note. According to early Grant Biographer Albert Richardson, the height of Grant's jump with York was a new record that stood at West Point for 25 years (Graduation Day: Ulysses S. Grant and the West Point Class of 1843 (U.S. National Park Service), 2020).

During the Mexican-American War, Grant was billeted as the quartermaster of his regiment, responsible for managing the mule teams used by the Army. Grant's duties included packing, inspecting, and caring for up to 50 mules (Dowdall, 2012). Grant was eager to put his horsemanship skills to use, so when a volunteer was needed to run dispatches at the Battle of Monterrey, Grant rose to the occasion, often riding hanging from the side of his horse throughout the battle to avoid lines of sniper fire.

As the Civil War broke out Grant was Colonel of the Twenty-first Illinois Volunteer Infantry. Over the course of the war, Grant owned ten horses, three of which became very significant to him. Different horses played different roles for Grant over the course of the campaign, some better fit for long-distance travel, some in more precarious situations. Several of Grant's horses were retired during the war, while others did not survive. Grant's first horse proved not to be battle worthy and was quickly retired. Fredrick Grant, Ulysses' son recalled: "This horse, though a strong animal, proved to be unfitted for the service and, when my father was taking his regiment from Springfield, Illinois, to Missouri, he encamped on the Illinois River for several days. During the time they were there, a farmer brought in a horse called 'Jack.' This animal was a cream-colored horse, with black eyes, mane and tail of silver white, his hair gradually becoming darker toward his feet. He was a noble animal, high spirited, very intelligent, and an excellent horse in every way. He was a stallion and of considerable value. My father used him until after the battle of Chattanooga (November, 1863), as an extra horse and for parades and ceremonial occasions" (Ulysses S. Grant Homepage – Grant the Equestrian, n.d.).

Jack was a distance-riding horse who famously carried Grant to the attack on Fort Donelson, through the Tennessee mud before the battle of Shilo, and through the Cumberland to the battle of Chattanooga. Grant utilized another of his horses, named Fox, during the actual siege at Ft. Donelson and Chattanooga.

During Grant's first battle engagement in the Civil War, at the Battle of Belmont, the now Brigadier General Grant had the issued horse he was riding killed out from under him. Grant resigned to using a pony he had purchased for his son, Fredrick, that was accompanying him as a pack animal. The pony was unfit for battle and later given to Grant's aide, Captain William Hillyer, in exchange for his steed. Author Ronald White in, his biography *"American Ulysses: A life of Ulysses S. Grant"* writes that during the final retreat at Belmont, at Camp Johnson, after the Confederates surrounded the Union troops, "Grant narrowly escaped on his horse by leading it down a steep riverbank. Grant recalled, my horse put its fore feet over the bank without hesitation or urging, and, with his hind feet well under him, slid down the bank and trotted aboard the boat, twelve or fifteen feet away, over a single gang-plank" (White, 2017).

It was after this that Grant purchased his most prized equine, Cincinnati. Cincinnati was 17.2 hands thoroughbred bay-colored horse and was the son of Lexington, the fastest-known thoroughbred horse in the United States at the time.

Grant called Cincinnati the finest horse he had ever seen. He only ever let two other people ride the horse when it was in his possession, one of which was Admiral Daniel Ammen, the other of which was President Abraham Lincoln. There were occasions when Grant was offered up to $10,000 in gold for Cincinnati, which he promptly refused. Grant loved Cincinnati so much that he was not willing to risk the horse in battle (White, 2017).

In 1962, before the siege at Vicksburg, Grant sent Jack away to rest for a month in Illinois. During the Vicksburg campaign, he acquired another horse, Jeff Davis, who was captured during a raiding party of a plantation in Mississippi. Grant found the horse delightful to ride and purchased him from the Army, riding Jeff Davis instead of Cincinnati on long journeys. Jeff Davis quickly became the second of General Grants most prized horses along with Cincinnati. The third of Grant's three favorite horses arrived to him a year later in 1963. While still in Chattanooga, the people of Egypt, Illinois, knowing Jack had been retired and Grant needed a replacement, sent a 16-hand 7-year-old dark bay. Grant named the horse Egypt, in honor of the residents who gifted the animal, which proved to be invaluable durring the campaigns in Virginia through the snow covered, winter months (White, 2017).

At the surrender at Appomattox, the two generals Grant and Lee at the picket lines between the armies sat on their horses for hours, Grant astride Cincinnati, and Lee on Traveler, and discussed the terms of surrender. Before departing, Lee requested that his officers be permitted to leave with their horses. Grant, having farmed with horses and knowing many of the Confederate officers were small farmers, allowed them to return home with their horses, swords, and their honor.

After being elected President in 1869, Grant's three favorite horses, now all veterans of the Civil War, Cincinnati, Jeff Davis, and Egypt, were brought to the White House stables.

Grant's first son Fredrick again recalls his father's relationship with Cincinnati in the archives, telling the story of Capitol stable master, Albert Hawkins. Hawkins noted, that in his second term Grant had commissioned a statue of himself on Cincinnati, and for nearly a month, would saddle up and ride out daily to meet the sculptor with his horse (Grant, n.d.). Nearly all depictions of Grant on horseback in drawings, granite, and bronze, are astride Cincinnati, including the Ulysses S. Grant Memorial in Washington, D.C. Cincinnati died in 1878 at the home of retired Admiral Amman, one of the three men to ever ride him.

Grant's relationship with his horses is another example of these special bonds between a military man and his steed. Grant and his horse Jack, as described by eyewitnesses, seemed to understand each other intuitively. Jack was known for his endurance and bravery, carrying Grant through numerous battles, including the pivotal Battle of Shiloh. Grant's men said that the horse would instinctively position himself protectively in front of Grant during the heat of battle. This anecdote not only highlights the deep trust and reliance that Grant placed on his horses but also demonstrates the profound emotional connection that can develop between a military leader and his equine companion. Grant continued to visit Cincinnati well after the war and, through his presidency, often visited the horse after retirement, highlighting the bond the man had with his animal. This further exemplifies the deep emotional connection that Grant had with his horses, highlighting the mutual trust and reliance that existed between them.

General Jack Seeley and Warrior

The First World War was the first transitional period into modern warfare. At the onset of the First World War, horses were essential in offensive military campaigns. Calvary and scout units were used to maximum effect. As the war went on and developments in machine guns, mortars, tanks, chemical gas, and other weapons caused warfare to evolve, horses were relied on less for use on the front lines and more for logistical support, as they were better than mechanized vehicles at traversing difficult terrain, carrying messages on reconnaissance missions, and in pulling artillery, supplies, and acting as ambulances. Battle losses of horses made up 25% of war-related equine deaths between 1914 and 1916. When the war began in 1914, the British Army had 25,000 horses; within 12 days, 140,000 additional horses had been purchased. Losses were so great that Britain began conscripting horses into service from farms around the country. Over the course of the war, Britain lost 484,000 horses, one horse for every two men (T. N. A. Web. (n.d.). *Horse Census—The UK National Archives)*.

Importantly, horses bolstered morale at the war front. Many soldiers had previous experience with equines before enlisting and had a great affection for horses. Some recruiting posters even featured horses, showcasing the relationship between horse and soldier. Perhaps the most famous military horse comes from the First World War, the inspiration for a book, hit Broadway play, and eventual globally famous film by Steven Spielberg. The real "War Horse" the Germans could not kill went by the name Warrior. Warrior was a bay of 15.2 hands born in the Isle of Wright in Hampshire on the Seely property. His owner, General Jack Seely, 1st Baron Mottistone, was an aristocrat and politician, first serving as Secretary of State of War prior to the First World War and later elected Member of Parliament after the war from 1904 to 1924. Jack Seely was a great friend of Winston Churchill and the only former cabinet member to join the war front and remain 4 years later.

General Seeley bred and rode Warrior himself, prior to the war. Seely rode the 15.2 hand thoroughbred charger for over 30 years, including all the major battles of the Western Front. There was a remarkable bond between the horse and the General, and Warrior became a symbol of motivation and endurance, not for the troops fighting on the front, but also one of hope for those back in England.

Brough Scott, a journalist, Seely's biographer, and grandson said of Warrior, "My grandfather was a flamboyant figure, he would be up near the front when they were parading and marching and very much not hiding and for the troops behind him, seeing the horse up there in front was something they found really inspirational and totemic, he was the ultimate mascot" (Lewis, 2018). In addition, he wrote, "My grandfather would say that when he rode up to the troops, they were saying 'here comes Warrior.' With a horse, you can go up to it and pat it and say 'good chap.'

There's no doubt for those cavalrymen their morale was kept up. Thinking about somebody else is helpful, no question" (Lewis, 2018).

Throughout the 4 years on the front Warrior participated in every major battle: Warrior led the Canadian cavalry forces at Salisbury Plain, was first off the boat at the landing at the fighting in Boulogne, fought in the trenches near Ypres, and galloped through the battle of the Somme. Warrior survived the attack at Guyencourt, getting stuck in the mud at Passchendaele, and fighting on the front line at Cambri, but perhaps Warrior's finest hour with the cavalry came on March 30, 1918, when he was ridden by Seely, commanding a number of Canadian regiments. He made one of history's last-ever cavalry charges against the Germans near Amiens. They checked the German advance and helped win the war.

After the war, Warrior and General Seely returned home to a quiet life. Seely continued to ride and even race Warrior, who won an Isle of Wight point-to-point race in March 1922.

When Warrior died in 1941 at the age of 32, The Times ran an obituary for him with the line: "*The Horse the Germans couldn't kill.*"

Warrior might be the most exemplary case of horse-human relationships. This horse was not just the connection to a single military leader, or to a garrison of troops he served with, but a beacon for an entire nation at war. All of England had a connection to Warrior, one that brought hope and bolstered the morale of the entire nation. Warrior became the symbol of the resilience of the British people during the First World War. Warrior was awarded the Honorary People's Dispensary of Sick Animals Dickin Medal in 2014, The "animals' Victoria Cross," regarded as the highest honor an animal can receive for serving in military conflict, to mark 100 years since the start of the Great War. The only recipient to pre-date the Medal's institution in 1943, Warrior received the Medal on behalf of all animals that served in the First World War (Ellis-Petersen, 2014).

Conclusion

Throughout nearly all organized military history, horses have played a vital role on the battlefield, treated with the same respect, and held in high regard as a military service member. Today, horses continue to serve in some capacity in militaries around the world, in parade and ceremony, if not in combat. The emotional bonds between horses and humans in the military are complex and highlight various psychological components: trust and dependence, emotional support, sense of purpose, companionship, symbolism, identity, and serve as a coping mechanism. The lives of the horses and fighting men and women become intertwined on the battlefield. Soldiers depend on the animals not only for transportation, reconnaissance, and protection but also for fostering strong emotional connections. Horses can provide emotional support for soldiers, have a calming effect, and help alleviate anxiety and fear during combat. A horse can provide a soldier with a simple sense of purpose among the chaos of war. The responsibility of looking after a horse and ensuring its well-being can give soldiers a sense of pride and accomplishment, strengthening their emotional bond with the animal. Horses serve as sources of companionship and solace for soldiers enduring the hardships of combat. The bond between a soldier and their horse can provide a sense of connection and belonging, offering comfort during lonely and challenging times. In addition to their practical military roles, horses can hold symbolic significance for soldiers, representing courage, loyalty, and resilience.

The relationship between a soldier and their horse can become deeply intertwined with their sense of identity and values, reinforcing the emotional bond between them. The emotional human-equine bond between a soldier and their horse can serve as a coping mechanism for dealing with the trauma and stress of war. The companionship and unconditional support provided by the horse can help soldiers manage their emotions and maintain their resilience in the face of adversity.

Equine-assisted therapy utilizes many of the same psychological components found in the emotional bonds between humans and horses in combat. However, in equine-assisted therapy, these components are intentionally harnessed to promote healing, growth, and well-being in individuals struggling with various mental health issues or emotional challenges.

Veterans utilizing equine-assisted therapy develop trust and dependence on the therapy horses, much like soldiers do in combat. Establishing a bond with the horse requires trust-building exercises, such as grooming, leading, and riding, which help individuals develop confidence and reliance on the horse as a therapeutic partner. Horses provide emotional support to individuals in equine-assisted therapy through their calming presence, nonjudgmental nature, and ability to mirror human emotions. Interacting with horses can help individuals regulate their emotions, reduce stress and anxiety, and increase feelings of comfort and safety. Engaging in activities with therapy horses gives individuals a sense of purpose and accomplishment. Caring for, training, and interacting with horses provides opportunities for personal growth, skill-building, and the development of a positive self-concept. Horses offer companionship and solace to participants in equine-assisted therapy, fostering feelings of connection, acceptance, and belonging. The therapy horses, often retired working horses from other trades, also get a sense of purpose and belonging with their veteran counterparts. Building a relationship with a therapy horse can provide individuals with a supportive and nonjudgmental ally, enhancing their sense of well-being and emotional resilience. The human-equine relationship can hold symbolic significance, representing themes of empowerment, healing, and personal transformation.

Working with these horses allows veterans to explore and express aspects of their identity, values, and emotions in a safe and supportive environment. Equine-assisted therapy can serve as a healthy coping mechanism for veterans struggling with mental health issues, trauma, or life challenges, and interacting with these horses can help veterans develop a new skill set, emotional regulation techniques, and problem-solving abilities, empowering them to manage stress, overcome obstacles, and navigate their life challenges more effectively.

In sum, equine-assisted therapy harnesses the therapeutic potential of the emotional bonds between humans and horses to promote healing, growth, and well-being in individuals facing a variety of psychological and emotional difficulties. Through meaningful interactions with therapy horses, veterans can cultivate resilience, self-awareness, and a sense of connection, leading to positive outcomes in their lives the same way soldiers on the battlefield have found deeper meaning in the human-equine relationship with their horses throughout history.

References

Bennett, E. A., Weber, J., Bendhafer, W., Champlot, S., Peters, J., Schwartz, G. M., Grange, T., & Geigl, E.-M. (2022). The genetic identity of the earliest human-made hybrid animals, the kungas of Syro-Mesopotamia. *Science Advances, 8*(2). https://doi.org/10.1126/sciadv.abm0218

Biography: Ulysses S. Grant | American Experience | PBS. (n.d.). www.pbs.org. https://www.pbs.org/wgbh/americanexperience/features/grant-biography

"Devil's Horsemen": Why Mongol Horse Archers Were History's Most Feared. (2023, July 24). *Big Think*. https://bigthink.com/the-past/mongol-archery-secret/

Dowdall, D. M. (2012). *From Cincinnati to the Colorado Ranger – The horsemanship of Ulysses S. Grant*. Lulu.com

Ellis-Petersen, H. (2014, September 2). First world war horse awarded "Victoria Cross for animals". *The Guardian*. https://www.theguardian.com/world/2014/sep/02/first-world-war-horse-awarded-victoria-cross-animals

Franco, S. (2023, January 6). The horse that became a staff sergeant for her service in Korea. *War History Online*. https://www.warhistoryonline.com/korean-war/sergeant- reckless.html

Graduation Day: Ulysses S. Grant and the West Point Class of 1843 (U.S. National Park Service). (2020). Nps.gov. https://www.nps.gov/articles/000/graduation-day-ulysses-s-grant-and-the-west-point-class-of-1843.htm

Grant, F. (n.d.). *Ulysses S. Grant and his horses during and after the Civil War* [Review of "*Ulysses S. Grant and his horses during and after the Civil War*"]. Archived from the original on 2011-07-19.

Lewis, B. A. (2018, November 9). World War One: "The horse the Germans could not kill". *CNN*. https://www.cnn.com/2018/11/09/sport/world-war-one-remembrance-horses- war--horse-spt-intl/index.html

Military Technology – The Age of Cavalry, c. 400 ce–1350 | Britannica. (2020). *Encyclopædia Britannica*. https://www.britannica.com/technology/military-technology/The-age-of-cavalry-c-400-ce-1350

The Paul Revere House. (2016). *Paul Revere – THe midnight ride*. Paul Revere House. https://www.paulreverehouse.org/the-real-story/.

The Real War Horses – Faithful unto Death. (2019, November 3). *Horse Journals*. https://www.horsejournals.com/popular/history-heritage/real-war-horses-faithful-unto-death

Raulwing, P. (n.d.). *The Kikkuli text. Hittite training instructions for chariot horses in the second half of the 2nd millennium B.C. and their interdisciplinary context*. http://www.lrgaf.org/Peter_Raulwing_The_Kikkuli_Text_MasterFile_Dec_2009.pdf

T. N. A. Web. (n.d.). *Horse census – The National Archives*. Home Front Stories. Retrieved June 5, 2024, from https://www.nationalarchives.gov.uk/first-world-war/home-front-stories/horse-census

Ulysses S. Grant Homepage – Grant the Equestrian. (n.d.). Www.granthomepage.com. Retrieved June 5, 2024, from https://www.granthomepage.com/grantequestrian.htm

War Horse Facts | Brooke. (2019). Thebrooke.org. https://www.thebrooke.org/get-involved/every-horse-remembered/war-horse-facts

White, R. C. (2017). *American Ulysses: A life of Ulysses S. Grant*. Random House.

Horse Well-Being in Therapies Integrating Horses

Ellen M. Rankins and Karyn Malinowski

Introduction

The well-being of horses participating in therapies such as psychotherapy, physical therapy (PT), occupational therapy (OT), and speech-language pathology (SLP) is critical because of its ramifications for the horses, clients, and industry. This chapter will consider why horse well-being is critical for these areas. A broad overview of welfare models is presented. This is followed by a summary of the measurements used in studies on welfare and stress and their physiological underpinnings. An overview of the literature on horses in therapies is provided. The consequences of horse well-being on human outcomes are discussed. This chapter concludes with a discussion of recommendations for future research and implications for practice.

The goal of every practitioner in therapy integrating horses and their environment should be a session that is engaging and leads to positive outcomes for the horse and human participants. Horses who are willingly engaged in the therapy session are more likely to reengage in future sessions. Additionally, if these horses are in a state of positive welfare—a positive mental state resulting from meeting or exceeding their nutritional, environmental, health, and behavioral needs—they are more likely to be able to continue to perform the work they are being asked to do. Distress, apathy, or confusion will detract from the session's success and may pose safety hazards to the clients and practitioners involved. Horses are more likely to

E. M. Rankins (✉)
Temple Grandin Equine Center, Department of Animal Sciences, Colorado State University, Fort Collins, CO, USA
e-mail: ellen.rankins@colostate.edu

K. Malinowski
Equine Science Center, Department of Animal Sciences, Rutgers, The State University of New Jersey, New Brunswick, NJ, USA
e-mail: karynmal@njaes.rutgers.edu

Y. Neria et al. (eds.), *Guide to Equine Assisted Therapy*,
https://doi.org/10.1007/978-3-031-74426-6_17

injure the humans working with them when poor or confusing communication exists between human and horse or the horse is in a state of poor welfare such as distress (Hawson et al., 2010; Thompson et al., 2015).

Positive horse welfare is also critical to the industry. The industry's ability to provide therapies integrating horses rests on a positive public perception of horses in these roles. Positive public perception is what gives industries or sports a social license to operate (Douglas et al., 2022). Loss of positive perception and a shift toward negative perception results in the loss of a social license to operate. This loss of social license to operate can result in government regulations, regulations from governing entities, or simply pressure from the public that results in changes to or loss of the ability to perform the service in question. Thus, the industry's ability to provide therapies integrating horses is dependent on its social license to operate and, thus, positive public perception (Douglas et al., 2022). This is particularly important in a field that has such routine and widespread interactions with various members of the public. Education regarding what positive welfare is and how it can be ensured for horses in equine-assisted services programs will be a critical part of this process.

Welfare Assessment

Welfare assessment of horses should be undertaken using a valid model of animal welfare. Two of the most used models are the Five Domains Model of Animal Welfare and the Five Freedoms Model of Animal Welfare (Farm Animal Welfare Council, 2009; Mellor et al., 2020). Both provide an overarching framework in which to assess and evaluate welfare, which is a multidimensional concept. These approaches are particularly helpful to practitioners, as the models can easily be used to evaluate a horse's welfare status and identify areas for improvement. At this point, research studies have not applied these models in studies investigating horses involved in therapy, although components of horse welfare and well-being have been investigated among these horses.

The Five Freedoms approach to welfare encompasses freedom from hunger and thirst; freedom from discomfort; freedom from pain, injury, and disease; freedom to express normal behaviors; and freedom from pain and distress. The Five Freedoms have routinely been adopted as a standard for welfare when enacting legislation or other policies with a focus on eradicating poor welfare conditions to achieve good welfare (Fig. 1).

The Five Domains Model comprises five categories for assessment: (1) nutrition, (2) physical environment, (3) health, (4) behavioral interactions, and (5) mental state. Under this framework, various items in categories one through four are evaluated to determine if they contribute toward a negative or positive welfare state and to what degree. These feed into and determine category five—mental state. This model allows for the determination of both positive and negative welfare states and moves beyond ensuring good welfare via the elimination of poor welfare states to

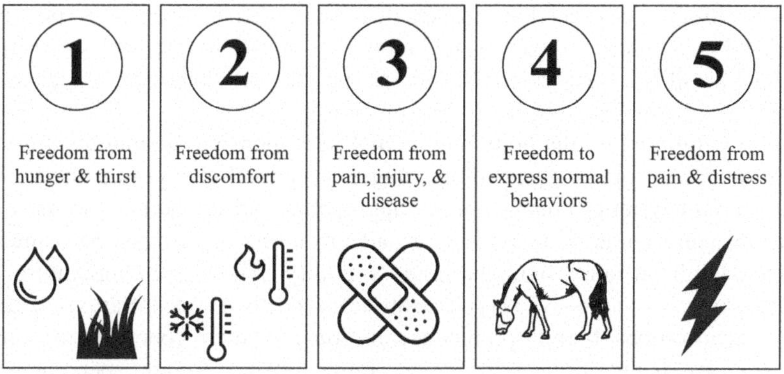

Fig. 1 The Five Freedoms Model of Welfare as proposed by the Farm Animal Welfare Council (2009)

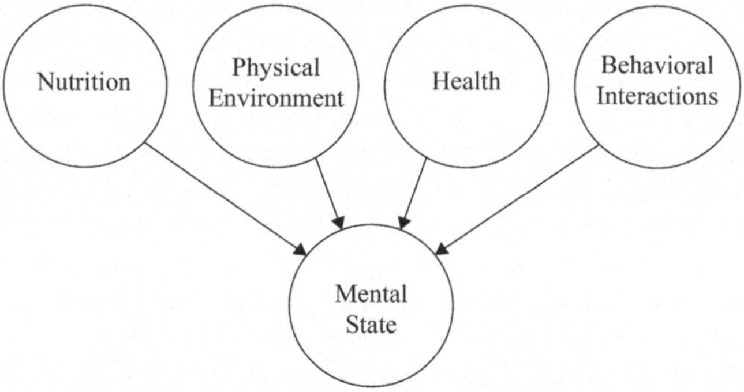

Fig. 2 The Five Domains Model of Welfare as proposed by Mellor et al. (2020)

creating space for recognizing and supporting positive welfare states and, thus, horse well-being (Fig. 2).

Research on horse welfare and well-being often focuses on acute responses to specific procedures, management strategies, or interactions. This information and other validated measurements that can be used to assess specific components of welfare can then be applied and used in more comprehensive welfare assessments (Harvey et al., 2020, 2023; Kelly et al., 2021; Lesimple, 2020). The focus when identifying acute responses or validating measures is most often on identifying situations and procedures that minimize negative affective states and distress rather than maximizing positive affective states. Affective states can be likened to mood states and reflect the animal's experiences with the stimuli around it. Affective states are defined along two axes: an arousal axis ranging from low to high and a valence axis ranging from negative to positive.

Stress is often used to connotate a negative state, when it is simply any change in the environment or an individual that alters homeostasis, thus causing the body to initiate a response to return to homeostasis (Koolhaas et al., 2011). Whether a particular situation or procedure invokes distress (negative) or eustress (positive) is determined by a number of factors, including the length and intensity of the stimuli, the animal's ability to respond to the stimuli, and even previous experiences with the stimuli (Bienertova-Vasku et al., 2020; von Borell, 2001).

Changes initiated by the body and animal in response to a stimulus during the stress response encompass physiological and behavioral changes. In the literature on therapies integrating horses, several approaches and methodologies have been used to measure animals' responses, usually in terms of distress. Measurements have included heart rate (HR), heart rate variability (HRV), eye temperature, adrenocorticotropic hormone (ACTH) concentrations, cortisol concentrations, catecholamine concentrations, β-endorphin concentrations, oxytocin concentrations, lactate concentrations, hemoglobin, erythrocyte count, leukocyte count, percent neutrophils, percent lymphocytes, and behavior (Rankins et al., 2023). Each of these measures is linked to the stress response in different ways and provides slightly different information about the horse's experience of and reaction to the stimulus.

The responses of the hypothalamic-pituitary-adrenal (HPA) axis and sympathetic-adreno-medullar (SAM) axes are the most common places to start when investigating the effects of a potentially stressful stimulus. In both axes, the brain initiates the response through recognition of the physical or psychological stressor. Activity in the HPA axis is initiated with the release of corticotrophin-releasing hormone (CRH) from the hypothalamus. This stimulates the cleavage of proopiomelanocortin (POMC), resulting in the release of ACTH and β-endorphins. ACTH stimulates the release of cortisol from the adrenal glands which has a number of peripheral effects in the body. Thus, increases in CRH, ACTH, β-endorphins, cortisol, or a combination thereof are characteristic of increased stress (Pilozzi et al., 2021). The response of the HPA axis to stress is relatively slow, occurring in the timeframe of minutes to hours. The response of the SAM axis, in contrast, is rapid and occurs within seconds to minutes. The primary products of the activation of the SAM axis are the catecholamines—norepinephrine (NE, noradrenaline) and epinephrine (E, adrenaline). Thus, increases in NE and E are also characteristic of increased stress. There is also direct action of the sympathetic branch of the autonomic nervous system (ANS) throughout the body. Many of the other measurements used in stress assessment are the result of the activation of the HPA or SAM axes (Fig. 3).

Heart rate is the number of beats per minute produced by the heart and is susceptible to a variety of influences, including regulation by the ANS. Heart rate increases with increasing stress but is a less sensitive and discriminatory measure than the related HRV. At its basis, HRV is a measure of the changes in time between consecutive heart beats with specific measures in the time and frequency domains as well as non-linear metrics. HRV is closely tied to ANS regulation and is generally thought to provide information on the balance and interplay between the parasympathetic and sympathetic branches (Shaffer & Ginsberg, 2017). Increases in sympathetic influence are indicative of greater stress. Increases in parasympathetic influence may be indicative of greater well-being, although this is much less commonly discussed and used.

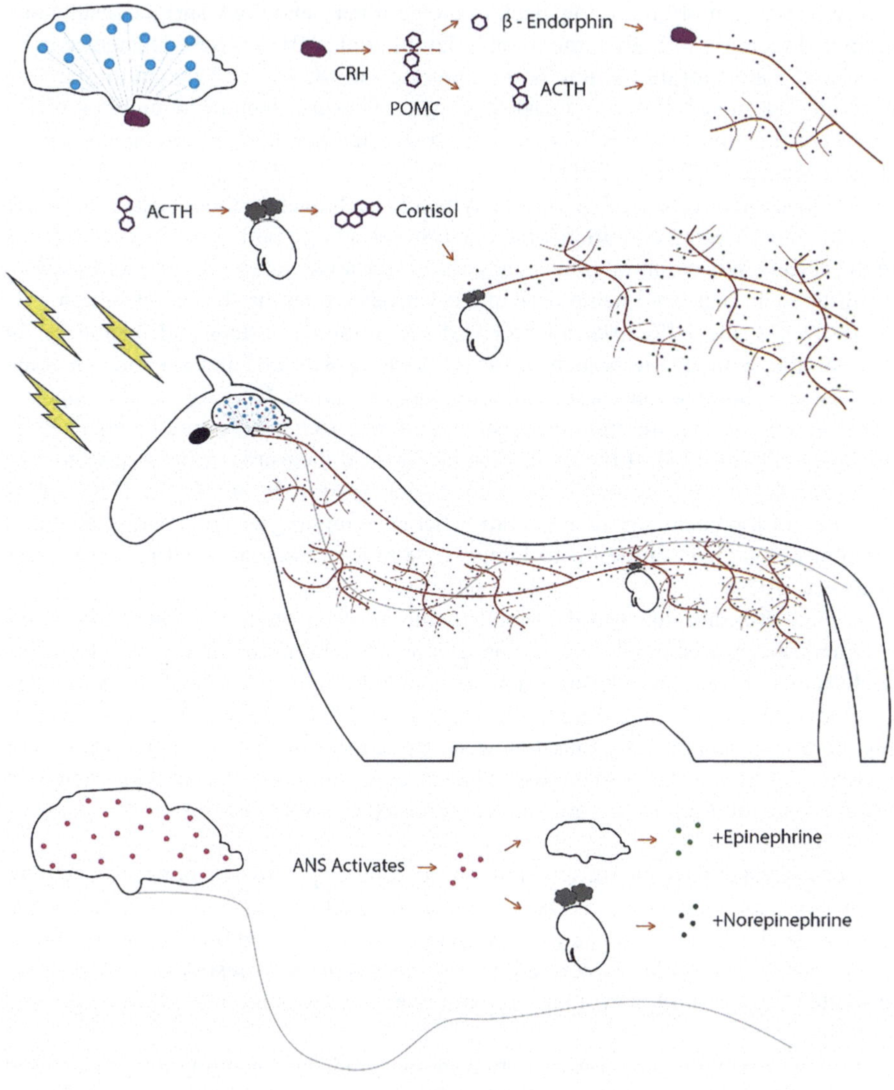

Fig. 3 Overview of the responses of the hypothalamic-pituitary-adrenal (HPA) axis and sympathetic-adreno-medullar (SAM) axis to stress. The HPA axis is depicted at the top of the figure. The SAM axis is depicted at the bottom of the figure. Figure design: Kyle Hartmann

Eye temperature is also closely related to and used as a proxy of the ANS and SAM axis functions. Activation of the SAM axis via the ANS results in a hyperthermic response and redistribution of blood flow. Immediately (milliseconds to seconds) following the encounter of a stressful event or stimulus, surface and peripheral body temperature decreases as blood is shunted to the core via vasoconstriction and vasodilation. The hyperthermic response produced by activation of the SAM axis and redistribution of blood flow back to the periphery and body surface results in a sustained increase in body temperature (Jerem et al., 2019). These changes can be measured using infrared scanners or cameras, and the eye or surrounding area is generally the most reliable and easiest place to measure changes in temperature. In studies using this methodology, increased eye temperature is associated with a stress response (Dai et al., 2015).

Another effect of the ANS via the sympathetic branch is the contraction of the spleen. Under resting conditions, the horse stores a large portion of its erythrocytes in the spleen. When contraction occurs, the erythrocytes are forced into circulation, resulting in an increased hematocrit and erythrocyte count in the blood stream.

The SAM and HPA axes interact with the immune system and responses. In general, the sympathetic branch of the ANS along with NE and E evoke an acute increase in inflammation via the inflammatory cytokines. Cortisol has the opposite effect of suppressing the immune system, and this occurs to restore balance (Reed & Raison, 2016). One of the more commonly used measures in the assessment of stress and the immune system is the ratio of neutrophils to lymphocytes. Neutrophils are a part of the innate immune system, whereas lymphocytes are a part of acquired immunity. A higher neutrophil-to-lymphocyte ratio is associated with greater stress (Zahorec, 2021).

Lactate concentrations in the bloodstream are most often associated with exercise and, more specifically, anaerobic glycolysis. The need for increased energy, such as that encountered during exercise, is met through a variety of endocrine and metabolic responses, including the increase in cortisol. Cortisol increases circulating glucose concentrations, making the substrate more available for glycolysis. The increased glycolysis leads to increased lactate concentrations, thus making increased lactate concentrations observable under increased stress and not just during exercise (Fig. 4).

Currently, the only measurement in use to identify positive responses to a stimulus is oxytocin concentration. Oxytocin is associated with affiliative behaviors and positive social interactions across a variety of species, including horses (Lansade et al., 2018). Oxytocin concentrations increase acutely in response to a positive stimulus. Lower basal or resting oxytocin concentrations are indicative of general well-being.

Behavior, usually in the form of observations guided by an ethogram, is also used to assess horses' responses to a stimulus. Ethograms used in studying horses' reactions to equine-assisted services and other stimuli typically focus on behaviors associated with negative affect and distress responses. Kaiser et al. (2006) developed perhaps the most used and well-known ethogram for horses in equine-assisted services. It has been used or modified for use in other studies. This ethogram focuses on behaviors associated with distress. While there are comprehensive and detailed ethograms for horses in natural settings (McDonnell, 2003) and for discomfort (Torcivia et al., 2021) in horses, there are currently no comprehensive ethograms focusing on horse-human interactions which would include positive, neutral, and negative affective states (Table 1).

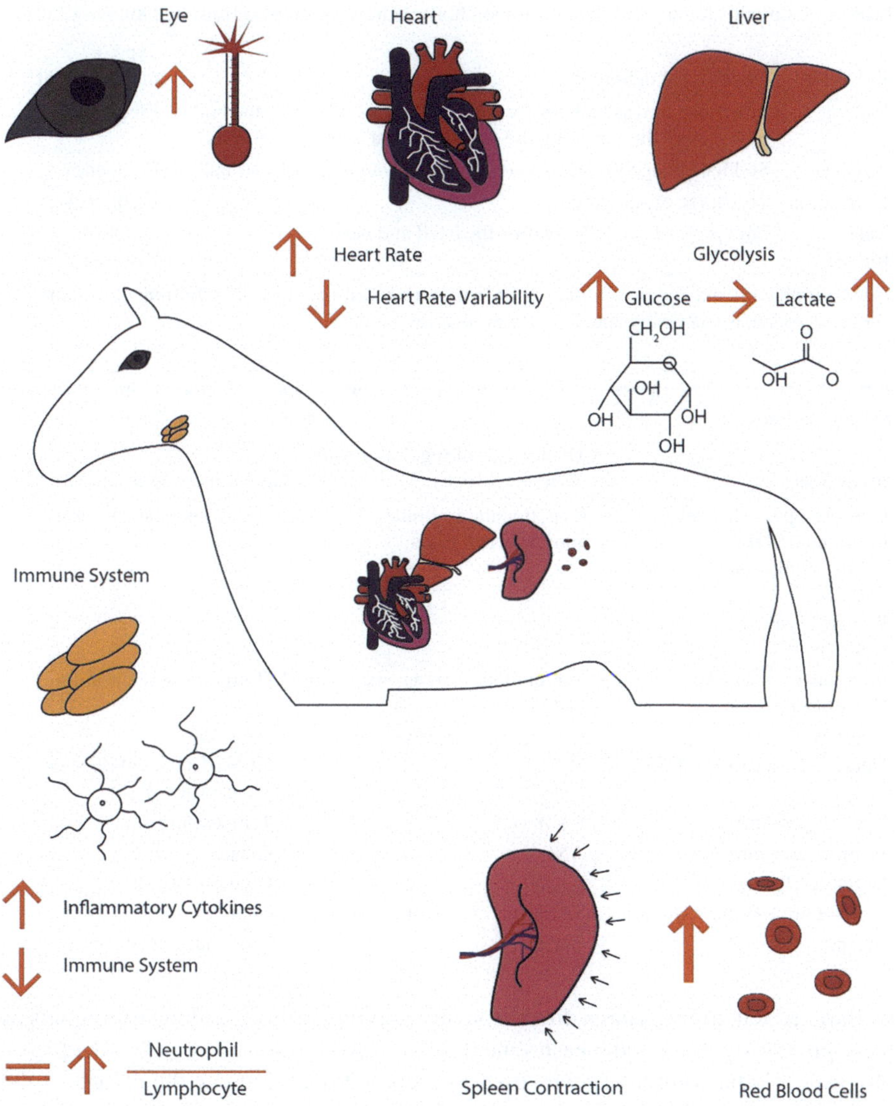

Fig. 4 The peripheral effects of activation of the hypothalamic-pituitary-adrenal (HPA) axis and sympathetic-adreno-medulla (SAM) axis measured for stress assessment. Figure design: Kyle Hartmann

The other subject receiving some attention in the literature on horses in equine-assisted services is kinematics or the movement of horses. So far, these investigations have been limited in scope. This area of research does offer valuable insights into horse welfare, as a horse's level of soundness and its ability to perform the movement in a comfortable, unrestricted manner is a critical piece of evaluating

Table 1 Example ethogram of some common horse behaviors adapted from McDonnell (2003)

Behavior	Operational definition	Type of measurement
Pawing	The horse moves its hoof forward and brings it back to the body by scraping the toe along the ground or just above the ground	Frequency
Shying	Sudden change in direction or sideways leap to avoid a stimulus	Frequency
Defecation	The horse expels feces	Frequency
Ears pinned	Ears pressed caudally against the head and neck	Duration, frequency

Videos or pictures may be used within or in lieu of a written operational definition. Observations can be recorded as frequency counts or duration of behavior

Table 2 Physiological measures used in the assessment of stress in horses during therapy integrating horses

Measure(s)	Mechanism of regulation and change	Indication of stress
Corticotropin-releasing hormone (CRH) Adrenocorticotropic hormone (ACTH) β-endorphins Cortisol	Hypothalamic-pituitary-adrenal (HPA) axis	↑ Hormone concentration
Norepinephrine (NE) Epinephrine (E)	Sympathetic-adrenal-medullar (SAM) axis	↑ Hormone concentration
Heart rate Heart rate variability (HRV)	Autonomic nervous system (ANS)	↑ Heart rate ↓ HRV (dependent on specific HRV measures)
Eye temperature	SAM axis	↑ Temperature
Erythrocyte count Hematocrit	ANS	↑ Count ↑ Hematocrit
Neutrophil: Lymphocyte ratio	SAM axis and cortisol	↑ Ratio
Lactate	Cortisol	↑ Blood lactate concentration

welfare. Kinematic measures differ from the previously discussed measurements as these previously discussed measurements characterize a stress response—the physiological or behavioral alterations used to prepare for or mitigate the effects of the stressor—whereas kinematic measures can highlight alterations caused by a rider, handler, or environmental and health issues (Table 2).

Overall, investigations of horse welfare in therapies integrating horses have focused on aspects and pieces of welfare and well-being rather than an integrated, multidimensional approach to welfare. Three main approaches to assessing horse welfare and well-being have been utilized: characterization of stress responses via measurement of physiological and behavioral changes, characterization of affiliative responses via changes in oxytocin concentrations, and evaluation of performance of movement via kinematics. While these types of studies have valuable insights to provide as we seek to evaluate horse welfare in therapies integrating horses, it is important to bear in mind that they need to be integrated into a larger framework of equine welfare where many or all aspects of welfare are considered. In general, the measures used in research investigating stress in horses can be thought to pertain to the arousal axis of affective states with other factors and measurements needed to determine a state's location along the valence axis.

Horse Well-Being in Therapies Integrating Horses: What We Know

The literature on horse welfare and well-being in equine-assisted services remains limited, and when this focus is narrowed to studies investigating therapies integrating horses, the literature becomes even more limited (Rankins et al., 2023). Six studies have focused specifically on therapies integrating horses with youth and

Table 3 Details of studies investigating horses' responses to therapies integrating horses

Author and year	Number of horses (*n*)	Client population	Type of therapy	Mounted or unmounted	Measurements taken
Ayala et al. (2021)	2	Youth with primarily physical disabilities	OT SLP Psychotherapy	Mounted and unmounted	T HR RR BP Behavior
Drinkhouse et al. (2012)	3	At-risk youth	Psychotherapy	Unmounted	HR
Malinowski et al. (2018)	9	Adult veterans with post-traumatic stress disorder	Psychotherapy	Unmounted	Oxytocin Cortisol HR HRV
Mendonça et al. (2019)	9	Individuals with various psychological and physical disabilities	Not reported	Mounted and unmounted	Behavior HR HRV
Suthers-McCabe and Albano (2004)	28	Not reported	Not reported	Not reported	Behavior Cortisol
Zagrai et al. (2022)	10	Youth with autism spectrum disorder	Not reported	Mounted	Hemoglobin Erythrocyte count Leukocyte count % Neutrophils % Lymphocytes

Abbreviations: OT occupational therapy, *SLP* speech-language pathology, *T* body temperature, *HR* heart rate, *RR* respiration rate, *BP* blood pressure, *HRV* heart rate variability adults (Table 3). Any survey of the literature on equine-assisted services is complicated by authors' use of differing terminology and the use of the same or similar terminology to describe different services (Wood et al., 2021). Even though some of these studies report the service provided as therapy integrating horses, it is possible a different form of equine-assisted services was provided, particularly if the type of therapy or therapist providing services was not reported.

The measurements used to characterize horses' responses to therapies integrating horses encompass most of the measurements used to characterize horses' responses to equine-assisted services in general (Table 3). Ayala et al. (2021) reported increases in respiration rate (RR) and the number of stress-related behaviors (two of the five measures) in horses during the anticipatory phase in which horses were present in the arena, but not directly interacting with the clients. Mendonça et al. (2019) reported increases in heart rate, the very low-frequency band of HRV, and the low-frequency to high-frequency ratio of HRV during the working phase when horses were ridden by the clients. These results are indicative of greater activation of the sympathetic branch of the ANS. The results of these two studies point toward greater horse stress during various phases of therapies integrating horses. In contrast, Malinowski et al. (2018) reported decreases in heart rate on day 2 of psychotherapy integrating horses, and Suthers-McCabe and Albano (2004) reported a decrease in cortisol concentrations from pre- to post-session. These results are more indicative of decreases in horses' stress in response to therapies integrating horses. The results reported by Zagrai et al. (2022) do not provide support to either conclusion, as no changes were reported in the group of horses engaged in the therapy sessions. The article by Drinkhouse et al. (2012) also fails to provide support for either conclusion, as the authors only analyzed and reported on the correlation between horse and human heart rates.

Since one half of the studies report results indicative of increased stress in horses and the other half report results indicative of decreased stress in horses, no firm conclusions can be drawn about the impacts of therapies integrating horses on equine well-being. Drawing conclusions from these studies is made more difficult by the variance in workloads across the studies with the horses ridden, sometimes at higher gaits and speeds, in some studies, and in other studies only performing unridden work at low gaits and speeds. As the literature on horse well-being in therapies integrating horses expands, the papers need to be critically evaluated and assessed on the quality of the experiment and reporting. Quality assessment, such as that conducted in a systematic literature review and meta-analysis that follows PRISMA (Moher et al., 2009) or similar guidelines, would aid us in understanding which results, if any, to place more weight on.

The Impact of Horse Well-Being on Human Outcomes

Research on the impacts of horse well-being on human outcomes during therapy integrating horses is still nascent. While it is promising to see research reporting on both human and horse outcomes, there is still a lack of work integrating these results in a meaningful way to describe or investigate how the horse and its behavior, well-being, and welfare impact the benefits afforded to the human participants. The horse is thought to help affect changes in clients through various mechanisms, including the horse-human relationship, the movement transmitted from horse to rider, the sensory input provided by the horse, motivation for the client, and the physiological coupling of horse and human. Many of these mechanisms rely on the transmittal of information and stimuli (physiological, behavioral, and movement) from horse to human. If even some of these theories prove to be correct when systematically investigated, then it becomes clear that human outcomes are heavily dependent on horse well-being. The welfare status of the horse determines what type and quality of physiological, behavioral, and movement information is transmitted from horse to human.

Challenges are necessary for growth and learning in humans and other animal species, but these challenges must occur in an environment where the individual feels safe and supported. In settings where horses experience poor welfare or less than optimal well-being, they are more likely to be in a state where learning is difficult and challenging. These types of scenarios are likely to lead to confusion and conflict behaviors that are frustrating and potentially dangerous for the client and horse handlers. This leads to an environment that is also less than ideal for the client and may limit progress toward their therapeutic goals. While eradicating poor welfare can lead to safer, more productive sessions, the end goal should be a state of maximum well-being for the horse. This approach moves beyond merely preventing harm, discomfort, and disengagement in horses during their time with clients to promoting positive engagement and comfort for horses with the result of potentially optimizing client outcomes.

Future Directions

There is a need for future research to explore and more fully establish the relationship between client outcomes and horse well-being, welfare, and affective states inside and outside of sessions. Such research efforts will need an expansion of the measures used to assess horse welfare and well-being, as simply determining horses are not experiencing stress during their interactions with human clients is insufficient to fully describe their state of welfare and offers little to no insight on their state of well-being. Even in research where human outcomes are the sole results of interest, monitoring, and reporting of variables and measurements related to horse well-being and care should be undertaken. The easiest to implement in most studies would be a report of horse behavior but would require the development and adoption of a standard ethogram encompassing behaviors indicative of negative, neutral, and positive affective states. Plasma cortisol and heart rate variability would also be useful for researchers to measure since robust protocols for measuring these variables in horses are established. More research is needed before a recommendation for markers of positive affective states and welfare to be used in research studies can be developed.

While further research is certainly needed, practices in the field also need to be adapted to consider and account for horse well-being. A practical step that practitioners and facilities can implement is the integration of routine horse well-being or welfare checks into clinical practice. These should be undertaken as part of larger, structured, periodic welfare assessments developed to encompass all aspects of our most current understanding of horse welfare.

References

Ayala, M. D., Carrillo, A., Iniesta, P., & Ferrer, P. (2021). Pilot study of the influence of equine assisted therapy on physiological and behavioral parameters related to welfare of horses and patients. *Animals, 11*(12), 3527. https://www.mdpi.com/2076-2615/11/12/3527/html

Bienertova-Vasku, J., Lenart, P., & Scheringer, M. (2020). Eustress and distress: Neither good nor bad, but rather the same? *BioEssays, 42*(7), e1900238. https://doi.org/10.1002/bies.201900238

Dai, F., Cogi, N. H., Heinzl, E. U. L., Dalla Costa, E., Canali, E., & Minero, M. (2015). Validation of a fear test in sport horses using infrared thermography. *Journal of Veterinary Behavior: Clinical Applications and Research, 10*(2), 128–136. https://doi.org/10.1016/j.jveb.2014.12.001

Douglas, J., Owers, R., & Campbell, M. L. H. (2022). Social licence to operate: What can equestrian sports learn from other industries? *Animals, 12*(15), 1987. https://doi.org/10.3390/ani12151987

Drinkhouse, M., Birmingham, S. S., Fillman, R., & Jedlicka, H. (2012). Correlation of human and horse heart rates during equine-assisted therapy sessions with at-risk youths: A pilot study. *Journal of Student Research, 1*(3), 22–25. https://doi.org/10.47611/jsr.v1i3.107

Farm Animal Welfare Council. (2009). *Farm animal welfare in Great Britain: Past, present and future*. http://www.fawc.org.uk

Harvey, A. M., Beausoleil, N. J., Ramp, D., & Mellor, D. J. (2020). A ten-stage protocol for assessing the welfare of individual non-captive wild animals: Free-roaming horses (Equus Ferus Caballus) as an example. *Animals, 10*(1), 148. https://doi.org/10.3390/ani10010148

Harvey, A. M., Beausoleil, N. J., Ramp, D., & Mellor, D. J. (2023). Mental experiences in wild animals: Scientifically validating measurable welfare indicators in free-roaming horses. *Animals, 13*(9), 1507. https://doi.org/10.3390/ani13091507

Hawson, L. A., McLean, A. N., & McGreevy, P. D. (2010). The roles of equine ethology and applied learning theory in horse-related human injuries. *Journal of Veterinary Behavior: Clinical Applications and Research, 5*(6), 324–338. https://doi.org/10.1016/J.JVEB.2010.06.001

Jerem, P., Jenni-Eiermann, S., McKeegan, D., McCafferty, D. J., & Nager, R. G. (2019). Eye region surface temperature dynamics during acute stress relate to baseline glucocorticoids independently of environmental conditions. *Physiology and Behavior, 210*, 112627. https://doi.org/10.1016/j.physbeh.2019.112627

Kaiser, L., Heleski, C. R., Siegford, J., & Smith, K. A. (2006). Stress-related behaviors among horses used in a therapeutic riding program. *Journal of the American Veterinary Medical Association, 228*(1), 39–45. https://doi.org/10.2460/javma.228.1.39

Kelly, K. J., McDuffee, L. A., & Mears, K. (2021). The effect of human–horse interactions on equine behaviour, physiology, and welfare: A scoping review. *Animals, 11*(10), 2782. https://doi.org/10.3390/ANI11102782/S1

Koolhaas, J. M., Bartolomucci, A., Buwalda, B., de Boer, S. F., Flügge, G., Korte, S. M., Meerlo, P., Murison, R., Olivier, B., Palanza, P., Richter-Levin, G., Sgoifo, A., Steimer, T., Stiedl, O., van Dijk, G., Wöhr, M., & Fuchs, E. (2011). Stress revisited: A critical evaluation of the stress concept. *Neuroscience & Biobehavioral Reviews, 35*(5), 1291–1301. https://doi.org/10.1016/j.neubiorev.2011.02.003

Lansade, L., Nowak, R., Lainé, A. L., Leterrier, C., Bonneau, C., Parias, C., & Bertin, A. (2018). Facial expression and oxytocin as possible markers of positive emotions in horses. *Scientific Reports, 8*(1), 1–11. https://doi.org/10.1038/s41598-018-32993-z

Lesimple, C. (2020). Indicators of horse welfare: State-of-the-art. *Animals, 10*(2), 294. https://doi.org/10.3390/ani10020294

Malinowski, K., Yee, C., Tevlin, J. M., Birks, E. K., Durando, M. M., Pournajafi-Nazarloo, H., Cavaiola, A. A., & McKeever, K. H. (2018). The effects of equine assisted therapy on plasma cortisol and oxytocin concentrations and heart rate variability in horses and measures of symptoms of post-traumatic stress disorder in veterans. *Journal of Equine Veterinary Science, 64*, 17–26. https://doi.org/10.1016/J.JEVS.2018.01.011

McDonnell, S. (2003). *A practical field guide to horse behavior*. Eclipse Press, A Division of the Blood-Horse Inc.

Mellor, D. J., Beausoleil, N. J., Littlewood, K. E., McLean, A. N., McGreevy, P. D., Jones, B., & Wilkins, C. (2020). The 2020 five domains model: Including human–Animal interactions in assessments of animal welfare. *Animals, 10*(10), 1870. https://doi.org/10.3390/ani10101870

Mendonça, T., Bienboire-Frosini, C., Menuge, F., Leclercq, J., Lafont-Lecuelle, C., Arroub, S., & Pageat, P. (2019). The impact of equine-assisted therapy on equine behavioral and physiological responses. *Animals, 9*(7), 409. https://doi.org/10.3390/ani9070409

Moher, D., Liberati, A., Tetzlaff, J., Altman, D. G., Altman, D., Antes, G., Atkins, D., Barbour, V., Barrowman, N., Berlin, J. A., Clark, J., Clarke, M., Cook, D., D'Amico, R., Deeks, J. J., Devereaux, P. J., Dickersin, K., Egger, M., Ernst, E., et al. (2009). Preferred reporting items for systematic reviews and meta-analyses: The PRISMA statement. *Annals of Internal Medicine, 151*(4), 264–269. https://doi.org/10.7326/0003-4819-151-4-200908180-00135/SUPPL_FILE/PRISMA_FIGURE-S1.DOC

Pilozzi, A., Carro, C., & Huang, X. (2021). Roles of β-endorphin in stress, behavior, neuroinflammation, and brain energy metabolism. *International Journal of Molecular Sciences. MDPI AG, 22*(1), 1–25. https://doi.org/10.3390/ijms22010338

Rankins, E. M., McKeever, K. H., & Malinowski, K. (2023). Equids in equine assisted services: A scoping review. *Journal of Equine Veterinary Science, 127*, 104825. https://doi.org/10.1016/j.jevs.2023.104825

Reed, R. G., & Raison, C. L. (2016). Stress and the immune system. In C. Esser (Ed.), *Environmental influences on the immune system* (pp. 97–126). Springer Vienna. https://doi.org/10.1007/978-3-7091-1890-0_5

Shaffer, F., & Ginsberg, J. P. (2017). An overview of heart rate variability metrics and norms. *Frontiers in Public Health, 5*. https://doi.org/10.3389/fpubh.2017.00258

Suthers-McCabe, H. M., & Albano, L. (2004). Evaluation of stress response of horses in equine assisted therapy programs. *Horses in Education and Therapy International Journal, 15*, 816–817.

Thompson, K., Mcgreevy, P., & Mcmanus, P. (2015). A critical review of horse-related risk: A research agenda for safer mounts, riders and equestrian cultures. *Animals, 5*, 561–575. https://doi.org/10.3390/ani5030372

Torcivia, C., Mcdonnell, S., Costa, D., Van Loon, T., & Paterson, M. (2021). Equine discomfort ethogram. *Animals, 11*(2), 580. https://doi.org/10.3390/ANI11020580

von Borell, E. H. (2001). The biology of stress and its application to livestock housing and transportation assessment. *Journal of Animal Science, 79*(Supplement E), E260–E267. https://academic.oup.com/jas/article/79/suppl_E/E260/4626044

Wood, W., Alm, K., Benjamin, J., Thomas, L., Anderson, D., Pohl, L., & Kane, M. (2021). Optimal terminology for Services in the United States that Incorporate Horses to benefit people: A consensus document. *The Journal of Alternative and Complementary Medicine, 27*(1), 88–95. https://doi.org/10.1089/acm.2020.0415

Zagrai, A. M., Cotor, G., Zagrai, G., Gâjâilă, G., Ghită, M., Ionescu, A. M., Cotor, D. C., & Damian, A. (2022). Evaluation of stress in riding horses, during the horse-assisted therapy activities in the case of children with autism spectrum disorders. *Bulletin of University of Agricultural Sciences and Veterinary Medicine Cluj-Napoca. Veterinary Medicine, 79*(1), 66. https://doi.org/10.15835/buasvmcn-vm:2021.0030

Zahorec, R. (2021). Neutrophil-to-lymphocyte ratio, past, present and future perspectives. *Bratislava Medical Journal, 122*(7), 474–488. https://doi.org/10.4149/BLL_2021_078

Index

A
Adults, 16, 59, 60, 75, 81, 83, 104, 112, 119–133, 173, 177, 245, 246, 270, 325, 326
Alternative therapeutic approaches, 97
Animal-assisted services (AAS), 232–234, 238–240
Animal therapies, 132, 252
Anxieties, 11, 13, 27, 29–31, 33, 35–37, 56, 68, 83, 86, 100, 102, 131, 140, 141, 148, 162, 164, 169, 175–177, 197–199, 201, 215, 216, 219, 220, 225, 231–241, 265, 268, 271, 272, 286, 291, 294, 295, 312, 313
Attention deficit hyperactivity disorder (ADHD), 12, 13, 245–261, 265–280
Autism spectrum disorder (ASD), 8, 325
Awareness, 5–7, 12, 15, 35, 62, 64, 67–69, 98–100, 104, 105, 107, 110, 113–115, 141, 143, 147, 162, 171, 178, 181, 182, 190, 200, 219, 220, 223, 250, 253–257, 259–261, 267, 269, 273, 279, 286, 288, 289, 293

B
Behaviors, 8, 25, 53, 77, 104, 124, 140, 162, 169, 187, 214, 232, 245, 265, 286, 318

C
Children and adolescent mental health, 231
Cognitive behavioral therapy (CBT), 31, 32, 119–121, 125, 163, 187, 232–234, 237
Cognitive processing therapy (CPT), 32, 39, 119–133
Communications, 7, 8, 35, 37, 62–68, 79, 82, 84, 87, 99, 108, 121, 123, 133, 141, 143, 152, 162, 173, 176, 178–181, 193, 196, 200, 214, 219, 220, 234, 253, 257, 258, 260, 261, 276, 289, 294, 307, 318
Controlled breathing, 11

E
Emotional regulation, 31, 56, 68, 102, 162, 177, 196, 197, 199, 234, 238, 239, 276, 279, 313
Empathy, 67, 87, 108
Empowerment, 125, 216, 313
Enlightenment, 4–6, 14
Equine, 3, 34, 53, 75, 100, 119, 140, 161, 176, 234, 251, 267, 286, 303, 318
Equine-assisted interventions (EAIs), 75, 76, 89, 91, 162, 285–298
Equine-assisted learning (EAL), 4, 14–17, 25, 26, 28, 30, 32, 70, 100, 103, 107, 115, 234, 240, 267, 286, 293, 296, 297
Equine assisted occupational therapy (EAOT), 267, 268, 270, 271, 274, 275, 277–280
Equine-assisted psychotherapy (EAP), 70, 75, 76, 81, 82, 86, 140, 176, 182, 218, 234
Equine-assisted services (EAS), 25–42, 76, 217, 234, 240, 267–268, 271–273, 275, 277–280, 318, 322, 323, 325, 326

Y. Neria et al. (eds.), *Guide to Equine Assisted Therapy*,
https://doi.org/10.1007/978-3-031-74426-6

Equine-assisted therapy/treatment (EAT), 3, 53, 75, 119, 140, 161, 176, 213, 251, 267, 286, 307, 313, 314
Equine facilitated cognitive processing therapy (EF-CPT), 119–133
Equine facilitated psychotherapy, 131, 225
Equine services, 141
Equine therapies, 69, 82, 131, 152, 162, 213, 252–253, 303, 306
Executive functions, 191, 192, 199, 245–249, 251–254, 259–261, 265, 272
Experiential awakening, 4
Experiential treatment, 155

F
Functional recovery, 189, 195

G
Grounded equine-assisted therapy (G-EAT), 53–71

H
Hippotherapy, 16, 25, 26, 53, 60, 71, 121, 123, 174, 175, 187–204
Horse assisted treatment, 218–219
Horsemanship, 3–6, 8, 10–15, 22, 26, 28, 30–33, 42, 55, 56, 58, 63, 70, 87, 98, 103–105, 111–113, 115, 141, 152, 162, 176, 235–237, 267, 289, 293, 294, 297, 298, 308, 309
Horse riding, 123, 174, 175, 181, 213
Horses, 33, 53, 76, 97, 120, 141, 161, 170, 192, 213, 234, 251, 267, 289, 303, 317
Horse selection, 4, 153
Human animal interaction (HAI), 183, 291
Human-equine relationship, 307, 308, 313, 314
Human–horse relationship, 77, 88
Hypothalamic-pituitary-adrenal (HPA) axis, 287, 290–293, 296

I
Implementation, 75, 82–87, 154, 155, 237, 249, 269, 293, 297, 298
Interpersonal relationships, 172, 252, 273
Intervention protocols, 235, 268–273

L
Limitations, 25, 76, 82, 83, 144, 147, 176, 178, 219, 220, 280, 296–297

M
Magnetic resonance imaging (MRI), 12, 13, 32, 38, 163, 164
Mental health, 3, 53, 76, 97, 121, 139, 161, 169, 190, 215, 231, 269, 286, 304
Mental health disorders, 4, 139, 140, 213–226
Military history, 312
Mindfulness, 11, 12, 30, 31, 35, 81, 98–100, 102, 104, 114, 236
Mounted-equine-assisted therapy, 295

N
Neurological deficits, 188, 195
Neuroplasticity, 190, 196, 266
Neurorehabilitation, 188, 189, 191, 192, 195–197, 199, 201, 202
Non-verbal communication, 7–8, 62, 64, 66, 162, 173, 175, 201, 218, 268, 288, 289, 307

P
Post-traumatic stress disorder (PTSD), 3, 81, 101, 120, 139, 163, 187, 215, 234, 303, 325
Psychiatric disorders, 25–42, 146, 155, 169, 171, 176, 286
Psychiatric rehabilitation, 172, 173, 176, 177
Psychotherapy incorporating horses (PIH), 25, 26, 30, 32, 41, 42, 234

Q
Quality of life (QoL), 27, 31, 38, 41, 81, 131, 172–174, 182, 190, 191, 202, 250, 265

R
Rationales, 25–42, 54, 57–63, 71, 91, 119, 120, 123–125, 148, 163, 245, 285, 287, 290–291
Reining in Anxiety (RiA), 56, 235
Rewards, 8–10, 14, 164, 165, 197, 198, 203, 251, 294, 297

S
Schizophrenia, 68, 170–181, 269
Self-control, 200, 254, 265
Self-worth, 83, 129, 246, 252, 258
Sensory processing and modulation, 249–250
Social competence, 285–298
Somatic awareness, 113, 115
Stress, 3, 36, 77, 100, 120, 139, 169, 191, 215, 234, 246, 285, 313, 317
Substance use disorders (SUDs), 101, 162, 214–215
Sympathetic-adreno-medullar (SAM) axis, 320–324

T
Thalamus, 36, 163, 164
Therapeutic riding, 29, 60, 70, 71, 120, 121, 153, 162, 170, 171, 173–179, 181, 234, 235, 238, 245
Therapy animals, 303
Training, 3–5, 9, 10, 13–22, 26, 28, 30, 32, 33, 35, 39, 58, 60, 63, 70, 75, 84, 87–90, 101, 103, 112–114, 121, 123, 126, 133, 141, 142, 152–156, 183, 189, 219, 221, 222, 233, 235, 237, 240, 241, 252, 266, 269, 286, 294, 304, 313
Trauma, 4, 32, 68, 75, 119, 139, 163, 187, 219, 234, 297, 303

V
Veterans, 3, 26, 68, 81, 97, 119, 156, 234, 303, 325

W
Welfare, 221, 233, 238, 317–325, 327, 328
Well-being, 7, 8, 15, 17, 27, 41, 53, 55, 65, 105, 107, 115, 122, 133, 161, 169, 173, 177, 201, 213, 225, 226, 231, 233, 273, 293, 307, 313, 314, 317–328
Working horses, 221, 313

Z
Zen Buddhism, 4, 6, 10–14

The manufacturer's authorised representative in the EU is Springer Nature Customer Service Centre GmbH, Europaplatz 3, 69115 Heidelberg, Germany. If you have any concerns regarding our products, please contact ProductSafety@springernature.com

Printed and bound by CPI Group (UK) Ltd, Croydon, CR0 4YY
30/09/2026
02225600-0009